LOUIS XIV AND ABSOLUTISM

LOUIS XIV AND ABSOLUTISM

Edited by
RAGNHILD HATTON

Ohio State University Press

First published in the United Kingdom 1976 by
THE MACMILLAN PRESS LTD
London and Basingstoke

Published in the U.S.A. 1976 by
OHIO STATE UNIVERSITY PRESS
Columbus

Printed in Great Britain

Library of Congress Cataloging in Publication Data
Main entry under title :

Louis XIV and absolutism.

Most of the essays are translated from French.
Includes bibliographical references and index.
1. France—Politics and government—1643–1715—Addresses, essays, lectures. 2. France—Economic conditions—Addresses, essays, lectures. 3. Louis XIV, King of France, 1638–
1715—Addresses, essays, lectures.
I. Hatton, Ragnhild Marie.
JN2369.L68   320.9'44'033   75–45158
ISBN 0–8142–0255–1

Contents

12 The French Navy under Louis XIV *Armel de
    Wismes*   243

13 The Protestant Bankers in France, from the Revo-
    cation of the Edict of Nantes to the Revolution
    J. Bouvier   263

    Glossary   281

    Chronology   287

    List of Persons   297

Preface

These essays are intended to put students in touch with important research in, or trends of thought on, the domestic reign of Louis XIV. Some will be familiar to academic teachers since they have already appeared in French; others have been commissioned for the volume. They differ in range and approach from extracts from books which were not annotated to contributions so condensed that the notes (printed after each essay) have to take up a good deal of space. There is even a printed lecture and a book review.

Kossmann's opening essay puts absolutism as a form of government into perspective and ranges therefore beyond Louis and France. Durand's 'What is absolutism?', after a general section, covers France up to the fall of the Ancien Régime, while Mousnier and Dumont deal specifically with French monarchy and society in the seventeenth century. With Bluche we reach a piece of detailed research focused directly on Louis XIV's secretaries of state.

The second section opens with Lossky's stimulating essay, 'The intellectual development of Louis XIV'. This is a slightly amended version (but with a briefer title) of his contribution to *Louis XIV and the Craft of Kingship*, but in view of its importance it is well worth reprinting. Three essays illustrating aspects of, or problems in, Louis' government follow : Levron's interpretation of the role of the courtier; Orcibal's detective work on the reasons for Louis revoking the Edict of Nantes; Livet's analysis of the compromise achieved in the frontier province of Alsace.

The last section deals with economic and financial aspects of the reign and opens with the late Jean Meuvret's discussion of fiscal policy and public opinion – the last article he wrote before his death. Deyon deals with the problems of the manufacturing industry; Baron de Wismes assesses the role of privateering within the framework of the navy, and the economy; while Bouvier's review article, centred on the work of Lüthy, discusses the significant role of the Protestant bankers – this, to give perspective, also extends beyond the reign.

The editor is grateful to the contributors for their help and co-operation in the rendering of their work into English. The translations have been made by Dr Geoffrey Symcox of the University of California at Los Angeles and Dr Derek McKay of the London School of Economics, in collaboration with the editor. A special word of thanks is due to Professor John Bromley of the University of Southampton who supervised the translation of Meuvret's contribution, and to Hamish Scott of the University of Birmingham who helped with the proof-reading.

For permission to reprint articles or sections of books the editor must thank the following: *Annales, Economies, Sociétés, Civilisations*; *XVIIe Siècle*; Armand Colin and Editions du Seuil of Paris; and the Ohio State University Press of America.

The editor has appended a glossary of French and a few Latin terms which occur in the text, a list of persons mentioned where they are not sufficiently explained already in the text or in the notes, and a chronology of significant dates for the domestic history of the reign.

Notes on Contributors

FRANÇOIS BLUCHE, Docteur ès Lettres, Professor of Modern History at the University of Paris (Nanterre). Specialises in social and institutional history. Author of *Les magistrats du parlement de Paris au XVIIIe siècle* (1960); *Le despotisme eclairé* (1968); *La vie quotidienne de la noblesse française au XVIIIe siècle* (1973).

JEAN BOUVIER, Docteur ès Lettres, Professor of Contemporary Economic History in the University of Paris VIII, secretary of the Association Française des Historiens Economistes. Specialist in financial and banking history from the eighteenth to the twentieth century. Author of *Finances et financiers d'Ancien Régime*, 2nd ed (1969); *Monnaie et banque en France au XVIIIe siècle*, in the series 'Histoire économique et sociale de la France', II : 1660–1789 (1972).

P. DEYON, Professor of Economic and Social History at the University of Lille. Author of *Amiens, étude sur la sociéte urbaine au XVIIe siècle* (1967); *Le mercantilisme* (1969); *La France Baroque*, in the series 'Histoire de la France' (1971).

FRANÇOIS DUMONT, Professor of History of Comparative Law at the Université du Droit d'Economie et des Sciences Sociales, Paris. Author of *Le bureau des finances de la généralité de Moulins* (1923); *Une session des Etats généreaux de Bourgogne: La 'terme' de 1718* (1936); *L'intendance de Dijon et le Maçonnais* (1945); *L'administration bourguignonne au XVIIIe siècle* (1947).

GEORGES DURAND, Agrégé d'Histoire; Maître-assistant at the University of Lyon II. Author of *Etats et institutions XVI–XVIIIe siècles* (1969); *Le patrimoine foncier de l'Hôtel Dieu de Lyon, contribution à l'étude de la grand proprieté rhodanienne* (1973). In preparation, *Vin, vigne et vignerons en Lyonnais et Beaujolais, 1500–1789*.

E. H. KOSSMANN, Professor of History at Groningen University, the Netherlands; formerly Professor of Dutch History, University College, London. Author of *La Fronde* (1954); 'Een blik op het Franse absolutisme', *Tijdschrift voor Geschiedenis* (1965); 'Typologie der monarchieën van het Ancien Régime', in *De Monarchie* (1966).

A*

JACQUES LEVRON, Conservateur en Chef Honoraire des Archives, Department of Seine-et-Oise. Author of numerous works on French palaces (one of which has been translated into English : *The Royal Châteaux of the Ile-de-France*, 1965, from the French original of 1964) and many guides to monuments and archives. Apart from *Les Courtisans* in the series 'Les Temps qui Court' (1961), from which our (abbreviated) essay is taken, he has also published *Versailles, ville royale* (1964), *La vie quotidienne à la cour de Versailles au XVIIᵉ et XVIIIᵉ siècles* (1965), and *Les inconnus de Versailles* (1968).

GEORGES LIVET, Docteur ès Lettres, Professor of Modern History at the University of Strasbourg. Vice-President of the Comité Française des Sciences Historiques. Author of *Le duc de Mazarin, gouverneur d'Alsace 1661–1713* (1954); *L'intendance d'Alsace sous Louis XIV, 1648–1715* (1956); *La route royale et la civilisation française de la fin du XVᵉ au milieu du XVIIᵉ siècle* (1959); Chapters VII and IX in *Histoire de l'Alsace* (1970) and Chapters IX, X and XI, in *Documents de l'histoire de l'Alsace* (1972).

ANDREW LOSSKY, Professor of History at the University of California, Los Angeles. Author of *Louis XIV, William III and the Baltic Crisis of 1683* (1954); 'The Nature of Political Power According to Louis XIV', in *The Responsibility of Power: Historical Essays in Honour of Hajo Holborn*, ed. Krieger and Stern (1967); 'Maxims of State in Louis XIV's Foreign Policy in the 1680s', in *William III and Louis XIV. Essays by and for Mark A. Thomson*, ed. Hatton and Bromley (1968).

JEAN MEUVRET was Director of Studies at the Ecole des Hautes Etudes, Paris. The essay in this volume was the last work by this eminent historian who died in October 1971. He contributed a chapter to the *New Cambridge Modern History*, VI (1970) entitled 'Prices, Population and Economic Activities in Europe, 1688–1715 : A Note'; for a selection from his many articles, see *Etudes d'histoire économique. Receuil d'articles* (1971).

ROLAND MOUSNIER, Docteur ès Lettres (Sorbonne), Professor of Modern History at the Sorbonne, Director of the Centre de Recherches sur la Civilisation de l'Europe Moderne. Author of *La vénalité des offices sous Henri IV et Louis XIII* (1946; 2nd ed. 1971); *Fureurs paysannes* (1968; English translation, 1971); *Les hierarchies sociales, de 1450 à nos jours* (1969; English translation, 1973); *La plume, la faucille et le marteau. Institutions et société en France du moyen-âge à la Révolution*, collected essays (1970); editor of and contributor to *Le conseil du roi de Louis XII à la Révolution* (1970).

JEAN ORCIBAL, Docteur ès Lettres, Dir. Pratique of Studies at the Ecole des Hautes Etudes, Paris. Specialist in religious history, editor of the volume *Problèmes et methodes d'histoire des religions* (1968). His best known works are *Fénelon et la cour romaine, 1700–1715* (1940); *Louis XIV contre Innocent XI. Les appels au futur concile de. 1688 et l'opinion française* (1949); and *Louis XIV et les Protestants* (1951).

BARON ARMEL DE WISMES, member of the Comité de Documentation Historique de la Marine Française. Author of *Jean Bart et la guerre de course* (1965); *Nantes et le pays Nantais* (1970); *Ainsi vivaient les marins* (1971); *Les Chevaliers de Malte* (1972); *Découverte de la Filibuste* (1973); *Les Grand Ports bretons du XVIIe et du XVIIIe siècles* (1973).

ENGLAND

FLANDERS

ARTOIS

Lille
Valenciennes
Arras
Amiens

THE THREE
ARCHBISHOPRICS

Metz
Strasbourg

Rouen

Caen

Paris

Châlons-
sur-Marne

ALSACE

Alençon

BRITTANY
Rennes

Orléans

Neuf-Brisach

Besançon

Tours

Bourges

Dijon

BURGUNDY

FRANCHE COMTÉ

Poitiers

Moulins

La Rochelle

Limoges

Riom

Lyon

Trévoux

Angoulême

Grenoble

Bordeaux

DAUPHINÉ

LANGUEDOC

Montauban

Auch
Toulouse

Montpellier

PROVENCE

Aix

Bayonne

Pau
BÉARN

SPAIN

FRENCH
CERDAGNE

Perpignan

ROUSSILLON

——————→ Districts under one intendant

—— —— —— Frontiers

● Towns in which local Estates and *Parlements* met

○ Towns in which intendant's office located

The administrative divisions of France

Source: La France au temps de Louis XIV, ed. Georges Mongrédien et al.
(Paris, 1966).

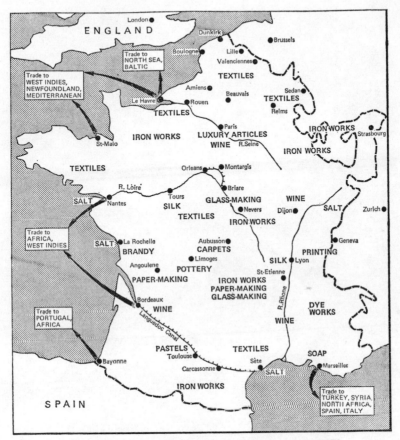

The economic life of France in the reign of Louis XIV

Source: As map opposite.

Part I

ABSOLUTISM AND SOCIETY

1 The Singularity of Absolutism*

E. H. KOSSMANN

In the international discussion among historians of the early modern period in recent years – a discussion which has proved destructive of many traditional concepts from 'renaissance' to 'mercantilism' – the term 'absolutism' has been spared. Absolutism still seems an undisputed historical fact, the defining of which has not given rise to substantial difficulties : it was and is considered to be a historical phenomenon connected with the aggrandisement and the centralisation of the state and with the increase of its power.

As soon as historians start to 'explain' absolutism and allocate it its proper place in historical development, however, agreement ceases. Even if the term is reserved for systems of government of the sixteenth, seventeenth and eighteenth centuries – and some writers are much less exclusive in their use of the label – absolutism is interpreted in mutually contradictory ways as feudal, aristocratic, agrarian, conservative, bourgeois, progressive, despotic, constitutional, monarchical, republican, an attempt to bring a modicum of order out of chaos, an effort to build on the ruins left by a collapsed economy, a triumphant step towards the rational modern state, an impartial and honest form of government, a systematic exploitation of the masses by a very small group of profiteers. Indeed, it would not be difficult for a diligent student of modern historical literature to expand this list considerably. This is not surprising. Anyone well versed in seventeenth- and eighteenth-century documents and printed works can, with the help of a little imagination, construct contrasting interpretations from varying contemporary attitudes. The problem is

* Specially commissioned for this volume.

not so much how to explain the large number of contradictory interpretations, since these have arisen out of Ancien Régime polemics rather than twentieth-century research; the problem is why we choose to continue thinking along these same lines.

Absolutism was the first political system able to profit from the printing press; it grasped its chance. In the sixteenth and seventeenth centuries a huge number of publications appeared which deal with absolutism. In countless universities lectures, dissertations, disputations, theses and the like were devoted to it. In the law courts specific problems relating to it were defined and redefined. In the churches its religious implications were emphasised and praised in innumerable sermons. For many decades absolutism provided major themes in art and literature, in theatre and music. For the first time in European history since Antiquity the state as such became the object of general discussion and propaganda. Thanks to this fairly massive interest, spread and stimulated by the printing press, a political terminology derived almost wholly from Aristotle, Cicero and the *Corpus juris* received coherent and readily understandable meaning. It was left to the nineteenth century to transform these terms into abstractions and 'isms' : not till then did *potestas absoluta* become absolutism, and *potestas mitigata, monarchia mixta, libertas,* etc. become liberalism. The essential concepts relating to political organisation were, however, rapidly adopted by all educated or half-educated men and need no translation even today. We still use the same terms. Not only the easy ones, such as monarchy, aristocracy, democracy, plutocracy or autocracy, but many more, as for example popular sovereignty (*majestas populi*), tyranny, despotism, fundamental rights, fundamental laws, natural law, arbitrary rule, prerogative, *raison d'état, coup d'état*, were so broadly circulated in the sixteenth and seventeenth centuries and proved so extraordinarily useful that they still strike us as much more familiar than the terminology of feudalism.

There may be a danger in this as it can mislead us into taking absolute monarchy and its opponents too much for granted. And that we should not do. We write with effortless ease of the 'new monarchy' and the 'new state' that took shape in the second half of the fifteenth century and rapidly developed into sixteenth- (and seventeenth-) century absolutism. Yet we realise that those states were 'modern' only in the indeed essential but still limited sense of being what we call 'states' at all. The aims and methods of their governments were far from modern. Nor were they medieval. In fact they were particular, singular and strange. The state of the Ancien Régime is a phenomenon *sui generis*. It is a truism to say that there are no isolated facts in history and nothing prevents us from forging our knowledge of the past into a long chain of continuity. It is pedantic to criticise some historians for linking absolutism – interpreted as a conservative feudal system – with the Middle Ages, and others for interpreting it as a centralising and progressive form of government and thus linking it with the nineteenth century. All I am prepared to argue is that it is also useful to look at absolutism as if it were a strange and dangerous beast, to examine it with caution and to study it as an isolated, short-lived type of state that, with all its glitter and display of power, was largely unsuccessful. There is nothing new in such an approach but it may be salutary to try it again.

That absolutism was short-lived nobody can deny. Fully developed in the seventeenth century in a number of European states, it started decaying in the early eighteenth century and failed in its attempt to adapt itself to the Enlightenment. Despite its ostentation and its undeniable success in advertising its wares, it was more ephemeral than medieval monarchy on the one hand and post-revolutionary constitutionalism on the other. This should not surprise us. The distinguishing features of absolutism is its pretension to rise above reality, to break out of the limitation of history, to transcend the community and the very foundation of political organisation, that is, human beings living together in a group. Absolutism was by definition an abstraction. There has never been another form of government for which its defenders have been bold enough to claim the absolute as its most characteristic quality. This element of intellectual pride and obstinacy weakened absolutism as a system. Not only were governments unable to realise their pretensions – even in the incomparably more sophisticated and better equipped state of the present day no one can rule so absolutely as intellectuals in the seventeenth century thought the monarch ought to do – still more dangerous for them was the fact that in modern times modes of thinking, fashions, philosophies and styles change more rapidly than forms of government, so that to associate a political system closely with a cultural development is to run the very real risk of soon making

that system look old-fashioned and thus rendering it unacceptable. This is what happened with absolutism. It was so thoroughly
embedded in renaissance and baroque thought, intellectually so
dependent on the Catholic revival and various forms of classicism
– whether neoplatonism or neostoicism – that it lost its meaning
and purpose as soon as men started moving beyond these particular ideologies.

The rise of absolutism remains a phenomenon difficult to describe and difficult to understand. In a broad sense the state is
supposed, in the course of the late fifteenth and sixteenth centuries, to have acquired more power than it possessed in the
Middle Ages; that is, to have obtained and developed better in-
struments for ruling large numbers of people. The growth of the
population, commercial expansion, improvements in banking,
better means of communication – including the spread of literacy
due to the new printing presses – increased the rulers' responsibilities, enabled them to get much closer to their subjects and generally made government more comprehensive. This was a relatively slow process and so hard to perceive that no one thought it
necessary to examine what ought to be done with the additional
power flowing to the state. At the beginning of the sixteenth
century it seemed not unlikely that princes and representative
bodies would share the new power. In England, France, the
Netherlands and other states parliaments and monarchs increased
their authority simultaneously without giving much thought to
the implications and theoretical justification of this situation. But
by degrees both prince and estates realised the awkwardness of
their position. Endless bickering over fiscal matters and financial
control debilitated government. Religious problems brought conflict to a head in France and the Netherlands. When the Protestant opposition to a Roman Catholic prince succeeded in associa-
ting itself with representative assemblies which were already more
powerful than in the past, the scope of the problem was im-
mensely widened : religion mattered incomparably more than
taxation. It was then that people felt the need to justify their
position in the conflict, and Europe was flooded by a torrent of
writings on political theory. Never before had such a perplexing
variety and quantity of political ideas been put forward; never
before had a controversy generated such an inexhaustible thirst
for theoretical justification. Europe had frequently been torn by

religious disputes and war; what was new was the dramatic expansion of political philosophy.

Not that political thought moved into totally new areas. The theoretical political discussion brought to such a climax by the religious strife borrowed many of its concepts and terms from early fifteenth-century debates in the Roman Catholic church. During the long struggles between the papacy and the councils of Constance (1414–18) and Basle (1431–49), conciliar theories approximating to the doctrine of constitutional and popular sovereignty and papal philosophies close to the idea of legislative sovereignty had developed.[1] These were either copied or rediscovered for different purposes by secular thinkers in the sixteenth century, and in a political framework they became much more explosive than they had been in their original ecclesiastical context. Power in the state was something altogether different from power in the church. The danger inherent in the adaptation of theories evolved in heated ecclesiastical debate to a political situation was that they acquired a degree of reality and carried consequences unthought of by the clerical philosophers who had formulated them. After all, to say that the pope possesses absolute legislative sovereignty is a relatively innocuous proposition compared to the statement that the king of France has this attribute. In France millions of men were dependent on the form of their government; outside France millions of Europeans were dependent on the ambitions of a French king holding absolutist doctrines. Papal claims had a strong indirect effect since these made it impossible for the reformers to keep their protest within the prescribed boundaries. State sovereignty, however, was experienced more directly. Religious dissent was caused by the pope's sovereign refusal to accept the reforms proposed to him. The religious wars, with all their misery and brutality, were caused by the sovereign refusal of the secular princes to admit dissent in their states. The philosophical principle of absolutism helped to wreck the unity of the church. When applied to secular government, it wrecked countries and societies and wrought havoc in the life of millions.

Of course the point is not that absolute rulers were particularly stupid, excessively cruel or exclusively responsible for the tragic turn taken by European history. If there is a point to be made, it is that such an abstract and extreme conception of sovereignty caused the rulers to formulate their policies on the strength of an idealised interpretation of what *dominium* ought to be rather than on a realistic assessment of their particular circumstances. It is perhaps vain to speculate whether French and Spanish kings who had not been taught that their authority was by definition limitless would have refrained from trying to enforce their will so tenaciously, but the question ought to be put. The bitterness of the conflicts might not have been less, but it would not have been further exasperated by the largely unsuccessful attempts of monarchs and governments of the late sixteenth and early seventeenth century generally to enforce policies based on principles that were becoming increasingly clear (thanks to the excellent and profound writers of the age), if impossible to put into operation because of the practical limits of power at the time. Because the theory could not readily be transformed into practice, wars lasted longer and their costs rose. Absolutism raised the rulers' objectives so high that the inevitable compromises which ultimately had to be agreed were extremely difficult to reach. It may sound reckless to say that in the absence of absolutist doctrine the settlement of 1598 in France could have been reached much earlier, or the truce in the Netherlands concluded long before 1609, but to this writer it seems not unlikely.

It is fair to suppose that for the masses of the population in any period of history the form of government under which they live matters only in so far as they experience its material consequences. Monarchy, however, usually aspires to be popular. Its defenders claim that it is rooted in the psychological need of most people to have some father-figure indicate the boundaries within which men are free to organise their lives, and argue that the monarch seeks to further the interests of the flock he is herding. Absolute monarchy raised itself above such trivialities. Medieval kingship kept intimate connections with heaven and earth. In the nineteenth and twentieth centuries, when heaven had moved so infinitely far away, royalty also sought and perhaps found support in the masses: the paternal monarchy of the Middle Ages became the popular, constitutional and national monarchy of the post French Revolution period. During the Ancien Régime monarchy was different. It had no connections with the people, it was not national in the modern sense of the word and of course it was not constitutional. If it looked up to heaven it did so without humility. It sought strength from a very distant God who provided help in as haughty a manner as that by which kings ruled the earth. Monarchy wanted to be isolated. It wanted to stand on its own. It was supported by educated men who were conversant with the latest cultural innovations, who read and wrote a language which no one outside a tiny élite was able to understand and who despised the *plebs* on the basis of arguments taken from ancient writers and repeated in Latin *ad nauseam*. These thoughtless vociferations against the ferocious, cruel, servile, corruptible masses – accompanied by neostoic praise of aristocratic virtue, endurance and wisdom – are shocking in their banality and in their humanist arrogance, but they served their purpose admirably. In this culture a lack of proper classical education and hopeless backwardness are convincingly demonstrated by unwillingness to equate democracy with anything but wild anarchy and despotism.

If no historian has seriously attempted to interpret French absolutism as a system particularly kind to the masses – though the early Stuart kings are supposed to have shown paternal if ineffective concern for the poor – there has been much learned discussion about its roots in other social classes. This is not the place to summarise the discussion or to make statements about whether French absolutism was feudal or bourgeois. Neither is this unpretentious essay intended as a contribution to the debate started by the researches of the Russian historian B. F. Porchnev into the French *soulèvements populaires* of the first half of the seventeenth century.[2] This much, however, must be said : it should be obvious to any reader of the numerous studies generated by this debate that it is not only more cautious but decidedly wiser to refrain from sociological generalisations wide open to attack from many different sides. Of course kings, and particularly French kings, enlisted the services of non-nobles who became excellent ministers. Of course the 'bourgeois' in Paris and the provincial towns disliked being disturbed by riots and pillage and welcomed royal help to keep order. Of course Henri IV, Richelieu and Mazarin refused to leave the high nobility as much power and independence as it wanted and thus provoked bitter conflict. It is perfectly true that social disturbances were rampant in France in the sixteenth and seventeenth centuries. Porchnev counted about a hundred *soulèvements* in French towns between 1623 and 1647

and interpreted these as parts of the perennial conflict between
'the people' and 'the absolutist system of exploitation'. In-
cidentally, textbooks on the history of the Dutch Republic –
decidedly a non-absolutist state – furnish examples of similar
'risings'. Between 1610 and 1635 the 'masses' of Dutch towns
rose in revolt at least twenty-five times and the Dutch population,
it should be noted, was ten times smaller than that of France.
Must we conclude that we find proof here of the perennial conflict between 'the people' and 'the bourgeois system of exploitation'?

Where in any case does this discussion lead us? Not to any firm
conclusion, it would seem. The pieces of the puzzle (which is
infinitely more complicated than can here be indicated) do not
help us to understand the refractory Ancien Régime reality. 'The
declining nobility', 'the rising bourgeoisie', 'the bourgeois character of the French Parlements', 'the rebellious masses', and many
other attempts to formulate a working hypothesis for further
speculation, have been abandoned by most historians; but they
have not been eliminated altogether and have proved remarkably
tenacious of life. It would seem that it is necessary for our age to
associate a form of government with a social reality and to explain
or understand that form as the expression or the result of deeper
forces working in society. The simplest way to do so is of course
by linking government to class. It is interesting to see Roland
Mousnier, whose knowledge of the period is unequalled and whose
opinions are both firm and subtle, succumb to this intellectual
obsession. In his famous polemic against Porchnev he at first held
that the whole idea of a French early seventeenth-century class
struggle, between feudal and aristocratic exploiters under the
king on the one hand and exploited masses on the other, was a
chimera because the concept of class was inapplicable to a society
differently articulated. Yet he leaves the impression that he is
making out a case for the 'progressiveness' of French absolutism
and emphasising the dynamic reality of 'the bourgeoisie' as a
social class.[3]

A crucial element of absolutist theory was its radical distinction
between government and subject, between state and society – a
distinction which led a consistent philosopher like Hobbes to
deny that society had an independent existence at all. Between
government and individual nothing was left. This of course was

not the 'official' theory of absolutism. For absolute power was considered to be of divine origin and Christian by its nature, which implied much more than a justification of limitless authority. It is no accident that Hobbes, whose idea of sovereignty was conceptually free from divine inspiration, made short work of the idea of community. 'Official' absolutism could not do this. God's purpose in investing absolute rulers with power was to establish a harmonious, hierarchical, political universe. In that universe Christian people were responsible individuals, having possessions, a place in society and an immortal soul. These must be recognised, as God wants Christians to have property and Christian society to be organised hierarchically. In this sense absolutism was 'constitutional' and conservative, the very opposite of un-Christian despotism. It is well known that for all his rash extremism Louis XIV refrained from abolishing elements in his state which were rooted, or supposed to be rooted, in constitutional tradition and did not seek to alter the old order radically. This was left for the enlightened despots of the eighteenth century to whom the *droit divin* theory mattered less and who thus felt less bound by the constitutional limits imposed by this doctrine.

But did this 'constitutional' character of absolutism draw the king nearer to the social organisation which he was committed to protect? This is not likely. For the paradox of absolutism was that even its 'constitutional' and conservative Christian nature tended to raise sovereignty to new heights not only in theory but in daily practice. Absolutism with its legislative sovereignty was by definition creative. If it was limited in the sense described, it had to seek other fields where it was allowed to operate more freely. For power, it was thought, tended to expand and extend itself and according to absolutists this was as it should be. This patently arbitrary statement is, strangely enough, still repeated in textbooks on political philosophy; though history, and daily life, show in endless variety another tendency of power, namely to wither away, disappear or abdicate. If sovereignty and power are to be dynamic concepts they must operate dynamically, and if they cannot do so on the level of organised institutions and hierarchic orders they have to rise above them. This they did in the seventeenth century when it was common practice to keep the existing institutions and social organisations virtually untouched but to superimpose new ideas, institutions and rules upon them

and so to create a whole new layer of government, a higher plat-
form of sovereignty. In this way absolutism was elevated above the
unreformed constitution that was spared and respected. In areas
of government where the constitutional tradition had not pene-
trated, the vital limitations of absolutism implied by its divine
inspiration and Christian character were to some extent reconciled
with its dynamic nature and its ambition to be limitless. The
result of this was that the isolation of absolutist government increased; it moved into unknown heights of abstraction.

Not only in France, but in most monarchical states of Central
Europe, the absolute princes proved unable and unwilling to
use the medieval representative assemblies in their original sense
as channels through which state power was drawn from and
flowed towards the subjects. Kings discovered other ways of making their will felt.[4] First they ruled in close collaboration with
their councils. When these bodies tended to become self-willed
institutions, ambitious of independent responsibilities, the absolute
king preferred to ignore them and to consult only his inner council
of ministers. Having previously created social institutions such as
the estates and even social groups such as the *noblesse de robe*
which filled *conseils* and *collèges*, monarchy withdrew into the
isolation and loneliness of absolutism. Louis XIV refused to listen
to organisations that claimed to be representative; he did not
often consult his council; he was reluctant to have a cabinet and
did his work mainly with the aid of individual ministers appointed
and dismissed at will. This was absolutism in its most perfect
form. It had cut its roots. It did not associate itself with any particular class or group of the French population. It withdrew
from society and from institutions which had been created by
the French monarchy and had long served it, acting on premises
about political power put forward by intellectuals since the sixteenth century. But to be alone and superior a king must also
withdraw from the centre of the country and build, at Versailles,
not just a new palace but the very symbol of absolutism. The end
of absolutism was symbolised equally clearly a century later by the
enforced return of the royal family to the national centre, to Paris.
Even for those unable to believe in the logic of history, it may
give pleasure to find that the most pompous decisions connected
with Versailles – the absolute monarchy, the establishment of the

German empire, the peace treaty of 1919 – were disastrous, ephemeral and too artificial to last.

It is rather doubtful if Central European princes achieved a similar measure of isolation as French kings. The Prussian monarchy, for example, probably leaned on the nobility to a greater extent than Louis XIV, although the Great Elector did so unwillingly. The English situation cannot easily be compared to that of France. Mousnier has emphasised the similarities of French and English royal absolutism in the early seventeenth century, and J. P. Cooper has denied them in essays[5] so erudite and subtle that it is not easy to define his conclusions. Stephan Skalweit has clarified in a paper he prepared for the international historical congress at Moscow in 1970[6] the points that must be taken into consideration in any comparison. These French, English and German endeavours are doubtless steps towards the synthetic explanation we need; but if comparative history has been rightly described as one of the most worthwhile historical pursuits, it is decidedly also the most difficult. Skalweit expects that new and important insights will clear up many of the uncertainties which still bedevil our thinking. But in order to carry through a satisfactory investigation into the effect of absolutism in various countries – for this seems now to be the direction into which we are moving – we must know what exactly we are trying to measure and lay down a yardstick by which we are to measure it. Until we agree on these matters, our discussion is bound to remain somewhat tentative. The problem itself becomes even more complicated, but also it would seem more interesting and more important from a general point of view, if we compare not only the European monarchies in their absolutist phase but also the republican forms of government of the period.

Can a republic be governed 'absolutely' and if so, is such republican absolutism more or less effective than a monarchical one? Recently Mousnier has stated that in England parliament exercised after 1640 'an arbitrary, absolute and truly sovereign power of which the kings had only dreamed, helped by ideas of using sovereignty and *raison d'état* in the name of the people'.[7] Indeed, one of the crucial developments in European, and for that matter world history, was the adoption of sovereignty by potentially democratic bodies or – to put it crudely – the suddenly discovered possibility that absolutist democracy might be a satisfactory form of government. 'Democracy' was, however, not necessarily defined in exact terms. It was possible for the post-1640 English parliament to claim that rather than being the representative of the people it was 'the people itself' and possessed absolute autonomous legislative sovereignty. In his *Observations upon some of His Majesties late Answers and Expresses* of 1642 Henry Parker defended an absolutism more absolute than Bodin's, and in other writings he claimed for parliament the power to abolish Magna Carta or the Petition of Rights. This was a theoretical position which had not been reached elsewhere. In the Netherlands discussion about sovereignty had not yet taken such a course. In his *Politica methodice digesta* of 1603 Johannes Althusius, whose system was inspired by the Revolt of the Netherlands, pointed out that all sovereignty was legislative and resided with the people. But what he meant was by no means what Parker meant forty years later. Althusius, as other publicists in the Netherlands of the sixteenth century, wanted to prove that a representative body, or a body considered representative, had the right to resist a despotic prince. Sovereignty was defined by him as popular in order to allow the so-called popular representatives to withdraw it from a ruler who exercised it in an illegal manner. Sovereignty was not used by Althusius as a creative and dynamic concept symbolising the soul of state power : sovereignty was not basically power to be exercised, it was power to resist illegitimate exercise of it. The concept was thus interpreted – quite differently from the way in which Bodin or Parker used it – as an instrument to defend the constitutional tradition and not as an instrument to unify and strengthen the state.

It was nevertheless in the Netherlands that democratic republican absolutism was for the first time investigated and defined in consistent theories.[8] The idea that democracy is a despotic form of government was not new; on the contrary, it was one of the major objections long raised against democracy. In the 1660s and 1670s several Dutch theorists argued that the absolute character of democracy was its greatest asset. They believed with Hobbes that power was needed to restrain men, but found it unwise to give absolute authority to one individual. For if man is perhaps not thoroughly bad he is at any rate capricious, unstable and unreliable. The more absolute a state, the more efficiently obedience and order can be organised. Monarchy, dependent as it is on one single person, is less absolute than aristocracy and aristocracy less absolute than democracy. Spinoza stated in his *Tractatus Politicus* (published in 1677) that 'the greater the right of the sovereign the more does the form of the state agree with the dictate of reason', and that 'absolute sovereignty (*imperium absolutum*) if any such thing exists, is really the sovereignty held by the whole people'.[9] However extravagant such a definition of absolutism must have seemed to most contemporaries, at least one of Spinoza's critics realised its crucial importance. Ulric Huber, who taught politics and law at the University of Franeker in Friesland, laid down in *De jure civitatis* (third edition, 1694) that although power is by definition absolute in all forms of government, it is exercised more absolutely in an aristocracy than a monarchy. A king always tempers the monarchical character of his government because, in spite of his pretensions, he is obliged to consult the nobles of the realm : if his rule degenerates into tyranny it is the great who will be his first victims. In an aristocracy the exercise of sovereignty is more intense (*intentior*) and more absolute (*absolutior*) because between the mass of the subjects and the rulers there is no intermediate class of people who mitigate power or who serve as the natural object of the monarch's hatred. In other words, the mass of the people tends to suffer more from aristocratic than from monarchical absolutism. Huber agreed however with Spinoza in thinking that the most absolute state is the best and that an aristocracy is thus preferable to a monarchy. Direct democracy, although admittedly the most absolute state, he held to be dangerous as the masses are unruly and rebellious. However, if in a democracy the obviously inadequate and irresponsible individuals were excluded from power, or if in an aristocracy all competent people move so easily towards high office that the distinction between aristocracy and democracy becomes insignificant, the best possible state is at hand, both freer and far more absolute and stable than a monarchy. It will become even better if one more element is introduced : a written constitution in which man's security, property and liberty are guaranteed.

It was by this type of reasoning rather than by *droit divin* theories that absolutism was brought back to earth. Eventually absolutist republicanism turned out to be more fruitful than the rarified extremism of absolute monarchy. In the seventeenth century it was still wholly inadequate to serve as a realistic alternative for most states. But in spite of its obvious limitations it contained elements which rendered the idea of absolutism viable. Absolute monarchy proved a failure. Already in the early eighteenth century it was becoming clear that the 'modern state' was by no means necessarily an absolute monarchy, although it was still widely thought that to achieve stability a state must be absolute. The 'absolute state' came to stand for 'the state' in general. When it was associated first with Hobbesian individualism and then with Dutch republicanism, the concept became so flexible and realistic that it lost its singularity. It could now be used to explain some important requirements of political life – the permanence of power as well as its functional limitations – without being elevated to the realm of juridical abstraction. Thus it was saved for posterity.

In yet another way absolutism deeply influenced European developments. In one of his interesting essays Gerhard Oestreich[10] has shown that for the present generation of historians it is difficult to believe in the merits for which absolutism was so often praised. Even if we assume (and it is not certain that we ought to) that absolute monarchy strove for 'centralisation', we know that it did not succeed. Much more important, as a result of absolute government and the absolutist spirit of the age, is what Oestreich has called *Sozialdisziplinierung*: absolutism helped to transform man into a socially disciplined being who learned to obey and to be obeyed, like law and order, to place the stoic virtues of self-control and reason above passion and lust. In his relations with superiors, equals and inferiors he was taught to keep to clearly defined rules. In the relations between the states, the *Jus Europeanum Publicum* and the slowly developing law of war were intended to clarify and put order into a chaotic situation. In military matters, in administration and in public or private morals discipline was thought to be of primary importance; it had to be furthered, if necessary, by harsh measures. This was, according to Oestreich, the lasting achievement of monarchical absolutism. He may well be right that this was a service absolutist monarchy rendered and one which benefited other forms of government: no democracy can function if its subjects have not learned to behave as socially responsible beings prepared to obey the rules. If Western democracy is at present (as is generally believed) going through a crisis that will transform it, we may be moving into a new post-absolutist era. Not only the exorbitant exaltation of sixteenth- and seventeenth-century monarchical absolutism but also the more realistic practices of democratic absolutism and discipline may disappear, though both have undeniably played a most significant role.

NOTES

1 A. J. Black, *Monarchy and Community. Political Ideas in the later Conciliar Controversy* (London, 1970).

2 Boris Porchnev, *Les soulèvements populaires en France de 1623 à 1648* (Paris, 1963). The original Russian edition was published in 1948.

3 Roland Mousnier, 'Recherches sur les soulèvements populaires en France avant la Fronde', *Revue d'histoire moderne et contemporaine*, v (1958) pp. 81–113; idem., 'Problèmes de méthode dans l'étude des structures sociales des XVIe, XVIIe, XVIIIe siècles', in K. Repgen and S. Skalweit (eds) *Spiegel der Geschichte. Festgabe für Max Braubach* (Münster, 1964) pp. 550–64.

4 F. Hartung and R. Mousnier, 'Quelques problèmes concernant la monarchie absolue', *Relazioni* (of the 10th International Congress of the Historical Sciences held at Rome, 1955) pp. 3–55; R. Mousnier, 'The Exponents and Critics of Absolutism', *New Cambridge Modern History*, IV (Cambridge, 1970) pp. 104–31.

5 J. P. Cooper, 'Differences between English and Continental Governments in the Early Seventeenth Century', in J. S. Bromley and E. H. Kossmann (eds), *Britain and the Netherlands* (London, 1960) pp. 62–90; idem., 'General Introduction', *New Cambridge Modern History*, IV (Cambridge, 1970) pp. 1–66; idem., 'The Fall of the Stuart Monarchy', ibid., pp. 531–84.

6 Stephan Skalweit, 'Frankreich und der Englische Verfassungskonflikt im 17. Jahrhundert', *Rapports* (of the 13th International Congress of the Historical Sciences held at Moscow, 1970) n.p.

7 *New Cambridge Modern History*, IV, p. 12 f.

8 E. H. Kossmann, *Politieke theorie in het zeventiende-eeuwse Nederland* (Verhandelingen Kon. Ned. Ak. van Wet., Amsterdam, 1960).

9 Benedict de Spinoza, *The Political Works*, ed. and translated by A. G. Wernham (Oxford, 1958) pp. 370–1, 372–3.

10 Gerhard Oestreich, 'Strukturprobleme des europäischen Absolutismus', in idem., *Geist und Gestalt des frühmodernen Staates* (Berlin, 1969) pp. 179–97.

2 What is Absolutism?*

G. DURAND

One historian's reply to this question is brief and to the point:
'Let us not talk of absolutism, that empty word into which everyone reads the meaning he wants, that favourite cliché of historians
in a hurry.' All the same, it might be useful to attempt a commentary on the term and reflect on its implications. At the very
least this exercise should make us more careful about the way we
use the word 'absolutism'. According to Littré the noun is a neo-
logism: it did not figure in the political vocabulary of the Ancien
Régime. Its late appearance therefore suggests an *a posteriori*
attempt to reconstruct a political system; the word itself reeks
of polemics, like totalitarianism, Machiavellism and similar
'isms'.

● Etymologically, the term absolutism denotes a form of power
which is unrestrained; more specifically it implies that no external
agency can suspend or delay the action of the sovereign power.
As a power which is free to act absolutism was, with the passage
of time, thought of as a power liberated from restraint. No
declaration, edict, charter or constitution ever established a system
of absolute power, but sovereigns gradually freed themselves from
the restraints imposed on the exercise of power by tradition, combinations of social forces, or the laws drawn up by their predecessors. Absolutism can therefore only be understood as a constant
struggle, an endless effort by the sovereign power to free itself.
This implies that the 'absolute' monarchies were continually moving in the direction of greater independence without ever
achieving complete freedom of action. They encountered serious
opposition. To regard absolutism as a 'constitutional system' is
to deal in myths rather than in realities. Absolutism is not so

* From G. Durand, *Etats et institutions XVIᵉ–XVIIIᵉ siècles* (Paris,
1969).

much a form of government as a tendency, a direction, which the exercise of power always seeks to take.

The progress of absolutism

Before we can describe absolute power we must examine the restrictions which hedged it about. In the late fifteenth century, from the Atlantic to the Urals, there were very few sovereigns who were masters of their own decisions and free to execute them. Louis XII, Henry VII, Ferdinand and Isabella, Maximilian I, and John Albert Jagellon (Jagillo) all had to reckon with their estates, their parliaments, their *cortes* or their diets. Only Sultan Bayezid II or Ivan III, whose marriage to Sophia Palaeologa in 1472 led him to assume the title of tsar, could claim to have overcome all resistance. But even they faced opposition : the support which the boyars or the janissaries gave them also hampered and troubled them, even if it did not actually restrict or halt the exercise of their power. All over Europe there were rival centres of power, relics of the long period of feudal anarchy – the great feudatories, the free cities, the privileged orders. The struggle amongst these rivals took place on three fronts :

1. The chief threat came from the nobles. Everywhere they based their independence on the possession of landed property, on the income from their estates, on their control of local government (i.e. their judicial and police functions in the countryside), but above all on their followings of retainers and clients which enabled them to remain in a state of near permanent conspiracy. Acting through their leaders, the magnates, and finding allies even within the innermost royal circles (such as Don Carlos of Spain or Gaston d'Orléans in France), the nobles exercised constant pressure on the monarchy. The most moderate of them demanded a seat on the royal council as a natural right, for in their view the feudal monarchy which they sought to preserve was no more than a contractual federation of a king and his peers. English lords, Russian boyars, the peers of France, the grandees of Spain, the German princes and Polish senators : everywhere the high nobility claimed to share the royal power. The monarchs strove, with varying success, to exclude the nobles from their councils, or at least to offer them seats by a supposedly free, spontaneous and revocable act. At the same time they also attacked the threat at its foundations : they struggled to develop their own competing

systems of administration in order to deprive the nobility of their local power. A new nobility of officials and commissioners, of *oprichniks*, fought the pretensions of the old nobles. The confiscation of apanages and great fiefs cut away their territorial and financial base. Finally domestication, working through their greed and vanity, completed the process of subjugation.

2. The sovereign was not truly free until he had achieved the right to tax at will. Fiscal absolutism faced great obstacles. No sovereign at the end of the fifteenth century dared to claim that he could raise taxes without consent. The permanent *taille* in France was levied in theory by an assumed extension of the consent of the Estates-General of 1439. Everywhere else it was the parliament, the *cortes*, the diet or the states which voted subsidies, *servicios* or the *Gemeine Pfennig*. The Spanish monarchy had to wait until 1624 before it could claim to dispense with the consent of the *cortes* in tax matters. The English parliament never permitted such laxity : the question of ship money in 1635–7 led to the English revolution of 1642. Only Louis XIV was able to impose new taxes (the *capitation* and the *dixième*), but the whole early modern period in France was punctuated by revolts against taxation. To escape from such decisive limitations sovereigns who were not absolute had to take refuge in expedients. Queen Elizabeth for instance shared in the profits of the companies she licensed, quite a sensible measure. The kings of Spain exploited their colonies by means of the 'royal fifth', or borrowed large sums and then declared themselves bankrupt as in the business of *asientos*. Kings issued state bonds such as the *rentes* of Francis I, secured on the *hôtel de ville* of Paris in 1523, tampered with the currency, sold offices, or obtained loans from financiers. All this indicates the real limits of absolutism.

3. The claims of the crown officials also had to be faced. To tame the nobles and draw freely on the sum of national wealth were enormous tasks : the monarchs needed assistants. All went well so long as the royal servants were conscientious. But revolt or recalcitrance on the part of these indispensable administrators posed the difficult question, 'Quis custodiet custodem?' Monarchs aimed at creating a type of official who would be amenable to control. Once the nobles, assistants by right of birth, had been removed or neutralised, the sovereign power was able to create officials. This method of recruitment proved unsatisfactory :

venality undermined the whole system by making the official independent and thus a potential rebel. Monarchies had to reckon with these bodies of officials, particularly after their assimilation into the order of nobility lent weight to their pretensions. In the end the state's only sure means was to create commissioners, revocable at will, without any special privilege and without any authority beyond a non-venal delegation of powers. This system spread through France under Richelieu, through Russia at the time of the *chinovniks*, Prussia under the 'sergeant-major king' (Frederick William, 1713–40), Spain under the Bourbons. For absolutism to achieve perfection it would have been necessary for the whole government and administration to consist only of officials of this type. It is worth noting that Maupeou's reforms (1771) aimed at nothing less than changing the hereditary and venal offices of the Parlements into commissions.

Resistance to absolutism
This striving towards absolutism – the struggles against the nobility, against the assemblies which voted taxes and against the crown's own officials – provoked the hostility and resistance of those who were excluded from influence, participation or control of government.

This opposition never ceased. Absolutism was always striving but never victorious, except perhaps in France under Colbert when there was no rebellious nobility, no parlements with political ambitions, no obstacle to the levying of taxes except for a few easily suppressed local revolts, as yet no Protestants in revolt, and no new masters on the scene – the bankers and financiers who had to be flattered and permitted to grow rich. Everywhere else experience showed that the strong positions of the enemy could not all be taken. Despite the myth of Enlightened Despotism, the eighteenth century even witnessed important reconquests by the anti-absolutist forces: the Polysynodie and the agitation of the parlements in France; the triumph of parliament in England; the charter of liberties of the Russian nobility, freed from their duty of service to the state; the defeat of Josephinism.

It is easy enough to enumerate these well-known instances of political history. The problem is to explain how, in a period when political theory justified and exalted the sovereign power of the prince to a degree which it had never attained before, those

deprived of power succeeded in organising general resistance or
in procuring the monarch's defeat. That there should have been
opposition is in no way surprising : the real question is why it was
so often successful. On the one hand, kings had developed the
means for exercising their power as never before through the
amounts of money at their disposal, the strength of their armies
and the efficiency of their bureaucracies; while the discontented
for their part were not numerous. In France the nobility and the
officials, together with their families, amounted to no more than
one million in a population of twenty million; everywhere else
the proportion seems to have been lower still. There are two possible explanations. The opposition, even when it was on the
defensive, may have felt itself to be inviolable because of ancient
privileges; or it may have been able, through demagogic methods,
to gain acceptance for the belief that any attack on its privileges
was an attack on the rights of all subjects of which it was the
guardian.

However absolutist a king might be in his aims and behaviour,
he never attacked the principle of privilege. The system of
privileges varied from one state to another. Fiscal privilege in
France was unbelievably absurd and unjust, while Spain had a
less inequable system; in England exemption from taxes was
unknown, each landowner paying a given percentage of the land
tax. Fiscal privilege was matched by claims to legal privilege. In
the twenty-seven articles of its 8 July 1648 Declaration the Paris
Parlement demanded the right of habeas corpus for officials of
the Parlement even though these were already outside the jurisdiction of the ordinary courts and could be tried only by the
chambre des requêtes.

The final establishment of absolutism required one essential
precondition : the destruction of the social order of the Ancien
Régime. If the king's authority was to be unlimited, he would
have to destroy every obstacle which the monarchy had created
– in other words, the whole system of privilege. How could the
law be applied equally to all, when it was understood in advance
that some were exempt from it ?

The opposition's most brilliant feat – a masterpiece of sleight-
of-hand – was to persuade public opinion that privilege and
liberalism went hand-in-hand, and that when the reforms instituted by the monarchy deprived a small group of the means of

opposition, this was an attack on the wellbeing of all. In a society immobilised and dominated by the privileged orders, the only hope for reform lay either in a revolution of the masses or in a government which refused to respect privilege – in other words, absolutism.

England provides the best example of the failure of absolutism. Yet here the conditions created by the slaughter of the nobility during the Wars of the Roses, and the absence of venal office-holding, should have opened the way to absolutism under princes as ambitious and authoritarian to the point of terrorism as were the Tudors. But there was parliament. It defeated these royal pretensions single-handed. Under the Tudors the crisis of the Reformation placed it in the role of arbiter between Henry VIII and the pope, making it indispensable to the king and forcing him to recognise its fiscal and legislative powers. Under the Stuarts, parliament acted as guarantor of the national religion and maintained its prerogatives – votes of supply, control of royal ministers through impeachment, and approval of bills. It mistrusted the autocratic tendencies of James I and Charles I, and the Catholic sympathies of James II. Absolutism in England was never more than an abortive attempt.

Absolutism: myth and reality
Viewed as a tendency rather than as a political system, absolutism is an undeniable reality. In every state the sovereign sought to free himself from pressure and control. The means were everywhere the same; the monarch tried to rule through councillors whom he chose rather than nobles who claimed such positions as their right. He also tried to recover control of the administration of justice which had been taken over by the feudal nobility and the church. These tendencies produced two institutions common to every state.

First a small, inner or secret council, a cabinet ('Conseil des Affaires'), distinct from the traditional councils which had grown from the division of the functions of the old *Curia Regis*. There is great similarity between, for instance, the *Consejo de Estado* in Castile, the inner circle of the privy council in England, the Austrian Council of State of 1748 and the Imperial council set up by Catherine the Great in 1769.

Second, a system of unifying and centralising judicial institu-

tions. In France the drafting of customary law in the sixteenth
century and the publication of the Codes and Great Ordinances
in the seventeenth, formed the basis for royal intervention in the
judicial process. The procedures of *évocation* to a higher court,
or judgement by special commissioners named by the king, were
specifically French; but an institution like the *conseil des parties*
had its counterpart in the Royal Council of Castile, the English
Star Chamber, or the Austrian *Hofrat*.

From this we may infer the existence of a general climate of
absolutism, more or less pervasive, which offered the monarch no
more than the opportunity to deliberate on matters of state without being affected by intrigue and pressure, and to ensure that
the judicial process followed his wishes and directives.

As an actual political system, absolutism is a myth. The monarchs themselves never regarded themselves as absolute, except
in the case of the autocrats of Russia, where the lack of fundamental laws, of established customs and corporate orders within
the state allowed the growth of a dictatorial form of government.
In France, however, even Louis XIV never planned to abolish
the Parlement, but merely curbed its pretensions and in December
1655 limited its right of remonstrance; nor did he try to abolish
the estates. Monarchs did not try to create a system of institutions
which would destroy any possibility of resistance through inertia.
They merely sought to restrict the activities of persons who might
cause trouble and to set up a new administrative structure parallel
to the old; a handful of commissioners directed, urged on and
controlled the system inherited from a time when counsel, remonstrance and shared power were the rule. Sovereigns also continued
to delegate their administrative powers through the sale of offices,
or to farm them out to financial potentates who became virtual
states within the state. The kings of Spain suffered the tyranny
of their own councils. In practice absolutism seems much more
the result of circumstances and personalities than of a deliberate
intention to revolutionise the whole structure of the state.

Two sets of circumstances, internal and external, favoured the
extension of absolutism. Every period of war, whether for survival
or for hegemony, was marked by the advance of absolutism.
Francis I and Henri II, Richelieu and Mazarin against the Habsburgs, Louis XIV striving for European supremacy, were all

obliged to extend their power in order to find the means with which to carry out their policies and to attempt to destroy the opposition and intrigues which might have thwarted them. During the intervals of peace the monarchy behaved more gently. Fundamentally, absolutism seems to have grown out of a balance of the dominant social classes which resulted from a particular economic situation. The state was seeking to free itself from the trammels of society. Any class will attempt to take over the machinery of the state when the opportunity is favourable in order to impose its own dominance. The opportunity is favourable for the state to free itself from class domination when two social trajectories cross : when the bourgeoisie is rising and the nobility is losing ground, the state can step between them as mediator. It can then try to prolong this moment of equilibrium, from which it benefits, by playing one class off against the other. At this point the natural dynamism of authority will blossom forth as absolutism.

THE PHYSIOLOGY OF THE FRENCH MONARCHY

Analysed in terms of the functions it fulfilled, the French monarchy – like any state structure – may be defined in part by its ability to control and mobilise national strength and resources, but in part also by the conflict between conservative and innovative tendencies which was inherent in it. In this way it should be possible to determine – as with a modern state – both its permanent, general direction, and its political orientation, which changed with time and was the result of a choice between resistance or movement.

Regulatory and mobilising functions

Legislative power. The regulations by which modern France was organised derived either from custom or from enacted law.

The whole of private law (professional, patrimonial or family law, and so on) was based on the codification of immemorial practices, and on their tacit acceptance. These customs did not originate in the authority of any individual or in the action of the sovereign power. In actual practice these customs would apply only for a limited area – a town or district, at the most a province. At the time of his coronation, or in the treaty by which he annexed a new province, the king swore to respect such customs.

Roman law, in force in the southern provinces, was merely one
local custom among many others; its strength came from traditional use, not from the authority of Justinian.

The monarchy had long been interested in customary law, for
if the king was to uphold it, he had to know it; if he was restricted
by it, his agents had to find ways around it while maintaining an
appearance of respect. The modern period marks a new departure.
The Ordinance of Montilz-lez-Tours of 1454 instructed the *baillis*
and *seneschals*, who were most immediately concerned, to codify
the customs in force in their areas of jurisdiction with the help of
men learned in the law and of representatives of the three estates.
From 1487 a procedure in four stages was followed : a project
would be drawn up, sent to Paris for scrutiny by the royal officials,
adopted by a local assembly, with the king giving the final decision
in any instance on articles which were deemed 'discordant'. This
royal arbitration represents an innovation when compared with
medieval practice. Royal intervention increased through official
codification and reform of customary law – particularly in the
work of Président Christophe de Thou between 1556 and 1582
– and by the establishment of general customary law which
eliminated the contradictions between different localities. This
prepared the way for *A Common Law of France*, the title of the
work published by Bourjon in 1720, who brought to a conclusion
the efforts of A. Loisel in the previous century. In his *Customary
Institutes* the latter had set forth as his aim 'to reduce to conform-
ity with a single law' the different French provinces 'which all
obeyed through the same king' (though in this he had only
limited success).

Total success would have entailed bringing custom into accordance with enacted law. 'As the king wishes, so wishes the law.'
Absolutism could not permit the existence of any source of law
but the royal will, whether in the sphere of general enactments
or in the acceptance of customs which therefore had to be transformed into local privileges. In theory at least the king could
intervene only in matters relating to the general welfare : in
questions of justice – the supreme kingly function; in matters of
policy, which included the whole range of administration (high-
ways, provisioning, public assistance, etc.) as well as in the maintenance of public order; finally in financial affairs, for without
finances there could be no judicial or administrative powers. The

royal will was expressed in 'letters', parchments or papers bearing
the royal seal or signature. The vast accumulation of royal acts
falls into three categories : individual enactments (decrees, orders,
commissions), such as appointments to offices, commissions for
intendants or *lettres de cachet*; collective privileges (which were
granted to groups and orders, or to cities) and general laws. These
last were the most important, because of their general application, and because they were political decisions made in response
to the needs of the state by the king and his council. They included letters-patent, with address, preamble, indication of the
council on whose authority the patent was issued, and executive
formula, all of which were subject to registration by the Parlement. They also included decrees of the council overriding the
decisions of the sovereign courts. Letters-patent dealing with a
single point were known as edicts, while those which covered a
whole series of subjects were called ordinances. They were the
product of long consultation and serious debate and were subjected to minute examination by the royal council. The ordinances
reveal long-term political purposes and reflect an underlying
scheme of organisation even where continual effort (demonstrated
by declarations, explaining and modifying the ordinances) was
required to put them into effect; whereas the decrees of the council and most edicts touch only on matters of immediate concern.

Mobilising functions. Once the royal will was clearly expressed,
its execution demanded the utilisation of resources, either human
or material.

   The king's subjects were at his disposition, and he could call
upon each one of them when the public good required. The difficulties inherent in such a summons had long ago led the monarchy
to demand permanent service from a certain number, while the
remainder provided the money to pay for such services. In theory
the nobility, as the feudal host, owed the duty of military service
but in practice the troops – national or foreign – were paid and
could not have existed without the support of the public finances.
The purchase of commissions turned the regiment or company
into the private property of the officer and made him a dealer in
armed men; the payment of a stipend allowed him to maintain
his force and, above this, to make a profit in proportion to his dishonesty. 'An officer is only concerned to have his money and not

B*

to keep his soldiers', Turenne complained in 1658. In the same way, legal and financial officials received a salary, commissioners were paid their emoluments, and the great nobles were awarded pensions as the price of their docility. The royal ministers were equally attentive to their own interests. All the provisions, materials, labour and services required by the state were handled by the treasury. It was a long time ago that subjects had served the king 'graciously and without reward, being content with the honour', as a *cahier* of the nobility asserted somewhat anachronistically in 1649, when they recalled 'the old order of things as they were practised before the reign of Louis XIII'. The reintroduction of the royal *corvée* on the roads proved a futile and unpopular attempt to reassert the principle of service without pay. The king in fact could only get what he was willing to pay for.

In other words, the king's power was directly related to his ability to tax the country. Mobilising the resources of the state meant raising taxes, negotiating loans, selling offices, exploiting crown lands, sometimes even reducing the value of the livre or recoining the money. How far did this fiscal system effectively mobilise the resources of the French state?

To answer this question we must examine the circulation of money. Modern economic theory has shown that it is absurd to speak of a nation's 'fiscal burden' : the state budget effects a shift only in part of the national wealth, since the state spends what it collects in revenue, and sometimes a little more; taxes are paid out as pensions, salaries, wages and profits. Although the machinery may seem complex, the circulation of money in France is simple. The peasantry provided the mass of direct taxes (the *taille* in particular) and also of indirect taxes (the *gabelle*, the *traites* and the *aides*). In addition the peasants paid various seigneurial dues, rents and tithes supposedly to compensate a feudal class for services, though in fact these services had fallen into desuetude. The peasants never received money; government concern for them went no further than occasional reductions of the *taille*. The bourgeoisie, officials and clergy contributed unequally, in the form of the 'free gift' paid by the clergy, the annual tax on offices, and a reduced *taille* or lump sums paid to compound for the *taille*. Their main contribution was in the form of loans, which brought them interest on a fairly regular basis, even though they could hardly hope for repayment in full. Two social groups

benefited handsomely : the nobility, who paid only a small indirect tax but received salaries and pensions; and the tax-farmers,
who merely made loans, but reimbursed themselves for the risk
involved by taking a big cut of the indirect taxes which they
contracted to collect. The *capitation* (1695) and the *vingtièmes*
(1741) did little to change the iniquities of this system. Fiscal
privilege and the awarding of pensions made the nobility the
principal beneficiaries of the budget. Below them the officials and
the bourgeoisie, and to a lesser degree the clergy, contributed loans
which were a disguised form of taxation, but which nonetheless
brought the state some relief and in any case enabled them to
bargain with the government.

Conservative tendencies

The mobilisation of national resources was thus inadequate; it
bore most heavily on the poor and spared the very rich. It was
possible to increase the level of taxation, but not to modify its
relative distribution. During the Ancien Régime the first priority
of the government was the preservation of the social order. This
does not imply a logical and rational organisation of the various
groups within the kingdom, but rather a static situation deriving
from the immobility of mental attitudes : social relationships were
accepted as part of the natural order when in fact they were the
product of a historical equilibrium.

The maintenance of public order. This function seems to have
been far more extensive under the Ancien Régime than it is today.
Murders, robberies, brawls and riots were far more frequent, but
were not tolerated. What stands out is the differentiation in the
state's repression. A commoner would be hanged for a crime for
which a gentleman would only spend a short time in the Bastille
or obtain the king's pardon. People of quality were scandalised,
as their correspondence reveals, when Richelieu punished duellers
or when Louis XIV imprisoned Fouquet at Pinerolo. The idea of
public order further comprised ethics, and was identified with
the moral and religious order. Concubinage, the acting profession,
or Protestant beliefs were considered, despite a *de facto* tolerance
at certain times, to be breaches of the prescribed faith and behaviour, and were punished by moral sanctions – refusal of
Christian burial, or insistence on burial at night; in times of fana-

ticism, even burning at the stake. Censorship hunted down sedi-
tious pamphlets and unorthodox books and ideas, even a straight-
forward economic analysis advocating reforms such as Vauban's
Dixme Royale. Witchcraft was still held to be a crime rather than
a symptom of mental disorder. Guild regulations fixed the system
of professional training, industrial organisation and production;
to contravene them was a breach of public order. Turgot's suppression of the wardens of guilds in 1776 seemed a 'horrifying
idea' to Séguier, the *avocat général*, who went so far as to argue
that 'it is these obstacles, hindrances and prohibitions which make
for the glory, security and immensity of the commerce of France'.
In the countryside there were many types of coercion : the pro-
hibition of enclosure, the observance of crop rotation, the fixing
of a date for the grape-harvest. Such regulations were also part
of an age-old order which was public and considered 'natural'.
To deter potential law-breakers, the state set up the machinery of
police and criminal justice. The cruelty of its methods (in preparatory and preliminary questioning) and of its punishments (the
galleys, the wheel, drawing and quartering or the stake) were a
normal part of this society in which gentleness played so small a
part. The army was used without hesitation for repressive purposes; military terror assured the return to their obedience of
subjects driven to despair by taxation, or the return to the fold
of heretics.

The maintenance of the social order. One of the state's functions
was to preserve inequalities and particularism. Society was based
on distinctions of office and rank. Absolutism tended in the end
to abolish these distinctions and reduce all its subjects to the same
level. In 1776, during the *lit de justice* in which he imposed his
reforming edicts, Louis XVI nonetheless asserted that he had no
intention of 'destroying differences of rank' or depriving the
nobility of its 'distinctions'. The sense of social differences was too
strong for the rulers to obliterate them, and the monarchy preferred instead to take advantage of social rivalries and conformism.
The nobility provides a good example of this. For a long time they
clung to the memory of their past power, which the monarchy
had increasingly whittled away. Despite various counter-attacks
– rebellions and plots during the Wars of Religion, the Fronde
and the Regency years – the nobility was ultimately forced to give

up its place within the political power system of the state. But it gave up none of its social prerogatives. The feudal reaction under Louis XVI was certainly self-interested; but the French aristocracy, protected by fiscal privilege and loaded with pensions, had never been treated unfavourably by the monarchy. The aristocracy's lavish spending, and its refusal to play an active part in the country's economy, are sufficient to explain its poverty which was in any case relative. The one area in which the nobles would not compromise was in that of 'quality'; and the constitution of 1791 did indeed offer the nobles in their capacity as landed proprietors what they had all along claimed by right of their birth. Similar analyses may be made in respect of the other classes or orders. The question is why the monarchy accepted this sanctification of the social order, and even favoured the subordination of one group to another on the grounds of 'prestige' or 'established greatness', at the very moment when the *philosophes* attacked, in the name of reason and social utility, the 'idleness' and privileges of the nobility as the judicial foundation of all particularism and inequality. The reasons for this are numerous. The monarchy was aware of the insuperable opposition offered by mental attitudes. The king and his ministers shared the generally accepted view of society and realised the danger of undermining the principle of inequality which was the ultimate guarantee of authority at any level of society. Here we meet the most deeply-felt justification for the existence of the Ancien Régime state : a static view of hierarchical orders whose equilibrium had to be maintained, a condition of rest in the Aristotelian sense of the term. The purpose of the state was the preservation of order and not the initiation of movement, as all motion was held to destroy a naturally established order. Conservation and restoration were the primary aims of the monarchy.

Nothing illustrates this attitude better than the meaning of the term reform or reformation in the Ancien Régime. For us, to reform is to change an unsatisfactory state of affairs, to adapt legislation to reality. Our reformers think that the future will be better if a different type of society is brought about by suitable measures. But in France before 1789 'reform' meant the return to an earlier condition of things which had been altered for the worse by social evolution. This was the spirit behind the great reforming ordinances of Villers-Cotterets (1539), of Blois (1579), and the Code Michaud (1629). Their purpose was always the same : to go back to original principles, and to restore and strengthen institutions which had been corrupted by the passage of time. Absolutism, however, was also capable of innovations since it asserted that the monarchy was not bound by any restrictions and that its will, like God's, was capable of new creations. From a 'simple paternal monarchy' we move here to the divine right monarchy, to a conception of the monarch as a demiurge who not only maintains and restores, but really governs and creates. The first signs of this revolution can be seen in the work of Richelieu, whose temerity was attacked by every upholder of the existing order.

Innovating tendencies

Although the theory of absolutism might allow for innovation, it was dangerous for it to clash openly with a static attitude of mind. Public opinion rejected new measures as a breach of the contract between the king and his subjects laid down in the coronation oath. Nonetheless the monarchy pressed forward, especially after 1750 when the idea of progress was gaining acceptance; the *philosophes* inspired some innovations at the time when the 'system', under Turgot in particular, attempted some forward-looking changes. The Paris Parlement, a reliable touchstone in such matters, expressed its anxiety and asked 'what necessity compels such simultaneous changes in every branch of the administration?' The innovations criticised were in any case only minor ones; and the Paris Parlement, which in 1776 condemned the abolition of the wardenships of the guilds as an innovation which would undo 'certain ancient and unchangeable principles', had used these same principles to oppose the institution of the wardenships in 1582 and 1583.

Despite opposition, the innovative impulse achieved some successes. In the field of education the state broke the clerical monopoly by setting up the Collège de France in 1530, established royal institutions like the School of the Corps of Royal Engineers in 1748 and the Royal School of Drawing in 1767, and created new disciplines, as in the teaching of French law by a professor at the Sorbonne (to be nominated by the king), under an edict of 1679. The economy was also affected by the current of reforming legislation, its ebb and flow dictated by the inertia of the popular mentality and the pressure of privileged interests. The results, however, were not negligible : the abolition of free pasture and rights of way in eastern France and Béarn between 1767 and 1777, the division of common lands, the free trade in grain (enacted in 1774, suspended in 1776, finally re-established in 1787). In general, agriculture and the exchange of its products were freed from century-old restraints written into local customs and considered by public opinion as part of a natural and beneficial order. The edict of 1759 on printed cloths opened the way for a gradual relaxation of industrial regulations. The abolition of guild wardenships in 1776 has already been mentioned, and we may note that the *corvée* was abolished in the same year. Temporary suspensions of such measures does not alter the fact that the will now existed to create a new order more in tune with social and economic movements of the time, even anticipating them in face of strong opposition. Although the government did not follow all the proposals which the marquis d'Argenson (minister from 1744 to 1747) made in his *Considérations sur le Gouvernement de la France* (Considerations on the Government of France), a new spirit animated it once Bertin became controller-general (1759–63). An effort was made, albeit belatedly, hesitantly and lacking in firmness, to endow the monarchy with 'all the virtues of a republic'. Thus may we sum up the political programme of enlightened despotism.

These successes were, however, offset by resounding failures. [These are dealt with in detail in Chapter xx of Durand's book.] We should note the victorious opposition of the parlements throughout the eighteenth century to any attempt to restrict their political role: the failure of the 1771 Maupeou revolution by 1774, the ineffective exile of the parlement to Troyes in 1787, and the short lifespan of the Laimognon reforms of 1788.

The real danger lay, however, in the tendency on the part of the privileged orders to take over and adapt to their own purposes the most promising royal innovations and reforms. Not the least of the paradoxes of the overhaul of the provincial and municipal administration was that it created the means and the pretext for the revolt of the privileged orders just before 1789. The principle behind the establishment of the provincial and municipal assemblies (1778–87) was clearly revolutionary. Among the innovations we may mention the doubling of the representation of the Third

Estate and the subordination of the intendant to the elected representatives. This was a royal commitment to a policy of liberalism which, by giving part of the nation a say in government, automatically limited absolutism and envisaged collaboration between social classes. The result was confusion and unrest. Revolts occurred at Dijon and Toulouse; the nobility of the local estates stirred up the mountain population at Pau; and at Grenoble the meeting of the local assembly provoked serious disturbances. The aristocracy, with ulterior motives, made conscious and skilful use of the new forum which the government had provided; as Soboul has pointed out, by demanding 'that local administration be handed over to elected provincial Estates, it intended nonetheless to retain its social and political dominance within these institutions' (*Histoire de la Révolution française*, vol. i, pp. 121–2). Reform became reaction.

In its desire for reform, neutralised by its role as guarantor of the *status quo*, the French monarchy was caught in an insoluble contradiction. Without equality, any liberty would inevitably act to the monarchy's disadvantage. This ambiguity was inherent in the very concept of liberty. For the revolutionaries of 1789 liberty was a metaphysical principle which stated that no citizen should suffer any restriction other than that imposed by a freely-made law. For the opponents of the monarchy liberty meant 'liberties', all those particular measures which defined the individual's status, in other words the very privileges which were the basis of inequality. This ambiguity took some time to clarify. Local, provincial and corporate liberties imprisoned the state within narrow limits which nullified its freedom to innovate and restricted its capacity to mobilise the nation's resources and talents. The state's primary function was the preservation of the *status quo*; its other functions of mobilisation and innovation were subordinated to this : hence the social crisis and financial collapse which destroyed the Ancien Régime.

STATEMENT OF THE ROYAL FINANCES FOR 1680

1. *Revenues*		*livres*
Section I, tax-farms		29,318,762
General farm, the five great farms		8,004,809
General farm, the *aides* (sales taxes)		9,520,725
General farm, the *gabelle* (salt-tax)		5,516,464
Royal demesne in France		1,600,900
Royal demesne in Flanders		1,087,666
Post office		1,220,000
Section II, general revenues		23,482,107
		+412,552
	Paris	2,206,000
	Soissons	520,000
	Amiens	456,000
	Boulonnais	nil
	Châlons	790,000
	Orléans	1,372,000
	Tours	2,199,000
	Bourges	342,000
	Moulins	933,000
	Lyons	890,000
	Riom	1,730,000
	Poitiers	1,615,000
	Limoges	1,439,000
	Bordeaux	2,409,000
	Montauban	2,402,000
	Rouen	1,540,000
	Caen	1,206,000
	Alençon	1,097,000
	Grenoble	327,000
Section III, general revenues and grants from the *pays d'états*		7,369,411
Languedoc		1,745,000
Ypres and Dunkirk		758,000
Franche-Comté		677,000
Artois		400,000
Flanders		647,000
Section IV, woods and forests		865,736
Section V, extraordinary revenues including *rentes* (government bonds) and alienations of royal demesne		15,481,265
		12,453,780
Section VI, anticipation of revenue for 1681		16,349,414
Tax-farms		5,478,703
Grants and revenues from *pays d'états*		6,755,335
Advances on the borrowing fund, on money promised by the farmers of the *gabelles*		4,115,429
Total revenues		91,759,460

2. *Expenses*   *livres*

The most important items, in descending order:

Extraordinary military expenses, including the artillery	31,233,000
Repayments	10,792,000
Royal household	9,184,000
Construction and repair of royal buildings	8,513,000
Navy	4,928,000
Fortifications	4,603,000
Galleys	2,869,000
Interest on advances and costs of collection	2,389,000
Garrisons	2,345,000
Salaries of the council and wages of officials	2,302,000
Payments in cash for secret affairs	2,224,000
Payments in cash for gratifications	2,176,000
Cash in hand of the king	2,030,000
Military depôts	1,509,000
Household of the queen	1,381,000
Pensions	1,215,000
Household of monsieur	1,198,000
Payment of arrears on *rentes*	1,182,000

The least important items:

Commerce	324,000
Roads and bridges	300,000
Paris streets	58,000

Total expenses   96,318,016

3 The Development of Monarchical Institutions and Society in France*

R. MOUSNIER

It is a great honour for me to take part in a series of lectures on legal themes, as I am a mere historian. I am fortunate, however, in that a large proportion of the documents which I, as a social and institutional historian, have had to use such as decrees of the Royal Council or notarial records are legal documents. Consequently I do not share that curious disdain in which some historians hold the study of law, but realise full well how much the historian can learn from the jurists, even though the historian has other ends in view and will use the documents they both study in a different context from that of the jurist. I have made a point of studying the jurists of the seventeenth century and the historians of law from the eighteenth century to the present day and I owe a debt of gratitude to them. But I have no legal training, and although I am appreciative of the honour of the invitation to speak to you today I am also very much aware of the responsibility you have put upon me.

The subject on which I have been asked to address you is one which deserves to be introduced by a comparison of French seventeenth-century society and its political and administrative institutions with those of other European states in the same century. Only such a comparison, supported by tables of similarities and dissimilarities, would enable us to identify and describe these functions fully. But I must confess that I had to give up so ambi-

* A lecture given at the Society for the Study of the Seventeenth Century on 20 January 1962 and first published in *XVIIe Siècle*, nos 58–9 (1963) under the title 'L'évolution des institutions monarchiques en France et ses relations avec l'état social'.

tious an approach as we have but a short hour at our disposal. I will, therefore, concentrate on a few major institutional changes which occurred in the course of the seventeenth century and try to examine their relationship to changes or periodic movements within French society. I realise that my choice – dictated by necessity rather than inclination – will not satisfy the expectations of all of you. I may well be accused of arbitrariness but I hope that you will sympathise with my predicament and judge me leniently.

The first great institutional change to which I should like to draw your attention is the disappearance of the Estates-General. Their last meeting in the seventeenth century was in 1614–15; from then until 1789 no representative assembly for the whole kingdom met with the sovereign. But we must be quite explicit and stress that no legal change occurred. As far as the law was concerned nothing had changed : the Estates-General continued to exist in principle, though the king no longer summoned them. Such summoning was his prerogative; there was no breach of the law. Ever since the Estates-General of 1439 it had been admitted that the king could call the estates when he pleased. Nothing had therefore changed in the customary constitution of the state, though in fact we are faced with an important institutional change which greatly strengthened royal authority.

Were there social factors behind this profound change in institutions, if not in the constitution? There were; and the clash of interests between the orders of the kingdom, and the consequent impossibility of their offering a united front against the king, is a crucial factor. The Third Estate was at odds with the Nobility on the one hand and with the Clergy on the other; and their very enmities made the king first the arbitrator between the orders and then their master, so that he could not be forced to accept the control of regular meetings of the representatives of France.

The Nobility, as constituted in the Estates-General before 1614, was made up of the aristocracy of the sword; while the Third Estate was drawn mainly from the office-holding bourgeoisie. Of the 187 deputies of the Third Estate in 1614–15, 115 were 'real' bourgeois, forty-one were bourgeois who owned *seign-euries*, and though a further thirty-one possessed both titles of nobility which went with their offices as well as *seigneuries*, all

187 were considered 'mere bourgeois' by the Nobility. It was above all a 'bureaucratic' bourgeoisie. The 187 deputies included 121 royal officials, nearly all of them magistrates of the *bailliages* and the *sénéchaussées*; with the addition of municipal officials the total reaches 139 out of 187; with the officials of the provincial estates, 147; with the lawyers (whose profession brought them into contact with the office-holders and who almost to a man aspired to office) the figure rises to 177 out of 187. For the rest there were two 'merchants' and one '*laboureur*', that is a well-to-do peasant who owned a plough team,[1] and who might be thought of as the equivalent of a yeoman farmer in England.

The Nobles were greatly incensed at this 'bureaucratic' bourgeoisie. They blamed it for dispossessing them of their manors and fiefs; though in fact many noblemen had been ruined by the Wars of Religion and still more by the aristocratic way of life which required that a gentleman be generous to a fault, spending vast sums on the celebration of marriages, on the pomp of funerals and on fitting himself out for war, while abstaining from any activity associated with demeaning money-making. Noblemen were therefore, by obeying their own code of honour, forced to borrow huge amounts from the officials; and if they could not repay their debts, they had to hand over lands and fiefs in settlement.[2] The aristocracy also blamed the officials for depriving them of government positions and public functions. The nobility held that most public offices should be reserved for gentlemen : all posts in the highway police; all provostships of marshals, along with their vice-bailiffs and vice-seneschals; all positions in the Department of Waters and Forests, all grandmasterships and special masterships; all chief positions in the municipalities; half the offices of the tax assessors, the *trésoriers de France*; at least one-third of the magistracies in the sovereign courts (*parlements, chambres des comptes, cours des aides, grand conseil*), as well as all magistracies in the judicial bodies.[3] The Nobility attacked therefore the system of venality of office, by which the king sold public offices and allowed private citizens to trade in them; and it inveighed against the high price of offices which by necessity excluded gentlemen in straightened circumstances. The Nobles assailed the *paulette*, the annual tax on offices (that insurance premium which gave the family of an office-holder the right to keep the office, and retain its value for his family, in the event of

early or unexpected death), and held it responsible for the un-
doubted rise in the price of offices and the supposed increase in
their heritability.

During the meeting of Estates-General on 13 November 1614
the Nobility demanded that the king suspend, as a first step towards abolishing the tax, receipts for payment of the *paulette*.
The Clergy agreed with the Nobles. The Third Estate dared not
oppose this move, but countered by a demand that the king
should reduce the *taille*, which bore heavily on the poor, by four
million livres. The Third Estate went on to request that the king
(who already stood to lose 1,600,000 livres through the abolition
of the *paulette*) should reduce government pensions by 5,600,000
livres. It is worth stressing that these pensions were mostly paid
to gentlemen, who could not remain gentlemen without them.

The Nobility termed the two proposals by the Third Estate
'ridiculous' and demanded that they be submitted separately. The
Third Estate refused. On 17 November the Nobility and Clergy
as one unit, and the Third Estate as another, presented themselves before the king. This was the decisive moment. The orders
had each put forward separate sets of demands, thus placing the
king in the role of arbiter between them. The government from
now on could keep the orders divided and thus control them. The
king replied evasively and requested the orders to draw up their
lists of grievances, after which the deputies were to be sent home.

The dispute between the Third Estate and the Nobility grew
very bitter. Président Jean Saveron, speaking for the Third
Estate, had on 17 November argued on the issue of the *paulette* :
'This was not the cause of the Nobility's withdrawal and removal
from the dignities of judicial office, rather, it was the result of the
Nobility's view (which they had held for many years) that study
and learning weaken courage and make a generous spirit base
and cowardly.' He went on to criticise pensions for gentlemen by
observing 'that it was neither just nor fitting that the services
which noblemen naturally owed to the king out of loyalty should
be rewarded with money, as they are through royal pensions.'
This was bad enough, but a still more insulting suggestion was
attributed to Saveron : 'that His Majesty had had to purchase the
fidelity of the Nobility with money and that the excessive cost of
this had reduced the common people to living on grass like cattle.'
The nobles were beside themselves. They abused and threatened

Saveron; one of their number suggested that he should be put at the mercy of their pages and lackeys. The Nobles as an estate demanded that the Third Estate by a deputation declare that they had not meant to insult the order of Nobility. The Clergy acted as mediator. The Third Estate gave in and sent Henri de Mesmes, the civil lieutenant of Paris, to address the Nobles on 24 November. But de Mesmes made matters worse by his contention

> that the three orders were brothers, children of the same mother, France . . . that the Clergy was the eldest, the Nobility the middle one and the Third Estate the youngest. That for this reason the Third Estate had always considered that the Nobility had been raised somewhat above them . . . but that the Nobility should also recognise the Third Estate as its brother and not hold it in such contempt as to think it of no worth, for it was composed of many notable persons holding offices and dignities . . . and furthermore [the Nobility might ponder that] it often happened in a family that the elder sons ruined the house, while the youngest retrieved it and brought it to the highest point of glory.'

His speech caused uproar among the Nobles, who on 26 November went in a body to complain to Louis XIII. Their spokesman, the baron de Sénecey, appealed to the king to confound the insulting propositions of the Third Estate : 'Render judgement, Sire, and by a declaration filled with justice recall them to their duty.' As they withdrew the Nobles made their point : 'We do not wish to be called brothers by the sons of shoemakers and soap-boilers. Between us and them is as great a distinction as between master and servant.' Louis XIII ordered representatives of the Third Estate to apologise to the Nobility; but though payment of the *paulette* was suspended, pensions were also reduced by a quarter. For a second time the orders had thus been forced to seek the arbitration of the king, and the Nobles had even asked for the support of his absolute power. To the very end of the meeting of the Estates-General the question of the *paulette* and of venal office was to keep the orders divided.[4]

The Third Estate bore a grudge against the Clergy for having sided with the Nobles. Moreover, the deputies of the Third Estate – for the most part guardians of the royal authority – were traditionally hostile to the immunities enjoyed by the Clergy, since these reduced their own influence. They now took advantage of the great dispute on what power the papacy could exercise over monarchs which agitated all Europe, to attack the Clergy, and in particular the Jesuits, as upholders of the doctrine of papal supremacy. On 15 December 1614 the Third Estate extracted one of the points from the *cahier* of the Ile-de-France and placed it at the top of their list of grievances :

> that the king be requested to draw up in the assembly of the Estates, as a *fundamental law of the kingdom* which shall be known and inviolable to all, that as he is sovereign within his own state and holds his crown from God alone, there is no power on earth, whether spiritual or temporal, which has any right over his kingdom, either to remove from it the sacred persons of our kings or to absolve their subjects from the obedience and loyalty which they owe them, on whatever pretext it may be. That all subjects, of whatsoever condition they may be, shall keep this law as sacred and inviolable, *as being in conformity with the word of God*, without any distinction, equivocation or reserve whatever; which law shall be sworn and signed by all the deputies of the Estates, and henceforth by all officials and beneficed clergy of the kingdom. . . .[5]

The Clergy protested and sent Cardinal du Perron to address the Third Estate on 2 January 1615. In his speech du Perron singled out three points from the proposition of the Third Estate. The first concerned the safety of the king's person. Clergy and Nobility both agreed that 'it is unlawful to assassinate a king for any reason', even if he were a tyrant (Council of Constance, session 15). This was a divinely ordained and theological truth. The Clergy and Nobility were also in agreement on the second point, that of the dignity and temporal sovereignty of the kings of France. 'Our kings are sovereign, enjoying temporal sovereignty over all things within their realm, and are vassals neither of the Pope . . . nor of any other prince; but that as concerns the administration of temporal things, they depend directly upon God and recognise no power but His above their own.' This too was 'established truth', and Pope Innocent III had affirmed it. But the third point was open to dispute. The problem was as follows :

> that these princes or their predecessors having sworn before God and their subjects to live and die in the Christian and

Catholic faith, if they should break their oath and rebel against Jesus Christ, levying open war against Him; that is to say, if they not only fall into manifest heresy or apostasy, but also seek to force the consciences of their subjects, by implanting Arianism or Mohammedanism or some similar infidelity in their state, and abolishing or destroying Christianity; whether their subjects for their part may be declared freed from their oath of obedience, and if this should occur, who it is that has the authority to absolve them from their oath.

The Third Estate opposed this: 'there is no case in which subjects can be absolved from the oath of fidelity they have sworn to their princes.' But the whole Catholic church affirmed

that when a prince violates the oath which he has sworn to God and his subjects to live and die in the Catholic faith . . . this prince may be declared deprived of all his rights, as one guilty of treason against Him to Whom he swore the oath for his kingdom, that is to say against Jesus Christ himself; and his subjects may be absolved in their consciences and before a spiritual and ecclesiastical tribunal from the oath of allegiance which they had sworn to him; that in this case it is within the authority of the Church here on earth, acting either through its head, who is the Pope, or through the whole body of the faithful, which is the Council, to declare them so absolved.

The arguments both for and against the proposal were inconclusive. The Third Estate's article was not at variance with religion. But it was nonetheless dangerous to go against the opinion of the vast majority of the Catholic church. What made the Third Estate's article completely unacceptable to the Clergy was its claim to be speaking in accordance with the word of God, and the demand that its proposal be imposed upon all the faithful. This was 'forcing the souls of the faithful and straining their conscience'. It would

turn the authority of the Church upside-down and open the gate to all kinds of heresies if laymen take it upon themselves, without being guided or preceded by any Council or ecclesiastical judgement, to decide in matters of faith, declaring that one side in a dispute is in accordance with the word of God, while the other is impious and detestable. We hold therefore that this is to usurp the functions of the priesthood. [Such conduct, they went on, would] plunge us into a clear and perilous schism. For since all other peoples of the Catholic faith holds this doctrine, we cannot declare it to be contrary to the word of God, impious and hateful, unless we cut ourselves off from the head and the other members of the Church, thereby declaring that the Church has been for so many centuries not the true Church but the synagogue of Satan, not the bride of Christ but of the Devil . . . instead of securing the life and state of our kings, it will involve them in the greatest danger, by reason of the wars and other discords which schisms have always brought in their train.[6]

The Clergy appealed to Louis XIII who, after submitting the question to his council, decided to order the Third Estate to withdraw the offending article. This caused a storm among the Third Estate, increased their hostility to the Clergy, and largely explains their refusal to associate themselves with the Nobility and Clergy (though they co-operated with the other orders, reluctantly, for short periods) in efforts to force the government to carry out desired reforms. The controversy also helps to explain the lack of interest shown by the Clergy and the Nobility in a second article, which sought to establish regular meetings for the Estates-General, proposed by the Third Estate.

Faced by such disunity, Louis XIII remained in control. The orders themselves had invoked his absolute power; they had declared that he had no temporal superior; each one of them had asked him to use his absolute authority against the pretensions of the others. On 24 March 1615 the government felt able to dismiss the deputies. In 1614 and 1615, therefore, it was the representatives of the kingdom who voluntarily handed over their authority to the king; it was the representatives of the kingdom who desired not only absolutism, but monocracy.[7]

The next great change was the establishment of the intendants and the systematic extension of the intendant system throughout the provinces. The king had long made use of commissaries to make his orders known in the provinces. During the seventeenth century a permanent network of these commissaries was established, the most important of them being the provincial intendants. Such a commissary was placed above the existing officials:

he supervised them, spurred them on and at times even took over the functions of some of them. In the seventeenth century it was fashionable to connect the use of commissaries with the *Missi Dominici*, in the same way as the origins of the monarchy were traced back to Charlemagne. Apart from the prestige deriving from the imperial title, and the need to build up the French king's claims to sovereignty and independence from the Empire – as against the claims to universal dominion of the Holy Roman emperor – we must also take into account the tendency of any society based on custom to favour whatever is old merely because it is old.

The commissaries were called intendants from the mid-sixteenth century onwards. From the beginning of Richelieu's ministry they became increasingly numerous, their powers were extended, and in fact after 1642 they carried out the duties of the *trésoriers de France*. A radical change had thus taken place : the intendant was no longer only a kind of trouble-shooter; he had taken the place of old established officials and carried out their functions. This is all the more remarkable since we know that Richelieu did not like the intendants and tried to use them as little as possible.[8] The intendants aroused the opposition of various groups of officers – of the *trésoriers de France*, of the *élus* and of the sovereign courts. This helped to provoke the Fronde and by a royal declaration of 24 October 1648 the rebels obtained the abolition of intendants, 'except in the frontier provinces'. However, in fact the government was still able to keep the intendants at work under different guises; and officially they were gradually re-established when the Fronde was over after 1654.[9] Between the Peace of the Pyrenees in 1659 and the outbreak of the Dutch War in 1672 Louis XIV tried to satisfy popular demands expressed during the Fronde. He therefore made use of the intendants, but sought to restore them to their original role of 'inspectors'. He also gave them larger areas of activity, at least two *généralités* each, left them in their districts for a shorter time, and rotated them frequently so that they should get to know the whole kingdom. He further restricted their authority within narrow limits : they were to conduct inquiries, gather information and send reports to the council, but were not to assume the functions of the ordinary officials. Colbert supervised them closely. But the Dutch War brought new financial problems and the need for

rapid decisions carried out without delay. The intendants now
had to take care of everything and continued to do so, despite
the efforts of Colbert, during the period after the peace of 1679.
Colbert, however, died in 1683, and the omnicompetence of the
intendants was finally established during the Nine Years War and
that of the Spanish Succession.

This change is an important stage in a general process of transformation : the movement from judicial to executive administration. Administration is executive when public functions are entrusted by the holders of executive power to agents whose directives have coercive power, and who are not subject to restrictions
which a judge could impose on them. All over Europe from the
twelfth to the twentieth century judicial administration, which
offers greater guarantees for the respect of individual liberties, has
given way gradually to the more rapid and efficient system of
executive administration. Seventeenth-century France saw great
advances in this direction. But we should stress that the administrative system of seventeenth-century France remained judicial:
the king was the chief dispenser of justice, and it was this which
gave him the right to command. According to contemporaries the
king 'judged' matters of state, even of foreign policy, just as he
judged between individuals.[10] The intendants were also judges,
not only because they were frequently magistrates and often
chosen from the *maîtres des requêtes* of the royal household, but
also because in their capacity as delegates of the king, the chief
justice, they too were judges. Their ordinances were therefore
those of judges. They followed judicial procedures in their work.
They all had a *procureur de l'intendance*, who initiated proceedings on behalf of the king as representative of the general interest.
The intendant pronounced judgement on the *procureur's* case
and thus ordered what was necessary for the general good through
a judicial decision. In the seventeenth century we are in the early
stages of the shift to executive administration; the crucial step,
the creation of the prefects of Napoleon when he was First Consul,
is still in the future, though we must admit that the intendants
represent a significant advance along the road.

Here too the institutional change corresponds to a social movement. The primary and most important reason for the proliferation of the intendants was the increasing difficulty of obtaining
revenue in a century of economic recession and long wars. The

élus and the *trésoriers de France* could not cope with the growing mass of taxes of every kind. They declared inability to pay and allowed arrears, discharged parishes where they, their relations, friends and connections had tenants or sharecroppers, and shifted the burden of payment on to the other parishes. They burdened the taxpayers with the cost of tax-collection, using court bailiffs or sergeants armed with the power of arrest to intimidate them. The intendants distributed taxes more evenly and used fusiliers to collect them; this method of levying taxes by military means was less costly in the long run.[11]

The burden of taxation, which rose continually, seems to have been all the harder to bear since from about 1625 France entered a long period of 'mortalities' : decades of dearth, famine and high grain prices, accompanied by epidemics which at times carried off as much as 30 per cent of the population in a single year. The principal cause of food shortages was a change in the European climate : the seventeenth century was a period of colder weather, with higher rainfall and the advance of glaciers. The 'mortalities' touched off a serious social and economic crisis, for the majority of victims came from the class of producers – peasants and artisans. Towns banned fairs and markets and the exchange of goods, for fear of spreading disease; the rich fled to their country houses; smallholders were turned into paupers and beggars, wandering in their thousands; the price of land fell, and large-scale transfer of ownership took place; city governments went into debt to pay for the care of the sick and the starving. These 'mortalities' were frequent and widespread; the most important were those of the years 1630–2, 1648–53, 1660–2, 1693–4, 1709–10. They were all the more serious because their effects were cumulative; the population had not yet recovered from one when the next struck. Moreover, the effects of the 'mortalities' coincided with a drop in bullion imports from the Americas and a decline in prices (reaching its lowest point around 1675) which discouraged production by decreasing profits. The France of Colbert was consequently in a state of real depression and suffered a severe shortage of manpower.[12]

One of the most serious results of this was the insolvency of the taxpayers which aggravated the continual conflict between royal and seigneurial taxation – the constant rivalry of the fisc and the rent-collector – for in a bad year a peasant could not pay both.

The government therefore had to redouble its efforts to increase the number of taxpayers, for instance by seeking out those who falsely claimed exemption on the grounds of nobility, or by taxing the nobles through various indirect taxes and impositions. The nobility protested and stressed its solidarity with the peasants. It aided them against the royal tax-collectors, encouraged them to refuse payment, to attack the bailiffs and commissaries charged with collecting the taxes, to wound and kill them, and even to rebel against the king. Royal officials, if they owned manors, acted similarly in the towns and countryside. The new taxes violated municipal or provincial privilege and sparked revolts of whole cities and provinces, where a spirit of localism united all classes of the population against the fisc and the king. Less frequently the lords' attempts to increase their revenues in a time of economic crisis led the peasants to rebel against the Nobility, as in Lower Britanny in 1675. Urban and rural revolts were thus frequent and often of a serious nature.[13]

The use of the intendants, those commissaries of unimpeachable loyalty, armed with the powers of decision and execution where necessary – and often driven by irresistible energy – was consequently required to suppress the rebellions and their causes; first by improving the fiscal system and then towards the end of the century by building up a wider base for taxation through economic development.

The third important change lies in the development of the feudal and seigneurial system, which not only survived, but grew and became more regularised in law, while yet undergoing some modifications.

The king tried to make use of this trend to increase his authority and revenues by means of the theory of his 'direct universal lordship'. At the end of the fifteenth century jurists had begun to differentiate between two levels of property rights : that of 'direct lordship' (which could be sold, bequeathed or given away), the property right of the lord, which permitted him to levy quit-rents (*cens*), dues, various other revenues and to demand services, and that of 'useful possession', the property right of the peasant – constituting for our purposes real ownership – which conferred the right to farm the land, to enjoy what it produced and to transfer it by inheritance, sale or gift. The king now announced that he was lord of the whole kingdom, and that all land was held

by him. But in Languedoc and other provinces where Roman
law had applied certain lands existed independent of any lord,
held in full ownership : the so-called 'free allods', the legal maxim
of that part of the country being 'no lord without title'. This
principle was quite unacceptable to the lawyers who served the
monarchy, since it denied the king's claims over all landowners
and the feudal rights due to him by reason of his 'direct lordship'. The king would not admit the right of free ownership.
From his point of view the holders of allods were only entitled to
'useful possession'; he, as king, held the 'direct lordship'. From
1626, as its involvement in the Thirty Years War grew deeper,
the government made great efforts to extend the 'direct lordship'
of the king. Colbert pursued this programme with particular
energy. The edict of 1667 obliged the holder of a noble allod to
present the royal title by which the land was held in free ownership. This was impossible in an area where this system of tenure
was the normal one, and where such titles had therefore never
existed. In practical terms therefore the edict of 1667 abolished
allodial tenures in favour of the king, though without saying this
in so many words. The edict did, however, allow for the possibility of an earlier title in the case of non-noble allods[14].

We find this same tendency on the part of the government to
make use of the concept of lordship or fief for the benefit of the
king in many other connections. The Midi Canal was declared
to be a lordship; New France was divided up into lordships.
This fitted in with contemporary thought. It was generally held
that lordship and feudal dependence provided the best way to
bring all kinds of property or organisations directly under the king
so that – in establishing a link of fealty and service – the king
could act in the common interest by control or direct intervention.

When we look at individual landlords, we need to distinguish
those gentlemen who served at court or in the army, and who were
often negligent in managing their lands, from those country
gentlemen who lived on their estates or those who stemmed from
the bourgeoisie, or were still part of it or of the office-holding
classes.

Landowners of this second type often revealed great avidity
and tenacity. When they had acquired a fief or a lordship, they
requested permission from the king to conduct notarial inquiry by
which their dependants and tenants would be forced to present

the titles by which they held their land : this permitted redrafting lists of possessors of fiefs and holdings with the rights, revenues and services – feudal or seigneurial – which were due from them.

Our archives contain masses of documents from numerous, long, even interminable lawsuits, ranging from quarrels over a rent of a few sous to disputes over life-time leases : 'You owe me your customary goose'; 'But I have sent it to you'; 'But it was brought by a servant in ordinary clothes, when in fact he should have been wearing your livery and arms'. Twenty years of legal consultations and memoranda committed to print by both sides often followed such exchanges.

Were economic motives at the root of such disputes? This would not seem to be the case, since we find that such litigation was as frequent and as long drawn out in regions where seigneurial rights had become very attenuated. As examples of such attenuations we can mention the following. In Paris the Hôtel-Dieu was 'useful possessor' of a house in the Rue de la Huchette called 'The Cauldron' which was rented for 350 livres a year; and in its turn the Hôtel-Dieu paid the 'direct lords', the monks of Longchamps, a quit-rent of two deniers per year. In 1646 the Hôtel-Dieu bought a house called 'The Cleaver' in the Rue de la Bûcherie, for which it paid 13,500 livres. To the 'direct lord' the Hôtel-Dieu was obliged to pay 12 deniers parisis in quit-rent, and 8 livres 15 sous tournois in ground-rent per year. Around Paris the normal quit-rent was a few deniers or a few sous per acre. On 1 September 1633 a property at Saclay – house, garden, 100 acres of ploughland, and two and a half acres of meadow – was let for 500 livres tournois a year, and sold for 13,000. Its quit-rent was 16 sous parisis, or one livre tournoi a year. The 'direct lord' would often wait twenty-five years to collect his dues, the period of prescription being up to thirty years. Other dues to be paid in kind, such as the *champarts, terrages* or *agrières*, were more substantial than the quit-rent, but still of small value. To the south of Paris, at Thiais or Avrainville, the *champart* was four sheaves per acre, at a time when the average return was from 72 to 140 sheaves per acre.[15]

Seigneurial rights seem to have been more of an obstacle to normal economic development in areas which had access to a market, and where a more commercialised form of agriculture was developing. In the southern part of the Parisian region, for instance in the Gâtine Poitevine, we note a tendency – albeit uneven – for larger units of land to be formed through purchase or exchange. While in the Gâtine itself, sharecropping farms of 30 to 60 hectares were the norm, in the region south of Paris we find estates of 200 to 500 hectares split between several farms. Such farms were generally leased in the Gâtine on a contract which divided the produce half-and-half or by some other form of sharecropping; and south of Paris for a money-rent to contractors with their own draught-animals, progressive in outlook, engaged in production for sale on the market. They provided food for the towns, supplying them with meat and grain, and with raw materials like wool for the cloth industries whose products were sold as far afield as the Levant, the Indies or the Americas. Here we find an agrarian system geared to the needs of commercial capitalism.

Now these lands, whether sharecropping or leasehold, were made up of a great variety of different tenures and sometimes of fiefs which were in turn part of other fiefs or 'superfiefs'. There was no longer any correlation between the productive unit and the *seigneurie*. The lords and the farmers found it increasingly hard to keep their relationship straight despite periodic inquests to unravel the various long-standing tenures which comprised each unit of production, to decide from which lordship these tenures were held, and to ascertain what dues they owed. The exploitation of seigneurial rights was becoming extremely intricate and time consuming. The business of collection was usually managed by a lawyer or a substantial farmer who acted as the lord's agent. It would seem as if fiefs and lordships were sources of trouble and obstacles to the lords themselves.[16]

But if this was so, how do we explain the passionate eagerness for fiefs and *seigneuries*? Possibly we can find the answers in certain mental attitudes of the period. The first of these is a lack of economic sense. The lords in general did not try to obtain the maximum return from their lands. Their sphere in the capitalistic development was limited to the partitioning of their land, to enclosures, to providing advances of seed or leases of livestock. They hardly ever took part in providing other means of production, like marl, tools or technical equipment; they lacked the spirit for material progress.

Secondly, they clung to their *seigneuries* and fiefs because they

c

were the source of fidelity and homage, of quit-rents and dues which constituted a symbol of the social superiority of one man over another, so that one owed to some degree (if only morally) allegiance and service to the other. The term 'superiority', used so frequently in the documents, for example occurs in a contract dated 20 April 1616 for the sale of two acres of ploughland at Sens, which were 'assessed at two sous tournois in sign and mark of superiority, payable each year to the said Prior of Saint-Loup, and another twelve deniers tournois in rent which shall be paid as a symbol of all rights of superiority'. Other texts specify that the tenants of a lord are 'his men' or 'his subjects'. To receive quit-rents had thus become the symbol of social position, rank and authority; and this was why such importance was attached to them. Furthermore, fiefs and *seigneuries* had long served as rewards for military services, and the seventeenth century still valued such services. We may quote in evidence the archbishop of Embrun, Georges d'Aubusson de la Feuillade, president of the Assembly of the Clergy, who in his reply to the Assembly of the Nobility on 15 March 1651 referred to

> that nobility which springs not from blood, but from your heroic souls, which was not buried with your forefathers . . . lives again in the consequences of your generous actions, has inspired you to gather together to preserve your privileges. Your ancient glory . . . can no longer suffer that the affairs of a state *which is military in its foundation,* and of which you form the most brilliant and powerful part, should be decided without your votes.[17]

It is also worth quoting the abbé François-Timoléon de Choisy of the Academy who went still further :

> My mother, who came of the house of Hurault de l'Hôpital, would often say to me : Listen my son, never try to be glorious and always remember that you are a bourgeois. I know that your fathers and grandfathers were *Maîtres des Requêtes* and Councillors of State, but learn from me that the only nobility which is recognised in France is that of the sword. Our warlike nation has placed all its glory in its arms.[18]

From such attitudes derived a particular reverence for the fief and the *seigneurie* as the traditional rewards of the soldier.

The survival of the seigneurial system was thus above all the survival in men's thoughts and feelings of the military foundation of society. Just as rank in the army was long linked to the hierarchy of landholdings, so the possession of land carrying a higher status meant a rise in social standing. In consequence, the hierarchy of landholdings was retained as a source of social prestige and esteem, though to the detriment of the national interest in view of the low profitability of such land. The underlying principle of social organisation determined everything, even the economic activity.

NOTES

1   H. Grelin, *Ordre de la Convocation des Etats 1615*: Bibliothèque Nationale, L° 17.34.

2   P. Goubert, *Beauvais et les Beauvaisis de 1600 à 1730*, 2 vols. (Paris, 1960) pp. 206–21.

3   'Cahiers de la Noblesse', printed in *Recueil des Monuments inédits de la histoire du Tiers-Etat*, ed. Aug. Thierry (Paris, 1857) i, clxvii–clxviii.

4   R. Mousnier, *La vénalité des offices sous Henri IV et Louis XIII* (Paris, 1945) book 3, ch. 4.

5   Thierry (ed.), *Recueil*, clviii.

6   *Harangue faite de la part de la Chambre ecclésiastique en celle du Tiers-Etat sur l'article du serment par Mgr le cardinal du Perron* (publ. by Antoine Estienne, Paris, 1615), B.N. L° 17.20, pp. 9–15.

7   P. Blet, *Le clergé de France et la monarchie*, i (Paris, 1959) pp. 3–11, 133.

8   R. Mousnier, 'Etat et commissaire. Recherches sur la création des intendants des provinces, 1634–1648', *Forschungen zur Staat und Verfassung. Festgabe für Fritz Hartung* (Berlin, 1958) pp. 325–44.

9   R. Mousnier, 'Recherches sur les syndicats d'officiers pendant la Fronde', *XVII° Siècle* (1959) 76–117.

10   R. Mousnier, 'Le Conseil du Roi, de la mort de Henri IV au gouvernement personnel de Louis XIV', *Etudes d'histoire moderne et contemporaine*, i (1947) 26–67.

11   Mousnier, 'Recherches sur les syndicats d'officiers'.

12   R. Mousnier, 'Etudes sur la population de France au XVII° siècle', *XVII° Siècle* (1952) 527–43.

13   R. Mousnier, 'Recherches sur les soulèvements populaires en France avant la Fronde', *Revue d'histoire moderne et contemporaine* (1958) 81–113.

14   P. Boutruche, *Une société provinciale en lutte contre le régime féodal. L'alleu en Bordelais et en Bazadais du XI° au XVIII° siècle* (Rodez, 1947).

15   L. Merle, *La métairie et l'évolution de la Gâtine Poitevine de la fin du Moyen Age à la Révolution* (Paris, 1958); M. Venard, *Bourgeois et paysans ua XVII° siècle. Recherche sur le rôle des bourgeois parisiens dans la vie agricole au*

sud de Paris au XVIIᵉ siècle (Paris, 1957); M. Fontenay, *Paysans et marchands ruraux de la vallée d'Essonnes dans la seconde moitié du XVIIᵉ siècle*, in *Mémoires*, published by the Fédération des Sociétés Historiques et Archéologiques de Paris et de l'Ile-de-France, IX (1958) 157–288.

16 *Journal de l'Assemblée de la Noblesse* (no place or date) B.N., Lᵇ³⁷, p. 79.
17 *Mémoires*, ed. J. F. Michaud and J. J. F. Poujoulat (Paris, 1847) p. 554.

4 French Kingship and Absolute Monarchy in the Seventeenth Century*

FRANÇOIS DUMONT

It is generally accepted that, from the seventeenth century on-ward, monarchical power in France was absolute, contrasting with earlier ideas of kingship. But in fact it seems more likely that the earlier conception of kingship, which we may call traditional, remained alive and opposed to absolutism throughout the seventeenth century. This ambivalence in the interpretation of royal power aroused the passions of contemporaries: it was generally agreed that kingship was necessary, and even holy, but the growth of absolutism was not readily accepted. Seventeenth-century men often preferred to think that the growth of absolutism was not the work of the king himself, but of ministers or officials who exercised in his name a power whose limits they exceeded.

It is not my aim, therefore, to study absolutism as such, but rather the degree to which it diverged in the course of the seventeenth century from the traditional views of French kingship, or from those practices which were held to belong to earlier ideas of royal power. This is a question which has been much debated following the excellent report, 'Some Problems of Absolute Monarchy', which Mousnier and Hartung presented to the Tenth Congress of the Historical Sciences at Rome in 1955.[1] I am in entire agreement with them on the need to draw a profound distinction between absolutism and tyranny; or, more precisely, to note the incomplete nature of absolutism in France as in England. Like them, I cannot accept W. Näf's theory, recently revived

* First published in *XVIIᵉ Siècle*, nos 58–9 (1963) under the title 'Royauté française et monarchie absolue au XVIIᵉ siècle'.

by Emile Lousse, that absolutism is the rule of a prince released (*absolutus*) from the obligation to share his power with an Estates-General.[2] The king of France was absolute, but he still had to deal with local estates – which presented the same difficulties as the Estates-General within the limits of a given province – up to the Revolution. In my judgement every European monarch was faced by estates in which the deputies of the various orders assembled, and the relations between these bodies and the ruler varied according to their relative powers under different circumstances. In any case, the 'orders' did not form the only opposition to the king. All rulers were aided or opposed by individuals such as personal relatives or chief advisers, and by 'bodies' other than Estates: government councils, courts of justice, guilds and corporations, none of which, however, claimed to represent the kingdom or the province as the estates did.[3]

It seems to me that estates, bodies or individuals accumulated power at times when the ruler was weak, and that their strength declined as the royal power grew. Already under Louis XI the French feudal nobility had lost strength in relation to the monarchy. Louis XI seems to some historians to have been an absolute ruler because he alone – or almost alone – imposed his will on the kingdom. But did the nature of kingship change? No: Louis XI's kingship was absolute only because it could affirm itself as such. In the sixteenth century economic upheavals, foreign wars and religious conflicts led to the replacement of the strong rule of Francis I and Henri II by a government of factions. Henri IV put an end to this, becoming an absolute ruler in his turn when he had gathered all power into his own hands. His tragic death was followed by renewed conspiracies and disorders. With Richelieu's help Louis XIII restored order rather late in his reign, in spite of foreign war. But during the regency at the beginning of Louis XIV's reign the same problems reappeared, and the same restoration of authority had to be undertaken by Mazarin. After Mazarin's death the king in the opinion of contemporaries and historians ruled as an absolute monarch. What then was this absolute monarchy which waxed and waned throughout the last three centuries of the Ancien Régime?

The term means literally a form of political organisation in which power is entrusted to a single person, who holds it completely; according to which, ever since the beginning of the Capetian monarchy, the king had held his crown from God.[4] This theory did not envisage any subordination of the French king to ecclesiastical authority : his independence had been asserted long before the famous dispute with Boniface VIII. The tenets attributed to Saint-Louis, and dating from the late thirteenth century, stated that the king 'holds his power of none save God and himself'.[5] Nor did he hold his power from the people. The early Capetians had certainly been elected, and the coronation ceremony preserved a trace of this election down to the eighteenth century;[6] but at least from the time of Louis VII the king's son (in this instance Philip Augustus) was considered his successor.[7] The doctrine of the delegation of power to the king by the people, first formulated by the Scholastics, was taken up again in the sixteenth century by the Protestants in order to justify tyrannicide,[8] and their use of it brought it into total discredit for a long time in France. Since the king held his power from God, there could be no limitation on his exercise of it; his power could only be absolute. Ordinary laws did not affect the king, for he was *absolutus legibus*, above the law.[9]

This authority, however, was in no way tyrannical. The duty of the prince was to uphold justice. His will must be just, bound by the divine and natural laws which would secure the welfare of his subjects, and by the fundamental laws of the kingdom which regulated the succession to the throne and the form of government – laws which, according to Bracton, after God made a true king.[10]

Such were the basic ideas of French kingship which went back almost to the origins of the institution : they were the concepts of absolute monarchy.[11] But their true nature was hidden by 'the rise of separate powers' and the fragmentation of authority characteristic of feudalism. During the period when the king was fighting to win back his kingdom, he had to rely on the help of his close relatives and share power with them. In this way the 'Capetian trinity' was born.[12] For the same reasons the king had to share his authority with his more distant relatives, the princes of the blood, and with his most loyal vassals, who had to be conciliated. As we know, once the king's situation became more favourable, all these accretions, these 'extras', were to disappear one by one.

French kingship was thus absolute – in origin and in the way it developed – but it had to work to develop this character and realise its true nature. If the seventeenth century was the period in which kingship restored itself in France, establishing the lines of its destiny for the last part of its existence, this success must be seen as a totality. Such a generalisation needs, of course, closer examination. Evidence exists which shows that the term seventeenth-century French absolutism has to be very carefully qualified. In the first place it should not be confused with the process of administrative centralisation which (following the pioneer work of Pagès)[13] we are still investigating. From the point of view of the officials originally charged with fiscal administration, the novelty of the intendants, who were directly responsible to the king, and of the intendant's agents, who took over the administration of taxes in a *généralité*, was a manifestation of 'absolutism'. But was not the king obliged to make every effort to assure fiscal justice, for the benefit of the kingdom as a whole? Even in those parts of France where the king's power was not shared, and therefore truly absolute,[14] there were differences of interpretation in respect of that power. We have already noted that the king had to follow certain rules of divine, natural or fundamental law. But how were these defined? Often in very dissimilar ways. Furthermore, the royal government was considered absolute by comparison with earlier practices and conceptions, dating usually from the beginning of the century. These earlier ideas and practices were held to represent the traditional form of kingship, and absolutism was deemed a result of recent changes. Although this view was inaccurate – for traditional kingship had been just as absolute in theory – it was generally accepted. But because it is inaccurate we need to proceed to a more detailed observation to ascertain how the sunrise of absolutism arose from the clouds of traditional kingship.

I

The contemporaries of Louis XIV based their ideas of traditional kingship on memories which survived for the early part of the century, recalling the general ideas which had dominated it and the rules which had controlled it.

These principles were inferred from the divine character of kingship, revealed in the coronation ceremony, during which the ruler was anointed[15] and received the power to cure scrofula, the king's evil.[16]

The divine grace which was vouchsafed the ruler in order that he might carry out his functions as king increased his responsibilities. In the course of the coronation ceremony he swore the traditional oath limiting his exercise of power, and he was enjoined to watch, in a general sense, over the wellbeing of the whole kingdom.[17] The awe attached to these ideas was recognised by all, rebels and Protestants included, and political commentators vied with one another in repeating them. Pithou declared that the king was 'a person consecrated, anointed and beloved of God as a being between men and the angels',[18] Richelieu called kings the images of God,[19] and Bossuet held that royal power was divine.[20] Under the influence of Roman law the conception of kingship became more and more of an abstraction : the power of the state existed of itself. The king symbolised God and the essence of power. At the same time, treatises on kingship no longer merely confined themselves to listing the rights of the king (the *Regalia*), but dealt with the question of the king's powers.[21] Even if Louis XIV did not say 'I am the state', he still spoke and acted in the service of the state.[22] And Louis XIII before him had actually said, 'It is not I who speak, it is my state.'[23]

The rules which governed the exercise of royal power formed what were called the fundamental laws of the kingdom.[24] They were expressed as maxims whose true meaning depended on their historical context, so that they always retained an air of mystery. They constituted the *arcana imperii*, towards which public opinion 'groped', to borrow the phrase of Cardinal de Retz, in times of crisis.[25]

They were concerned with the succession to the throne, with the position of the crown in relation to the other powers within or without the state, and finally with the manner in which he should conduct policy.

Succession to the throne was regulated by the principles of heredity, legitimacy and orthodoxy, against which there was no opposition by the king in the early seventeenth century. To these principles must be added those of the impossibility of disposing of the crown, and the inalienability of the royal domain,[26] with its corollary of the union of the king's personal lands with those of the crown. This was not implemented by Henri IV except in the

c*

case of a few *seigneuries*; but in 1620 Louis XIII incorporated the kingdom of Navarre and the lordship of Béarn, hitherto independent, into the kingdom of France.[27]

In his relations with other powers, inside and outside the kingdom, the king's duty was to maintain the independence of his crown.[28]

Within the kingdom the powers that confronted him were his own family and his immediate advisers : the princes of the blood and the great officers of the crown.

Was the king really independent of his closest relatives? After the end of their respective regencies, both Marie de Medici and Anne of Austria shared in the exercise of power, or sought to do so. The long series of plots directed by Marie de Medici after Louis XIII's majority is well known,[29] as are the endeavours of Anne of Austria, the queen, in favour of Spain.[30] Louis XIII is thought never to have forgiven her. The delight in intrigue and conspiracy of Monsieur, Louis XIII's brother, is also notorious.[31] On the death of Louis XIII his various acts of treason were pardoned, he was made lieutenant-general of the kingdom and given a rich apanage, the Orléanais. The same degree of importance and unreliability can be observed in the princes of the blood and the great nobles. Henri IV had a difficult time with them, and after his death it was said : the day of kings is past, that of princes and nobles has come. This was borne out when Condé, Soissons, Vendôme and Bouillon formed the league of princes, backed by their powerful retinues; when Marshal Montmorency raised Languedoc in revolt; when, later, the great Condé led the Fronde of the princes.[32]

But apart from these open shows of force, the princes and great nobles were traditionally the governors of provinces.[33] Montmorency lost both his province of Languedoc and his head, but the Condé family remained in Burgundy, except for a few short interruptions caused by their revolts against the crown, which brought them imprisonment or relegation to other provinces. Burgundy seemed to be their own personal property, and they built up wide popularity there with the help of favours obtained from the king on behalf of the province. Burgundians seeking advancement or favours applied directly to them and not to the crown.

All this was regarded with a certain degree of tolerance, as was the power of the great officials of the crown.[34] The chancellor could be removed from his position only by execution (which happened on occasion), but usually he was deprived of the seals, leaving him with a title but no functions.[35]

In military affairs the Capetian monarchy had been forced to accept co-operation with a high command, comprising the constable and his marshals, under the orders of the Seneschal, who assisted the king in his traditional role as leader of the army. This organisation fell out of use in the twelfth century,[36] but the title of constable remained until the death of Lesdiguières in 1626.[37] The captains, as owners of their companies, recruited their own troops. They were under the orders of the colonels, who likewise owned their positions and chose all the officers.[38]

Louis XIII, the 'company-officer king' as Tapié so well describes him,[39] managed the army well in war and peace – in so far as its organisation allowed him. The navy was under the control of the admirals,[40] the admiral of the *Ponant* for the Atlantic, and of the *Levant* for the Mediterranean. They too owned their offices.

In respect of foreign powers, France no longer faced the problem of Imperial claims to suzerainty over the kingdom.[41] Even so, Roman law had not been taught at the University of Paris after 1220, lest recognition be given to the theory that laws made by the successors of Justinian were binding on territories which had once been Roman provinces.[42] This created an awkward situation for students, who had to go to Orléans to take their degrees in civil law after working up the *Institutes* under the guidance of Parisian crammers, nicknamed 'whistlers' or 'hissers'.[43]

The relationship between the spiritual and temporal powers, always so delicate because of the sensitivity of the contending parties, seemed settled at the end of the sixteenth century. The excommunication of Henri of Navarre, accompanied by declarations of Sixtus V and Gregory XIV which barred him from the succession, had been quashed by the parlements and rejected by a considerable part of the French clergy.[44]

But the dispute flared up again in the seventeenth century, sparked by treatises which argued for the indirect power of the pope over the king. The Estates-General of 1614 had proposed that the king declare his independence. But the clergy was reluctant to re-state a principle which was already held to be valid, having been asserted in *The Liberties of the Gallican Church* of

Pierre Pithou and the subject of commentaries since the end of the sixteenth century. The government concurred.[45]

In 1626 the publication of a work by the Jesuit Santarelli, supporting the pope's right to depose kings in cases of heresy or schism, and even to sentence them to death, led the Paris Parlement and the Sorbonne to condemn this doctrine.[46] Richelieu wished to avoid trouble with Rome, and, acting on his advice, Louis XIII imposed a pacification : the Sorbonne was ordered to rescind its censure and the Parlement was silenced.

The fundamental laws of the kingdom also dictated how the king should conduct himself, obliging him to respect the laws of God, the status and customs of the realm, and the Catholic faith. They reminded him that he was the source of all justice and that he must govern 'with his great council'.

Respect for the law of God demanded that the king should govern in accordance with his conscience as a Christian. This was one of the 'restraints' noted by Bodin.[47] Guez de Balzac declared that the king ruled 'by divine right according to the principles of our faith'.[48] Richelieu stressed the particular gravity of errors committed by the king, adding that 'many would be saved, if they were merely private persons, who are damned because they are public figures'.[49] Finally Bossuet eloquently expounded the duty of kings to render account to God.[50]

We cannot say that the respect for custom which was enjoined on the king was confined to his exercise of the power of legislation, for this power was not distinguished from the other aspects of kingship. Custom was a reality which had defined itself over a long period of time, and the respect which the king owed it was in harmony with his duty to make decisions – his 'Establishments' – which would apply to the whole kingdom. The power of custom was balanced by the king's obligation to act for the welfare of all, so that the king could abolish bad customs, suspend them by letters of justice, or change and codify them with the aid of the three estates. The promulgation of 'Establishments required the participation of the Estates-General. The great ordinances of the sixteenth century were drawn up on the basis of the demands of the estates, and the ordinance of Marillac (the *Code Michau*) was founded on the *cahiers* of 1614–15.[51]

As well as custom, the king was bound to respect 'status'.[52] This was the organisation of the state into bodies, grouping the king's subjects according to their social position, residence, trade or occupation. Each body had its particular position, fortified by privileges known as 'liberties'. All these separate liberties had to be kept within the limits of the common good, the king being sole judge of the balance between privilege and general welfare. This balance was maintained through judgements made in council on pleas of individuals. Even though the three orders of the kingdom no longer met in the Estates-General, the clergy kept up its own assembly, instituted to implement the Contract of Poissy of 1561.[53] The nobility similarly held assemblies in 1649 and 1651.[54] Some provinces had their own estates,[55] set up at the time of the absorption of the province by the crown, or maintained by tradition. During the seventeenth century some of these fell into disuse : in central and western France, and in Normandy and Dauphiné. But those affected by this change do not seem to have protested. Even the towns, parishes and rural communities had their own assemblies.[56] The towns opened or closed their gates to royal troops at will; and the parishes at times resisted the levying of taxes. The judicial and financial officials formed corporations which claimed a share of public authority and whose importance was enhanced by the system of venal offices.[57] The *paulette*, 'annual levy', payment of which allowed the holder to transmit his office to a designated successor, provided the monarchy with its only means – through the threat of non-renewal – of moderating the inordinate demands of officeholders right down to the end of Louis XIV's reign. Even so there were many occasions when the corporations of officials adopted a hostile stance towards the king. The union of the sovereign courts which produced the ordinance of 1648, the Fronde of the Parlement, the syndicates of financial offices and *élus*, all show how extensive was their power.[58]

The king's solemn oath to uphold the Catholic faith raised the problem of religious unity, compromised since the Edict of Nantes of 1598. The assembly of the clergy frequently took up the question. Richelieu's hostility to the Protestants did not, however, spring from religious considerations but was the result of his fear of a too powerful political group. The war against the Protestants ended with the destruction of their fortified towns, and the Gracious Peace of 1629 formally repeated the terms of the edict.[59] In the realm of religion therefore the king had not upheld (or had not been able to uphold) his coronation promise.

The king's power embraced the administration of justice, which included general administration. There were indeed other systems of patrimonial or ecclesiastical justice not vested in the king,[60] but the theorists of royal power made use of the maxim that all justice derived from the king to reserve the right of 'ultimate jurisdiction' to him, and thus to establish the sovereignty of his courts.[61] Most frequently exercised in the form of 'delegated justice' the system of royal justice always included the right of the king to intervene in the judicial process, either in a *lit de justice* or through his general supervision of the judges. The latter were also the king's counsellors, for the courts were in fact no more than institutions that had developed out of the old *curia regis*.[62]

In the earliest days of the monarchy the *curia regis* had been the king's council, which he was supposed to consult on all matters of government. The parlements, *Cours des Comptes* and other courts took over the special task of reviewing the judicial process, leaving the king's council or council of state to deal with political questions.[63]

Such an important central council posed a problem of organisation. The tendency of the king's immediate circle to control the council had to be resisted. At times of political upheaval and during regencies the council tended to become engulfed in a riotous 'mob'. It had always been the practice therefore to form several councils, some of which remained easily accessible, while entry to the others was restricted, to provide an atmosphere of calm in which to decide the most important affairs. But in spite of this separation the royal council remained one in theory, and its unity was expressed in the formula in which decrees were made by 'the king in his council'.[64]

In administrative matters the courts maintained a close watch on the government, by virtue of the principle that royal decisions had to be registered and through the rights of remonstrance. The courts were thus enabled to suspend the publication of edicts or ordinances. These practices made the courts, as they themselves were quick to claim, a real 'second power' in the state. The lower courts showed the same desire for independence in financial matters.

Certain assemblies did possess special rights. The Estates-General claimed that their approval was necessary to legalise the raising of taxes. After the failure of the Estates-General of 1614,[65] the crown avoided calling this assembly and tried to use smaller assemblies – the Notables as they were called – for the same purpose.[66] But these assemblies, called for instance in 1617 and again in 1626, offered the king little more than moral support and refused to authorise any extra taxation.[67] The assemblies of the clergy, on the other hand, continued to vote and administer the tax levied directly on all holders of benefices.[68] The local estates, where they existed, agreed to the sums demanded of them, and levied them.[69] What exactly was understood by taxation at this time? The principle that taxes should be voted by the estates was still voiced. But these taxes comprised in our period the *taille*, voted long ago by the deputies of the three orders, and still levied on a quasi-customary basis.[70] To increase the *taille* would be difficult; and the government tried to meet its financial needs by raising those 'domainal duties' which the king could claim as a feudal lord, as for instance the taxes on wine, spirits, and salt.[71] The creation of offices for sale was also used on a large scale[72] and did not encounter any real opposition, except among certain groups of officials who did not like to see their numbers increased. In fiscal matters the *pays d'élection* were always at a disadvantage, as their only possible form of opposition to governmental exactions was popular disturbance. But in the *pays d'états* constant negotiations between the estates and the government legitimised royal demands and provided some protection for the taxpayers.[73] The estates would often dispute such royal demands. In 1650 the estates of Burgundy asked for information on how the moneys requested by the government were to be spent and refused to vote the full sum.[74] In 1658, at the time of the famous 'journey to Lyons' during which Louis XIV's engagement to Margaret of Savoy was to be discussed, the estates negotiated for a long time over a subsidy requested to defray part of the cost of the journey[75] and did not grant it until the king had exiled them to Noyers.[76]

II

Our sketch has shown how tradition forced the monarchy on to the defensive on certain points : there were stringent fundamental laws regulating the succession, not enough clarity in regulations as to the king's power, divided authority and fiscal impotence. The

sixteenth century bequeathed to the seventeenth all these dis-
advantages of the traditional system of monarchy. The disadvan-
tages were aggravated by the weakness of the crown during
minorities, and by the urgent financial and other needs of the
kingdom, beset by domestic troubles and civil war – the Frondes
of the Parlement and of the Princes – and long drawn out foreign
wars. The crown had to react, and in the eyes of contemporaries
this reaction took the form of absolutism. As soon as absolutism
became apparent in royal policy, political writers, encouraged by
statesmen, formulated it into maxims.

For a statesman's view, let us look at Richelieu's *Political Testament* : the king must command 'absolutely'; certain circumstances 'demand the voice of a sovereign possessed of absolute
power'.[77] The declarations of Louis XIII and Louis XIV on the
subject of their own sovereign power pointed in the same absolutist direction.[78]

At the same time the doctrine that the policies of the state
should be dictated by reason within the framework of Christianity
was upheld.[79] Montaigne did not believe that this was possible,[80]
while Bossuet was convinced that reason of state and divine wisdom were identical.[81]

From 1632 political theorists, led by Le Bret, identified the
person of the sovereign with the sovereign power itself, thus stressing its essential indivisibility.[82] Le Bret asserted that sovereignty
is 'no more divisible than a point in geometry'. He extolled the
supreme and perpetual character of royalty, but believed that the
attribute of indivisibility was conferred only by time and that
royal supremacy must remain 'an ideal'. He held that royal power
was incommunicable and not patrimonial – that is, it could not
be transferred – thus strengthening its indivisibility.[83] The restraints
which Bodin had enumerated[84] (fundamental laws, divine law, the
duty of giving justice, the estates and assemblies of orders) were
also accepted by Le Bret as the limits of sovereignty which ensured
that it did not develop into despotism or tyranny.[85] Such was the
climate of opinion in which royal power would whittle away
traditional rules and practices, especially after 1660, although the
process had begun well before that date.

Let us now examine the attitude of the monarchy to the fundamental laws. The laws of succession were applied less strictly as

the principle of the independence of the crown came more and more into prominence. In the end, the king treated lightly those principles which had traditionally governed his conduct.

We may note two attacks directed by the ruler against the laws of succession; they concern the legitimised princes and Philip V, king of Spain. The first instance is that of the natural sons of Louis XIV and Mme de Montespan, the duc du Maine and the comte de Toulouse. The fundamental laws of succession barred them from the throne because of their illegitimacy. In a series of edicts from 1711 to 1715, however, Louis XIV made them eligible to succeed, though after the princes of the blood.[86] His actions caused Saint-Simon the greatest alarm and revulsion. The attempt did not succeed since the royal dispositions were annulled after Louis XIV's death by the edict of 1717, but it reveals a very cavalier attitude to the fundamental laws of the kingdom.[87]

The same tendency affected the rule that the crown was inalienable. At the request of Louis XIV, Philip V renounced his claim to the French crown at the Peace of Utrecht, although he was in the line of succession as son of the grand dauphin. His renunciation was not considered binding in France or even in England : the English government, which had demanded this renunciation, asked in vain that it be ratified by the Estates-General.[88]

The general principle of the independence of the crown was extended, in both internal and foreign policy. The king's authority was held to be indivisible, and could not be 'shared' by his family or his associates, although a new political figure was making his appearance – the first minister.

Louis XIII's well-founded mistrust of his mother led to a series of quarrels and reconciliations, the latter taking the form of virtual peace treaties. The Day of Dupes was a turning point in the struggle between the king and those who sought to influence him, and it was the king who emerged victorious.[89] Later Louis XIII had to deal with plots centred on his queen. The confession made by Anne of Austria on one such occasion was drawn up in a formal report, and she was not restored to favour until she had agreed to conditions which ensured her submission.[90] Louis XIII also had to impose his authority on his brother; agreements were drawn up between them, and Gaston was forbidden to marry Margaret of Lorraine. In his turn Louis XIV had to impose his will on his own mother and refused to allow the marriage of the grande mademoiselle. Princes of the blood were imprisoned on slight pretexts, but were pardoned with equal facility. The great magnates were in Louis XIII's reign subjected to royal authority : one need only point to the executions of Chalais, Montmorency and Cinq-Mars.[91] The provincial governors also saw their powers reduced, being obliged to obtain the king's permission to reside in their governorships. Their administrative functions were taken over by lieutenant-generals and commanders appointed by the king.[92] But there was no clean break with the past : Marshal Villars wielded great influence in Provence, as did the Condé family in Burgundy.

Even though the governor might still remain the sole representative of royal authority in a province, a new figure had in fact supplemented him : the *maître des requêtes,* given a temporary commission, who gradually assumed permanent functions and became an intendant.[93]

The sweeping away of the great officials of the crown by absolutism was especially noticeable in the sphere of military organisation, giving the army a new character. The colonel-general of cavalry remained, but the colonel-general of infantry disappeared, and with him went the contingents of troops provided by the nobles and the towns. The civil power took over the control of purely administrative matters from the military. The king, who no longer directed campaigns, became the real head of the army, acting through the *commissaires des guerres* and through the intendants of the armies who were responsible directly to the secretaries of state.[94]

Within the king's immediate circle a new figure emerged : the first minister.[95] Was Sully, as he claimed, Henri IV's 'first minister'? This is difficult to decide, but we do know how strong was the influence of Concini over Marie de Medici and of Luynes over Louis XIII; Louis himself used to refer to 'King Luynes'.[96] Richelieu certainly played a leading part in the government : he was both first minister and head of the council, as was Mazarin in the reign of Louis XIV. After him, both Colbert and Louvois exercised extraordinary authority, although without these specific titles.[97] The use of a 'first minister' did not constitute an encroachment on the king's authority, as the king alone made decisions.[98] Nonetheless, the belief in the ultimate responsibility of the first minister came to be widely held; it was convenient to let him bear the unpopularity of certain measures.[99] Guez de Balzac sought to demonstrate that the rule of 'first minister' was an 'institution'. We may easily understand why his work attracted Richelieu's hostility, for he was well aware how the absolutism of a minister could mask that of the king.[100]

The same tendency of growing royal power is discernible in the conduct of foreign policy, particularly in relation to the Holy Roman Empire and the papacy. Louis XIV was sufficiently sure of his independence from the former to allow the teaching of Roman law to be resumed at the University of Paris; an edict of 1679 restored it, along with canon law.[101]

In more practical matters the dispute with the duke of Lorraine over the frontiers of the Three Bishoprics, where territory was claimed both by the Empire and by France, was settled by le Bret, the future *doyen* of the council, who was at that time the king's commissary.[102] His chief argument was the French king's independence of any external authority, and the denial of the emperor's prescriptive right to lands once conquered from France.[103]

The conflict with Rome, which the government had long sought to play down, burst into prominence once more as a result of the 1663 declaration of the Sorbonne and the 1682 declaration of the Assembly of the Clergy on the limits of papal power. Colbert had engineered the latter in order to justify the French position in respect of the *régale*. It was made a law of the kingdom as well as being designated 'a certain and incontestable truth', but in 1693 it was in part abandoned by Louis XIV in an autograph letter to the pope in which the king undertook not to demand the teaching of, nor to uphold officially, the 1682 declaration.[104]

The power of the French clergy did prevail in one sphere, however. As we noted above the king's promise in his coronation oath to maintain the unity of religion had not been kept since the Edict of Nantes. Was this due to the king's wish to assert his independence against Rome or the Catholic church in France, or did he feel bound by the edict? Possibly opportunism counted most. Certainly Louis XIII's policy ensured that the Protestants remained faithful to the crown throughout the Fronde.[105] The king was careful to refer to them as his 'loyal subjects'. But religious feelings still ran high and the Assembly of the Clergy was able to

foment a number of persecutions and finally obtain the revocation of the edict in 1685.[106]

In the field of customary and statute law the king acted with
increasing freedom, in both public and private law.[107] Bad customary law was now assailed with vigour. The various corporate
bodies within the state were subjected to close supervision, which
necessitated government approval of publications, regularised
procedures to be followed in the courts,[108] and rules for guilds
and corporations.[109] After 1660 came the series of great ordinances which were promulgated without consultation with the
three estates.[110] In 1665 Louis XIV, aided by Colbert, announced
his intention of reforming the judicial system. Various commissions
worked to prepare these reforms, with the king settling disputed
points. The first ordinance was ready in 1667, and was followed
by others: that of 1669, dealing with civil procedure; that of
1670, for criminal procedure; the commercial code of 1673,
drawn up by Savary; the ordinance of 1681 which organised the
merchant marine; that of 1685 for the colonies. All were drawn
up without prior consultation with the estates.

In the area of statute law the king showed a similar disregard
for tradition; the Estates-General were no longer called, and
the assemblies of the nobility were not permitted; only the
Assembly of the Clergy and the local estates survived. The latter
were considered a 'quaint archaism', relics of less sophisticated
times, and were increasingly supervised and controlled.[111]

In judicial matters the growth of monarchical absolutism was
characterised by the increased use of 'reserved justice', and of the
king's right to delegate justice. 'Reserved justice' took the form
of the procedure of submitting *placets*[112] which were then answered, a system which Louis XIV increasingly applied. *Lettres
de cachet* were another manifestation of the king's justice;[113] they
were used in the private interests of families and were employed
also for political as well as judicial purposes, being considered as
direct manifestations of royal legal decisions taken by the king's
council. 'Delegated justice' was represented by the frequent transfer of proceedings to ordinary or extraordinary judges. Regular
judges were frequently sent on *Grands Jours*[114] in the seventeenth
century to make up for the weakness of the parlements and local
courts in Auvergne and Languedoc, at le Puy, Périgueux and
Poitiers. Extraordinary judges, commissaries chosen for their

devotion to the king's interests, were entrusted with the great political trials, like that of la Valette, 'who would not take Fuenterrabia'.[115] As revolts grew in intensity, the use of such special commissions was extended to the point where the chancellor Séguier was sent to deal with the revolt of the *va-nu-pieds* at Rouen, with full judicial powers and the ability to punish without legal proceedings.[116] The supervision of justice became tighter once the organisation of final appeals to the king's council had been put into effect.[117] Police powers were increasingly taken out of the hands of the local courts. In 1667, for example, a lieutenant of police, responsible directly to the king, was appointed at the Châtelet, thus encroaching on the jurisdiction of the Parlement.[118]

Within the government itself, the king's authority grew at the expense of a council now organised more in accordance with the royal will. The principle that the council should be composed of men the king had chosen gained increasing acceptance, as did the view that the king was in command of the decisions made by his council.[119]

The reaction against too easy access to the council, noticeable before 1630 in regulations unearthed by Mousnier,[120] manifested itself after 1643 in revisions of commissions. The Fronde put a stop to this for a while, but the process was resumed in the edicts of 1655, 1657 and 1673.[121] These edicts created two different kinds of councillors: those who held the title of *conseiller d'état* and performed functions, and those who held a commission granting a honorific title 'without the right of entry or session' to high officials, bishops and other important persons.

Birth did not automatically confer the right of entry to the council, and the exclusion of princes of the blood and *ducs et pairs* (dukes and peers) gave great offence to Saint-Simon. Louis XIV's own son did not gain entry to the *conseil des dépêches* for a long time, and only after that to the council of state. Louis' grandson, the duke of Burgundy, however, was admitted at a much earlier age to the *conseil des dépêches*, and soon after that to the *conseil des finances*. The king's brother, whose lack of discretion was notorious, was only admitted to the *conseil des dépêches*.[122] This was because secrecy was one of the most vital rules of the council, a tradition that went back to Francis I.[123] Secrecy had to be especially observed in governmental decisions,

which were always made by a small council called successively
council of the chamber, council of affairs, cabinet council, secret
council, and high council (*conseil d'en haut*). As for the other
councils, they were assisted by specialised bodies forming the
nucleus of the administrative machine.[124]

The king would allow cases submitted to the council, if they
concerned individuals,[125] to be settled by a majority vote. If the
king were judge in his own case, he would only decide in favour
of himself if his rights were clear and indisputable, but this was a
delicate question; reason of state or the needs of the community
could make the king decide against his councillors. And in many
cases the king decided and issued orders alone. The issuance of a
lettre de cachet could be decided either in the council, or by the
king consulting an individual minister. Similarly general or particular rulings could be drawn up under the aegis of the council
acting on orders from the king, or by the controller-general or a
secretary of state, as part of the day-to-day process of administration or in response to special circumstances.

The superiority of the council's decisions over those of the
sovereign courts was continually reaffirmed. In 1631, when the
Paris Parlement refused to register an edict against the accom-
plices of Gaston d'Orléans, the king overruled its deliberations by
a decision of the council. A decree was issued declaring that
affairs of state and administrative matters were not within the
competence of the parlements. Such matters were the sole prerogative of the king who had been 'established and set up by
God, to whom alone he was responsible'.[126] The records of the
Parlement's deliberations were destroyed, and some of its members were exiled. Later, in an edict of the *conseil d'en haut* issued
on 8 July 1661, Louis XIV ordered the sovereign courts to accord
the decrees of his council the same respect and obedience as ordinances of state.[127]

There was a feeling the courts could not be completely trusted.
Louis XIII frequently excluded members of the parlements from
special commissions,[128] and in a famous speech at Metz he stressed
that it was not for the parlements to question what the king had
decided and ordered. Their function was to judge: 'If you continue meddling, I will clip your wings.' The many creations of
new offices were also a source of humiliation for the magistracy,
and in 1641 the Paris Parlement was expressly forbidden to take

cognisance of matters of state. Remonstrances were 'tolerated' for a time, but in 1653 they were forbidden in a *lit de justice*.[129]

A decree issued by the council in 1661 laid down the principle of the superiority of conciliar edicts: another, of 1668, struck from the registers of the Paris Parlement all decisions taken during the Frondes between 1648 and 1652. In 1673 remonstrances were only permitted after registration of edicts: from this time, there were to be no more 'noises from the Parlement'.[130]

The royal victory over the judiciary corresponds to a similar victory in financial matters. Although the king made increasing use of the sale of offices and other financial expedients, he in fact also established his right to create new taxes for which the approval of the Estates-General was necessary in theory. The same lack of respect for the forms of old marked the king's relations with the provincial estates. During the Nine Years War the *capitation* was levied for the first time in 1695 : it became a permanent tax in 1701. The clergy, however, compounded for payment of the tax and thus purchased complete exemption. The nobility were taxed directly by the intendant of each *généralité*. For the members of the Third Estate the *capitation* was first levied in proportion to their social position, but in time became another tax like the *taille* and levied in proportion to it. Thus it became a general tax. The same thing happened to the first tax on incomes, the *dixième*, levied in 1710 at a critical period of the War of the Spanish Succession.[131] The original idea behind this tax can be found in the proposals put forward by writers like Vauban and Boisguilbert.[132] It was abolished after the Peace of Utrecht but later reappeared, improved and augmented.

In the *pays d'états*, where local estates survived, the situation of the taxpayer deteriorated. In all the local assemblies it became standard practice to vote the 'free gift' (the sum to be paid by the province over and above the cost of its own administration) by acclamation and without debate. To encourage this the monarchy adopted the practice of awarding the province a reward for its loyalty, while at the same time increasing its own demands. For example, for a million livres demanded and granted, the king would remit a gracious 80,000, 100,000 or 150,000 depending on the circumstances.[133] And in direct contravention of their privileges the king did not hesitate to extend new taxes to the *pays d'états*, as to the other parts of the kingdom. Local estates com-

pounded for the *capitation*[134] and the first *dixième*[135] by paying
either an annual amount or a fixed sum. In return for such 'com-
mutations' the estates were permitted to collect the taxes themselves. In this way the 'liberties' of the provinces were preserved
– at least in appearance.

III

The political system of the later seventeenth century was thus
the traditional system of kingship freed from the limitations it
had suffered hitherto. It was, as we term it, 'absolute monarchy',
though to be exact we should qualify the term by saying 'more
absolute' than before as the government as we have seen still had
to act with considerable restraint. How can we explain the movement and what were its consequences?

In the first place the monarchy appears to have been encouraged to expand its authority as a reaction against the humili-
ations suffered during the Fronde, and also by the recollection of
the strength of the neighbouring monarchies, Spain and England,
in the sixteenth century.

Extraordinary financial pressures also led the government to
increase its demands. Under Louis XIV it had a free hand to do
this for the upper bourgeoisie, made up mainly of officials and the
high nobility, was almost completely excluded from political
decision-making. The officials were now concerned with little
more than their personal interests, while the court had absorbed
the representatives of the great noble families.

We should note that absolutism seems to have developed in a
direction which was actively desired by the great majority of
Frenchmen. The chaos of the Wars of Religion had left scars
still felt in seventeenth-century France. The loss of Henri IV, a
king who had known how to make himself loved, alarmed a
people with civil war still fresh in their memory. The improvements in the economic life of the country achieved in the first
years of the century were soon nullified by an excessive fiscal
policy.[136] Revolts were caused by poverty, which touched even
those who should have prospered, and in turn contributed to the
general misery. The disorders of the Frondes also increased the
distress of the majority of the population. In the towns control
of public funds had for a long time been monopolised by a bour-

geois oligarchy, which pilfered and peculated shamelessly and openly.[137] The parlements did nothing to deal with the problem; the bailiwicks and the bureaux of finance refused to take action. This caused general despondency and disgust among the people at large: the public wanted a stronger government to correct abuses. In towns where a royal commissary was able to act we find a pattern of initial hostility, stirred up by the local notables, followed by popular trust when he was seen to be a reformer counteracting the indifference, greed and neglect of the municipalities. Thanks to the efforts of such commissaries the great cities gradually ceased being open sewers,[138] a fact which tells us something about the use former administrators made of liberties now vanished.

But although the new political system brought benefits, it also brought long wars. In their train came the scarcely-forgotten exactions of the fisc, rebellions harshly suppressed (as in Guyenne or Brittany), and general misery. Opposition, in word and in deed, raised its head as public opinion became disillusioned.

In the realm of active opposition (even if there was no massive rising of the *noblesse de robe* against the government) a general, deep-rooted hostility can be discerned in all the parlements. The local estates, whose docility we have noted, concealed a secret opposition. At each meeting the monarchy had to scrutinise carefully their composition and exclude undesirables. The voting of 'free gifts', unanimous in form, was in fact obtained only after long bargaining.

Ideological opposition did not spring from the *libertines* or the Jansenists, even though – as Villers has argued – their protestations of loyalty were suspect 'because of the rather artificial and academic nature of their submission to the king'.[139] From the Fronde onwards, however, there had been numerous critics of absolutism who took as their central point the limitations set by God on the exercise of royal power. De Retz set forth this doctrine in his *Mémoires*, where he also stressed that the authority of the prince is limited, 'moderated by customs generally accepted and enshrined, first in the Estates-General, and then in the Parlements'.[140] Claude Joly went further than this in a significant work, his *Maximes véritables et importantes pour l'instruction du roi* (True and important maxims for the king's instruction).[141] He was not afraid to assert that kings were made for the benefit of the people who had received the gift of sovereignty from God and had then transferred it, with divine approval, to their kings. He therefore held that there were strict and firmly fixed limits to royal power. We know that the book was burned at the Châtelet and that his *Réponse* (Reply) to the condemnation, published in 1663, suffered the same fate in 1665.

Criticism of absolutism came also from the Protestants. The work entitled *Les soupirs de la France esclave* (The sighs of enslaved France) stressed the limits on the king's power and argued the right of revolt if these limits were infringed : the king must not become the 'idol' of the people. The former elective character of the monarchy was recalled, and the undermining of the social hierarchy was lamented. In the Dutch Republic Jurieu published his *Lettres pastorales adressées aux fidèles de France qui gémissent sous la captivité de Babylone* (Pastoral letters addressed to the faithful in a Babylonian captivity) in which he stressed, like Joly, that sovereignty belonged to the people, who delegated it to their kings and could resume it if the king 'failed in their trust' : the people were the ultimate arbiters of government.[142]

These works were to some extent inspired by English writings in the Protestant and anti-absolutist tradition, foremost among them Hobbes (d. 1679) whose celebrated work *The Leviathan* enjoyed a wide reputation.[143] *Leviathan* dealt with a giant state created by individuals in order to protect themselves and especially their property. The sovereign to whom they entrusted the state was without supernatural attributes and did not wield limitless power, however 'absolute' he might be. Locke, the apologist of the 1688 revolution, took an even more radical view : the prince's powers derived from the contract by which property-owners had entrusted him with the task of maintaining order; if the sovereign did not defend and respect natural rights, his subjects had the right to revolt.[144]

Apparently not directly influenced by these ideas, another movement of opposition to absolute monarchy developed within the French aristocracy; its most notable exponents were Fénelon[145] and Saint-Simon. The former accepted that the monarchy of France was absolute in principle but did not admit that it was so in practice. The state and the principles of government were superior to the king. Fénelon wrote to Louis XIV that 'your chief ministers have undermined and overthrown all the ancient maxims

of state in order to raise your power to its greatest heights.'[146]
Fénelon's ideal was government by an aristocracy which would
include estates and parlements playing their accustomed roles,
and in which taxes would be voted by the estates. Saint-Simon
was an outspoken critic of the policy of conquest, and of the consequences rather than the spirit of absolutism – central control
of the army and the growing powers of ministers. He could not
reconcile himself to the absence of the high nobility from the
royal councils.[147]

It is difficult to assess how 'public opinion' viewed absolutism.
The fear of offending those in power, coupled with close police
surveillance, should make us wary of placing too much trust in
contemporary correspondence, including that of Mme de Sévigné.
Can we say anything about feeling in educated circles? I believe
that men living in the last years of Louis XIV's reign were reflecting on dictatorship, as Corneille had done before them.[148] Perhaps they did not dare to repeat de Retz's judgement, that 'the
most scandalous and dangerous tyranny' had overtaken 'the most
legitimate of the monarchies',[149] but they contrasted the new
political system with an idealised memory of feudal monarchy
which had been less powerful and more easy-going. Like Alceste
they realised that one could not swim against the current,[150] but
resistance to oppression nonetheless seemed more glorious than the
misuse of power. Was this not a theme close to Corneille's heart?

'This absolute empire . . . this sovereign power . . .' seemed too
overbearing. Absolutism verging on despotism struck men as im-
moral; they could no longer rely on the king's Christian conscience
as a restraint on the use of power. Looking back with nostalgia to
ancient Rome,[151] where all-powerful princes had ultimately been
brought low, they waited. For what? The king's death.

NOTES

1 F. Hartung and R. Mousnier, 'Quelques problèmes concernant la
monarchie absolue', in Comitato Internazionale di Scienze Storiche,
Rome, 4–11 September 1955, *Relazioni*, vol. IV, *Storia Moderna*
(Florence, n.d.) pp. 3–55. See also the discussions on this report, in
Atti del X Congresso Internazionale (Rome, n.d.) pp. 429–43.
2 W. Näf, *Die Epochen der neueren Geschichte* (Aarau, 1945); E. Lousse,
'Absolutisme, droit divin, despotisme éclairé', in *Schweizer Beiträge
zur allgemeinen Geschichte*, XVI (1958) 91–166.

3 See F. Olivier-Martin, *L'organisation corporative de la France d'Ancien Régime* (Paris, 1938), and the same author's *Histoire du droit français des origines à la Révolution*, i, pt 2 (Paris, 1948) ch. ii, 'La nation organisée', pp. 357–427; his 1948–9 doctoral lectures (mimeographed) follow up the themes of this volume, 'Les ordres, les pays, les villes et communautés d'habitants'.

4 Olivier-Martin, *Histoire du droit français*, p. 338.

5 *Etablissements de Saint-Louis*, ed. Paul Viollet, 4 vols (Paris, 1881–6) i, p. 83; iv, p. 14.

6 Olivier-Martin, *Histoire du droit français*, p. 329 ff.

7 C. J. Declareuil, *Histoire générale du droit français des origines à 1789* (Paris, 1925) p. 397.

8 Olivier-Martin, *Histoire du droit français*, p. 338.

9 Ibid., p. 346.

10 J. Touchard *et al.*, *Histoire des idées politiques*, i (Paris, 1959) pp. 225–6, 238.

11 F. Olivier-Martin, 'L'absolutisme français', mimeographed notes for doctoral lectures 1950–1, pp. 7–9.

12 A. Luchaire, *Histoire des institutions monarchiques de la France sous les premiers Capétiens, 987–1180*, i (Paris, 1891) p. 134.

13 G. Pagès, *La monarchie d'Ancien Régime en France de Henri IV à Louis XIV* (Paris, 1928); and the same author's 'Essai sur l'évolution des institutions administratives en France du commencement du XVIe siècle à la fin du XVIIe siècle', *Revue d'histoire moderne* (1932).

14 Olivier-Martin, 'L'absolutisme français', pp. 93–5.

15 Ibid., p. 211.

16 Cf. M. Bloch, *Les rois thaumaturges*, 2nd ed. (Paris, 1961).

17 Olivier-Martin, 'L'absolutisme français', pp. 222–5, 231–41.

18 Quoted by J. Declareuil, 'Les idées politiques de Guez de Balzac', *Revue de droit public et de la science politique*, 24 (1907) 642–3.

19 Ibid., p. 653.

20 G. Pagès, *Les institutions monarchiques sous Louis XIII et Louis XIV* (Paris, 1962) pp. 20–1.

21 Ibid., pp. 9–10. Cf., for instance, the differences between the work of Charles de Grassaille, *Regalium Franciae libri duo, jura omnia et dignitates christianissimi Galliae regis continentes* (Lyons, 1538) and that of Claude d'Abbon, *De la Maïesté royale* (Lyons, 1575).

22 F. Hartung, 'L'état c'est moi', *Historische Zeitschrift* (1949) 130; Olivier-Martin, 'L'absolutisme français', pp. 38–47.

23 Quoted in V.-L. Tapié, *La France de Louis XIII et de Richelieu* (Paris, 1952) p. 424.

24 A. Lemaire, *Les lois fondamentales de la monarchie française* (Paris, 1907); B. Basse, *La constitution de la monarchie française*, Law thesis (Paris, 1959).

25 Quoted by Lemaire, *Les lois fondamentales*, p. 319.

26 Olivier-Martin, *Histoire du droit français*, pp. 307–23.

27 Olivier-Martin, 'La réunion de la Basse-Navarre à la couronne de France', *Annuario de Historia del Derecho Español* (1932).

28 Olivier-Martin, *Histoire du droit français*, pp. 335-6.
29 E. Préclin and V.-L. Tapié, *Le XVIIe siècle* (Paris, 1949) pp. 145-6.
30 Tapié, *La France de Louis XIII*, pp. 445-9.
31 Préclin and Tapié, *Le XVIIe siècle*, pp. 78, 84, 127, 150.
32 For these events, see ibid., pp. 149-57.
33 Olivier-Martin, *Histoire du droit français*, pp. 567-9.
34 Ibid., pp. 446-7.
35 Ibid., pp. 451-3.
36 Ibid., p. 220.
37 E. Escalier, *Lesdiguières, dernier connétable de France* (Paris, Lyons, 1946).
38 Olivier-Martin, *Histoire du droit français*, p. 507.
39 Tapié, *La France de Louis XIII*, p. 117.
40 Olivier-Martin, *Histoire du droit français*, pp. 509-11.
41 Ibid., pp. 206-8.
42 Ibid., pp. 612-13.
43 M. A. Le Masne-Desjobert, *La faculté du droit de Paris aux XVIe et XVIIIe siècles*, Law thesis (Paris, 1966).
44 R. Villers, 'Aspects politiques et aspects juridiques de la loi de Catholicité', *Revue de l'Histoire du Droit* (1959) 196-213.
45 Olivier-Martin, 'L'absolutisme français', pp. 68-71.
46 Ibid., pp. 73-5.
47 Touchard *et al.*, *Histoire des idées politiques*, I, pp. 290-1.
48 Quoted by Declareuil, 'Les idées politiques de Guez de Balzac', p. 653.
49 Quoted by R. Mousnier, 'Le testament politique de Richelieu', *Revue historique* (1949) 70.
50 Touchard *et al.*, *Histoire des idées politiques*, I, p. 244.
51 Olivier-Martin, *Histoire du droit français*, pp. 331-8, 524-8, 420-4.
52 For these developments see ibid., pp. 360-3, 387-90.
53 Cf. the recent work by P. Blet, *Le clergé de France et la monarchie. Etude sur les assemblées générales du clergé de 1616 à 1666* (Rome, 1954).
54 J.-D. Lassaigne, *Les assemblées de la noblesse de France aux XVIIe et XVIIIe siècles*, Law thesis (Paris, 1965).
55 Olivier-Martin, *Histoire du droit français*, pp. 262-332.
56 Ibid., pp. 414-16.
57 R. Mousnier, *La vénalité des offices sous Henri IV et Louis XIII* (Paris, Rouen, 1945) and works cited therein; ibid., pp. 208-86.
58 R. Mousnier, 'Recherches sur les syndicats d'officiers pendant la Fronde', *XVIIe Siècle* (1959) 76-117.
59 Préclin and Tapié, *Le XVIIe siècle*, pp. 149-50.
60 Olivier-Martin, *Histoire du droit français*, pp. 149-50.
61 Ibid., pp. 518-19.
62 Ibid., pp. 221-31.
63 Ibid., p. 436.
64 See R. Mousnier, 'Le Conseil du Roi de la mort de Henri IV au gouvernement personnel de Louis XIV', *Etudes d'histoire moderne et contemporaine* (1947) 28 ff. See also Olivier-Martin, 'Le conseil d'etat du roi', mimeographed notes for doctoral lectures 1947-8, pp. 43-4 and his *Histoire du droit français*, pp. 438-40, 444.

65 Olivier-Martin, *Histoire du droit français*, pp. 541–52; V.-L. Tapié, *La France de Louis XIII*, pp. 94–7; C. Alzon, 'Quelques observations sur les Etats généraux français de 1614', *Schweizer Beiträge zur allgemeinen Geschichte* (1958) pp. 66–73; A. Lublinskaya, 'Les Etats Généraux de 1614–15 en France', in *Album Helen Cam*, I (Louvain, Paris, 1960) pp. 229–46.

66 See B. de Chantérac, *Les assemblées des notables dans l'ancienne France*, Law thesis (Paris, 1919).

67 J. Petit, *L'assemblée des notables de 1626–1627*, Law thesis (Paris, 1937).

68 See Blet, *Le clergé de France*, p. 12.

69 J. Meuvret, 'Comment les Français du XVIIᵉ siècle voyaient l'impôt', *XVIIᵉ Siècle* (1952) 64–5.

70 Ibid., pp. 59–64.

71 Ibid., pp. 74–8.

72 Olivier-Martin, *Histoire du droit français*, pp. 403–6.

73 Meuvret, 'Comment les Français . . . voyaient l'impôt', pp. 64–5.

74 *Procès-verbal de l'assemblée des états tenue à Dijon aux mois de mars et avril 1650 sous la présidence de César, duc de Vendôme, commandant pour le roi en Bourgogne*, Archives Départementales de la Côte-d'Or, C 3028, f. 164 ff, and C 3095, f. 75 ff.

75 *Procès-verbal de l'assemblée de 1658, tenue à Dijon au mois de novembre, au couvent des Cordeliers sous la présidence du duc d'Epernon, gouverneur de la province*, A.D. Côte-d'Or, C 2996, f. 100 ff.

76 Ibid., f. 105 ff.

77 Quoted by Mousnier, *Le testament politique de Richelieu*, p. 61.

78 Cf. Pagès, *Les institutions monarchiques*, pp. 10–13.

79 Mousnier, *Le testament politique de Richelieu*, pp. 59–60.

80 I have attempted to show this in my study 'Royauté française et auteurs littéraires au XVIᵉ siècle', *Etudes historiques à la mémoire de Noël Didier* (Paris, 1960) p. 70.

81 Declareuil, 'Les idées politiques de Guez de Balzac', p. 657.

82 G. Picot, *Cardin le Bret, 1558–1655, et la doctrine de la souveraineté* (Nancy, 1948) pp. 125–31.

83 Quoted in Picot, *Cardin le Bret*, pp. 73, 127; ibid., pp. 132–6, 145–79, 117–23.

84 J.-J. Chevalier, *Les grandes oeuvres politiques, de Machiavel à nos jours* (Paris, 1950) pp. 48–9.

85 Picot, *Cardin le Bret*, pp. 183–210.

86 F. A. Isambert *et al.*, *Recueil général des anciennes lois françaises*, 29 vols (Paris, 1821–33) xx, pp. 585 ff.

87 Olivier-Martin, *Histoire du droit français*, p. 325.

88 Ibid., p. 324.

89 Tapié, *La France de Louis XIII*, pp. 284–8; G. Mongrédien, *La journée des Dupes* (Paris, 1961).

90 Tapié, *La France de Louis XIII*, pp. 445–9.

91 Ibid., pp. 192–200, 367–75, 509–16.

92 Olivier-Martin, *Histoire du droit français*, pp. 568–9.

93 Pagès, *Les institutions monarchiques*, pp. 78–96, 115–22.

94 Olivier-Martin, *Histoire du droit français*, pp. 506–9.
95 Pagès, *Les institutions monarchiques*, pp. 23–4; Declareuil, 'Les idées politiques de Guez de Balzac', p. 638.
96 Tapié, *La France de Louis XIII*, p. 154.
97 Pagès, *Les institutions monarchiques*, pp. 24–40, 41–9, 62–5.
98 Declareuil, 'Les idées politiques de Guez de Balzac', p. 662–98.
99 Ibid., pp. 663–8.
100 Ibid., p. 637.
101 Olivier-Martin, *Histoire du droit français*, p. 613.
102 Picot, *Cardin le Bret*, pp. 45–50, 142, n. 3.
103 Ibid., pp. 141–4.
104 Olivier-Martin, *Histoire du droit français*, pp. 487–9.
105 Olivier-Martin, *L'absolutisme français*, pp. 223, 320.
106 Préclin and Tapié, *Le XVIIe siècle*, pp. 262–4. In respect of the Jews, however, the clergy were content to issue declarations of principle. Although the Jews had been formally banished from the kingdom by royal letters of 25 April 1615, they remained in several cities under the king's protection. See Olivier-Martin, *Histoire du droit français*, pp. 498–500.
107 Olivier-Martin, 'Les lois du roi', mimeographed notes for doctoral lectures 1945–6, pp. 90–100.
108 Olivier-Martin, *Histoire du droit français*, p. 354.
109 Olivier-Martin, *L'organisation corporative de la France d'Ancien Régime*, pp. 205–13.
110 Olivier-Martin, 'Les lois du roi', pp. 227–40.
111 Olivier-Martin, *Histoire du droit français*, p. 395. The abolition of the estates of Franche-Comté was in part a consequence of their disloyalty, but in its dealings with other estates the royal government also sought to demonstrate its authority. In Burgundy, for example, when in 1661 the *élus* were slow in levying taxes, threatening despatches were sent to them. The *élus* were denied the right of deputations to protest the tax burden, but were required to send such deputations to explain what measures were in hand for the more rapid collection of taxes due. If delays were prolonged, the king would send troops to consume on the spot the moneys which had not been paid (A.D. Côte d'Or, Correspondance des élus, C 3952, 1614–75, nos 115–31; Cf. C 3353, for strong demands in respect of tax payments 1676–1715). In the case of Provence Louis XIV, in 1671, when the Assembly had had 'the audacity to discuss his orders', went so far as to send the lieutenant-general, M. de Grignan, blank *lettres de cachet* to exile the most 'ill-disposed' deputies to Brittany. See B. Hildesheimer, *Les assemblées générales des communautés de Provence* (Marseilles, 1935); for Brittany see A. Rébillon, *Les états de Bretagne de 1661 à 1789* (Paris, 1932); for Languedoc see E. Lavisse (ed.), *Histoire de la France*, 9 vols in 17 parts (Paris, 1911–26) VII, pt 1, pp. 280–7.
112 Olivier-Martin, *Histoire du droit français*, pp. 519–20.
113 Ibid., pp. 520–2.
114 Ibid., p. 524.

115　Tapié, *La France de Louis XIII*, p. 468.

116　Ibid., pp. 493–4.

117　Olivier-Martin, *Histoire du droit français*, pp. 540, 525.

118　Olivier-Martin, 'La police sous l'Ancien Régime', mimeographed doctoral lectures 1944–5, pp. 102–18.

119　Olivier-Martin, 'Le conseil d'état du roi', pp. 60–4; ibid., p. 305.

120　R. Mousnier, 'Les règlements du conseil du roi sous Louis XIII', *Bulletin de la Société de l'Histoire de France* (1946).

121　Olivier-Martin, 'Le conseil d'état du roi', pp. 56–7; see also R. Mousnier, 'Le conseil d'état du roi de la mort de Henri IV au gouvernement personnel de Louis XIV', *Etudes d'histoire moderne et contemporaine* (1947) 54–5.

122　Olivier-Martin, 'Le conseil d'état du roi', pp. 67, 77.

123　N. Valois, *Inventaire des arrêts du conseil d'état*, I (Paris, 1886) p. xl.

124　Olivier-Martin, 'Le conseil d'état du roi', p. 59. For greater detail, see R. Mousnier 'Le conseil d'état du roi', pp. 39–44. Mousnier adds that the king sometimes took the most important decisions with the help of only a small number of ministers; the decisions were then 're-ferred to the *conseil d'en haut* for approval'. This meant, ibid., p. 39, that there was a sort of 'upper section of the *conseil d'en haut*'.

125　Ibid., p. 44 ff. On all these points, see Olivier-Martin, 'Le conseil d'état du roi', pp. 304–14.

126　Quoted in J.-H. Mariéjol, *Histoire de la France* (ed. Lavisse) VI, pt 2, p. 293.

127　Olivier-Martin, *Histoire du droit français*, p. 547.

128　J. H. Mariéjol, *Histoire de la France*, VI, pt 2, pp. 394–9.

129　Olivier-Martin, *Histoire du droit français*, p. 547.

130　I summarise here the passage in ibid., pp. 547–0; see also the same author's 'L'absolutisme français', pp. 297–8.

131　R. Villers, 'Histoire comparée des finances publiques européennes aux XVIIᵉ et XVIIIᵉ siècles', mimeographed doctoral lectures 1960–1, pp. 203–10, 211–13.

132　R. Villers, 'Opposition et doctrines d'opposition aux XVIIᵉ et XVIIIᵉ siècles', mimeographed doctoral lectures, 1960–1, pp. 203–10.

133　The sum of 1,053,000 livres voted by the estates of Burgundy as a 'free gift' at the tumultuous assembly of 1659 became traditional. It was demanded in 1662 (A.D. Côte-d'Or, C 2997, f. 2). In 1665 1,103,000 livres were required (ibid., f. 61) and in 1668 1,253,000 (ibid., f. 94); in 1674 1,053,000 once more. After 1685 the 'free gift' required by the government was always 1,000,000 livres, plus the 53,000 traditionally voted since the beginning of the seventeenth century.

134　In Burgundy, for example, after many difficulties with the intendant over the levying of the capitation, the *élus* were forced to accept the amount for which the tax was compounded, 1,000,000 livres per year from 1696. Of this sum, 400,000 was compounded for a total payment of 2,400,000 livres. The sum compounded thus amounted to 600,000 livres. Except for the privileged classes, who were taxed by the commissaries of the nobility, the *élus* drew up rolls of taxpayers in the same way as for the *taille*, parish by parish. In Burgundy, therefore, the *capitation* had already become an assessed tax before 1701, the date at which this became true for the kingdom as a whole (A.D. Côte-d'Or, C 3353, f. 85; C 3141, ff. 46–80; C 5573). For the *capitation* in general, see G. Lardé, *La capitation dans les pays de taille personnelle*, Law thesis (Paris, 1906), and S. Mitard, *La première capitation*, Law thesis (Rennes, 1934).

135 The same occurred with the *dixième* from the very beginning (A.D. Côte-d'Or, C 3330, ff. 37, 60). All these compounded taxes were levied and adjudicated by the provinces concerned, except for the right of appeal to the council. For this point, see Olivier-Martin, *Histoire du droit français*, p. 399.

136 Tapié, *La France de Louis XIII*, pp. 432–3, gives an example for Périgueux.

137 This was the normal condition of towns in the sixteenth century. Henri IV and Richelieu made some attempts to remedy the situation, but without much success: see for example the methods used by the governor de la Vallière at Moulins to nominate the mayor and *échevins*, before the arrival of the intendant le Vayer: P. Baer, *Les institutions municipales de Moulins sous l'Ancien Régime*, Law thesis (Paris, 1906) pp. 110–11. For Dijon, see M. A. Millotet, *Avocat-Général au parlement, Vicomte mayeur de Dijon, Mémoire des choses qui se sont passées en Bourgogne depuis 1650 jusqu'à 1668* (Dijon, 1886), which gives a lively description of the intrigues which prevented the author from being elected. The investigation begun in 1662 into the financial administration of the cities brought to light many scandals.

138 Cf. for example the situation of Dijon at the beginning of the seventeenth century: 'one great hospital', almost 'a great charnel-house': G. Roupnel, *La ville et la campagne au XVIIᵉ siècle. Etude sur la population du pays dijonnais* (Paris, 1955) pp. 29–30. For the great public works 'imposed from above' on the cities at the end of the seventeenth century, see F. Busquet, *Histoire de Marseille* (Paris, n.d., [1945]) and F. Lot's review of this book in *Revue Historique* (1948) 114. See also P. Wolff, *Histoire de Toulouse*, 2nd ed. (Toulouse, 1961) p. 279.

139 R. Villers, 'Opposition et doctrines d'opposition', pp. 100–7.

140 Quoted by Lemaire, *Les lois fondamentales*, p. 168.

141 R. Villers, 'Opposition et doctrines d'opposition', pp. 116–25.

142 Ibid., pp. 127–33.

143 G. Davy, 'Sur la politique de Hobbes. La technique et les principes du droit public', *Mélanges Scelle*, i (Paris, 1950) pp. 207–12; J.-J. Chevalier, *Les grands oeuvres politiques*, pp. 52–69.

144 Ibid., pp. 85–99.

145 R. Villers, 'Opposition et doctrines d'opposition', pp. 135–45; R. Mousnier, 'Les idées politiques de Fénelon', *XVIIᵉ Siècle* (1952) 140–66.

146 Quoted by Mme Gallouedec-Genuys, *La conception du Prince dans l'oeuvre de Fénelon*, mimeographed Law thesis (Paris, 1961) p. 143, n. 2.

D

84 *Louis XIV and Absolutism*

She provides a careful study of Fénelon's conception of absolute, but not arbitrary, power: ibid., pp. 140–66.

147 R. Villers, 'Opposition et doctrines d'opposition', pp. 145–53.
148 P. Benichou, *Morales du grand siècle* (Paris, 1948) pp. 52–76.
149 Ibid., p. 71.
150 Ibid., pp. 209–17.
151 Ibid., pp. 74–6.

5 The Social Origins of the Secretaries of State under Louis XIV, 1661-1715*

FRANÇOIS BLUCHE

This study is not directed towards the elucidation of the concept of social origin as such. It is concerned with the distinction – which some may consider somewhat too legalistic – between the second estate (the nobility) and the commoners (the *roturiers*) among the ministers and high officials of Louis XIV during his personal reign. Were the French chancellors, keepers of the seals, controllers-general and secretaries of state between 1661 and 1715 'bourgeois' or not?

Contemporaries who discussed the social composition of Louis' advisers after the death of Mazarin (9 March 1661) did indeed at times use the label 'bourgeois', justifying themselves by reference to the triumvirate of Fouquet, Lionne and Le Tellier in the *conseil d'en haut*. The verdict of the upper aristocracy has come down to us in the following memoir – entry of Canon Hermant. 'The great persons of the court, and among them Monsieur de Turenne, were by no means pleased, and asked whether it could be true that three bourgeois had the chief voice in governing the state.'[1]

Saint-Simon – as one would expect – is even more sweeping, seeing all Louis' ministers and secretaries of state as sprung 'from the most utter and abject commonalty', or 'from nothing'; a condition of nothingness to which the king could at any time reconsign them if they incurred his displeasure.

Even today informed opinion still inclines to the prejudices of a Turenne or a Saint-Simon and historians find confirmation in

* First published in *XVII° Siècle*, nos 42–3 (1959) under the title 'L'origine sociale des secrétaires d'Etat de Louis XIV (1661–1715)'.

the oftcited sentence from Louis' *Mémoires for the Instruction of the Dauphin*, 'it was not in my interest to choose men of outstanding eminence to be my ministers'. One has only to open Lavisse's *Histoire de la France* to read 'Colbert was forty years old; he had been born at Rheims, a *petit bourgeois*'.[2]

Let us briefly examine the first two quotations. Both contain a good deal of deliberate exaggeration. Saint-Simon, born in 1675, is not a very reliable witness. He belongs to the generation between Fontenelle and Montesquieu, and at the time of Colbert's death in 1683 he was only eight years old. In addition he is apt to dismiss as plebeian anyone who does not belong to the charmed circle of *ducs et pairs* (dukes and peers). What of Turenne? We know that, apart from a small group of great nobles, he preferred to choose his intimates from among the magistrates and members of the Parlement. Louis XIV is supposed to have observed that 'Monsieur de Turenne loves me, but he gives much consideration to the gentlemen of the gown (*gens de robe*)'.[3] Are we to conclude from Hermant's memoirs that the marshal regarded the guests at his table, Lamoignon, Boucherat, Harlay, Lefèvre d'Ormesson, as 'bourgeois'?

It is clear therefore that what our two texts indicate is that the king chose as ministers of state neither princes of the blood nor the great nobles, but men of lesser birth. It should also be noted that when Saint-Simon says that Louis XIV raised up his assistants 'from nothing', he assumes that the king deliberately chose them. This is where the objections build up. Loménie de Brienne had been granted the reversion (*survivance*) of the secretaryship of state since 1615 : how could Louis XIV – or for that matter Louis XIII – have chosen him? Louis Phélypeaux de la Vrillière had taken office in 1629. Séguier, chancellor since 1635, had been keeper of the seals since 1633. Guénégaud and Michel Le Tellier had exercised their functions since 1643. Fouquet was superintendant of finances from 1653 onwards; Lionne, a minister of state after 1659. These men were thus all in office before 1661. The king dismissed Fouquet but kept the others; that is, he continued them in office but he did not raise them up 'from nothing'. The custom of *survivances* dates from long before Louis' personal rule and reversions had been agreed before 1661 : Louvois, for example, had been designated as successor to his father Le Tellier in 1655.

We may therefore ask, first, whether 1661 was really such a crucial date in the development of the French ministry, or whether we should stress it as the year of Fouquet's disgrace : the abolition of the superintendancy – the end of the idea of 'ministerial rule.'

Secondly, we may ask whether Louis XIV had a personal policy when choosing his ministers, or whether he made do with the men he inherited from Mazarin, utilising families whose political fortunes were already well established; and later, when he favoured others like the Colberts, the Le Peletiers or the Boucherats, choosing them from a social stratum which had already provided most of the ministers and secretaries of state in the first half of the seventeenth century. Let us next examine more closely the way in which these great officers were chosen within the framework of the upward movement of families.

Chancellors, keepers of the seals, superintendants and controllers-general, secretaries of state 1661–1715: were they noblemen?
They claimed to be. Not one of them admitted to plebeian origin; the majority claimed titles of nobility going back several centuries. This is not surprising. Those who reached the pinnacle of honour in the seventeenth and eighteenth centuries usually sought to create a long line of illustrious forbears for themselves, even if this to some degree diminished their own achievement.

In the judicial sense the French nobility was one single order. As d'Aguesseau put it : 'the nobles of the kingdom form the estate of nobility, which when considered in a general way exhibits no distinctions of rank'.[4] But in a social sense the order of the nobility did contain degrees of rank. A deeply rooted and easily understood prejudice took ancientness of lineage as the first qualification for membership of the second order. For this reason most of Louis XIV's ministers claimed antiquity for their families. They were powerful enough to have this accepted, if not by everyone, at least by their clients and those owing them obligations, by the naïve or the easy-going, and even by great nobles eager to marry off their daughters to the heir of a ministerial family. They could also convince, or buy off, obliging genealogists. To appear in a printed almanac of nobility indicated a great elevation above the common herd.

Thus we find the Guénégaud family claiming descent from a

clan of the same name, holders of the fief of Guénégaud, near Saint-Pourçain in Bourbonnais, since 1300.[5] The Lionnes liked to believe that they could trace their descent even further back, and the almanacs of the nobility of Dauphiné compiled by Chorier and d'Allard supported their pretensions. Chorier linked them to a family of ancient Rome, while d'Allard accepted a noble connexion documented from 1367.[6]

The Arnauld family was just as ambitious. Arnauld d'Andilly tells us in his *Mémoires* that his family came from Provence and had been noble since 1195, with proof going back to 1340.[7] Such lack of modesty seems odd in a solitary of Port-Royal, a follower of the author of *Twenty-three reasons to be humble.*[8]

The other ministerial families were not to be outdone. The Desmarets were supposedly descended from a governor of Laon, while the Fouquets, the Loménies, the Séguiers continually improved on their family trees, and Colbert claimed in all seriousness to be descended from a king of Scotland.[9]

What are we to make of this almost unanimous scramble for illustrious ancestors? It would seem indiscreet, to put it mildly, if one were really descended 'from the most abject and utter commonalty' to spread tales of one's knightly origins and ancient lineage. But it becomes 'normal' if one has already achieved noble status, of however recent a date. Public opinion was uncritical; the authorities were indifferent and even co-operative. For fiscal reasons the state had an interest in maintaining the distinction between nobles and commoners. But once a family had obtained exemption from the *taille*, the state did not trouble itself with the actual degree of nobility involved. Indeed, Louis XIV frequently issued patents of ennoblement which flattered the holder by recognising his ancient nobility, either by confirming it or by removing a supposed derogation.[10] Moreover, although the pretensions of Colbert did arouse disbelief, most claims were less blatant. Though actual proof was missing, it could be argued that the cases of Fouquet, Séguier, Lionne and Guénégaud were at least plausible. Even today genealogists are sometimes not sufficiently alert and mistakenly, if unwittingly, concede too elevated an origin to one or another of these families.[11] It is not strange that seventeenth-century genealogists should, unwittingly or not, have proved inventive when faced with powerful clients. But between the branches of their mythical family trees, and the 'nothingness' from which Saint-Simon conjured up Louis' ministers, there are many intermediate steps. It is in this wide space that we must place the families of the secretaries of state.

They were indeed noble, but their families had only recently attained that rank. Some went back to the sixteenth century : the Arnaulds[12] and the Lionnes[13] by letters-patent; the Boucherats,[14] the Fouquets,[15] the Le Telliers[16] and the Séguiers,[17] through judicial offices; the Loménies[18] and the Voisins,[19] through the post of private secretary to the king. The rest did not gain entry to the second estate until the seventeenth century, and again by means of offices : the Chamillarts through their positions in the sovereign courts;[20] the Guénégauds[21] and Le Peletiers[22] by purchasing offices which conferred enoblement; the Phélypeaux, in 1610 and 1621, via the office of secretary of state;[23] Desmarets, the controller of finances, was the son of a *trésorier de France*, and marks the second generation of a family in the process of becoming ennobled.[24] The only case where commoner origin is demonstrable is that of the two elder Colberts – the controller-general and his brother Croissy. But even here it should be borne in mind that their father, Colbert de Vandières, from 1652 held a commission as councillor of state. This honorific title did not confer nobility on its holder, as did the letters-patent of nominated councillors of state, but it did grant him certain personal privileges which placed him half way, as it were, between the upper bourgeoisie and the nobility.

We can now go on to consider whether these recently ennobled families in fact counted as members of the second order. The chancellors, controllers-general and secretaries of state from 1661 to 1715 were clearly of newly ennobled families, but this does not make them merit the label 'bourgeois', nor give others the right to over-emphasise their plebeian origin. Aristocratic pretensions are usually in inverse proportion to antiquity of lineage (*vide* Colbert); and the feudal reaction of the eighteenth century demonstrated that the newest nobles were the least willing to compromise with the reform movement. The men we are discussing were of the nobility of the robe; but how much of a defect was this? We forget too easily today that nobility was defined not merely in terms of privilege, but even more by intellectual and moral outlook. 'What is the nobility?' asked the marquis de Mirabeau. He went on to give his own answer : 'I believe it may be defined as that part of the nation which is most usually presumed to possess valour and loyalty.' This presumption of loyalty was not restricted to the military field; the question of service, of service to the crown, was central. Unlike Leporello in *Don Giovanni* who protests : 'I want to play the gentleman; I will serve no longer', the newly-made nobleman of seventeenth-century France wished to serve in order to play the gentleman. He willingly performed services as a nobleman of the robe, while his brothers or his sons served in the army. Even though a distinction still existed between the military and the civilian branches of the king's service in Louis XIV's reign, the monarch himself worked continually to reduce the difference in prestige between the two branches; and at the high level represented by the secretaries of state the division had already disappeared. A comparison between the recruitment of Louis XIV's ministers and that of the eighteenth century is useful.[25] It is true that between 1661 and 1715 the secretaries came from families which had held titles of nobility for an average of just over three generations, that is ennoblement going back as far as the grandfather of the man in question. It is also true that not one nobleman of an old-established family figures among them; the only apparent exception being the duc de Beauvilliers, who was a minister only and not a secretary of state. During the eighteenth century, however, members of the old noble families of Broglie, Choiseul, Saint-Germain and Quelen de la Vauguyon held office as secretaries of state. But we also know of eighteenth-century secretaries who were commoners, as for example Dubois or Necker. This situation is the opposite of that of the seventeenth century. In fact, Louis XIV's personal reign does not provide a single example, in the upper reaches of government, of a 'base plebeian' or a 'new man' in the social, if not the juridical, meaning of the term.

We thus reach a conclusion directly at variance with that which has generally been accepted : Louis XIV ruled without relying on the assistance of a single 'bourgeois'.

So far we have only been considering the question of nobility and have seen that all the ministerial families of Louis XIV were of noble rank. They had, however, all been bourgeois in the more or less recent past. Does an investigation of their rise lead straight back to the 'utter and abject commonalty' and the 'nothingness' of Saint-Simon? This point is crucial. Within the bourgeoisie, just as in the ranks of the nobility, time was of prime importance. It is not enough to say 'families of bourgeois origin' : we must consider what sort of bourgeoisie, and the point at which they entered the bourgeois order.

Again the conclusions we arrive at contradict Saint-Simon. The bourgeois lineage of the Phélypeaux family goes back uninterruptedly to 1399. The Phélypeaux were a good bourgeois family from Blois, fief-holders, with office in the local presidial court, in the habit of contracting good marriages.[26] Therefore, when the family attained noble rank in the last years of the sixteenth century, there was no abrupt transition from one social status to another.

The bourgeois status of the Fouquets, the Aligres and the Séguiers dated from the fifteenth century. The Fouquets were cloth merchants from Anjou,[27] and their attainment of offices in the Parlements of Rennes and Paris in the second half of the sixteenth century is in no way unexpected. The Aligres had figured among the bourgeoisie of Chartres since the fifteenth century, moving from the legal bourgeoisie into the nobility of the parlements, buying fiefs in the Chartres region, continually extending their patrimony.[28] The Séguiers came originally from Bourbonnais. They were established as apothecaries in Paris before the end of the fifteenth century, had acquired seigneuries and were thus well established in the bourgeoisie before they rose to the distinction of the nobility of the gown.[29] The Boucherats attained bourgeois status in the first half of the sixteenth century. They lived 'nobly', having pretensions to noble rank, and their accession to the second estate merely regularised a condition which already existed.

The case of the Colbert family is the same, or very nearly so. They were well known in the commercial circles of Rheims from the mid-sixteenth century. One member of their branch was ennobled by letters-patent in 1603 : Oudart II Colbert, lord of Villacerf, silk manufacturer. Another, the grandfather of Jean Baptiste Colbert, achieved distinction while remaining a commoner : he was controller of the *gabelles* in Burgundy.[30] During the sixteenth century the Desmarets passed from the mercantile bourgeoisie into the legal bourgeoisie of Laon, producing a *procureur du Roi* of the *bailliage* of Vermandois (the grandfather

D*

of the controller-general) who sought, sometimes successfully, to style himself 'esquire', The Le Peletiers held legal offices at Le Mans from the early sixteenth century. The Le Telliers from Paris, merchants in 1535, are found among the legal bourgeoisie in 1551, and rose to nobility via office in the *chambre des comptes* twenty-five years later.

All the above families were thus of well-established bourgeois rank. Were they wealthy? In the seventeenth century they were clearly very rich as the prices they paid for the offices prove. In 1663 Lionne bought his secretaryship from Loménie de Brienne for 900,000 livres, and in 1669 Colbert bought the office of secretary of the royal household from Guénégaud for 700,000 livres.[31]

How these fortunes were amassed is not always immediately clear. Sometimes it was through the exercise of some lucrative post in the royal finances : Guénégaud, the father of the secretary of state, was *trésorier de l'épargne*.[32] Henri Arnauld, the ancestor of Pomponne, was originally a notary and later adviser to the duc de Beaujeu; he probably helped in the running of the ducal finances. His son Antoine, *procureur général* of Catherine de Medici, was also involved in financial affairs. The founder of the dynasty of Lionne was *receveur général* at Grenoble and con-troller of the salt storehouses.[33] Sometimes it was the slow, steady labour of several generations of a bourgeois family – thrifty, econ-omical, cutting back on every expense, continually increasing its income, its houses, its lands – for which, more than for any other class, marriages were part of the obligatory expansion of the patrimony.

The fundamental conditions for advance into the second estate were thus a solid bourgeois tradition and an accumulated fortune large enough to buy increasingly prestigious and costly offices. But what really consolidated – in every sense of the word – the family fortunes of Louis' secretaries of state was their dynasticism and the tightly-knit system of alliances within their group. Etienne d'Aligre, keeper of the seals in 1672, chancellor in 1674 (who died in office in 1677), was the son of a previous keeper of the seals and chancellor. Jean-Baptiste Colbert set up his son, Seignelay, in the navy, and his brother Croissy and nephew Torcy in the department of foreign affairs. All four were to become ministers of state. The Le Tellier dynasty only produced two ministers (Le

Tellier and Louvois) and one secretary of state (Barbezieux) but controlled the department of war through three successive generations, from 1643 to 1701. The Phélypeaux surpassed every other family in the number and duration of offices held, with five secretaries of state, the first of whom assumed his functions in 1629,[34] while the last – to go no further than the seventeenth century – died in office in September 1725, having achieved the rare feat of being the only secretary of state not dismissed or deprived of office in 1715.

But besides the dynastic proclivities of these families one must also note their relationships and alliances. Louis' policy in the *conseil d'en haut* is frequently explained by his exploiting the rivalries of the Colbert and Le Tellier clans; but the factors which held these clans together and counteracted their hostilities should also be stressed : in 1628 Nicolas Colbert, an uncle of Jean-Baptiste, married Claudine Le Tellier, sister of the future minister and chancellor. Through their connection with the Le Telliers, the Colberts were also related to the Le Peletiers. At the same time they were connected to the family of Arnauld de Pomponne and closely related to the Desmarets. In 1646 the father of the future controller-general Desmarets married Marie Colbert, sister of the Jean-Baptiste who later became controller-general and minister. The Desmarets in their turn were allied to the family of the chancellor Voisin. By following their direct or indirect family relationships one may indeed compile a complete – or almost complete – list of the ministerial personnel of Louis XIV.

Nevertheless the hereditary element, the nepotism or favour shown by those in power to their relatives or connections, were by no means unlimited. The effect of such links was probably less evident, less effective and less openly displayed than was the case with the similar network of relationships discernible in the sovereign courts. In the Parlement there were scarcely any obstacles to the transmission of an office, while among the secretaries the choice of the king was decisive. This explains the aborted careers of certain ungifted sons of ministers, for instance Le Tellier de Courtenvaux, who gave up his position to Barbezieux, his younger brother; or the younger Chamillart, even less suitable than his father for high office in the state.

But whether these high posts in government were obtained through a successful career, family support or direct royal favour, the result was the same from a social point of view. Via their offices the ministerial families, even if still close to their past as commoners, undeniably and clearly moved up into the highest noble society. This is the real reason which led Saint-Simon to protest so bitterly against their rapid advancement.

Marriages of ministers or their sons into old noble families also played a considerable part in the rise of the 'new men'. Louis Phélypeaux de la Vrillière (secretary of state from 1700 to 1725) married a Mailly-Nesle; his cousin Jérome Phélypeaux de Pont-chartrain (secretary of state from 1699 to 1715) married as his first wife a La Rochefoucauld; while Guénégaud married into the Choiseul-Praslin family. There are numerous examples in the next generation : one of Le Tellier's daughters married the duc d'Aumont; one of Voisin's daughters married the son of a Broglie; Chamillart married a son to a Rochechouart (the oldest family of the French nobility after the Capetians) and a daughter to the duc de Quintin of the house of Durfort. The success of Colbert's matrimonial policies, which made him father-in-law to three dukes, is too well known to need elaboration.

The pinnacle of these careers was crowned by marks of distinction. The role of titles need not be over-emphasised. The fact that Boucherat was given the title of comte de Compans, or that Nicolas Desmarets became marquis de Maillebois, is of minor importance. These titles reveal the significance of landed property and demonstrate that their holders were better placed than most of the French nobility to obtain what they wanted. The pains-taking repetition of these 'officialised' titles betrays some *parvenu* insecurity, and up to and including marquisates the titles were not of great social importance. Louis did not make any of his secretaries of state dukes, though the Phélypeaux were to enjoy that good fortune in the next reign.

On the other hand the secretaries of state were able, with the backing of Louis XIV, to obtain special privileges which placed them *de facto* on an equal footing with dukes. The most famous instance of this, and the one which caused the greatest furore at the time, was the right to the title of *monseigneur*. From the time of Louvois, thanks to the support of the king, the secretaries of state were permitted to address dukes as *monsieur*, instead of *monseigneur*, while in their turn being addressed as *monseigneur* by others, with the exception of foreign princes, ecclesiastical peers, dukes and the high officers of the crown. This achievement was indeed significant. Similarly, when the ministers and secretaries of state put forward pretensions to be allowed to dine at the king's table, to ride in his carriages and to obtain audiences at court for their wives, such requests were usually granted. It was virtually impossible, once the etiquette of the court had been strictly codified in the eighteenth century, to call an existing privilege in question. The families of ministers were thus dispensed from furnishing proofs, and were allowed by reason of their position to follow the king to the hunt and to be presented to their majesties.

In comparison with these rare privileges, the other marks of distinction accorded to the families of secretaries of state (outstanding episcopal careers, promotion to the highest ranks in the army, entry to the Order of the Knights of Malta) seem nearly commonplace. But here again we are dealing with rewards normally reserved for the highest nobility of the realm, and must conclude that the only real issue was not whether a minister was of noble rank, but whether he was the equal of a duke.

This brief examination is no more than an introduction to the problem, but since historians have concerned themselves with the social origins of Louis XIV's secretaries of state, we have considered it essential to dispel certain prejudices, and modify some judgements (though experts will have to pardon us for having expressed what to them are self-evident truths). It is abundantly clear that in Louis XIV's reign it is not the bourgeoisie, but the nobility of the robe, which arrived at the summit of power. At the level of the highest positions in government and the state, representatives chosen from this social group were permitted to integrate with and become the equal of the highest nobility of the realm; from this time onward their status was so high that they dominated the Second Estate. Louis XIV did not thrust the 'bourgeois' into power; but he used his authority to make government service equal in prestige to antiquity of lineage. By putting his ministers of the robe nobility on an equal footing with dukes, he gave the civil service a hitherto unheard of importance and removed the inferiority hitherto imputed to it. The history of the great offices of government in the eighteenth century shows the continuance of Louis XIV's policy and demonstrates, despite a few anomalies, that the royal service was from now on unified : the kingdom needed administrators as much as soldiers.

NOTES

1   Quoted by G. Pagès, *La monarchie d'Ancien Régime en France* (Paris, 1928) p. 142.
2   E. Lavisse (ed.), *Histoire de la France* (Paris, 1920–2) vii, pt 1, p. 142.
3   M. Weygand, *Turenne* (Paris, 1929) p. 144.
4   H. F. d'Aguesseau, *Deuxième Instruction*, in *Oeuvres Choisies* (Paris, 1863) p. 280.
5   J. B. Bouillet, *Nobiliaire d'Auvergne* (Clermont-Ferrand, 1846–53) iii, pp. 224–8; Henri Jougla de Morenas, *Grand Armorial de France* (Paris, 1934–49) iv, p. 240.
6   Quoted by Marquis Louis Etienne Gustave Rivoire de la Batie, *L'Armorial de Dauphiné* (Lyon, 1867) pp. 354–5.
7   L. Delavaud, *Le Marquis de Pomponne* (Paris, 1911) *passim*; Eugène and Emile Haag, *La France Protestante*, 2nd ed. (Paris, 1877–88) i, 355; accepted somewhat carelessly by Jougla de Morenas, *Grand Armorial de France*, i, p. 238.
8   The author of this work is Jean Haman (1618–87), *solitaire* of Port-Royal.
9   Though Saint-Simon exaggerated in telling a good story, it is clear from documents in the *Cabinet des Titres* that this pretension was put forward.
10 One instance of this – among many others – is found in the 1666 ennoblement of Pierre Paul Riquet, the entrepreneur of the Canal du Midi.
11 Cf. the example in Jougla de Morenas given above (note 7); it should be stressed however that his is one of the best works in the genre published in this century.
12 Haag, *La France Protestante*, i, p. 355 ff; Bibliothèque Nationale, MSS. Nouveau d'Hozier, 12; papers of Colonel de Bellaigue, a specialist on the Auvergne nobility.
13 Rivoire de la Batie, *L'Armorial de Dauphiné*, pp. 354–5.
14 P. Anselme, *Histoire généalogique . . . de la maison royale de France* (Paris, 1726–33) vi, p. 584.
15 Jougla de Morenas, *Grand Armorial de France*, iv, p. 49; B.N., MSS. Chérin, 84.
16 L. André, *Michel Le Tellier et Louvois* (Paris, 1943) pp. 579–83.
17 B.N., MSS. Nouveau d'Hozier, 303.
18 *Annuaire de la Noblesse* (1877) p. 391.
19 B.N., MSS. Chérin, 187; A. Tessereau, *Histoire chronologique de la grande chancellerie de France* (Paris, 1710) i, pp. 242, 289, 345.
20 B.N., MSS. Fr. 32353.

21 B.N., MSS. Pièces originales, 1425; and Dossiers Bleus, 236.
22 F. Bluche, *L'origine des magistrats du Parlement de Paris au XVIII* siècle* (Paris, 1956) pp. 271–2.
23 Hélion de Lucay, *Des origines du pouvoir ministériel en France. Les Secrétaires d'Etat* (Paris, 1881) p. 592; B.N., MSS. Chérin, 155.
24 Bluche, *L'origine des magistrats*, p. 147; Jougla de Morenas, *Grand Armorial de France*, III, p. 15.
25 For this topic see the author's article 'L'origine sociale du personnel ministeriel français au XVIII* siècle', *Bulletin de la Société d'Histoire Moderne* (1957) 9–13.
26 B.N., MSS. Chérin, 155; Bluche, *L'origine des magistrats*, pp. 345–6.
27 Jougla de Morenas, *Grand Armorial de France*, IV, p. 49; B.N., MSS. Chérin, 84.
28 Series E of the Archives d'Eure-et-Loir has much information on this.
29 B.N., MSS. Nouveau d'Hozier, 303; MSS. Chérin, 188.
30 For the Colberts, Jougla de Morenas, *Grand Armorial de France*, III, p. 15 is reliable, being based on the researches of the famous genealogist Chaix d'Est-Ange.
31 Lucay, *Des origines du pouvoir*, p. 60 and note; Lavisse (ed.) *Histoire de la France*, VII, pt 1, p. 155 n.
32 B.N., MSS. Dossiers Bleus, 336.
33 Rivoire de la Batie, *L'Armorial de Dauphiné*, p. 354.
34 The text only takes note of those of the family who held office as secretaries of state.

Part II

PROBLEMS OF
INTERPRETATION

6 The Intellectual Development of Louis XIV from 1661 to 1715[*1]

ANDREW LOSSKY

To avoid a misunderstanding that the title of this essay may suggest, let us point out at once that Louis XIV was not an intellectual in the true sense of the word. Though endowed with an intelligence above the average (and here we venture to disagree with Saint-Simon's appraisal) the king laid no claim to be either an original or a profound thinker, let alone a professional philosopher. In his *Mémoires*, written when he was barely thirty years old, Louis spoke with the weariness of a schoolboy of 'some dark and thorny regions of science . . . where the mind attempts with effort to raise itself above its reach, most often to accomplish nothing; their uselessness, at least their apparent uselessness, repels us as much as their difficulty.'[2] But, illustrating Descartes' famous dictum, Louis thought himself abundantly provided with good sense. This was rather important, since 'the principal function of kings is to let common sense work, and it always works naturally and without strain'.[3] Louis XIV found many occasions to congratulate himself on faithfully discharging the principal duty of his office; this is, in fact, the main theme of his *Mémoires*. True enough, the same *Mémoires* contain some passages from which it appears that the *bon sens* did not always operate with such ease; less than ten years after completing the main body of the *Mémoires*, the king drafted some pages on the difficulties and torments of decision-making.[4] Yet to the end he remained the apostle of common sense; only to give it effect he

* Reprinted from *Louis XIV and the Craft of Kingship*, ed. John C. Rule (Columbus, Ohio, 1969).

put more and more emphasis on continuous and unremitting application to his work.

A man of action, believing in rational common sense, seldom has an elaborate and consistent philosophical system worked out to the last detail. But he cannot fail to have a set of assumptions, or 'mood-thoughts', which may or may not be consistent with one another, and which form the basis of most of his conscious actions. To the process of decision-making of such a person we cannot deny the name of thought, though it is not of the same quality as the ratiocination of a philosopher. It is legitimate for a historian to enquire into this domain, for there is no other way to understand the idiosyncrasy of his actors. In the case of Louis XIV such an enquiry is made possible by the fact that the king liked to reason things out, either in oral discussions or on paper; as he himself said, it helped him to clarify his own mind when he had to express his thoughts in words.

Louis XIV looked upon himself as an incarnation of classicist reason. All might change around him, but the king remained always the same, upholding, under God's dispensation, the immutable principles of reason and justice, a vigilant guardian of the interests of his state. Since Louis sincerely believed that he was cast for this role, he convinced most of his contemporaries that this was indeed a faithful representation of him. The same impression, moreover, was passed on to many of the historians who have written about him. This is not the place to discuss the historiography of Louis XIV. Let us merely note that to most historians, regardless of whether they have praised or damned Louis, the king remained a static figure throughout his personal reign. G. Lacour-Gayet, in his *Education politique de Louis XIV*, has shown how the king had got to the point where we find him in the 1660s; regrettably, however, he never followed up his work to show Louis' further growth. Lavisse, in volumes vii and viii of his *Histoire de la France*, gives an excellent panorama of the whole period, in which the king receives the attention he deserves. The reader cannot fail to be taken in by Lavisse's picture of the monarch growing old and more devout; but, apart from this, there seems to be very little change in Louis' outlook and ideas. Yet no one denies that changes were occurring in the France of Louis XIV. Since the first half of the reign was spectacularly successful and the second half just as obviously unsuccessful, it is generally taken for granted that these changes were for the worse. Many explanations have been advanced to account for the deterioration of Louis' fortune : the king's health, absolutism becoming 'over-ripe' and drying up initiative in the country, irresistible trends and forces changing the face of Europe. The royal advisers also figure prominently : thus Colbert's influence is usually supposed to have been good, Louvois', evil, Madame de Maintenon's, either good or evil, depending on the historian's predilections and degree of acquaintance with her.[5] In most of these interpretations, however, it is tacitly assumed that the king's own basic ideas – if he had any – remained the same from 1661 to 1715.

To suffer no alteration in one's beliefs in the course of fifty-four years of adult life is a sign either of extreme stupidity or of grave mental derangement. Since neither of these descriptions fits Louis XIV, we can take it for granted that changes did in fact occur in his thinking. The problem, therefore, is to detect and to define them. At this point we must admit that if we adhere rigorously to the formalist method of research, the sources available to us may appear to be inadequate both in their quantity and in their quality. Unfortunately for us, members of the *conseil d'en haut* guarded well the secret of the deliberations in that body, which seem to have been remarkably free and candid. No minutes were kept of its meetings. For the early 1660s, the papers of Colbert and of others contain summaries of several conversations held in the council. We also have the *Journal* of Torcy from November 1709 to May 1711, where he reports what was said there. For the rest, we have only a few scattered glimpses of the proceedings in the king's chief council. The king, however, liked to let his trusted subordinates know the reasons for his decisions, and in his correspondence we find a number of arguments and digressions on various subjects, with the aid of which it is possible to reconstruct some of his assumptions and mental processes. Leaving aside for the moment the question of authenticity of royal correspondence, let us note that it contains one group of letters which forms a class apart. Between 1701 and 1715, Louis XIV sent over five hundred letters to his grandson, Philip V of Spain, whom he tried hard, though with little success, to teach the art of kingcraft.[6] Here, if anywhere, we can come close to the real thought of Louis XIV.

Unlike Philip II or William III, Louis XIV rarely held the

pen in his hand. Instead, he preferred to dictate his memoranda, or to give orally the substance of the amendments and insertions to be made in the dispatches. The main autographic writings that remain from Louis comprise the guide to the gardens of Versailles; some military memoirs of the war of 1672–8; the 'Métier de roi' (1679), short letters to persons in his immediate entourage; the advice to Philip V in December 1700 and some of the subsequent confidential letters to him; and a draft of a harangue (1710); to these we must add the purely formal messages of congratulations or condolence to other reigning monarchs. Most of the letters in this last category were not even written by Louis himself, but by special secretaries, like Rose or Torcy, who were skilled in counterfeiting the king's hand. Even the bulk of the *Mémoires* was penned not by the king, but by Périgny or by Pellisson, a fact that has led some critics to attack their authenticity.

The autographic material we have enumerated is clearly inadequate for an analysis of Louis' ideas, especially if we wish to follow their evolution throughout his reign. Before embarking on such an enterprise, we must cast off the fetters of indiscriminate and hypercritical formalism, which can be as noxious to history as is naive credulity or carelessness. Even if Louis XIV was not the clerk who wrote out every word of his *Mémoires* and of every letter that he signed, this does not mean that his role in their composition was perfunctory. The various drafts of the *Mémoires* and of the more important outgoing dispatches contain many marks of the king's pencil. Sometimes Louis merely changed some expressions, for he was an accomplished stylist; elsewhere he deleted whole passages, or altered or expanded a paragraph. It is fairly obvious that wherever we find the king's pencil or pen at work, we have a document whose final version Louis fully approved.

This is not all, for there are many documents not marked by Louis' pencil that, nevertheless, can be attributed to him. When any matter of importance was decided in the council, the minister concerned drafted the king's letter. Sometimes he did it in the king's presence; in the later part of the reign one or several ministers might repair to Mme de Maintenon's room in the evening, where they would do their homework under the king's eye and in consultation with him; some of these sessions were indistinguishable from the regular meetings of the council. At other times the minister would bring his finished draft to the king, who would read or listen to it, and then either approve it as it stood or order some changes to be made; these changes would then be entered in the minister's hand. It is not always possible to ascertain whether a substantial alteration in the draft originated from Louis or from his minister, or from a consultation between them. But in most cases there can be little doubt that the final product was fully approved by Louis; this is especially true of the passages that were added as amendments. Occasionally one comes across a dispatch that has been completely rewritten, sometimes in the sense opposite to the original draft; this was usually the result of lengthy deliberations in the *conseil d'en haut*.[7]

The true authorship of the king's letters hinges on the nature of relations between Louis and his ministers: did the ministers shape the royal mind and express their own ideas in the letters they drafted, or were they merely the mouthpieces of the king? Louis himself entertained no doubts on that score: it was he who moulded his counsellors, and he himself was the ultimate author of the good advice that came to him. The function of the ministers was to give candid advice, and then to find the suitable expedients to carry out the royal decision, seeing to it that no detail or difficulty was overlooked. The actual situation was not quite so simple, for most of Louis' ministers, with the exception of the rather colourless Phélypeaux family, were strong men who held well-defined views of their own. Lionne, Le Tellier, Colbert, Seignelay, Croissy, Louvois, Pomponne, Torcy, Beauvilliers, Desmarets were not mere file clerks. Since these advisers were more or less evenly distributed throughout the reign, the belief that Louis was served by capable ministers in the first half of his reign and by feckless time-servers in the second lacks foundation, unless we choose to single out Colbert for a solitary pedestal.[8]

In the first half of his reign Louis seems to have kept or chosen his ministers because their main ideas were consonant with his own; in the second half, because they reflected some aspect of his personality, which, in maturing, had become more complex and liable to combine contradictory elements. The king, however, did not expect his servants to agree with him in all matters; what he demanded of them was loyal and prompt compliance with his decision once it was made. Torcy's *Journal* records many instances where he disagreed with his master,[9] and, in the earlier part of the reign, there are indications that Lionne did not always agree with the king. But when it came to writing the royal letters, the same Torcy or Lionne faithfully followed Louis' decisions and views. This could hardly have been otherwise, for Louis would not have been slow to discover his minister's deviation and to correct it. Yet, the degree of Louis' supervision varied from department to department, and from one period of the reign to another. Only in foreign affairs did his attention remain constant throughout.

The supervision of the king explains why changes in ideas underlying his letters did not always coincide with changes in the ministry; this is a further indication that these ideas belonged mainly to Louis, at least by adoption. Against this it may be argued that one of the most striking changes came about when Colbert de Croissy replaced Pomponne as foreign secretary in November 1679. But the change in the king's ideas that resulted in Pomponne's dismissal had occurred before that date.[10] Moreover, in the first few months after Croissy had taken over Pomponne's job, the number of corrections in the drafts drawn up by the minister increased drastically. More often than not, these corrections altered the mode of expression rather than the basic meaning of the document: Croissy's original words were often appallingly brutal and insulting, while the final versions stated the same thing in courteous, though forceful and unambiguous, terms. Since these corrections, just as the original drafts, are in Croissy's hand, we cannot affirm with certainty that Louis was the author of them all. Yet the corrections often bear the imprint of the royal style, and we are probably witnessing the lessons of polite international intercourse which the king administered to his servants.

Of course, Louis did not read all the letters that all his secretaries wrote. But we can assume that he read those in which an important new departure was made; at other times he proceeded by the method of spot-checking, which he recommended in his *Mémoires*. There were some departments that he always kept under close surveillance: he never let foreign policy out of his hands, and the same is true, to a lesser extent, of army administration. In other departments, as has been said before, the degree of his attention varied in different periods of his reign. For instance in the several versions of the memoirs for 1661 it is stated that 'no matters of real consequence' passed through the hands of the secretaries of state for the royal household and for Huguenot affairs.[11] Between them, these two secretaries were responsible for much of the internal administration of the realm. It is unlikely that Louis would have rated their departments so low in the later 1670s. When Louis liked and trusted the archbishop of Paris, as he did François de Harlay (1671–95), this prelate was in fact the king's minister for ecclesiastical affairs and received many confidential communications from Louis. Needless to say no such relations existed between Louis and Harlay's successor, Cardinal de Noailles, who was strongly suspected of Jansenism. In the later years the functions of a minister for ecclesiastical affairs were in practice exercised by the king's confessor, Père La Chaise, while Bossuet continued to set the ideological tone in these matters. In the last ten or fifteen years of Louis' reign, some of the late-comers to the ministry, like Desmarets or Voysin, developed a new manner of writing which was in striking contrast with the style of Colbert, Le Tellier, or even Louvois. While these early ministers had ascribed all decisions and directives to the king, many of the later ones developed the habit of writing and issuing orders in their own name; their occasional references to the king sound like afterthoughts.[12] However, this was not true of Torcy, the foreign minister; in his department Louis' presence remained undiminished and constant to the end. In the documents dealing with foreign affairs we thus have a source of more or less uniform value for tracing Louis' intellectual development throughout his reign. It is mainly on impressions gathered from this source that the following sketch is based; it is necessarily incomplete.

We can classify Louis' beliefs into three categories, considering not their contents, nor the intensity with which they were held, but only their persistence. The king held some of his beliefs and attitudes fairly consistently throughout the personal reign; others underwent one or two major changes; still others changed at relatively frequent intervals, leaving, nevertheless, a distinct imprint on royal policy.

Among the permanent elements of Louis' idiosyncrasy was the belief in the 'natural order of things' which God had established; it comprised a set of norms reflecting the ideal state of the world. These norms, however, were not self-enforcing; they required either a human agency or a special intervention of the Divine Providence to make them operative. But the Divine Providence usually worked through intermediary agencies, by endowing some persons with certain gifts: 'God does not do our work without us.'[13] The 'natural order of things' could best be discovered by reason, and, in this sense, Louis remained a rationalist all his life. The application of reason demanded incessant labour on his part, which consisted largely in gathering information, for 'he who is poorly informed cannot help but reason poorly'.[14] Louis' rationalism also showed itself in his faith in calculation in mathematical or mechanical terms. The 'geometric spirit' pervaded his personal tastes and his view of human nature, and it inspired his predilection for siege warfare. The same spirit also resulted in perfectionism, which at times bordered on indecision: the king did not like to act rashly, before all the pieces were set in their appointed positions on his chessboard. When, on a few occasions, he took precipitate action, the results were usually harmful to him; these deviations from the path of reason occurred mainly in the later 1680s when he was passing through a period of confusion.

Louis did not have a high opinion of human nature. Man was above all an egoistic creature, whose chief drive was to procure private advantage for himself and to gratify his passions which sprang from his unreasonable nature. Most of man's actions, however, were controlled by the two mainsprings of fear and hope; the latter, depending on one's inclinations and social status, assumed the form of ambition, vanity or greed, or a combination of these vices. The art of governing or of influencing people consisted in a large measure of applying these stimuli in the right dose and at the proper time. Though some of Louis' worst miscalculations can be traced to this naive mechanistic view of human nature, he persisted in it; in fact, it deepened in his old age, to the dismay of his most devoted servants like Torcy, who complained bitterly about the king's cynicism and distrust.[15] In what measure these attitudes were real or affected is hard to tell; the evidence is contradictory.

Louis' belief in royal absolutism was closely connected with his view of human nature. A private individual if allowed any share in the sovereign power was bound to misuse it, that is, to divert it to serve his personal ends to the detriment of the public good. Even if he turned out to be that rare bird, a man of integrity, his virtue could not long withstand such a temptation unless his master watched closely over him, ever ready to apply the standard stimuli. The prince, therefore, had no right to alienate any part of his sovereign power, for fear that society would disintegrate into 'a thousand tyrannies', so oppressive to the common man. As for the prince, his own self-interest, regardless of any other considerations, induced him to work for the public good since the good of the state made for the glory of the prince. An absolute monarch, brought up in sentiments of honour, jealous of his glory, endowed with intelligence and addicted to hard work was bound to rule for the public benefit. Even if he was stupid, indolent or vicious, his rule was preferable to that of a thousand tyrants : the harm inflicted by the latter was so much more difficult to repair, as Louis knew from his own experience during the aftermath of the Fronde. These were the theoretical grounds for Louis' dogged pursuit of absolute sovereign power.

There was one permanent element in the policy of Louis XIV which is apt to confound all attempts to find any neat formula explaining his behaviour (it may also raise some doubts about the sincerity of his attachment to some of his principles) : Louis XIV was an opportunist. At least, an element of pragmatism was always present in his policy to a greater or lesser degree. In his *Mémoires* Louis repeatedly proclaimed that reason of state was the first of all laws; in following its dictates the prince had to adapt his conduct to changing circumstances and to the spirit of the times, and, if necessary, to do violence to his natural inclinations in order to derive the greatest possible benefit for his state from every turn of events.[16]

Opportunism, however, can never be an absolute rule of behaviour, for it must always serve some fixed end. Thus Louis held an unshakeable belief in God, in the 'natural order of things', in the rightful pre-eminence of France and of the Bourbons in Christendom, in reason of state serving the public good, and in royal absolutism. These disparate elements formed an integral whole in his mind, and a clash between any two of them was unthinkable to him. Louis preached opportunism only in the sphere of those principles that were designed to serve this set of values. But even here he was not a wholly consistent votary of opportunism, for in nearly every major decision his motives were mixed.

For example, the Cretan expedition of 1669, though it was undertaken partly for unadulterated political motives, was also necessary to discharge the king's obligations to God and to enhance his reputation in Christendom. In 1683, had Louis been an out-and-out opportunist, he would have crushed the emperor, who was hard pressed by the Turk; yet the Most Christian King did not do it. When Louis had concluded that the regime set up by the Edict of Nantes was an evil, there was no major external obstacle to prevent him from revoking it outright well before 1685; for instance, right after the Peace of Nijmegen in 1678. Likewise the recognition of the Old Pretender as 'King James III' of England in September 1701 was not a purely opportunistic move, even though it could be argued that it improved Louis' standing with Pope Clement XI, whose support was necessary to strengthen the Bourbon hold on the Spanish monarchy and to buttress their position in the Mediterranean generally. But, at that time, the French king stood well with the pope anyhow, for Clement XI feared the Habsburgs more than the French. It can further be argued that Louis' quixotic move was not only unnecessary but harmful, since it was apt to cause complications away from the main theatre of action, which was in the Mediterranean area. These examples, and many others, indicate that Louis was fairly moderate in his opportunism; the record merely shows that, in espousing different principles, he never lost sight of the interests in his state as he understood them, and that these interests influenced some of his changes. This, however, does not warrant the conclusion that Louis' principles served him only as a hypocritical cover.

We have discussed some of the main permanent features of Louis XIV's thinking. Most of them helped to shape the form of his beliefs; but this form could accommodate many different contents, which could exist harmoniously together, succeed one another, or clash and produce confusion. Three of Louis' beliefs underwent major changes or received new emphasis in the course of his reign : the doctrine of the 'true maxims of state', the concept of the fundamental laws, and the appraisal of the role of Providence in human affairs.

From the 'natural order of things' one could deduce certain 'true maxims' for every community or geographical area. If faithfully followed, these maxims would procure the community the greatest benefits that it was capable of receiving. Prior to the Peace of Nijmegen, Louis held that the 'true maxims of state' could change with the times. In the 1680s, however, he acted for the most part on the assumption that they were immutable. But the ossification of at least one compartment of the royal mind did not last very long. In the 1690s and especially towards the end of his reign, Louis had managed to free himself from this rigid doctrine, and the 'true maxims' once again came to express the living, and changing, interests of the state.[17]

The notion of the fundamental laws of the state was perhaps not wholly absent from Louis' mind at the beginning of his personal reign; but it was overshadowed by other interests and considerations, the first of which was to destroy all obstacles to the free exercise of sovereign power, which was then to be used to reform the realm and to bring it into line with the 'natural order' : 'Since the main hope of [accomplishing] these reforms rested on my will, their first prerequisite was to make my will quite absolute . . . [at the same time letting it be known] that though I rendered account to no one, I nonetheless governed myself by [the precepts of] reason'.[18] In consonance with this line of thinking was Louis' conviction, repeatedly proclaimed in the *Mémoires*, that he was the only depositary of all property in the realm, a part of which he left in the usufruct of his subjects; hence he had an inherent right to tax all his subjects, lay and ecclesiastical, at will. He was also the sole source of equity, of '*my* justice', as distinct from that enforced by the courts. All of this is a far cry from the situation in 1710, when the Sorbonne was asked whether the king had the right to levy the *dixième* on his subjects; much to Louis' relief, the answer was in the affirmative.

The king's concern for fundamental law began to grow in the 1680s, and reached its peak in the early 1700s. It is possible that it had an influence on his vacillating procedure in revoking the Edict of Nantes. At least, this can help to explain his psychological need to show to himself that this edict no longer served any purpose, since virtually all the Huguenots had been converted: strange as it may be, Louis seems to have believed that this was indeed so in 1685. There is not much doubt that Louis' concern for fundamental law was spurred on by his interest in claiming the whole of the Spanish succession for the dauphin; this question began to preoccupy him seriously in about 1685. It cannot be stressed too often that the dauphin's claim, as far as Louis XIV was concerned, was not based on the Spanish failure to pay the dowry of Queen Maria Teresa. Nor was it based on the testament of Carlos II. It rested on the fundamental laws of the Spanish monarchy, which no testament, renunciation or treaty could set aside. According to the doctrine of fundamental law, which is here closely bound with the divine right of kings, a reigning monarch could abdicate, but could not change the law of succession. By 1688 Louis envisaged that if Carlos II left no children after him, the dauphin would take over the Spanish monarchy, and then arrange, in concert with his eldest son and with the various *cortes*, the transference of the succession to his second son. Thereafter, if either of the two branches of the Bourbons died out, the other would be able to succeed it. The inconvenience of heedless adherence to the strict dictates of fundamental law was all too obvious to Louis : hence the elaborate scheme to transfer the Spanish monarchy to the duc d'Anjou. At no time did Louis entertain the chimerical notion that a Spanish monarch could reside in France, or *vice versa*. The idea of fusion of the two monarchies found currency only among some French merchants and among some later historians.

With regard to the role of Providence, there is very little that we can say at this time, not because the subject is unimportant, but because we know so little about Louis XIV's religious beliefs, beyond the obvious fact that he believed in God, suscribed to the standard dogmas of the Catholic church, and disliked extremist movements whether of the Jansenist or of the Quietist variety. As sovereign, and as God's vice-regent in France – the first realm in Christendom – he often quarrelled with the pope and held the papacy, as a human institution, in low esteem.[19] There was, however, at least one perceptible change in Louis' religious views. In his *Mémoires* the king, from time to time, paid obeisance to Divine Providence, usually in a rather perfunctory manner; but in the drafts of this work he repeatedly struck out or toned down many of the passages dealing with Providence.[20] On the contrary, in Louis' correspondence during 1702–12, Providence became the decisive factor in human affairs; all events were in the hands of God, who disposed them for our benefit; it remained for us to worship God's judgements without murmuring.[21] When exactly this change in Louis' thinking came about is hard to determine. In the letters that his secretary Toussaint Rose wrote imitating the king's hand, the theme of Providence is scarcely detectable prior to the spring of 1676; in May of that year it makes itself felt *à propos* of the capture of Bouchain by the French, and then it becomes ever more prominent in 1677 and 1678.[22] This piece of evidence would be significant if it could be proved that Louis set the tone of his formal letters of acknowledgement sent in response to messages of congratulation he received on his victories; in the absence of such a proof, its value must remain in doubt.

Side by side with these big shifts in Louis XIV's thinking, it is possible to distinguish a number of relatively smaller changes which allow us to discern at least nine periods in his personal reign. The first of these is the early formative period, extending from the death of Mazarin to about 1665–6, that is, to the time when the king began a more or less systematic ordering of his ideas. In the early 1660s many of Louis' traits that later became marked were present in inchoate form. This was the time of the first joys of power and of the first assertions of sovereignty. The theme of fundamental law, most unexpectedly, cropped up in Louis' immediate entourage, to disappear just as quickly.[23] There were elements of opportunism and of royal Gallicanism, encouraged both by Lionne and by Colbert. Towards the very end of this period the king developed a certain curiosity for history and arranged to receive some instruction in this subject. But his interest in it was hardly profound : history provided some knowledge useful in peace and in war and a number of examples for the pursuit of virtue.[24] 'Virtue' was of paramount importance to Louis in this period : it showed the path to glory and to the pinnacle of success. The achievement of Charles V and of Philip II haunted him in 1661–2 : through their extraordinary virtue these two monarchs had managed to raise Spain to a station above that warranted by the natural order of things.[25] Louis' '*vertu*' was thus synonymous with Machiavelli's '*virtù*'.

In the second period (1666–73) we meet the 'classical' Louis XIV, who is the model for the standard portrait of his admirers. This is the Louis of the *Mémoires*, who had more or less put his ideas in order. The themes of natural order, of common sense and of mathematical perfectionism reached their full development. It was also the time when the assertion of absolutism proceeded according to plan, and culminated in 1673 in the virtual suppression of the right of parliamentary remonstrance.

The third period extends roughly to the end of the Dutch War in 1678. One of the key figures in it was Pomponne, who, with the backing of the king, developed the principle of opportunism and erected it into a consciously held doctrine. More than ever before, considerations of legitimism were explicitly put aside, and replaced by those of naked expediency.[26] Probably both Louis and his minister were put on this path by the French failure to overwhelm the Dutch Republic in 1672, in spite of all the well-laid plans and thorough preparation. Nevertheless, Pomponne did not lose sight of the system of Europe. France, to him, was merely the chief member of the community of European states, not an entity apart from it, nor its oppressor. It was within this system that Pomponne played his game of procuring for his country the greatest possible advantages, but always in such a way as not to damage, let alone destroy, the fabric of Europe. This is what gained for Pomponne the reputation of being a moderate, as well as an honest man. But Louis XIV seems to have travelled much further than Pomponne along the road to reckless opportunism, and this is what was probably at the bottom of the divergence between the king and his servant. Most of Louis' charges against Pomponne have a hollow ring,[27] except the accusation that the minister failed to press every claim that Louis could have derived from his military and diplomatic superiority in 1678–9.

There was another element that began to creep into Louis' character towards the end of the Dutch War. In spite of the position of strength from which he negotiated the peace treaties of Nijmegen, his original goal – the abasement of the Dutch Republic – remained unachieved. That the war had not gone according to plan was apparent to all, including Louis. It was natural that the king should have sought to discover the reasons for this state of affairs by writing a history of his campaigns; for this effort he first obtained some memoranda from his close advisers. But what is noteworthy is that in 1677–9, when Louis was at work on his military history, his memory, remarkably good in normal times, began to play tricks on him. The king's manuscript contains a number of errors, and the writer is obviously looking for scapegoats.[28] Thus an element of confusion began to appear in Louis' thinking towards the end of the 1670s. Earlier we have noted the increased importance of the Providence theme about the same time. There is no logical connection between the belief in Divine Providence and confused thinking. Nevertheless, in Louis' case, in the late 1670s, the simultaneous appearance of these two tedencies seems to indicate that the king was groping to understand something beyond his mental reach.

The fourth period of Louis' development covers most of the decade of the 1680s and is rather complex, with overtones of incipient confusion becoming much more marked. The decade as a whole was characterised by the activities of Colbert de Croissy and of Louvois.[29] We have already noted the temporary ossification of the doctrine of 'true maxims of state' in this period. The other salient feature, especially in the early years of the decade, was the preoccupation with limited strategic objectives on the French frontiers. The rounding off of French territory through 'reunions' was based mainly on positive customary law and on purely legalistic interpretation of treaties and of other documents. In all of this we can detect the work of Colbert de Croissy – a forceful and rather unscrupulous lawyer, whose sole interest was to win lawsuits for his client and to score points against the other side, and who was utterly oblivious of all other considerations. The same narrow legalism appeared in the French dealings with Pope Innocent XI; it was only two decades later that Louis XIV and his entourage realised that 'the maxims of France' in matters ecclesiastical were best left undefined if they were to be an effective shield against papal pretensions. Moreover, the violent measures and arrogant language of Colbert de Croissy and of Louvois were in strange contrast with the very limited and modest, not to say petty, aims pursued by the French government in the 1680s.

These policies were carried on in utter disregard of the system of Europe and even of the broad international interests of France. As a result, France was but a passive observer of the momentous changes in central, south-eastern and northern Europe : the first successful counter-offensive of the Christian states against the Turk; the gradual transformation of the Habsburg state into a great military monarchy; the reform of the Swedish realm along new lines; and the re-entry of Russia into the system of Europe. For France, her virtual absence from the scene of these great events entailed the crumbling of her system of alliances on the

E

Habsburg borders. At the same time, France's near-sighted isola-
tionism helped to bring about a split of the European system into
three more or less independent zones : the west, the north and the
south-east; this division was to subsist until the end of Louis XIV's
reign.

In spite of what has just been said, let us note that in 1682
Louis raised the siege of Luxembourg, apparently so as not to
impair the concerted effort of Europe in repelling the Turkish
onslaught. But in the next year, he destroyed whatever advantage
he might have reaped from this gesture : he invaded the Spanish
Netherlands before the Turks had been driven away from the
walls of Vienna. Shortly thereafter, his interest in fundamental
law began to make itself felt. This development cannot be connected either with Colbert de Croissy or with Louvois; it is hard
to ascribe it to the chancellor, Michel Le Tellier, or to any of the
other intimate advisers. The first impetus may conceivably have
come from Bossuet, but in the absence of any direct evidence to
support such a hypothesis the most likely explanation is that this
was a spontaneous growth in the king's mind, prompted by his
interest in the Spanish succession; it is worth noting that in pursuing this great aim Louis showed himself moderate in his methods
as well as in his words. Whatever the origins of the fundamental
law theme or of Louis' outburst of magnanimity in 1682–3, these
developments did not fit in well with Louis' other assumptions
at the time and contributed to the mounting confusion in his mind
and in his policy.

This leads us straight into the fifth stage in the evolution of
Louis XIV – the period of total confusion from early 1688 to
1691, which landed him in the Nine Years War (1688–97), commonly called the 'War of the League of Augsburg'. While the
king sought to disengage himself in the east in order to concentrate
on wooing Spain, he allowed the small military operation that he
undertook against Philippsburg at the end of September 1688
to be escalated into a major war; and finally he managed to get
himself embroiled with Spain in 1689. According to Louvois, the
little war in the east was to have lasted four months; it lasted nine
years. France was militarily unprepared for a major war;[30] her
diplomatic preparation for it had been even less adequate : she
had virtually no allies. While Louis posed as an international
champion of the Catholic cause, his relations with the Holy See

were of the worst, and he had incurred a secret sentence of excommunication by Innocent XI. In one respect only can Louis be absolved of the charge of improvidence: few rational men could have foreseen in 1688 that William III's expedition to England would be anything but political suicide. The French king was therefore quite right in not interfering with his enemy's enterprise.

Heedless violence is not an uncommon reaction in a proud man caught up in the coils of his own contradictions. Of Louis' advisers only Louvois believed in premeditated, systematic violence as an effective instrument of policy: suffering inflicted on enemy subjects would induce them to press their sovereigns to comply with French desires. As for Colbert de Croissy, his brand of violence was that of the tongue rather than of action, except on a small scale; for instance, when he took up the cudgels in Hendaye's quarrel with the Spanish city of Fuentearrabia, which had been going on for decades. Louis XIV himself did not subscribe wholeheartedly to the favourite methods of either minister; occasionally he seems to have held them in check. Yet in the 1680s, acts of violence committed, or at least authorised, by Louis XIV were on the increase. Although the systematic burning of dwellings in the Spanish Netherlands in 1683–4 bears the distinct imprint of Louvois, most of the other violent proceedings – the destruction of three-quarters of the city of Genoa by bombs fired from the French fleet in May 1684, the massacres of the Vaudois in Savoy in 1686, the fantastic schemes in 1687–9 to browbeat Pope Innocent XI (only a few of which were put into effect) – appear to be irrational outbursts, with little or no premeditation. The devastation of the Palatinate, which has made more noise than Louis' other acts of violence, was also one of such outbursts. But at least it can be explained by fear: the French government suddenly found itself on the verge of a major war, for which it was unprepared, and its first reaction was to cut the enemies' lines of communication, regardless of political consequences or moral considerations.

We could lengthen the list of inconsistencies and of acts of violence of Louis' administration in the later 1680s; but it would add nothing to the impression that the confusion in Louis' mind and his tantrums, especially towards the very end of the decade, bordered on mental derangement; they were quite out of keeping with Louis' character during the rest of his reign, both before and after the 1680s. Fortunately for the king and for his state, this condition did not last long. Even while he himself was hitting out indiscriminately in all directions, Louis XIV was capable of giving advice full of good sense and moderation to his weak-minded English cousin, James II. And of course he could not help being disappointed in his own servants Louvois and Colbert de Croissy in the first place. But something had happened to Louis : he could not bring himself to dismiss them as he had dismissed Pomponne in 1679. It was death that relieved him of Louvois on 16 July 1691.

The sixth period in Louis' development extends from 1691 until about 1696. Its primary theme was the liquidation of the legacy of the 1680s. Within a week after the death of Louvois, the king called Pomponne back into the *conseil d'en haut*. Though Croissy retained the secretaryship of state for foreign affairs and his place in the council, Pomponne's hand was soon felt. Beginning with 1691 we can discern in French foreign relations a policy rather than a set of erratic expedients.

There was another change in 1691 : the duc de Beauvilliers joined the king's council a few days after Pomponne. Pomponne and Beauvilliers resembled each other in their judicious, mild temperament and in their polished manners. Both were gentlemen, even great lords, rather than assiduous clerks. Both believed in the system of Europe, though Beauvilliers was apparently inclined to lay more stress on fundamental law as its basis. However, in matters ecclesiastical, which at that time were of paramount importance for the internal structure of France, the two men stood for opposite tendencies. Arnauld de Pomponne certainly was not an out-and-out Jansenist; nevertheless, by his education, family ties and personal tastes he was drawn to that movement. His children were brought up as moderate, but devout, Jansenists; among them was the future wife of Torcy. Beauvilliers, on the other hand, had some Quietist leanings, as his religious writings indicate. He was a close friend of his brother-in-law, the duc de Chevreuse, whose Quietist tendencies and connections were quite pronounced. Chevreuse – and through him Beauvilliers – was continuously in touch with Fénelon; both men openly proclaimed their attachment to him, even when Fénelon was *persona non grata* at court.

The ministerial shake-up of 1691 was significant of Louis' state of mind, because the king was well acquainted with Pomponne and Beauvilliers and with their views. Thus there was nothing fortuitous about the opposite tendencies for which they stood being brought simultaneously into Louis' inner council. Moreover, this enfranchisement of opposite views was not a passing phenomenon, for it subsisted almost to the end of the reign. Did the king try to institutionalise, and thereby to put into more orderly channels, the confusion of his own mind, or did he seek to dominate his council that much more effectively by maintaining discordant views in it? For the years 1691–6 we cannot answer this question with any certainty. But taking the period from the 1690s to 1715 as a whole, it is fairly clear that Louis sought to assert his control, as well as to gain information, by encouraging disputes between the ministers in his presence. In the *Mémoires* Louis had said that rivalry between the ministers helped to unite the full authority of the master in the king's person.[31] The *Mémoires*, however, are apt to be a misleading guide for the later part of Louis' reign, unless they are corroborated by other evidence. In this instance we can draw on Torcy's *Journal* for an account of the sessions of the council in 1709–11. Torcy's descriptions, as well as some fragmentary indications in the dispatches, show that the clash between opposite views in the royal council was open and strong, that the king's decisions, after he had heard the debates, were indeed his own, and that he did not side consistently with any one adviser or group of advisers. No doubt the king's view of human nature was partly responsible for his technique of arriving at decisions : one self-interest would cancel out another. This system could not guarantee Louis from vacillation and even from taking contradictory measures; but it did safeguard his personal exercise of the sovereign power.[32]

To return to the years 1691–6 : the task of liquidating the legacy of the 1680s was facilitated by French military victories in the Low Countries[33] and by a series of diplomatic successes in Italy; these successes began in 1692 and culminated in the Peace of Turin in June 1696, which exploded the anti-French coalition. At the same time the centre of French political attention shifted definitely from north to south, from the Holy Roman Empire to Italy and Spain. Louis could thus afford to be moderate in his peace aims in the north, while being victorious in the field in that quarter; with regard to Spain, his policy had been moderate throughout the Nine Years War anyway. The king achieved this position of strength by following the restrained opportunism of Pomponne. Yet, at the same time, the theme of fundamental law and legitimacy was on the rise, which made it difficult for Louis XIV to recognise the kingship of William III. A further element of confusion continued to plague Louis XIV's ecclesiastical policy. Admittedly, the theological quarrels that agitated the church of France in the 1690s were involved enough to have taxed the ingenuity of a professional theologian : it is enough to mention the ever-changing nature of the Jansenist movement and the Quietist scare. Since most of these issues carried political overtones, the king could not afford to ignore them, even if he had wished to do so. But the persistent confusion in the royal head, now heightened by confusion built into the council, resulted in such ill-considered measures as the appointment of de Noailles to the see of Paris in 1695. Only in one respect did Louis succeed in solving the ecclesiastical imbroglio : he cut the Gordian knot of his relations with the Vatican by a virtually total surrender to the pope in 1693; true enough, the pope was no longer Innocent XI, but Innocent XII.

The seventh period covers the time from the last stages of the negotiations at Ryswick to the acceptance of the will of Carlos II of Spain. The theme of legitimacy, though not altogether discarded, was overshadowed by a concern for the system of Europe within which France would occupy a place of honour, but not of hegemony. This was the background of the Spanish partition treaties and of the close co-operation between Louis XIV and William III. Such a policy was clearly inspired by Pomponne. This minister, freed from interference by Croissy, who had died in 1696, and ably seconded by his son-in-law, Torcy, was now in a position to make his ideas prevail.[34] The king, for his part, wished above all to avoid getting involved in a war like the one from which he had just extricated himself, and he was glad to take shelter in Pomponne's ideas, for they seemed to guarantee him from precisely such a predicament. Moreover the Spanish partition treaties held out the prospect of a considerable accretion to French territory and power without overturning the European system. The Spanish partition policy was Pomponne's greatest achievement in diplomacy, as well as his swan-song. He died in

September 1699, when the Second Partition Treaty had already taken shape in its main outlines.

It was not Pomponne's fault that the will of Carlos II put such a severe strain on his policy. In fact, Carlos' will made the policy of partition virtually unenforceable : not by the bequest of the Spanish monarchy to the duc d'Anjou (which was, indeed, highly desirable for a smooth working of the partition policy), but by the clause that transferred the entire succession to Archduke Charles if the grandsons of Louis XIV refused to accept the inheritance in its entirety. The adamant refusal of the Austrian Habsburgs to consider any division of the inheritance at this time was well known. The French rightly judged that, to enforce the partition treaty, it would have been necessary to conquer all of the far-flung lands of Spain, and then to proceed to dismember them. The best military opinion of the time held that Frence stood little chance of winning such a war, in which the Spanish nation (that is, the political classes of Spain) would be on the opposite side; and, anyway, Louis' object was to avoid war. It is to the honour of Louis XIV and of his council that it took them several days of deliberation to reach this embarrassing conclusion : their first decision had been to adhere to the Second Partition Treaty. Apparently it was Torcy who first saw the absurdity of such a course and began to argue for an acceptance of the will of Carlos II. The irony of it all was that neither Louis XIV nor his councillors believed in the validity of this will : no legitimate king could alter the law of succession by such a document. But the will could be used as a powerful propaganda weapon to misguide the Spanish public, and as such it was feared by the French.

Under the circumstances there was only one thing that Louis XIV could do, which was to take a strong stand on the issue of fundamental law and legitimacy. The various tactical mistakes that he committed in pursuing this course, leading to the outbreak of the War of the Spanish Succession (which could have been avoided, or at least localised), need not concern us here. We have already dealt with some of the aspects of Louis' preoccupation with fundamental law in the second half of his reign; what we should note here is the intensity of this reaction, which forms the main theme of the eighth period of his reign, until about 1712. Louis' belief in Providence reached its greatest intensity at the same time (1702–12). Of the many examples of Louis' preoccupation with fundamental law let us cite his injunctions to Philip V to govern himself in accordance with the laws and maxims of Spain, the safeguarding of Philip's right of succession in France, and the recognition of the Pretender's royal title.[35] Later on, it was necessary to maintain that Francis Rákóczi was not really a rebel, but a defender of the ancient constitution of his land; to the best of my knowledge no such arguments had been invoked before in order to justify French aid to the Sicilian rebels in the 1670s or to the remnants of 'Cromwell's faction' in England. To have been so thoroughgoing the resurgence of the fundamental law theme must have answered some deeply-felt need of Louis' mind. There was, however, at least one deviation from the general course: after the battle of Almanza in 1707, Louis encouraged the revolutionary schemes of the court of Madrid to introduce Castilian laws and form of government in Aragon and Valencia. But, in 1711, after Philip's second reconquest of Spain, Louis took up the defence of Aragonese laws and privileges against the threat of Castilianisation; he recommended to modify only those of the privileges of Aragon, and later of Barcelona, that were directly harmful to royal authority and to the whole state, and were therefore contrary to nature.

The transition from the eighth to the ninth period in Louis' development was not as abrupt as that of 1700. In this last period the preoccupation with fundamental law was tempered by other considerations and inclinations: by historical reasons, rational analysis of existing conditions, a grain of opportunism, and humanity. For the first time all these elements were combined in the spirit of compromise, not of confusion.

French military defeats and deaths in the royal family made it impossible for Louis to adhere strictly to the fundamental laws, not only of Spain, but even of France, without endangering the very existence of his state. First he had to press Philip to abandon most of his kingdoms, satisfying himself with a small state in Italy; failing this, he had to insist that Philip give up his right of succession in France. Of course, if one chose to stand firmly on the ground of divine-right constitutionalism, one could maintain that Philip's renunciation of his right to succeed to the French crown was null and void, though it was drawn up in strong terms and duly registered in the Parlement of Paris. Whether Louis, at the back of his mind, regarded it as such, we shall never know for certain; here, more than ever, he would have needed to exercise all his powers of dissimulation if this were so. Judging by the appearances, however, Louis sincerely believed that the renunciation was valid, for it had been inspired by Divine Providence.[36] Moreover, Louis knew that Philip's accession to the French throne might well spark off a general war in Europe, and even civil wars in Spain and France; all of this Louis XIV was determined to prevent at almost any price.

Philip V's renunciation of his rights to the French crown and the series of deaths in Louis' family in 1711–14 brought the question of the French succession to the forefront. The situation became critical in May 1714 when the duc de Berri, Louis' third grandson, died leaving no son. There was little hope that the sickly four-year-old child, the future Louis XV, would be spared. The next lawful heirs after him were Philip V of Spain and his two sons, followed by Louis' nephew, Philip of Orléans, and his son, and then several young princes of the Condé branch. The inconvenience of Philip V's succession was clear, and the extinction of the other lines was a distinct possibility. The Capetian dynasty would then come to an end in France. The election of a new dynasty would have necessitated a convention of a body like the Estates-General. Barring a miracle, such a body was certain to undo the work of the three Bourbon kings. It was likely to inaugurate aristocratic rule in France and to set up institutions limiting the powers of the monarch. To Louis, this meant government by pressure groups, which would ultimately have reduced the realm of France to anarchy and degraded it to the status of England, or even Poland. Louis had already firmly rejected the English proposals that the Estates-General be convened to confirm Philip V's renunciation – proposals as naive as they were insulting to Louis.

It is against this background that we must interpret the edict of July 1714 declaring the duc du Maine and the comte de Toulouse, Louis' illegitimate sons, capable of succession to the crown after the princes of the blood. At about the same time, Louis drew up his will, which was dated 2 August 1714. In it the king enjoined his great-grandson to repair as soon as possible any degradation that might occur during his minority in the status of the duc du Maine. In the same document the king also appointed the future Council of Regency, seeking thereby to ward off the

E*

more imminent danger of aristocratic government during the coming minority. Not that the king had much faith in the efficacy of all these measures, but to avert the calamities threatening his realm he had to erect every barrier he could devise, however unconstitutional or feeble.

Military defeat was not the only reason that made Louis press his grandson to give up some of the Spanish lands. As early as 1703, he began to urge Philip to cede the Spanish Netherlands to the elector of Bavaria. In this he was moved not only by the strategic need to keep this prince fighting on the Bourbon side, but also by the lessons of history : the Burgundian lands of Spain had been the main reason for Franco-Spanish enmity in the past. A complete liquidation of this heritage would help to prevent the same kind of enmity arising between the two branches of the Bourbons in the future. Though historical thinking had not been entirely alien to Louis XIV before, it had appeared only sporadically and seldom left a significant mark on him. Traces of such thinking can be seen in some passages of the *Mémoires*, and, more clearly, in his analysis of Franco-Spanish relations undertaken in the mid-1680s, when he wished to compose the differences between the two countries. It is not clear whether or not it was Torcy, an addicted student of history, who now guided the king on the path of historical speculation. The fact remains that towards the end of Louis' life a historical view of the changing scene became an ingredient in his thought. It showed itself in his approach to Vienna in 1715, when he sought an alliance with the Austrian Habsburgs. The only trouble with this policy was that neither the contemporary statesmen nor Louis' immediate successors possessed his penetration; the great diplomatic revolution had to wait until 1756. Yet it is remarkable that at no time was the mind of Louis XIV so clear as in the last year of his life.

Though Louis had not been a total stranger to enlightened humanity, this feeling finally broke surface towards the end of his life. Nowhere did it appear more clearly, and to his greater credit, than in the intercession he made for the citizens of Barcelona in 1714. Philip V intended to stage a general massacre in that city as soon as it would fall into his hands. The old king was outraged by his grandson's callousness, and told him so in two forceful letters.[37] To appreciate the full import of Louis' plea for clemency, we must consider that there was no doubt in his mind that

Barcelona was guilty of rebellion against its lawful sovereign; to Louis, the perpetrators of such an action were always 'infinitely criminal'.

One further remark needs to be made. It concerns Louis' personal character rather than the contents of his ideas. A reader of the king's *Mémoires* cannot fail to be impressed by some penetrating passages; but he will also find it difficult not to be suffocated in the fumes of the incense that the brash young man keeps burning before his own image. The panegyrics addressed to him by great and small men in every walk of life, the palace of Versailles, where every courtier, every picture, every ornament, every statue, almost every tree was dedicated to the single theme of the worship of Louis – all this should have redoubled Louis' propensity for self-adulation. It did nothing of the sort. Instead, as the king grew old, wisdom and even humility gradually replaced the themes of pride and self-worship in his words and actions. It is one of the ironies of human affairs that so many historians have sung the praises of Louis XIV for the first part of his reign and have deprecated him for the second.

The picture of Louis XIV that emerges from this sketch is not a tidy one. It was not meant to be, for our main purpose has been to show that, behind the impassive classical façade he presented to the world, Louis was a human being, as full of contradictions, passions and confused thoughts as other mortals.

NOTES

1   This essay summarises some of the conclusions of the *Studies in the political beliefs of Louis XIV* which I am preparing.

2   '. . . quelques endroits obscures et épineux des sciences . . . où l'esprit tâche à s'élever au dessus de sa portée, le plus souvent pour ne rien faire, et dont l'inutilité, du moins apparente, nous rebute autant que la difficulté'. J. Longnon (ed.), *Mémoires de Louis XIV* (Paris, 1927) p. 22; Ch. Dreyss (ed.), *Mémoires de Louis XIV pour l'instruction du Dauphin*, 2 vols (Paris, 1860) II, p. 428 (hereafter cited as Longnon and Dreyss respectively).

3   'La fonction des rois consiste principalement à laisser agir le bon sens, qui agit toujours naturellement et sans peine': ibid.

4   Commonly known as the 'Réflexion sur le métier de roi' (printed in Longnon, pp. 280–2; Dreyss, II, pp. 518–21) for which see note 10 below.

5 The problem of Mme de Maintenon's influence on Louis XIV and *vice versa* is rather complex. She changed, as did Louis himself, in the course of their married life. Though there are instances where their opinions differed, Philip V of Spain, who knew Maintenon well, wrote to Cellamare in 1715 that she was 'unicamente vinculade à la voluntad y gusto del Rey Christianisimo': A. Baudrillart, *Philippe V et la cour de France*, 5 vols (Paris, 1890–1901) I, p. 648. Maintenon's full correspondence, especially for the later years, would have made an excellent source for a study of Louis XIV. But, in 1713, she burnt many of the king's letters to her, and in the following year Louis did the same with Maintenon's letters to him. It is also regrettable that the critical edition of her letters undertaken by Marcel Langlois, *Madame de Maintenon, Lettres*, vols II–V (Paris, 1935–9) stops in 1701. Some of Maintenon's letters for the 1700s are scattered in several *fonds* of the manuscripts department of the Bibliothèque Nationale; even these few letters are of great interest, and show her familiarity with what went on.

6 Baudrillart tracked down a total of 538 letters of Louis XIV to Philip V; 401 of them, addressed to Philip or to Queen Marie Louise of Spain, are at present in the Archivo Historico Nacional in Madrid, Estado, Legajo 2460 *bis* (transferred from the General Archives of Alcalá de Henares); only five of the letters in this bundle date from before 26 June 1703. Some of Louis' letters to Philip are in the collection of the duc de la Trémoîlle. The Archives of the Ministry of Foreign Affairs in Paris have 514 drafts and copies of Louis' letters to his grandson. They duplicate the vast majority, though by no means all, of the originals in Madrid. For a discussion of these materials see Baudrillart, *Philippe V*, I, pp. 11–15, and idem., *Rapport sur une mission en Espagne aux Archives d'Alcala de Hénarès et de Simancas* (Paris, 1889) pp. 25, 49–70.

7 See, for instance, Louis XIV to the comte d'Avaux, ambassador at The Hague, 2 Sep 1688, Archives des Affaires Etrangères, Correspondance Politique, Hollande, vol. 155, ff. 351–4; this letter, bearing many alterations and pencil marks, is the one that instructed d'Avaux to declare to the States-General that Louis had an alliance with James II of England. Another example is the letter to the comte de Briord, also ambassador at The Hague, dated 10 November 1700, but obviously sent a little later (ibid., vol. 190, ff. 14–17); it informed Briord of the death of Carlos II of Spain and of Louis' decision to reject Carlos' will and to adhere to the Second Partition Treaty. However, the draft of this letter was rewritten at least twice, and in the final text the theme of adherence to the Partition Treaty is much less prominent than in the original version.

8 A history of the Colbertian myth would provide a most instructive insight into the 'middle-class interpretation of history' fashionable in the nineteenth and twentieth centuries.

9 See F. Masson (ed.), *Journal inédit de Jean-Baptiste Colbert, Marquis de Torcy* (Paris, 1884) *passim*.

10 In this connection it is interesting to note that Louis' original draft of the 'Réflexion sur le métier de roi' was written in the present tense; see

Bibliothèque Nationale, MS. Fr. 10,331, ff. 125–30. An exact copy taken from this draft exists in A.A.E., Mémoires et Documents, France, vol. 297, ff. 206–10. At some later date the section dealing with Pomponne's inadequacy was changed into the past tense, the accusations against Pomponne were toned down considerably, and the whole document was given the form in which it is usually published. This correction of the original text was made in a trembling hand, probably when the king was already old. The 'Métier de roi' was thus originally a memorandum of the king to himself on what to do about Pomponne, who had ceased to satisfy him – an instance of the king trying to clear his ideas by expressing them. It was against Louis' principles to consult his advisers on matters of appointment or dismissal of the ministers and other high officials, as such matters affected the personal interests of the advisers. Hence Louis had recourse to pen and paper: see Longnon, pp. 228–9, 271; Dreyss, II, pp. 238–9, 341–2; cf. ibid., pp. 22–3.

11   Longnon, p. 30; Dreyss, II, p. 391.

12   This is an aspect of the much wider and little investigated process of administrative decentralisation that set in during the last two decades of Louis' reign. The king conferred more and more initiative on his trusted advisers and ambassadors. At the same time the intendants were beginning to behave like fully-fledged governors of provinces, and even the governors, whose office until then had been mainly honorific, were beginning to acquire a certain structure in the administration of the provinces. Anyone reading the day-to-day correspondence of the intendants and governors in the early 1700s cannot fail to be struck by the difference in tone between their letters and similar documents for the 1670s.

13   Longnon, p. 118; Dreyss, II, p. 565.

14   See draft for the *Mémoires* of 1666, Dreyss, II, p. 95; cf. ibid., p. 429; Longnon, p. 23.

15   See, for example, Torcy, *Journal*, p. 172 and *passim*.

16   See, for example, Longnon, pp. 43, 113–14, 117–18, 208; Dreyss, I, p. 229; II, pp. 444, 561–2, 564–5; cf. ibid., II, pp. 104–9. Most of these passages appear in the later version of the *Mémoires*, written by Pellisson. The inspiration of Machiavelli is fairly obvious. On Machiavelli's influence on Louis XIV's *Mémoires* see Paul Sonnino, 'The Dating and Authorship of Louis XIV's *Mémoires*', *French Historical Studies*, III (1964) 303–37.

17   On Louis' doctrine of 'true maxims' see my 'Maxims of State in Louis XIV's Foreign Policy in the 1680s', *William III and Louis XIV. Essays by and for Mark Thomson*, ed. R. M. Hatton and J. S. Bromley (Liverpool, 1968) pp. 7–23.

18   '. . . que pour ne rendre raison à personne, je ne me gouvernais pas moins par la raison': Longnon, pp. 20–1; Dreyss, II, 382–3. This text is Pellisson's and dates from about 1670.

19   A promising beginning of an enquiry into some of Louis' religious views has been made in Jean Orcibal's *Louis XIV contre Innocent XI* (Paris,

1949) and *Louis XIV et les Protestants* (Paris, 1951), and in Paul Sonnino's *Louis XIV's View of the Papacy (1661–1667)* (Berkeley, Los Angeles, 1966).

20 For example, in the draft of the *Mémoires* for 1661, prepared by Pellisson about 1670–1 (B.N., MS. Fr. 10,332) there were eleven references to Providence. Five of them received the king's special attention. Three passages were suppressed entirely (ff. 16, 23, 290–1; in this last instance a whole long section on belief in God was eliminated: ff. 268–92); one passage was drastically curtailed, so that only its weaker part remained (ff. 231–3); one passage bears the mark of the king's black pencil (f. 35).

21 For examples of Louis' stress on Providence in 1702–12, see Baudrillart, *Philippe V*, I, pp. 116–17, 121, 259, 276, 499.

22 See copies of the royal letters '*de la main*', written by Rose in 1674–8, B.N., MS. Fr., Nouv. acq., 20, 215.

23 Colbert recounts how on 11 November 1661, the day the dauphin was born, news was brought from Spain of the death of the only son of Philip IV (the future Carlos II was to be born a little later): the dauphin 'étoit né par ce moyen héritier naturel et légitime des deux couronnes de France et d'Espagne' (A.A.E., Mémoires et Documents, France, vol. 296, f. 90). Since Colbert himself was the last person on earth to have bothered about fundamental law and legitimacy, it is improbable that this reflection originated with him; however, we cannot impute it with any certainty to the king either.

24 Dreyss, II, p. 96.

25 See Louis' reflections in his council in October–November 1661, as reported by Colbert: B.N., MS. Clairambault, vol. 485, pp. 54–6; printed in P. Clément, *Lettres, Instructions, et Mémoires de Colbert*, 8 vols in 10 (Paris, 1861–82) VI (1869) p. 490. The reader should, however, be warned that in editing Colbert's notes for the history of the king, Clément changed the order of several paragraphs and altered some expressions; as a result, his text is more orderly than the original Colbertian document. See also A.A.E., Mémoires et Documents, France, vol. 296, ff. 89–94. Cf. Longnon, pp. 54–5, 87–8; Dreyss, II, pp. 452, 542; cf. ibid., pp. 16–17.

26 This development can be traced, for instance, in A.A.E., C.P., Liège, vols 8, 9, 13 and Supplément, vol. I. In the years 1676–9, which this correspondence covers, Liège was undergoing a series of revolutionary upheavals. The Archivo Historico Nacional in Madrid holds several bundles of letters of Louis XIV and of his ministers to the rebel senate of Messina in 1674–7 (Estado, Legajo 2264): they reflect the same assumptions.

27 For example, in the 'Métier de roi', Louis said that he disliked Pomponne's style of writing; but, as we have seen above, he apparently had no more reason to be satisfied with Croissy's style in the first months of his ministry. The other charges, like lack of diligence or of *capacité* (which was later struck out by the king), were just nebulous expressions of general disagreement.

28 For this information I am indebted to Paul Sonnino who has let me peruse the manuscript of his article 'Louis XIV's *Mémoires pour l'histoire de la guerre de Hollande*', before publication in *French Historical Studies* (1973).

29 Without going into the controversy over the role of Louvois, it can be stated that we know much about his military activity thanks to Rousset's work; we also know that his manners were brusque. But of Louvois' actual political role we know, as yet, next to nothing; no doubt the difficulty of deciphering his handwriting is partly responsible for this state of affairs.

30 My impression of French unpreparedness for a big war in 1688 has been borne out by the findings of Geoffrey Symcox, who did research in Parisian archives on relations between Louis XIV and James II in 1688–92; it appears that the French navy, like the army, was caught unprepared in 1688 and was reduced to hasty improvisations.

31 Longnon, pp. 25, 246; Dreyss, II, pp. 267–72, 385–6.

32 Whatever may be said for this manner of decision-making in the central government, where Louis could dominate the scene by his physical presence, its defects were all too evident in Spain when in 1703 it became clear that Louis would have to take over the administration of that realm. At the time, the French establishment at the court of Spain consisted of three great personages, all of them directly in touch with Versailles: the cardinal d'Estrées (the official ambassador, and member of Philip's Council), the princesse des Ursins (the queen's *camarera mayor*) and Louville (Philip's former tutor). To these must be added two understudies: the abbé d'Estrées (the cardinal's nephew and successor as ambassador), and the financial expert Orry (more or less a protégé of Ursins). The three prima donnas could never get along with one another: the cardinal and the princess hated each other blindly, while Louville detested Ursins and disparaged the cardinal. As a result, the entire French establishment in Spain collapsed in the summer of 1703 at a critical juncture in the affairs of the Bourbons.

33 The battles of Fleurus (1690), Steenkerk (1692) and Neerwinden (1693), and the capture of the key cities and fortresses of Mons (1691) and of Namur (1692).

34 Perhaps it was not altogether fortuitous that the second rout of the Quietists, with the condemnation of Fénelon's *Maximes des saints* by the pope, also occurred at this time; we must hasten to add that, in spite of this discomfiture, Beauvilliers retained his post in the council.

35 Louis maintained that this step involved neither a withdrawal of his recognition of William III nor any design to help the Pretender to establish himself in England. See, for instance, Louis to Chamilly, postscript to the letter dated 15 Sep 1701, A.A.E., C.P., Danemark, vol. 66, ff. 393–4.

36 See Baudrillart, *Philippe V*, I, p. 499.

37 Louis XIV to Philip V, 2 July and 1 August 1714, quoted in part in Baudrillart, *Philippe V*, I, pp. 652–3.

7 Louis XIV's Courtiers*

J. LEVRON

No place could be more accessible to the public than the Louvre
and (even more so) Versailles. Such an observation is in no way
original. But the usual picture is still that of the kings of France
surrounded by a whole hierarchy of guards, ushers and soldiers
whose duty it was to carry out stringent security checks, demand
passwords and watch the movements of every visitor. In fact, the
royal palace of Versailles was far more open to the public than
the presidential palace of the Elysée is today. Security measures
were extremely haphazard. Certainly there were wrought-iron
gates at the entrance, but they were always open. When Louis
XVI wanted them closed in October 1789, it was discovered that
their hinges were so rusted that it took a number of men several
hours to make them work after a fashion.

The royal palace was not in theory open to all comers without
exception, but all that was required was for ladies to be in court
dress and with an escort, and for gentlemen to be wearing a
sword. If this were so, the guard at the gate would let you pass
without a second glance. In any case the *concierge* (porter) – a
man of importance – would hire out swords to those who had
'forgotten' their own. There were also continual comings and
goings of tradesmen and workmen – for Versailles always remained a huge building-site – and of innumerable servants, who
were never questioned. One could stroll along the great avenues
of the park or through the main apartments without being subject
to any kind of check.

The ready access allowed to the public helps explain the swarm-
ing crowds that filled the palace. Quite apart from the courtiers
many loitered in the corridors, went up and down the staircases
or lurked behind pillars in the hope of catching a quick glimpse
of the king and his companions. The sightseers were legion;

* From Levron's *Les Courtisans* (Paris, 1961).

Parisians who wanted a fleeting taste of life 'out there', hoped to pick up a witticism to carry fresh to the salons of the capital, or wanted to ferret out the latest scandal.

The permanent members of the court proper comprised first the households of the king, the queen, the princes of the blood and other members of the royal family; then, the great nobles who deemed it necessary to reside close to the king; next, all the favourites and intimates of these personages; finally, once it was realised that Versailles was the sole source of all favours and benefits, all the great families of France.

At the beginning of Louis XIV's reign the real court was not very large, and was still very much as in the time of Louis XIII. It was still nomadic; it moved from the Louvre to Saint-Germain, from Compiègne to Fontainebleau, from Saint-Cloud to Chambord. Because of this continual movement, it had to be small. 'There are hardly any ladies here and very few gentlemen', the duc d'Enghien wrote on 27 June 1667 to the queen of Poland, 'the court has never been so small, we scarcely know how to occupy ourselves.'

In 1667 the great building programme at Versailles had hardly begun. Everything was to change once the young king had decided to turn the *piccola casa* of his father into the most magnificent palace in the world. From that time the population of the court began to increase, and soon the French nobility had but one aspiration : to live at Versailles. They pursued long intrigues to obtain permission to occupy an apartment or at least a room or two at the palace. This mark of favour was eagerly sought and was granted only grudgingly. The apartments at the palace provided the minimum of comfort, yet this took second place to vanity.

The court now began to be crammed with an endlessly changing crowd. The great mob of men and women, and the freedom of access, deeply offended one Italian duke; while a cardinal from the same country was moved to compare the court to the land of Cockaine. A foreigner described the free-for-all of the king's afternoon walk : 'It is a fine sight when he leaves the palace, with his bodyguards, the carriages, the courtiers, the lackeys and a crowd of other people surging and making noise all around him. It reminds me of a queen bee flying across the fields surrounded by her swarm.'

Although exaggerated, such a comparison was not inaccurate. The king wanted to be surrounded by his most loyal courtiers, yet at the same time to remain accessible to all. It was not always easy to reconcile these two requirements; and the result was, at certain moments, chaotic.

In these first years at Versailles the king's court was by no means formal. There was a continual round of festivals, balls, equestrian sports and hunting. The reigning mistress of the moment, first Mlle de la Vallière and then Mme de Montespan, spent much of her time devising entertainments for the king and took her part in all of them attended by a large following.

Nonetheless the king's day was as carefully regulated as it had been in the time of his ancestors and Louis XIV even increased the strictness of court etiquette. There were still the lesser and greater *lever* and the lesser and greater *coucher*. Only certain members of the royal family and the princes of the blood were admitted to the latter, while admission to the former was arranged in rotation. Every activity of daily life was transformed into ritual and ceremony.

The restrictions that the king imposed upon himself hedged his presence with awe and made his glance more majestic. It was easy enough to get into the palace; but it was hard to catch sight of the king, even from a distance, as he was continually surrounded by attendants. The courtiers felt somehow diminished before him : 'One is a small man at court, and whatever self-esteem one may possess, one feels oneself to be humble. But this is a common complaint; even the great are little here.' One had to accustom oneself to being with the king, Saint-Simon noted, if one did not want to lose one's tongue when talking to him. The respect that his presence commanded imposed silence and even a kind of awe. When Louis XIV approached, the lackeys at the doorways would announce : 'Gentlemen, the king.' And the noise of the courtiers, the ceaseless hubbub of conversation that rolled like thunder, was immediately still, so that nothing was heard but the tap of the king's walking-stick on the floor.

There may seem to be a contradiction between what we have said about the court during the early years of the reign, and the reverential and almost adoring attitude of the courtiers described by Mme de Sévigné, La Bruyère or Saint-Simon. The truth is that we have come a long way from the days of La Vallière and

Montespan, from 'The Pleasures of the Enchanted Isle', from the ballets and dances, to the rigid ceremonies of the court after the climacteric of the reign. This turning-point, which is rightly associated with Mme de Maintenon's influence, comes in the years around 1684. It matters little whether the former governess of Mme de Montespan's natural children became the king's wife at that time, or remained the king's mistress until 1697. What is certain is that she effected a transformation in the king's behaviour and endowed the court with the atmosphere it was to retain until the end of the reign.

There is no doubt that the everyday existence of the courtiers was profoundly changed by this. In the first place, the court expanded enormously. It is very hard to give any precise figures, but if we include all the 'households' of the princes, all the guards, lackeys and hangers-on, we reach a total of nearly ten thousand people gravitating around the palace, crowded into houses (*hôtels*) and furnished rooms, residing in the *château* and in other buildings in the park of Versailles.

The king had achieved his aim which, as we know, was not merely aesthetic, but fundamentally political: he had successfully domesticated his nobles. In every corner of France anyone with an important name or title now had one single aspiration – to appear at Versailles and be accepted. 'The great question', Georges Mongrédien comments, 'was to see who would present the king's shirt at his *lever*, who would hold the candlestick at the *coucher*.' Intrigues would be conducted for weeks on end to secure one's turn at these fleeting honours, or to obtain the right to wear the famous *justaucorps à brevet*, the 'royal coat' which gave its wearers exemption from sumptuary laws. A courtier would not forget his own interests and would try to draw minor advantages from his presence at court. The king was well aware of this, but there were not enough favours and pensions to go around. He therefore exercised his ingenuity in order to set a value on the smallest marks of favour. 'He knew', says Saint-Simon, 'that there were far from being sufficient favours to dispense to gain general goodwill. Instead he created imaginary ones out of little distinctions – based on envy – that arise every day, and so to speak, on every occasion. The hopes that grew out of these little preferences and the effect he was able to draw from them . . . I know that no one was more ingenious than he in devising this sort of thing.' This is a harsh accusation and may not completely express the reality of the situation : Saint-Simon's view of Louis XIV and his court was affected by his own rage and bitterness. But La Bruyère is hardly more gentle when, in a famous passage, he describes the courtiers in the royal chapel :

> The great persons of the nation assemble each day in a temple that they call a church. At the far end of this temple stands an altar consecrated to their God, where a priest celebrates the mysteries they call holy, sacred and fearful. The great ones form a huge circle at the foot of this altar and stand erect, their backs turned to the priest and the holy mysteries, their faces lifted towards their king who is seen kneeling in a gallery, and on whom they seem to be concentrating all their hearts and spirits. One cannot help but see in this custom a sort of subordination, for the people appear to be worshipping their prince while he in turn worships God.

A less well-known passage, attributed to the abbé de Saint-Réal and dating from the last decade or two of the reign, may also be quoted as it is an acute analysis of the courtier's mind :

> The people of the court are like a foreign nation within the state, made up of men drawn from many different places. They are not all men of intelligence, but they are all possessed of an admirable politeness which serves them in its stead. They are not all worthy men, but they have the air and manner that make one think them such. Their obliging and accommodating spirits can adopt any kind of behaviour so that it is impossible to discover their true feelings. Their contempt for anything that is not of the court is unimaginable and goes to the point of extravagance. There is nothing well said or well done, except what is said and done among them. Everything that comes from outside is ignorant or boorish. It is however true that, with the best taste in the world, they are for the most part without any kind of learning, and they only make themselves out to be knowledgeable in all manner of subjects by reason of a few well-turned phrases and because of the respect they induce which causes everyone else to fall silent in their presence.

The court became formal and depressing. The courtiers were prey to a profound boredom, but they would not leave for anything in the world. Even officers in the services were attracted by the court's magnetism. As soon as a campaign was over, the colonels would abandon their regiments to pay court at Versailles. A good many captains did the same. They left their men to the care – or lack of it – of the lower-ranking officers and ended up knowing nothing of their soldiers' condition. Louvois, resolved to reform the army, was offended by this and upbraided the over-assiduous courtiers. Mme de Sévigné noted the following:

> Monsier de Louvois said the other day to Monsier de Nogaret: 'Sir, your company is in a very poor state.' 'I did not know that, Sir,' replied Nogaret, somewhat impertinently. 'Then Sir, you should have known it,' retorted Louvois, 'Have you seen your company?' 'No Sir.' 'Then you should have done, Sir.' 'Sir, I shall give the requisite orders.' 'You should have done so already, Sir. You must choose, Sir, either to be an avowed courtier, or to perform your duties if you are going to be an officer.'

The real trouble was that officers preferred to lose their companies and expose themselves to Louvois' reprimands, rather than lose their place at court. The bishops behaved as badly. How many of them made only brief and fleeting visits to their dioceses? But we must not exaggerate. During Louis XIV's reign there were, besides these 'court prelates', others who were virtuous, conscientious in their duties, and devoted to their flocks (like Neufville de Villeroy at Lyons or Henri Arnauld at Angers) who never left their sees for the whole of their episcopate. And the king did not hold it against them.

Although boredom might weigh heavily at Versailles, intrigues and plots abounded and were the everyday occupation of the courtiers. The fall of a favourite was predicted, the disgrace of a minister foretold. Men manœuvred to advance someone in order to reap a reward once he had arrived. The king did not discourage this attitude on the part of his courtiers, realising that they needed some form of distraction. He played the occasional game of cards or billiards with them. The stakes were high and cheating was common, even at the king's table. Good courtiers were careful to let the king win, and it was said that Chamillart's promotion to minister was the reward for his skill in letting Louis XIV win at billiards. His epitaph bears witness to his adroitness:

Here lies the famous Chamillart
The old king's protonotary
A hero with a billiard cue
A zero in the ministry.

Thus the courtiers enjoyed their petty revenge. Verses and epi-
grams passed furtively from hand to hand, provided the court
with moments of light relief; they were exchanged in whispers.

Then there was Marly. There it was possible to unbend a little,
even in the king's presence, once he had uttered the ritual phrase :
'Gentleman, put on your hats.' At Marly there were pavilions
radiating from the royal residence like stars grouped around the
sun. At Marly conversation was less restrained; one could drop
a well-chosen word or make a request with more chance of success
than at Versailles. But there was room for very few people at
Marly, so that to be invited there was a great honour. The king
asked whomever he wanted, without regard for precedence or
privileges. What beseeching looks, therefore, among the courtiers
when the king named those who were to accompany him : 'Sire,
Sire, Marly. . . .' No more needed to be said; this was enough to
make the request plain. A place on the list for Marly was the
most precious favour that the king could bestow. Never to be
invited there was a sign of royal indifference that filled a courtier
with despair. But the interludes at Marly were short; soon it was
necessary to return to Versailles and servitude.

It would be a mistake to assume that the courtier's life was one
of ease. In the first place he had to be ready to adapt instantly
to any situation. The right reply, calculated to flatter the king,
had to be on the tip of his tongue. A good many sayings have
come down to us from Louis XIV's court, or have been attributed
to his courtiers. Nothing is more revealing than the following
examples of repartee; they permit us to get the feel of the court
and its relationship to the king.

Cardinal d'Estrées had the honour to dine at the king's table
when the latter was old and toothless. Louis complained bitterly
of this disability and bemoaned his lack of teeth. 'Teeth, Sire,
teeth?' exclaimed the Cardinal, displaying a magnificent set of
dentures, 'nowadays nobody has any teeth of their own.'

This reply was more witty than servile, and d'Estrées was well
aware that the king would not be taken in. But the courtier's

desire never to utter anything but flattering words in the king's presence frequently produced absurdities. The duc d'Uzès, asked by Louis XIV when his wife would give birth, replied : 'Ah, Sire, whenever Your Majesty pleases.' The duke's reply was even more ridiculous when the queen asked him the time : 'Whatever time it pleases Your Majesty.' Such servility served no purpose for the queen did want to know the time, and the duke's reply did not enlighten her in the least.

Some remarks by courtiers amuse by their childlike desire to please the king. On his deathbed Racine declared his loyalty to his teachers at Port-Royal by deciding to be buried there. This decision implied a definite rejection of the king's religious policies, and naturally made the courtiers' tongues wag. The king did not hide his disapproval. 'Oh, Sire', Monsieur de Coustine hastened to say, 'Racine would never have done that in his lifetime. . . .'

Not all the courtiers were stupid; in fact most of them were very intelligent. They knew how to act their part from a very early age. The young Créqui was clever, though he pretended otherwise. One day he was target-shooting with the dauphin. Créqui's turn came and he missed by six feet, although he could easily have scored a hit. 'Young serpent', exclaimed the duc de Montausier, who had been watching and had guessed Créqui's purpose, 'you should be strangled.' In this instance the flattery was crude and obvious; but Créqui was still young. The older courtiers were subtler. The duc d'Antin, superintendent of buildings, knew his master's taste for architecture; he was well aware that the king loved to give advice, to check for errors and to put things to rights. Antin therefore placed tiny wedges under the plinths of statues set up in the park of Versailles, so that the king might notice that they were slightly out of true. He would then hasten to congratulate the king on his perfect eye, pretending to blame the contractors, and give orders to have the mistake corrected. Is this story true? We may be inclined to doubt it, but several memoir-writers record spectacular stunts of his of a similar kind.

Here is one of them, from the time when Versailles was being laid out. On several occasions the king had been heard to complain about a small wood that blocked his view. Antin had the trees sawn almost through at ground level, so that they were ready to fall, and then had ropes attached to the tree tops in such a

way that they could not be seen at a distance. When the king
next walked by, surrounded by his courtiers, with Antin by his
side, he once more complained of the wood and wished it would
vanish. 'Really Sire?' was Antin's comeback: 'Your wish will
come true at once.' The superintendent blew his whistle and every
tree disappeared as if by magic. Pleased, Louis XIV exclaimed:
'Ah, that is the prettiest sight I ever saw.' Antin was overcome
with joy; but he did not have the last word. The duchess of
Burgundy, who had been watching the whole performance, turned
to her companions and remarked, with a feigned shudder: 'Truly,
ladies, I think that if the king wanted our heads to fall, Monsieur
d'Antin would manage that just as cleverly.'

The best courtiers knew that the way to flatter the king was by
a quick reply, avoiding exaggerated praise which Louis disliked.
Racine, the king's historiographer, preferred to follow the Dutch
campaign of 1677 at a safe distance in Paris. Louis on his return
commented on Racine's lack of curiosity. 'Did you not want to
see a siege? You would not have had to travel far afield.' 'Sire',
replied Racine, 'my tailor was too dilatory. I had ordered cam-
paigning clothes from him, but by the time they were ready all
the towns that Your Majesty had besieged were already taken.'
The duc du Maine, the king's son by the marquise de Montespan,
was equally adroit: 'Sire, I shall remain ignorant; my tutor gives
me a day's holiday every time Your Majesty wins a battle.'

The courtiers took a real pleasure in praising Louis XIV for
his victories, and this was the kind of compliment he liked best.
On one occasion Boileau was able to turn an elegant compliment
on this subject. The word *gros* [literally, 'fat'] had recently become the fashionable adjective, both at court and in Paris. Everything was *gros* just as today everything is *formidable*, and the
word had become everyone's favourite cliché. Its continual use
finally aroused Louis XIV's irritation; he held that the word was
being used improperly and in the wrong context. Mentioning
this to Boileau, he expressed his desire that the Académie Française would lay down the correct meaning and usage for the word.
'Sire', replied Boileau, 'Your Majesty need have no fear. Posterity
will never confuse Louis the *Gros* with Louis the Great.'

Again, it was by referring to military successes that Lebrun,
Louis XIV's favourite painter, was able to transform an awkward
moment into a well-turned compliment. Lebrun had started yet

another portrait of the king, in the later years of the reign. 'Do
you not find that I have aged?' the king suddenly asked. Lebrun,
too frank to lie but too clever to give a direct answer, avoided the
pitfall with consummate skill : 'It is true, Sire, that I can trace
the marks of a few more campaigns across Your Majesty's brow.'

The king was not deceived by this sort of flattery. But it was
he who had made the court what it was; he had created it in his
own image, and he could not complain of the result. He did,
however, possess a few companions whose frankness appealed
to him. One of the best known of these was the comte de Gramont,
whose wit pleased Louis. One day they were walking in the gardens of Versailles when the king remarked. 'Do you remember,
Monsieur de Gramont, there was once a windmill here at this
spot?' 'Yes, Sire', replied Gramont, who loathed the draughts at
Versailles, 'the mill has gone but the wind remains.'

That response was merely witty. But consider another, by the
same man, which goes much deeper, for it shows how this perfect
courtier could judge the minds and spirits of his fellow courtiers.
One evening Louis XIV was playing tric-trac when a dispute
arose; none of the courtiers taking part dared give an opinion.
Then Gramont appeared and the king asked him to decide the
point at issue. Gramont immediately replied : 'Sire, Your
Majesty has lost.' 'How can you decide against me before you
know the details?' asked Louis. 'Sire, you must understand that
if there had been even the slightest element of doubt, these gentlemen would have hastened to find in your favour.'

It is incorrect, therefore, to think of Louis XIV's court as in-
habited solely by servile flatterers singing endless eulogies to their
king. There were ambitious and astute individuals, certainly. But
there were also disinterested servants of the monarchy and the
country who belonged to the court because there was no other
place where they could display their real talents. Versailles and
the court of Louis XIV can be compared to Paris today; every
high-ranking civil servant, every capable official has to live there
if he wants to be appreciated at his true value. These loyal servants had to be courtiers, too.

The others fulfilled their function, which had a certain use-
fulness, as we shall see in a moment. Perhaps they were sometimes
unattractive toadies and sycophants, but there was an excuse for
this. It was so easy to fall into disgrace; court life was exhausting,

full of continual tension. The older courtiers grew tired of this demanding existence, but yet they could not make up their minds to leave Versailles. They were born courtiers, and knew no other profession.

THE COURTIER'S FUNCTION

In the course of Louis XIV's reign, as a result of the king's expressed wishes, the most important elements of the French nobility were concentrated at Versailles : princes of the blood, scions of ancient families, newly-created nobles, officers who hastened to abandon their military duties if they had the choice, servants of the bureaucratic monarchy – all were transformed into courtiers. They were obliged to appear at court whether they liked it or not. From this time, courtiers became a social class rather than a caste. But did this class fulfil any function?

It is generally agreed that the courtiers were very busy. From morning to evening their life was an endless round of visits to the king or the great personages of the court. 'This winter is like the others : in the morning I wait upon the king; from there I go to the Cardinal's apartments, but largely for form's sake, because it is usually impossible to see him; then to Monsieur Le Tellier's or occasionally to the Marshal de Turenne.' That is how Bussy wrote to his cousin, Mme de Sévigné. The ideal courtier must pay his court before all else. But it would be wrong to assume that his visits were purely formal. The courtiers were not just the backdrop in the great theatre that was Versailles; they had their parts to play. They acted as intermediaries, and sometimes as a screen, between the king and the mass of his subjects. They had a definite role, therefore, in the society of seventeenth-century France.

Life at court was inordinately expensive. The ritualised existence demanded enormous expenditure from those who took part in it. The most insignificant courtier was obliged to maintain an elaborate retinue if he was not to lose prestige : household servants, coaches and horses, the clothes he had to wear, as elaborate as they were varied, the jewels that had to be worn – all this required a large fortune.

Meanwhile the incomes of the French nobles were declining throughout the century. The fall in prices discernible after 1650 had its first effects on the income from landed property, which was the main source of noble wealth. But since the nobility no longer resided on its estates it had no means of recouping its losses. Furthermore, most rents and dues payable in money had been fixed at the end of the Hundred Years War, in monetary units which had continually depreciated. Many dues had fallen into disuse. Finding it impossible to maintain close control over his tenant farmers, the landowner generally leased out the right to collect his revenues to an agent, a *fermier général*, or a superintendent. He usually struck a good bargain with the peasants but handed to the landowner only the sum that had been fixed by their agreement, naturally after subtracting all the expenses incurred for the upkeep of the family seat and the administration of the estate.

As a great many noblemen found it necessary to live at Versailles as courtiers, they were obliged to engage in business deals and make their living by financial transactions. The mere fact of belonging to the court constituted a financial advantage in itself. Georges Mondgrédien has called this their 'capital', and capital has to be employed. The courtiers therefore turned all their efforts towards drawing profit from their positions at Versailles. They peddled their influence and exploited their places close to king, ministers and their underlings. They also became *donneurs d'avis*, literally translated 'providers of information'. They were in effect paid informers, since we learn from Trevoux's Dictionary that this somewhat euphemistic and vague term indicates one who 'offers advice which increases the revenues of the royal fisc', and that for this service the informer was paid a bounty, a bounty intended 'to stimulate his activities'.

It has always been the task of the financial administration to ferret out abuses. A chronicler already in the reign of Philip Augustus sighed, 'O France, tormented by tax-gatherers'; and today the inspectors of finances of the rue de Rivoli are not among our most popular figures. One of the salient characteristics of the bureaucratic system instituted by Louis XIV was the lack of any thorough control. Public functions were largely unpaid, and many offices had no real purpose. Informers would therefore point to abuses in the fiscal system in the hope of receiving in return for their services a reward, euphemistically known as the 'fee for information' (*droit d'avis*).

Such a state of affairs strikes us as extraordinary, or even repellent, but seemed quite natural to contemporaries. Everyone, from the most august to the most humble, would offer his information if he thought it of value to the state. The king's grand equerry, brother of M. de Marsan and brother-in-law to the marshal de Villeroy, Monsieur le Grand as he was called, was in 1683 awarded a hundred thousand livres for information provided by him a dozen years earlier; in 1685 he received ten thousand livres for denouncing the embezzler de Bauyn; in 1691 four thousand *pistoles* for another piece of information; in 1698 another reward of forty thousand *écus*, and so on. All these figures are taken from Dangeau's *Journal*. The abbé de la Proustière obtained the huge sum of forty thousand *écus* for a piece of information given during Pontchartrain's ministry. The abbé was a parvenu and Saint-Simon scornfully stressed his lowly origins. But even the royal family was not above such practices. 'In 1693 Monsieur [i.e. Louis' brother Philippe] proposed that the king carry out an investigation of the treasurers for extraordinary war expenses (who were in fact notorious profiteers), hoping to receive an informer's fee of a million livres', writes Georges Mongrédien. It is only fair to add that Louis XIV did not fall in with his brother's plan.

The informer's fee was an exceptional windfall, however; for the most part the court nobles made use of their positions to act as intermediaries between those seeking an office, a monopoly, or the right to market a new invention, and the king or the minister who could grant the required favours or privileges.

Consider for example what Saint-Simon has to say about the de Noailles family and their financial dealings.

'Monsieur de Noailles eagerly pursued anything that had to do with the ministries, and particularly that of finance. He, or rather his wife, who had more business sense and talent for intrigue than he had, was always involved with those in charge of the finances . . . They had worked on Madame de Maintenon to such good effect that the King gave instructions to Pontchartrain, and later to Chamillart when he succeeded as Minister of Finances, to approve any arrangements that she and her daughter might propose, and to encourage them to suggest as many as possible. They made incredible profits in this way.

Saint-Simon's information is in this case quite accurate. In 1693 Marshal de Noailles was granted the right to install a new kind of machine to work the hammers in a paper-mill or fulling-mill without the aid of wind or water power. In 1703 he received a present of fifty-thousand *écus* from the manufacturer of Saint Gobain mirrors, for whom he had obtained a patent from the king. Industrial concerns regarded the payment of these huge sums as perfectly normal and were quite willing to enter into a contract, drawn up in due form by a notary, with those who had offered to exercise influence on their behalf. To give an example : 'We hereby promise and engage that we shall honestly pay the sum of . . . livres in return for the trouble and solicitations which . . . (here follows the name of the court lady) has promised to undertake in our interest. . . .'

Mongrédien, who published this example, expressed a certain misgiving at discovering in such contracts the names of the most illustrious families in France – Rohan, Noailles, Lorraine. But this was commonplace; at court everyone was involved in deals and sought to make use of his influence. As we have just seen, setting up monopolies brought large profits. Even foreign ambassadors took part in this : 'Primi Visconti interceded with the King on behalf of two Parisian booksellers to obtain the right to print a weekly report of the capital's news.' His request was granted and the grateful booksellers paid Visconti his agreed commission of four hundred *pistoles* per annum. But the most fertile field of operations lay in the marketing of new offices and functions. The courtiers watched for the establishment of new offices and were quick to inform those who might be interested, in return for a generous reward.

The importance of this side of Louis XIV's financial policy cannot be over-emphasised. To obtain revenue the king was continually creating new positions in the state, sometimes of a strange or surprising nature. These offices entailed functions similar to those of notaries or brokers today; they carried small salaries but offered honours and privileges, social prestige, exemption from the *taille*, and could provide the means for rising in society, even as far as the court. This was why the king could always find an aspiring gentleman willing to become 'Guardian of the Royal Carp', 'Captain of the King's Minor Diversions', 'Chief Goblet-holder to the Queen' : all these positions with their odd-sounding titles admitted their holders to membership of the royal household.

'Every time Your Majesty creates a new office, God creates a

fool to buy it.' Pontchartrain's witticism is well known, but it is
also indicative of the situation. Quite apart from court offices
there were innumerable provincial offices. As soon as the decision
had been taken to set up new offices there was a rush to inform
possible candidates. To give an example, ten new presidial courts
were to be set up. A whole hierarchy of magistrates would have to
be created : presidents, assessors, counsellors, royal attorneys,
ushers, registrars and so on. A little syndicate immediately formed
amongst the courtiers to obtain the management of the affair.
First they had to out-manœuvre the ministers concerned and take
control of the distribution of the offices, then word had to be sent
to possible aspirants. Finally each courtier received a handsome
commission : ten per cent of the cost of each office. In the syndicate figured a financier, an abbé, a marquis and one of the
queen's maids of honour. All these fine people regarded their behaviour as perfectly normal. 'The royal household is like a great
market where one must of necessity go to buy and sell in order to
make a living, or to look after the interests of those whom duty
or interest attach to us.' These are the words of Mme de Motteville, who found nothing wrong in such behaviour, and who in
fact was ready to justify it. We should note, however, that the
king tried to prevent such operations. A syndicate of courtiers
could run into trouble; and even though its leading personages
might escape punishment, some shady financier, worldly abbé
or lady-in-waiting of dubious virtue would be sent to the Bastille
to repent his or her temerity. It was better therefore to carry on
business alone; the risks of being found out by Louis XIV were
less.

Lieutenant-General of police Argenson, who did not miss much,
has preserved among his notes a record of some of the activities
of great ladies and gentlemen who had no scruples about profiting
from their prestige and accepting 'presents'. The duchesse de
Guiches, the daughter of Marshal de Noailles, made twenty-five
thousand *écus* out of the creation of inspectorships to supervise
'the removal of the night soil and the lighting of the street lamps'.
The inspectors in their turn more probably than not passed on
the cost of their outlay to their clients. Officials also tried to make
a profit by methods of dubious legality. Narbonne, the commissioner of police at Versailles, noted in his diary that on the
occasion of a ball given by the duc de Berry during the carnival

of 1714 officials known to him were able to recover the cost of their offices out of what was paid for decorations, the buffet and so on.

Everything was negotiable; anything could be the subject of a deal. The ladies of the court were the most eager for profit, and would often act as marriage-brokers. The comtesse de Gramont agreed to negotiate the marriage of the son of a registrar of the Paris Parlement, a rich youth but not yet of age. Her commission consisted of a decent percentage of the dowry of the bride-to-be.

That commissions in the army and navy were the objects of business deals is easy to understand at a time when commissions were always purchased. The comtesse de Fiesqe offered to obtain a commission as *capitaine de frégate* for two thousand livres; the princesse d'Harcourt, less demanding, demanded only fifteen hundred. Saint-Simon, a peer of the realm, was not in the least ashamed to admit having paid 3100 livres informer's fee to the person who advised him of a regiment being for sale. Even the king's mistresses were grasping. The delicate La Vallière, that angel of tenderness, was quite ready to pass to Louis petitions (*placets*) handed to her, so long as she was paid her commission. Mme de Montespan, who was always in need of money, never obtained an office or position for a petitioner without claiming her percentage. People were even willing to pay to gain admission to a particular celebration: the duchesse du Lude wanted to be invited to Marly; and the princesse d'Harcourt promised, for a consideration of two thousand *écus*, to intercede with the king. This princess had quite a reputation at court. 'She was a gambler and even a cheat', Saint-Simon noted, 'and she made it her business to arrange any deal, charging from one *écu* to the highest possible sums.' Such behaviour had become so customary that nobody was shocked.

We should not deduce, however, that Louis XIV's court was nothing but a den of gamblers and speculators, or that all courtiers were rogues. A great many were honest and upright and would use their influence with the king without seeking to profit. Here is one example. In 1685 a group of erudite and cultivated men of the city of Angers decided to found an academy on the model of the *Académie Française*. It was necessary to obtain letters-patent from the king authorising the new foundation. The leading spirits in the enterprise charged Grandet, the mayor of Angers, with presenting their petition to Louis XIV.

It was, as we have seen, a simple matter to stroll around the grounds of Versailles, but it was far from easy to catch the king's attention. For this it was essential to find a courtier in good standing who would be willing to station a would-be petitioner where he could meet the king and hand him a petition. In normal circumstances the mayor of Angers could have asked the governor of the province of Anjou to do this for him. But Louis XIV had forbidden the governors to reside in their province, because of the dangerous part they had played in the Fronde. They lived at Versailles, where they usually carried out certain duties at the palace while their functions as governors were discharged by lieutenants, who kept them informed of events in the province.

In 1685 the governor of Anjou was none other than the king's grand equerry (Monsieur le Grand), the prince of Armagnac. He was far from obliging and refused to importune the king 'on whatever pretext it might be'. But by good fortune Grandet, on arriving at Versailles accompanied by two other magistrates, happened to meet one of the king's gentlemen attendants, Chevais du Boullay, who hailed from Anjou and whom he knew well. Du Boullay offered to station Grandet 'advantageously' near the king's table when he ate in public. This was done. The mayor was a fine-looking man. Louis XIV noticed him, and recalled, since he had an extraordinary good memory for faces, that he had seen him several years before. Grandet had in fact then had a personal interview with the king for the purpose of settling a Jansenist dispute at the seminary of Angers. Louis called for the prince of Armagnac and asked 'who was this man from his governorship?' The grand equerry was stunned; he had not imagined that the king would recognise Grandet. Next morning Grandet presented himself at the prince's *lever*. 'Good morning, you accomplished courtier', said Monsieur le Grand, 'since the King already knows you, you had better carry on paying court on your own. I haven't spoiled things for you, and I know plenty of men who have done well here without the advantages that you have to start with.' Grandet quickly seized his opportunity: 'Then it only requires Your Highness' assistance to carry on from such a favourable beginning.' The prince enquired why the mayor had wanted to present a petition to the king. Grandet explained the plan for founding an academy, adding, 'I know that Your Highness sets little store by the solicitations that are made to you.'

The grand equerry burst out laughing, and promised to present Grandet at the conclusion of the king's dinner that day. We know this from Grandet's own account :

> In fact, it was done when the fruit was served. The prince approached the captain of the guard, who was standing behind His Majesty's chair, asked to be permitted to present me, and this was granted. His Majesty rose from the table and started to walk towards his apartments. The captain of the guard followed him, with Monsieur d'Armagnac close behind. At the door of the ante-chamber he told the usher to let me pass, after which the door was closed. The King then sat down in an armchair, the two gentlemen at his side, whereupon I asked his permission to set up an Academy of the Humanities in the city of Angers.

Louis XIV at first made objections recalling the rebellious past of the Angevins. But Grandet was able to reply so adroitly and convincingly that the king agreed : 'So be it. You may have the letters-patent.' He then went into his chamber. The grand equerry expressed surprise at Grandet's presumption in daring to argue with the king. Here we may observe the difference between the professional courtier, accustomed to bowing before the king's will, and the temporary visitor at court who had not developed the same flexibility of mind and would defend his position. Grandet, euphoric by success, was bold enough to retort : 'His Majesty displayed greater insight than some. I comported myself like a man of *esprit*.'

The prince thereupon took Grandet to dine with him. A large company was present, for it was his normal practice to keep open house. The grand equerry treated all the gentlemen present to an account of what had transpired in the king's ante-chamber, and they all praised the mayor and approved his conduct, 'saying that there were few at court, even amongst those who were accustomed to speaking to the king, who would have argued a point with His Majesty, as I had.'

This naive tale, which comes from Grandet's *Mémoires*, tells us a good deal about the manners and customs of the court. It might even serve as an argument for the existence of courtiers,

F

for Grandet would never have had the chance to see the king without the aid of du Boullay and then of the grand equerry. Neither of these charged the mayor of Angers for their services, which had, moreover, entailed a certain amount of risk : for one could never be quite sure how the king would react to an introduction. They had helped Grandet out of a willingness to oblige him, their only recompense the opportunity to show the mayor of an important city how influential they were at court.

Life at court was trying. Though one might be content to live without making large profits, and merely keep an eye open for those minor advantages that were more or less essential to keep one's connections happy, the unremittingly theatrical existence finally wore down even the hardiest. But nothing in the world could make the courtiers abandon Versailles. Louis XIV's secret was his ability to attach the courtiers to himself. 'I would rather die than go two months without seeing the King', the duc de Richelieu confessed to Mme de Maintenon. To be exiled was the great fear of every courtier. True wisdom would have been shown by knowing when one had ceased to give pleasure at court and withdrawing gracefully; when, in the phrase of the police commissioner Narbonne, 'the air of the court no longer agreed with you'. But how many courtiers actually possessed this wisdom? No courtier went willingly into retirement.

The case of Claude Le Peletier, comptroller-general of finances after Colbert, is an exception and was much talked of. He set a good example by giving up an office of his own accord, with no threat of disgrace hanging over him. Saint-Simon wrote movingly describing his retirement, though long after the event. Le Peletier had discharged his burdensome office to the general satisfaction of the country at large, but a time came when he felt he could no longer carry a responsibility which seemed beyond his capacity. In spite of pressure from the king, he resigned from the comptrollership, to which Pontchartrain was appointed in his place. But Le Peletier remained at court. With the title of minister of state he directed the postal service and enjoyed the friendship and trust of the king, who, in 1697, considered making him chancellor. Le Peletier refused. 'He had always intended to set an interval between the affairs of this world and the next. The negotiations for the peace detained him in office; he did not think it right to leave such an important task half-done. But as soon as he had seen it to its completion, he requested permission to retire from court.' Louis XIV tried for two months to dissuade him in private conversations, but in the end he let him go, on condition that he returned to visit him two or three times a year.

Nobody at court had been told of Le Peletier's decision. On Wednesday 18 September 1697, he took his leave of the king, and without a word to anyone entered his carriage and departed to his house at Villeneuve-le-Roi. Thereafter he divided his time between his residence in the capital and his estate in the country, where he could indulge his passion for horticulture.

Courtiers of the more usual sort were amazed by Le Peletier's behaviour. The minister for foreign affairs, Pomponne, declared : 'Le Peletier's retirement is as admirable as my own lack of courage to imitate him at my age is shameful.' Pomponne, seventy-nine years old at this time, waited another two years before handing over his office to his son-in-law, Torcy.

It sometimes happened, however, that a courtier fell from the king's favour without being aware of what had happened; and he would then receive a sudden order to leave the court. This was the most terrible fate that could befall a courtier, and as an offender was not given advance warning, life at court was felt to be precarious. Secure in his place for the time being, the courtier could never know whether tomorrow he might be sent into exile. The sword of Damocles was ever poised over his head, which explains why so many courtiers betrayed a constant feverishness and agitation : they were always anxious for the future.

Disgrace usually overtook a courtier just when he expected it least. The night before, he had left Versailles with fortune apparently smiling on him : the king had favoured him with a gracious word, a minister had received him cordially; next morning at dawn one of the royal messengers would come to inform him, suddenly and without warning, that he was not to reappear at court.

Saint-Simon has described how Louis XIV exiled his first physician, Antoine d'Aquin. The office of chief physician to the king was an important one. Living close to his royal master, supervising the work of all his physicians, surgeons and apothecaries, the chief physician was in a better position than anyone else to flatter his royal patient and thereby obtain considerable benefits. D'Aquin was well aware of this and quite willing to use his position. According to Saint-Simon, he was grasping, self-seeking and ambitious to establish his family in whatever way he could. He owed his advancement to Mme de Montespan. She had obtained the post for him, and that alone was reason enough to arouse the hostility of Mme de Maintenon. But Mme de Montespan's final departure did not impair d'Aquin's standing; it was his overweening ambition that ruined him. At a moment when it would have been more prudent to remain quiet and unobtrusive, he took it upon himself to importune the king on behalf of his son, a mere abbé, for whom he wanted the archbishopric of Tours. This was tantamount to an affront to all the other abbés and bishops in the kingdom; but d'Aquin continued to press vigorously, even urgently, his son's case. Louis XIV was already tired of his endless demands and solicitations and this one proved the proverbial last straw. Let Saint-Simon decribe the scene: 'Madame de Maintenon wished to control the King by whatever means were available to her, and felt that one of the most important of these lay in the choice of the King's chief physician, now that the King was ageing and his health was beginning to decline . . . She therefore seized the opportunity d'Aquin himself had created and made full use of the King's anger.'

D'Aquin's fall was decided on Sunday 1 November 1693. The evening before, Louis XIV had received him with his usual affability: in fact, never had the king treated him with so much favour or conversed more familiarly with him at supper and at his *coucher*. Never had d'Aquin seemed more secure. Next morning, before seven o'clock, Pontchartrain who as comptroller-general of finance was also in charge of the court and the royal household knocked at the door of d'Aquin's apartment. Without ceremony he informed him that by the king's order he was to withdraw at once to Paris. He was not to attempt to see the king or write to him. The information that he would be compensated for the loss of his position was the parting shot. As d'Aquin was not malevolent and had never done any harm at court, his fate aroused a certain sympathy and a few courtiers – the bolder ones – even had the courage to call on him during the brief interval before he left for Paris. But all guessed 'where the thunderbolt had come from'. Two hours later the announcement of Fagon, Mme de Maintenon's physician, as d'Aquin's successor, removed any possibility of doubt.

The king's behaviour in this affair may seem surprising. But less so if we recall that he was following the advice of his godfather, Mazarin, who had often told him : 'Cultivate that kingly quality of dissimulation which nature has so lavishly bestowed upon you. Surround your decisions with an impenetrable veil of secrecy.' This was the maxim that Louis XIV followed in dealing with his courtiers. Knowing all too well their greed and duplicity, he adopted an attitude towards them which may seem cruel, but which was in fact a defensive reflex.

Few courtiers recovered from such crushing blows. D'Aquin died three years after his fall; he was not so much ruined in a material sense as defeated morally. The prestige and social functions of this artificially created class disappeared once its members were removed from court. 'Sire', said Vardes when he returned from exile, 'away from you one is not merely unhappy; one is ridiculous.' And in the France of the Sun King ridicule was a deadly weapon. Stendhal made the point crystal clear with his remark, 'Louis XIV's real genius lay in creating *ennui* – in the original sense of the word – the *ennui* of exile.' Banished from court, the courtier was nothing.

It is curious to observe that, while exile could drive a courtier to despair, court life too would end by overwhelming him. The less conventional, at least, admitted that they were bored at court. 'I am half a courtier', wrote Racine in 1663, 'but in my opinion it is a pretty tedious life.' And as the king grew older and misfortunes gathered around him, boredom descended on Versailles like a leaden cloak. The mechanism still worked with its accustomed regularity. Protocol was maintained punctiliously. Louis XIV did not give up any of his daily round of public ceremonies : the lesser *lever*, *entrée*, dinner, *coucher*. But once these public duties had been performed, he preferred to withdraw from the crowd. He was scarcely seen any more.

The galleries of Versailles were still thronged with noblemen. 'The court has never been so large', wrote Mme de Maintenon in 1714. The courtiers sought to escape from the monotony, gladly welcoming even the smallest distractions : a group of gypsies who told fortunes, or a mountebank who claimed to have found the philosopher's stone. In 1708 one of these tricksters even managed to dupe Chamillart, the comptroller-general of finance, though it is true that the latter was particularly hard up that year. A furnace and the necessary materials were procured for the mountebank and ministers, princes and nobles of the court went to watch him at work and were taken in by his double-talk. It took the rough common sense of police commissioner Narbonne to put a stop to the deception, and the charlatan – having profited handsomely at the expense of the court for a couple of months – was finally sent to prison. This minor news item gives a good idea of the credulity of the courtiers, eagerly seizing on anything that might ease the deadening boredom of life at Versailles.

On 26 August 1715 the illness that had hit Louis XIV a few days earlier took a turn for the worse, and it became clear that the king was dying. The courtiers, who foresaw great changes in the government, began to dash hither and thither in a frenzy. We have many descriptions of Louis' last hours, but historians have had little to say about the courtiers and their behaviour. Narbonne enlightens us.

> The days when the King appeared to be at death's door, his chamber was empty of courtiers and gentlemen, who had all rushed in a crowd to wait upon the duc d'Orléans. But as soon as word spread that the King was better, the same crowd of gentlemen could be seen leaving the ducal apartments to return to the King. This scene repeated more than once, so that the duc d'Orléans was sometimes quite alone, and sometimes courted by all the great men of the state.

If Louis XIV had ever cherished the slightest illusion about the disinterestedness of his nobility, this rapid succession of departures and returns must have destroyed it.

Louis XIV happened to die on the same day that a devaluation of the currency was announced. A witticism circulated among the courtiers: 'he wanted everyone to feel a loss at his death'. He had reigned too long.

Louis XIV had barely expired before the final exodus of courtiers from the palace took place. The regent, who had assumed full power and intended to rule with the backing of a haughty and intemperate aristocracy, did not hide the fact that he planned to abandon Versailles.

For seven years afterwards there was no court in France. The regent took the young Louis XV away from Versailles and, after a period at Vincennes, established him at the Tuileries while taking up his own residence at the Palais-Royal. The gentlemen of the court were scattered all over Paris, to meet only at balls or at the Opéra. Only the young king's household remained with him : his governor, old Villeroy, and his governess, Mme de Ventadour, grown devout with age. 'Frivolous and foppish', Villeroy was principally concerned to teach his charge courtly manners and contempt for courtiers and others who served him. His advice was forthrightly put, 'You must hold the chamberpot for your ministers, Sire, as long as they are in office; then you can empty it over their heads once they are out of office.'

Paris high society saw many scandals between 1715 and 1727 – so many indeed that Mme de Sabron commented that 'God at the Creation had made two kinds of matter; from one He created men, from the other He created princes and lackeys' – and financial speculations which gripped all classes during Law's Bubble. The years when the duc d'Orléans had been regent had left a bad taste; and when the young king was twelve and nearing his majority the decision was taken to move him, and with him the court, back to Versailles.

Once more the Sun King's city took on life and animation. The salons of Paris, however, did not lose their appeal; indeed, they were to keep it throughout the eighteenth century.

Life at Versailles had changed. Louis XV was shy, crowds alarmed and terrified him. Throughout his youth, which was chaste and much more studious than is usually believed, he led a sheltered and retired life. He had no idea of the intrigues which had developed once the court had been re-established.

8 Louis XIV and the Edict of Nantes*

J. ORCIBAL

Even if the Edict of Nantes of 1598 seems, in historical perspective, to be the French equivalent of the Peace of Augsburg of
1555, it is important to note that to contemporaries it represented a definite novelty: whereas religious and political unity had
been closely identified until then, the edict imparted a federal
character to the French state.[1] Like those of Beaulieu (6 May
1576) and Poitiers (September 1577),[2] the Edict of Nantes recognised the weakness of the central power, unable to make either
party lay down its arms without the guarantee of places where
it could worship in security according to its own religious choice.
Mayenne, Joyeuse and Mercoeur were won over by such concessions between January 1596 and March 1598, and on 13 April
1598 Henri IV had to grant his former co-religionists the Edict
of Nantes before proceeding to make peace with Spain, the
Empire and Savoy at Vervins on 2 May. The use in the edict of
the terms 'perpetual' and 'irrevocable' denoted the intention –
sincerely held by Henri IV – of not resorting to force, but it did
not imply the abandonment of hopes of achieving religious unity
within the state. Henri III's formula of 'provisionally and while
awaiting a Council of the (general or national) Church' was
echoed in a clause of the Edict of Nantes: 'God has not seen fit
that my subjects should as yet worship and adore him under one
form of religion.' Pierre de Beloy, a lawyer from Toulouse, was
therefore right to conclude in 1600 that 'the Edict will lapse as
soon as there is no longer reason for it to exist among us'.[3] In a
conversation with the cardinal of Florence on 2 September 1598,
Henri IV pointed out that the grant of the 'places of security' was

* Specially commissioned for this volume.

only temporary, and that he hoped to see heresy extirpated from his kingdom by 1606.[4] He and the legate probably attached different meanings to this statement, but the king certainly gave his support to the work of publicists who sought to reconcile the two creeds, particularly in 1607 and 1608.[5]

Both Catholic and Protestant leaders had accepted the edict with reluctance, regarding it as a temporary consequence of the balance of forces and hoping to use it as a basis from which to make further advances.[6] Although the regent Marie de Medici was quick to confirm the edict (22 May 1610), this did not stop the Protestants from rebelling in 1615, 1621, 1625 and 1627. Backed by a succession of foreign powers they aimed at setting up a state of their own within France. The Peace of Montpellier (19 October 1622) still left them a chance to achieve this, but the fall of la Rochelle seemed to open the way for the 'great stroke' desired by Cardinal de Berulle – one which would have been the equivalent of the Imperial Edict of Restitution of 6 March 1629. Richelieu decided, however, that alliances with Protestant powers were vital to his war policy, and he therefore came to terms with the Huguenots by the Grace of Alais (27 June 1629).[7] Even if he did not prevent the parlements and Clergy from demanding a restrictive interpretation of the edict during the following years,[8] he devoted much time to preparing a conference at which he hoped that French Protestant pastors (many of whom had been won over in advance) would be induced by new arguments and judicious concessions to rejoin the Catholic church.[9] The inspiration for Richelieu's efforts came not so much from the writings of La Milletière as from those of Grotius.[10] When criticised by intransigent Protestants like A. Rivet and the Parisian pastor J. Daillé, Grotius had felt obliged to remind them that members of the French Reformed church were not protected 'by treaties', but only by edicts promulgated by kings in the public interest, and therefore revocable if their interpretation of the public interest should change.[11]

Richelieu's premature death enabled the Huguenots to maintain that he had believed himself bound by the Edict of Nantes.[12] The weakness of Anne of Austria's position obliged her to reconfirm the Edict of Nantes on 8 July 1643; and in fact during the Fronde the Protestants, well represented in government finance

F*

and hostile to Spain, were among Mazarin's most loyal supporters.[13] At the point when he most needed their help, he issued the
declaration of 21 May 1652 which 'seemed to abolish with a
stroke of the pen all the restrictions imposed by Louis XIII on the
exercise of the Protestant religion'.[14] The Assemblies of the Clergy
were forced on to the defensive and protested that they 'were
not demanding the revocation of the Edict which had been publicly sanctioned by the divisions within the state'.[15] The concession which the Clergy obtained in return – that commissions
composed of members of both religions would be sent to the provinces to enquire into the 'activities' of the Huguenots – was not
put into effect before the cardinal's death.[16] But his declaration of
18 July 1656 went back on that of 1652, and was followed by
several restrictive measures reminiscent of those enacted in the
previous reign.[17]

Louis XIV had been brought up on the *Vie de Henry le Grand*
written by his tutor Péréfixe. It condemned the Massacre of Saint
Bartholomew outright,[18] but was factual and noncommital on the
edict which 'factious and powerful Huguenots' had obtained from
Henri IV who 'could not disappoint them' because of 'reason of
state and the great obligations he owed them'.[19] According to the
Mémoires Louis XIV dictated in 1671, he had determined that
he would respect his grandfather's promise, though he would try
'to restrict its execution within the narrowest limits' and would
reserve 'the graces which he could personally grant' for 'those
who showed submissiveness'. But he admitted that 'changed times
and circumstances could produce a thousand alterations . . . in
his plans'.[20] Although for stylistic reasons Louis placed these and
other declarations of principle under the year 1661, they belong
to a later period of his thinking :[21] at the beginning of his personal
reign he had noted that 'nothing of much importance' occurred in
the department of La Vrillière, who was in charge of matters
relating to the R.P.R. (*Religion Prétendue Reformée*, the official
nomenclature for the Huguenot faith).[22] Commissions of inquiry
were, however, sent to the provinces in accordance with the 1652
provision; and in the course of the next few years they settled
many local disputes. Faced by the exceptional degree of agreement between the Clergy and the parlements, the royal council
always gave verdicts in favour of the Catholics. One result of this
was the destruction of dozens of Protestant temples.[23] Although

the Protestants received favourable judgements in some other cases,[24] the trend in these years differed so much from that of the preceding period that already by 6 October 1665 the orator of the Assembly of the Clergy could characterise Louis XIV as 'the invincible hero destined by eternal wisdom to destroy the terrible monster of heresy'.[25] The question seemed as good as settled when on 2 April 1666 the king signed a declaration – to please his dying mother as well as the Assembly of the Clergy – renewing all the earlier restrictions on the Protestants.[26] But it was still too early for the Catholics to claim victory. Louis did not wish to have the reputation abroad of a persecutor of Protestants,[27] and he therefore on 1 February 1669 withdrew his declaration of 1666 and forbade the proselytising of children of Huguenot parents.[28] In 1670 the Assembly of the Clergy 'in the most profound consternation' deplored 'this extraordinary transformation', but in vain; and despite the generosity of its 'free gift' in 1675 the assembly could not prevent the rebuilding of the temple at Rennes.[29]

Yet it would be wrong to assume that the Sun King was prepared to accept the permanent religious division of his kingdom. In 1670 Pierre Bayle warned the Huguenots that their very existence depended on the king's tolerance,[30] and by this time Louis had in fact already conceived the 'grand design' which, as his *Mémoires* show, he believed he could achieve by peaceful means.[31] He had some reason for such optimism. Bossuet's conciliatory *Exposition* had enjoyed an enormous success. The pope, who long continued to hope that the Most Christian King would act against the Turks (as he had done in 1664 and 1669), could be expected to grant Louis dispensations calculated to bring the Huguenots back into the Catholic church at the conference table.[32] But the synod of Ile-de-France, meeting at a moment (1673) when the French frontiers were menaced by hostile armies, halted the king's plans; and Turenne's death in battle in 1675 further removed the possibility of their coming to fruition. The projects for reunion were not abandoned;[33] but after the Peace of Nijmegen Louis XIV, triumphant over the whole of Europe, was no longer willing to wait with the same patience as before.

It is therefore not surprising that between 1679 and 1685 Louis XIV signed about a hundred edicts against heresy, for he was no longer prepared to tolerate opposition of any kind.[34] In vain did Innocent XI, preoccupied with the Turkish threat to

Europe, tempt Louis with approval for Bossuet's *Exposition* and
for the irenian plans advocated by Rojas de Spinola: Louis
proved hostile to anything that might increase the power of the
Habsburg emperor and refused to commit himself to help Leopold I against the Ottomans.[35] The year 1683 marks a turning
point since Louis now expected the German princes to beseech
him to become their protector in place of a weakened Austria.
Sobieski's victory, however, upset his calculations and Louis now
began to side more openly with the Turks.[36] For this behaviour
the French king seems to have felt no remorse: a concern for his
gloire was uppermost in his mind.[37]

At this very time conflicts over the *régale* and the four Gallican
articles (see Chronology) brought an almost complete breakdown
in Louis' relations with Rome,[38] and there was speculation as to
whether the Huguenots would have the satisfaction of driving the
king into a schism. Such speculation rested, however, on slender
foundations. Louis was more likely to proclaim himself more
Catholic than the pope and to prove this by assuming leadership
of a crusade against his own Protestant subjects, to compensate
for his lack of participation in the crusade against the eastern
infidel.[39] Such a domestic venture held less political danger and
promised, moreover, the greater glory of achieving lasting
results.[40]

The choice before Louis was not at first as clearcut as the above
analysis might imply.[41] Bossuet's opening address to the Assembly
of the Clergy, the report of G. de Choiseul, and the 'pastoral
advertisement' (*Avertissement Pastoral*) of 1 July 1682, all show
that the assembly was aware of the ecumenical possibilities inherent in Gallicanism.[42] In the following year the revolts in Vivarais and Dauphiné demonstrated that the spirit of Rohan and
Soubise was not dead, and further that such rebellions – which
were unimportant in peacetime – could be dangerous when
France was involved in foreign war.[43] In August 1684 the Truce
of Ratisbon gave Louis complete freedom to act. He now thought
of nothing but his 'great work', while remaining for some time
undecided as to the means by which he would execute it.[44] In late
1684 a council of conscience, which included two theologians and
two jurists, declared that the king could legally revoke the Edict
of Nantes and that – since he was able – this obliged him to do
so.[45] This, however, was also the time when 'all the talk at court

was of amicable conferences to bring an end to differences of religion'.[46] It would have been easy to have proposals of this nature put forward in the Assembly of the Clergy of 1685.[47] Rome feared that the assembly might move in the direction of a schism, while the pastor J. Dubourdieu hoped it would bring the work begun in 1682 to fruition by reforms and by showing latitude on points of dogma.[48] The issue still seemed undecided when the archbishop of Paris, acting on his own initiative, on 8 June announced that a commission selected for its loyalty to himself was to draw up a profession of faith.[49] It was probably on the archbishop's orders that its draft project amplified Pius IV's profession by the addition of conciliatory glosses. Of these only one was crucial in that it touched upon the limits of papal power.[50] However, these glosses were not included in the official text which was of the profession issued : in this a denunciation of the 'slanders of the heretics' loomed large.[51] The chairman of the commission admitted on 18 June that its members had had to grapple with serious problems, but that the archbishop had settled every difficulty.[52] The real question here is whether the archbishop's hand had been forced by the king. On 18 and 28 June, Louis had in fact listened graciously to the arguments of the papal nuncio,[53] who seems to have been supported by the archbishop of Rheims, by Bossuet and by the chancellor, Le Tellier. The draft project for a profession of faith had indeed been schismatic enough to avoid any reference to Bossuet's *Exposition*, which the pope had already accepted.[54] Harlay's annoyance was increased by his being obliged on 8 August to issue a condemnation of the draft project which had clandestinely appeared in print.[55] It would seem that the archbishop's attitude made Louis hesitate, for on 17 August the king wrote to Cardinal d'Estrées that 'the affair is not as yet completely perfected'.[56] But on 23 August Louis issued an edict which reaffirmed the position he had adopted at the end of June, namely in the direction of revoking the Edict of Nantes. This therefore was the decisive moment.[57] The abandonment of Harlay's draft project was definitive and indicated the triumph of the nuncio, of Le Tellier, of Roman orthodoxy, and of the 'armed apostles'.

Was Louis XIV's decision based on reports which daily announced the conversion of thousands of Huguenots?[58] He could hardly have been ignorant of the fact that these conversions were caused by the presence of troops, a method he had condemned in

1681 at the time of the *dragonnades* in Poitou, and of whose unpleasant features he was well aware.[59] The voluntary reuniting of the Huguenots with the Gallican church, on the other hand, would – so their theologians promised – have been celebrated as the most glorious action in the world.[60] This could have been achieved at the price of small concessions. Would the pope have agreed to such a compromise? We know that he was afraid of a schism,[61] and with good reason : when Louis XIV was excommunicated in 1688, he called for a general church council and planned an invasion of the papal states. Louis was not yet restrained by devout religious feelings, although these began to make themselves known after his illness in 1686;[62] and his theologian advisers would have proved to him that he could perform no action in 1685 more pleasing in the eyes of God than that of bringing the Huguenots by peaceful means back to a 'more pure' form of Catholicism. We may therefore conclude that neither religious motives nor regard for public opinion, which was in any case impotent,[63] dictated the Sun King's decision.

The international situation would seem to have been far more important in bringing about the revocation. The traditional policy of alliance with the Protestant states against the Habsburgs no longer offered any advantages : William of Orange was Louis XIV's implacable enemy, while in Brandenburg patriotism had triumphed over the desire for subsidies.[64] The elector of the Palatinate was now a Catholic, and the shaky alliance of Bavaria with the emperor would have been strengthened by a schism in France.[65] On the other hand, a schism would have serious repercussions among the Italian princes and – more significantly – would ensure the permanent exclusion of the Bourbons from the Spanish succession. The accession of a Catholic prince to the throne of England also affected the international situation. From May 1685 Louis XIV had represented himself at Rome as the protector of James II, who, he argued, was unable to survive without French aid.[66] The news of Monmouth's rebellion and its defeat in June–July[67] contributed to Louis' choice of the rigid orthodoxy of Le Tellier in preference to the semi-Anglicanism, now seemingly obsolete, of the archbishop of Paris.[68]

Although de Cosnac, the spokesman for the Assembly of the Clergy, was incautious enough to announce on 14 July 1685 that England was 'about to offer' Louis XIV 'one of the most glorious

opportunities he could wish for . . . to restore true religion everywhere',[69] he was at least careful not to associate this prophetic
utterance with the demand for 'the revocation of any Edict'.[70]
Government departments at Versailles continued to act throughout
the summer of 1685 as if the Huguenots would remain part of
the body politic.[71] After the decree of 16 June, that of 15 September established regulations for their baptisms and marriages.[72]
But by this date Louis XIV was receiving almost daily reports of
the 'conversion' of whole towns to the Catholic church.[73] The
king, somewhat taken aback, concluded that God wished to make
use of him 'to bring to perfection the holy work he had begun,
which was the conversion of all his subjects'.[74] During his stay at
Chambord from 3 to 30 September he was little occupied with
affairs of state:[75] the supposed meeting there of the Council of
Conscience to draw up an edict of revocation, granting extraordinary powers to the Jesuits and the Assemblies of the Clergy,
took place only in the hostile imagination of a Protestant pam-
phleteer.[76]

Louis XIV kept in touch with the archbishop of Paris; but the
latter's reports to the king were concerned, not with anti-Protestant legal measures, but with news of secret negotiations with
influential Huguenots[77] and of the violently Gallican theses put
forward by Berthe, rector of the University of Paris.[78] The initiative
for the judicial persecution of the Huguenots seems in fact to have
come from the archbishop's opponent, the chancellor Le Tellier,
who – feeling himself close to death – was eager that his name
should be associated with a measure he considered both pious and
glorious.[79] His letters from this period have not survived, but we
possess one from his son, the archbishop of Rheims, of 30 September, addressed to the *procureur général* Achille III de Harlay,
in which the former thanks the latter for a memorandum sent to
the chancellor on 25 September and which the archbishop was to
pass on with comments of his own.[80]

The Protestant issue came to a head at a meeting held in the
afternoon of 8 October at Fontainebleau. For the past few months
the council dealing with Huguenot affairs – to which the archbishop of Paris had been specifically invited since the beginning
of August[81] – had been meeting regularly every Monday,[82] but
the session of 8 October was of particular solemnity and importance.[83] Louis XIV summoned the dauphin to it at a time when

his heir had not yet started to attend any of the king's councils;[84] and the king presided in person though he did not normally attend the meetings of the council on Huguenot affairs. The duke of Burgundy's account of the meeting stresses the part played by the dauphin who came armed with a memorandum received the day before (possibly from Seignelay), emphasising the political and economic dangers of a revocation. The king replied that 'he had taken this into account long ago . . . and that questions of temporal interest were of little account beside the advantages of a measure that would restore the splendour of religion, bring peace to the Church and recover authority that the state had lost'.[85] This is all the information Burgundy gives. The *controleur-général* Le Peletier later claimed that he had opposed the revocation, but his account is not trustworthy.[86] We do not know if anyone spoke of the desirability of depriving the many newly-converted Huguenots of their fiscal privileges, though this was in effect done.[87] Apparently the main point discussed on 8 October was how to deal with the Huguenot pastors.[88] The archbishop of Paris wanted to imprison them,[89] and his view might have carried the day had not Châteauneuf pointed out that the cost of their subsistence would be too heavy.[90] Several issues were deliberately omitted from the discussion, as can be deduced from Louis XIV's letter to the archbishop of Paris of 28 October : 'the matter of burials and marriages which is thought to have been overlooked, has been left out on purpose and for good reason'.[91] The fate of the Huguenot pastors was not decided till 15 October when the king adopted the project submitted by Le Tellier, with additions which Rulhière attributes to Châteauneuf. The new draft was sent by Louvois to his father[92] who, racked by illness, added the clause stipulating registration by the *chambre des vacations* (see glossary). In the opinion of Benoist, Le Tellier speeded up the promulgation of the Edict of Fontainebleau by six or seven weeks;[93] but against this it should be stressed that, on the chancellor's instructions, the *procureur-général* had been summoned as early as 14 October for Thursday the eighteenth.[94] This did not please the archbishop of Paris, who still hoped to arrange – with the help of spokesmen won over in advance – a meeting of the Parisian Huguenots. But the king's 'sole response' to a memorandum Harlay wrote was to let him know on 16 October, 'in extreme secrecy, that next Monday the great Declaration would be laid before the Parlement without further delay'. The archbishop's two letters to Louis XIV of the nineteenth, announcing his intention of going to Charenton the following Sunday, had no effect.[95] The Protestant temple remained shut,[96] and the Edict of Fontainebleau was registered on 22 October.

After that day the Huguenot leaders on whom the archbishop had been relying proved uncooperative and on the 27 October Seignelay gave up the idea of a meeting with them.[97] Their disappointment stemmed perhaps from the fact the archbishop of Paris had not been given enough time to reassure his future flock.[98] Furthermore, since Harlay in Paris was closely watched by the papal nuncio he dared not – as was possible in the provinces – interpret Pius IV's profession of faith in the spirit of the draft project of the commission.[99] All he could do for the moment was to make slight alterations in the translation of the pope's profession;[100] though less than a month after the Edict of Fontainebleau he grew bold enough to order the printing of a very short formula allowing great latitude.[101] On this Louis XIV congratulated him on 20 November : 'There are none of those details which could cause difficulties to those of the Protestant religion', a clear indication of the irresolution and theological incompetence of the Sun King.[102] The formula would no doubt cause annoyance in Rome; but, as the chancellor had died a week after his triumph, the archbishop had been able to recover some of the ground previously lost.

We must therefore revise the accepted opinion that the archbishop of Paris pressed Louis XIV to take extreme measures against the Protestants. It might seem justified by Harlay's hostility towards Bossuet, Le Camus, Fénelon and all 'accommodators' suspected of Jansenism.[103] But the archbishop had been the ally of Colbert;[104] his special form of Gallicanism was well adapted to win over 'anti-papalists' whose support he could then hope to use against Rome. It was, however, precisely this tactical possibility that aroused opposition to him by the chancellor and by the archbishop of Rheims : the dread of a schism which they had shown in 1682 was bound in 1685 to make them hostile to the plans of 'the future Patriarch'.[105] It is true that Spanheim[106] and the abbé Legendre[107] have tried to explain the part Harlay played in the revocation by his desire to vindicate, at little cost to himself, his orthodoxy in Rome. But this judgement is based

mainly on Louis XIV's rejection of the archbishop's draft project
of the profession of faith. In fact, the Edict of Fontainebleau was
the work of laymen; the archbishop of Paris was hardly con-
sulted, and the expulsion of the Protestant pastors was decided on
against his specific recommendation.[108] The early publication of
the edict, at the chancellor's instigation, prevented Harlay from
achieving an amicable union with the Protestants which would
have been more in line with the statement in the preamble to the
edict : that the religious dualism on which the Edict of Nantes had
been founded no longer existed.

Should Louis XIV, as the Huguenot argument ran, have regarded Henri IV's edict as perpetual and irrevocable?[109] It is
hard to believe that the king could have done so, since – regardless of the opinions of theologians – the jurists had all along
emphasised that such an edict could only be valid in a federal
state. Henri IV's concessions had been necessary because his
authority was not respected in many parts of the kingdom. Once
this authority was restored, the king was obliged to act only in
the interest of the general welfare; and subjects could no longer
make use of 'treaties' which presupposed the existence of two
equally sovereign contracting parties. The evidence at our disposal would seem to indicate that Louis XIV never accepted the
Huguenot argument; certainly in his *Mémoires* he said that even
in respect of international treaties 'there is no clause so clear that
it cannot be interpreted in different ways. . . . When the reasons
which led men to make a certain promise no longer subsist, there
are few who will keep the promise.'[110] It is worth stressing that
for a long time Louis XIV had treated the Edict of Nantes in this
way, claiming to 'interpret' it without actually 'abolishing' it,[111]
declaring that he 'wished to see it obeyed, so long as it was nullified in a thousand ways' and 'overturned on the pretext of
enforcing it'.[112] The very way, therefore, in which the edict had
been implemented in Louis' reign made it seem as though there
was no longer any reason to maintain it. No doubt this was
hypocritical, but it shows that the king had more respect for the
edict than the circumstances of its enactment actually warranted.[113] Successive re-enactments had endowed it with a prescriptive character which influenced Louis XIV's attitude to it.
Richelieu had renewed the Huguenots' privileges at a moment
when he had very good reasons for wishing to see them

abolished.[114] Like Mazarin, Louis XIV had repeatedly proclaimed his determination to uphold his grandfather's edict,[115] and his proclamations are not explicable only by foreign policy motivation.[116] Initially regarded as a sign of weakness, and without parallel in western Europe, the French religious settlement had gradually come to be looked upon as an example for other states once the ideal of a Christian, united Europe gave way to the concept of the diversity of separate European states.[117] Louis XIV must have found it all the more difficult to abolish the edict since the Huguenots had been among his most loyal subjects during the conflict with the Habsburgs, and since public opinion was no longer accustomed to the use of violence in matters of religion.[118] This last factor probably explains why the final clause of the Edict of Fontainebleau pretended that freedom of conscience was preserved.[119]

It could be argued that the many executions which followed the Popish Plot in England had revived the religious fanaticism of the French lower classes, who in any case resented the economic superiority of the Huguenots.[120] Certainly the Clergy and the parlements had kept up their campaign against the privileged status by which the Huguenots were protected from their jurisdiction, their corporate will and their desire for prestige, which was greater than their concern for their religion.[121] C. Rousset is of the opinion that

the Revocation was the only major decision not completely controlled by the French government . . . [which] was carried along by the actions of its subordinates. . . . The tide rose in the provinces and engulfed Paris. . . . There are signs of disruptive forces acting from below. This explains the hesitations, the confusion, the contradictions . . . the fragmentary plans which do not agree among themselves, the cross-currents, the collisions and clashes – in a word, there was miserable and repugnant anarchy.[122]

I would add that despite the unity implied in Louis XIV's 'great design' – the outcome of his inordinate desire for *gloire*[123] and the length of time he had been pondering it – the king never sought to remedy the confusion that marked its execution. His policy was always too closely affected by the immediate political situation and was too empirical and even impulsive.[124] It underwent successive modifications to accommodate chance happenings and counter currents, so that possible courses of action were progressively narrowed down.

The first choice facing Louis XIV was between a crusade abroad or one at home. The former project, encouraged initially by the victory on the Raab, was virtually abandoned after the setbacks, unnecessary as they were, in Candia. Sobieski's victory at Vienna closed the possibility of pursuing this policy, and Louis' need for psychological compensation led him to allot to the Huguenots the role that the Turks could no longer play. But there was a difference. The chance of a negotiated union between the Huguenots and the Gallican church still existed : and the coercion, mixed with bribery, employed against the Huguenots could only have led them, according to Augustinian psychology, to come the sooner to terms.[125] In the course of 1685, however, a series of unforeseeable circumstances made it extremely dangerous from the point of view of international politics to pursue a policy which might lead to a schism. Since Louis XIV could not hope to win glory by the religious unification of France through peaceful means – a task that five of his predecessors had found beyond their powers – he fell back on the superficial success of conversions, soon revealed as forced and insincere.

But here also the king came up against obstacles that he had himself created before *dragonnades* had ever been used, such as the ban on emigration and the measures against lapsed Catholics. In 1681 he had publicly condemned the violence of Marillac's troops. As soon as this became known, retractions had followed in large numbers.[126] When in 1685 forceful methods were used almost everywhere – and even if Louis tried to ignore this, he cannot have been completely unaware of what was going on[127] – discreet warnings were sent to those responsible : it was not fitting that the victims should think that 'the King disapproved of anything that was made in order to convert them'.[128] Royal disapproval would have stemmed the flow of conversions and would, moreover, have led many converts to retract : a distasteful situation would have become ludicrous. A great many Frenchmen desired the achievement of religious unity without bloodshed and they too sought to deny the evidence of violence. It is fair to say that Louis XIV 'was imperceptibly encouraged and pressed to revoke the Edict by the complicity of almost all those around him'.[129] The consequence was an action unparalleled in the way in which it was generally praised by contemporaries[130] and universally condemned by posterity.[131]

NOTES

1 E. G. Léonard has compared it to the Anglo-Scottish connections at the accession of James I: *Revue Historique* (1948) 155 ff, 166. The situation in Poland, with semi-independence for the nobility, should also be borne in mind: see A. Jobert, 'La tolérance religieuse en Pologne au XVI⁰ siècle' in *Studies in onore di E. Le Gatto e G. Maver* (Florence, 1969) pp. 337–43; and J. Lecler, *Histoire de la tolérance au siècle de la Réforme*, I (Paris, 1955) pp. 364–98.

2 For these see Lecler, *Histoire de la tolérance*, II, pp. 120–30; see also C. Brousson, *Etat des réformés de France où l'on fait voir que les édits de pacification sont irrévocables* (The Hague, 1685) p. 93.

3 *Conférence des édits de pacification des troubles de France pour le fait de la religion et règlements faits par Charles IX et Henri III et de la déclaration d'iceux de Henri IV* (Paris, 1600) pp. 38 ff. Cf. C. Ancillon, *L'irrévocabilité de l'Edit de Nantes prouvée par les principes du droit et de la politique* (Amsterdam, 1688) pp. 2, 31.

4 *Lettres du cardinal de Florence sur Henri IV et sur la France*, ed. Raymond Ritter (Paris, 1955) pp. 247 ff.

5 See my *Louis XIV et les Protestants* (Paris, 1951) p. 29. Mme E. Labrousse has shown that the *Discours au Roi* of 1607, summarised by Tabaraud in *Histoire critique des projets formés depuis trois cents ans pour la réunion des communions chrétiennes* (Paris, 1824) pp. 195 ff and 253 ff, is the work of the councillor Guillaume Ribier (Ribbier). Cf. also E. G. Léonard, *Histoire générale du protestantisme*, II (Paris, 1961) pp. 315 n., 325.

6 The contradictions within the edict have been stressed by C. de Rulhière, *Eclaircissements historiques sur les causes de la révocation de l'Edit de Nantes*, I (no place of publication, 1788) p. 13. For the Protestant attitude see Elie Benoist, *Histoire de l'Edit de Nantes* (Delft, 1695) p. 361, and H. Tüchle, *Nouvelle histoire de l'Eglise*, III (Paris, 1968) p. 268; for that of the Catholics see my *Louis XIV et les Protestants*, p. 21, n. 49.

7 Tüchle, *Nouvelle histoire*, III, pp. 259, 269, and my *Louis XIV et les Protestants*, p. 30 ff. L. Dedouvres in *Le P. Joseph et le siège de La Rochelle* (Angers, 1903) pp. 70 ff, 111, 122, has stressed the irenic disposition of his hero. Lecler, in *Histoire de la tolérance*, concentrates on Richelieu; one of his sections (II, pp. 130–5) is entitled 'Richelieu et le triomphe du système des politiques'.

8 P. Blet, *Le clergé de France et la monarchie*, II (Rome, 1959) pp. 342–5; cf. Brousson, *Etat des réformés*, I, p. 72.

9 My main source of information is the letter addressed by Richard Simon to the abbé de la Roque, 12 September 1665: *Lettres choisies*,

ed. Bruzen de la Martinière, ɪ (Amsterdam, 1730) pp. 1–11, 26; cf. also pp. 30–3 and 276 ff. Simon had been told by Richelieu's collaborator, du Laurens, that the cardinal would have tried in these discussions to have the natural sense of the Holy Scriptures accepted on six or seven specific points. For Richelieu's willingness to substitute 'real change' for the phrase 'transubstantiation', a step which eighty pastors had approved, see A. Rébelliau, *Bossuet, historien du protestantisme*, 3rd ed. (Paris, 1909) pp. 9, 11; and my *Louis XIV et les Protestants*, p. 13, n. 14. The most effective opposition came from the 'devout' party: see my *Origines du Jansénisme*, ɪɪɪ (Paris, 1948) p. 143 ff, and the François Hallier letters of December 1640 and, in particular, that of 20 January 1645, published by P. Ceyssens in *Bulletin de l'Institut historique belge de Rome*, xɪ (1969) 157–264; cf. also Tabaraud, *Histoire critique*, p. 202.

10 A good source of information are the letters addressed to A. Rivet in November and December 1642 by Daillé and Sarrau: *Correspondance du P. Marin Mersenne*, xɪ, ed. P. Tannery and J. De Waard (Paris, 1971) pp. 168, 293, 297, 361 f. Grotius' attitude to religion has been studied by Levesque de Burigny; and, more recently, by R. Pintard, *Le libertinage érudit* (Paris, 1943) ɪ, pp. 17, 19, 50, 305, 308, 324; and by L. Polman in *Studia Catholica*, xxɪx (1954) 134–5.

11 *Rivetiani apologetici pro schismate contra Votum pro pace facti discussio* (no place of publication, 1643) p. 22.

12 Ancillon, *L'irrévocabilité de l'Edit de Nantes*, p. 43. See Chamlay's response – not convincing – cited in Léonard, *Histoire du protestantisme*, ɪɪ, p. 31 n.

13 The best account is in Blet, *Le clergé de France*, ɪɪ, pp. 346–69, 379–80. He has not, however, dealt with the new projects for a reunion which Du Laurens, Gaffarel, Sorbière and Marca put to Richelieu, but these would in any case seem to have had no effect. Cf. Simon in de la Martinière (ed.), *Lettres choisies*, ɪ, pp. 5, 33–4; Tabaraud, *Histoire critique*, pp. 204 ff; Rébelliau, *Bossuet*, p. 19; Pintard, *Le libertinage érudit*, ɪ, pp. 273, 278.

14 Cf. Blet, *Le clergé de France*, ɪɪ, pp. 348–53, 368, 379 f.

15 Ibid., ɪɪ, pp. 356, 359, 362.

16 Ibid., ɪɪ, p. 358 ff.

17 The list is printed in [—] Soulier, *Histoire du Calvinisme* (Paris, 1686) pp. 559–65. Mme E. Labrousse holds that Mazarin underwent a real change of heart and attributes this to his second treaty with Cromwell.

18 'An execrable act which can never, and will not – if it so pleases God – be equalled': p. 29 of the Paris edition of 1661.

19 Ibid., p. 219.

20 *Mémoires*, ed. Charles Dreyss, ɪɪ (Paris, 1860) pp. 453–7.

21 Ibid., pp. 418–19. On the composition of the *Mémoires* see Dreyss (ed.), ɪ, xxviii–xxxv, cxlvi–clii and Paul Sonnino in *French Historical Studies* (1964) 303–37.

22 Dreyss (ed.) *Mémoires*, ɪɪ, p. 391.

23 Blet, *Le clergé de France*, ɪɪ, pp. 370–2.

24 Most importantly of 28 September 1663 and 24 April 1665 on the education of their children and the freedom of livery companies: ibid., pp. 374–5, 381, 383.

25 Ibid., pp. 378, 384.

26 This declaration of 59 articles was, according to its preamble, 'accorded at the request of the Assembly of the Clergy': ibid., pp. 385–7.

27 Dreyss (ed.) *Mémoires*, I, p. 206; C. Rousset, *Histoire de Louvois*, III (Paris, 1863) p. 434; my *Louis XIV et les Protestants*, p. 98 ff.

28 See E. Haag, *La France protestante*, IV (Paris, 1859) p. 377.

29 Léonard, *Histoire du protestantisme*, II, p. 359; my *Louis XIV et les Protestants*, p. 23, n. 54.

30 *Louis XIV et les Protestants*, p. 20, n. 42.

31 Ibid., p. 91; Dreyss (ed.), *Mémoires*, I, p. 155 ff; II, pp. 232, 418; Paul Sonnino, *Louis XIV's Views of the Papacy, 1661–1667* (Berkeley, 1966) pp. 15, 22, 28.

32 See, in particular for the plan of Daguesseau, Rulhière, *Eclaircissements historiques*, pp. 62–6; Tabaraud, *Histoire critique*, pp. 207–8; P. Gachon, *Quelques préliminaires de la Révocation de l'Edit de Nantes en Languedoc, 1661–1685* (Toulouse, 1899) pp. lxxx–lxxxv; and my *Louis XIV et les Protestants*, pp. 32–7, 40.

33 Cf. *Louis XIV et les Protestants*, p. 85; and below, notes 35 and 48 ff.

34 Cf. ibid., p. 57.

35 Cf. ibid., pp. 58–62, 82–5.

36 Cf. ibid., pp. 103–5 and my commentary to Fénelon's letter of 8 October 1686 in *Revue de l'histoire littéraire de la France* (1969) 436, 439.

37 E. Spanheim, *Relation de la Cour de France* (Paris, 1883) pp. 5–9, 25 ff. For Louis' passion for glory see also my *Louis XIV et les Protestants*, p. 96; Dreyss (ed.), *Mémoires*, I, p. 289; P. Goubert, *L'avènement du Roi-Soleil, 1661* (Paris, 1967) pp. 58 f, 135, 140–1, 143–4, 147, 150.

38 Cf. my *Louis XIV et les Protestants*, pp. 62, 65, 77.

39 For the substitution of one kind of crusade for another, see commentary on Fénelon's letter cited in note 36 above.

40 Innocent XI declared that the revocation was more important than the conquests of towns (à propos Cassovia) or provinces (à propos Hungary) 'which are gained and then lost': the despatches of the brothers d'Estrées in Archives des Affaires Etrangères, Correspondance Politique, Rome, vol. 294, f. 275v; 393 n°; vol. 296, f. 253v; cf. L. von Pastor, *Storia dei Papi*, XIV, pt 2 (Rome, 1943) p. 241.

41 In a frequently quoted letter, Mme de Maintenon writes on 5 April 1681: 'If God grants the King life, in twenty years time there will not be a single Huguenot in France' (see my *Louis XIV et les Protestants*, p. 101); but Louis himself on 10 July 1682 ordered the bishops 'to do nothing against the edicts and the declarations by virtue of which those of the *R.P.R.* are tolerated in the Kingdom': Rébelliau, *Bossuet*, p. 359, n. 3.

42 Tabaraud, *Histoire critique*, p. 481; A. G. Martimort, *Le gallicanisme de*

170 *Louis XIV and Absolutism*

Bossuet (Paris, 1953) pp. 393, 423, 463; my *Louis XIV et les Protestants*, pp. 62, 77ff, 101, n. 49.

43 Rousset, *Histoire de Louvois*, III, p. 452ff: Léonard, *Histoire du protestantisme*, II, p. 367.

44 Lavisse (ed.), *Histoire de la France*, VII, pt 2, p. 57; my *Louis XIV et les Protestants*, p. 91, n. 1.

45 We possess only one piece of evidence for this, but it is absolutely reliable: the 'Mémoire du duc de Bourgogne sur le rappel des huguenots', cited in my *Louis XIV et les Protestants*, p. 107, n. 71. Confirmation is found in J. Claude's letters of December (ibid., n. 72) and in a despatch of Cardinal Pio's from early January 1685, welcoming rumours of the revocation: Vienna, H.H. St. A., D. K. Rom, f. 13. I have found nothing to confirm Daguesseau's conclusion that the archbishop of Paris and Père de la Chaise inspired the revocation: *Œuvres*, XII (Paris, 1789) pp. 50–1. On the contrary, their influence was much weakened during October 1685: see infra, notes 82ff.

46 Apart from the references cited in my *Louis XIV et les Protestants*, pp. 70 n., 84f, see Benoist, *Histoire de l'Edit de Nantes*, IV, p. 712.

47 See the despatches of Cardinal Pio, edited by Ch. Gérin in *Revue des questions historiques*, XXIV (1878) 387–401, of 12 Aug, 16 Sep, 11 Nov, 9 Dec 1684, 27 Jan, 17 Feb and 3, 17, 24 Mar 1685; also my *Louis XIV et les Protestants*, p. 102, n. 53.

48 *Louis XIV et les Protestants*, pp. 81, 85, n. 16 and n. 17. The collection of Joly de Fleury, 1678, ff. 100–16, contains J. Dubourdieu's letters from Montpellier to 'Those of the *R.P.R.*' of 4 May 1684 and February 1685, and also a paper from March 1685 entitled 'Conversations which the Assembly of the Clergy propose to hold with those of the Reformed Religion', attributed to E. Benoist. In the Morel de Thoisy collection, vol. 31, no 380, there is a Protestant 'Project for a reunion of the two religions'. The 'Nouvelles ecclesiastiques' of 3 February 1685 notes that 'those of the *R.P.R.* propose articles': Bibliothèque Nationale, MS. Fr. 23,498, f. 9r. According to *Les larmes de J. Pineton de Chambrun* (Paris, 1854) pp. 117ff the Huguenots were waiting for the Assembly of the Clergy to suggest reforms in the Catholic cult. Daguesseau for his part had, through de Bagnols, requested the assembly to take such an initiative: see my *Louis XIV et les Protestants*, p. 84, n. 14.

49 The president of the commission was the archbishop of Auch, Hyancinthe de Serroni: see *Procès-verbal de l'assemblée du clergé de 1685 à Saint-Germain-en-Laye* (Paris, 1690) p. 35.

50 The text is in B.N., MS. Fr. 7057, ff. 94v–95r; and in the despatches of the Venetian ambassador: B.N., MS. Italien 1897, pp. 247–51.

51 Dated 11 July this became the subject of an edict of 23 August 1685: *Procès-verbal*, pp. 154–90; cf. Benoist, *Histoire de l'Edit de Nantes*, V, pp. 847ff. and (181).

52 *Procès-verbal*, p. 63ff.

53 The 'news at hand' of 23 June 1685 (E. Griselle, 'Avant et après la Révocation de l'Edit de Nantes', *Société de l'histoire du Protestantisme française, Bulletin historique et littéraire* (1907) p. 271) is confirmed by the

despatches of the nuncio Ranuzzi himself: see L. O'Brien, *Innocent XI and the Revocation of the Edict of Nantes* (Berkeley, 1930) p. 65; by the despatches of Cardinal d'Estrées to Louis XIV of 10, 17 and 24 July 1685, see A.A.E., C.P., Rome, vol. 294, ff. 168r, 177v–79r, 188r; by Louis' answer of 3 August 1685, ibid., f. 175v; and the letter of Abbé Servient of 14 August 1685, ibid., vol. 297, f. 191v. For echoes of the audiences see the Venetian dispatches of 20 and 27 June, 4, 11 and 18 July 1685 in B.N., MS. Italien 1897, ff. 185, 198, 208, 219, 227.

54 There is a version of 'Nouvelles ecclésiastiques' in a damaged, undated letter of Fouquet, B.N., MS. Fr. 23,498, f. 26. It should be noted that Fouquet, who was passionately opposed to the Jesuits, incriminated not only Maimbourg but the whole company. Cf. B.N., MS. Italien 1897, f. 184ff, despatch of 20 June 1685. On the chancellor's anti-Huguenot views see P. Blet, 'Le conseil du Roi et les protestants de 1680 à 1685', *Bibliothèque de l'Ecole des Chartes*, cxxx (1972) 159ff, and on his son's rivalry with the archbishop of Paris, Spanheim, *Relation de la Cour de France*, p. 248.

55 For the condemnation see *Extrait des registres de l'officialité de Paris*: B.N., Imprimés, E. 3572; a copy is appended to the despatch of 19 September 1685 in B.N., MS. Italien 1897, ff. 325ff. This measure was the result of a visit of the nuncio to Croissy; the Venetian ambassador reported on 1 August 1685 that Ranuzzi had been met with hard words, had been unable to learn the author, and had not dared to ask to see the king on the matter: B.N., MS. Italien 1897, ff. 239, 248ff.

56 A.A.E., C.P., Rome, vol. 297, f. 205r; Cf. O'Brien, *Innocent XI*, p. 66.

57 E. Benoist does not discuss the importance of this moment, contenting himself (*Histoire de l'Edit de Nantes*, iv, p. 709) with stating that he 'will later divulge the reasons which put so sudden an end to the Dagnesseau's negotiations'; cf. my *Louis XIV et les Protestants*, p. 84, n. 14.

58 L. L. Bernard, 'Foucault, Louvois and the Revocation of the Edict of Nantes', *Church History* (1956) 26–40, attributes all responsibility to Foucault.

59 See my *Louis XIV et les Protestants*, pp. 70–4, and n. 41 above.

60 J. Dubourdieu, *Lettres de quelques protestants pacifiques* (no place of publication, 1685) p. 1ff. For Aubert de Versé being of the same opinion, see my *Louis XIV et les Protestants*, p. 98, n. 32.

61 *Louis XIV et les Protestants*, p. 102, n. 54 and n. 47 above.

62 Ibid., p. 93. See also the letter of Mme de Maintenon to Noailles, 27 Dec 1695, in *Lettres*, ed. M. Langlois, iv (Paris, 1937) p. 479.

63 See my *Louis XIV contre Innocent XI* (Paris, 1949) p. 62ff.

64 Louvois, informed by the ambassador Rébenac, passed this on to his father on 17 September 1685: Rousset, *Histoire de Louvois*, iv, p. 21; cf. my *Louis XIV et les Protestants*, p. 105, n. 63.

65 Louis' efforts to gain Bavaria (see Dreyss (ed.) *Mémoires*, i, pp. 113, 236) had resulted in the treaty of 28 October 1670. Bavaria fought

172   *Louis XIV and Absolutism*

against France in the Nine Years War, but became France's ally in
the War of the Spanish Succession.

66 See his letters to the duc d'Estrées of 18 May and 1 June 1685:
A.A.E., C.P., Rome, vol. 295, ff. 226r, 252v, 253r; cf. his letter to
Cardinal d'Estrées of 13 June 1685: ibid., vol. 294, f. 86v. For the
duc d'Estrées reporting the pope's indifference to the news from
London, see ibid., vol. 295, ff. 205r, 301v, despatches of 10 April and
12 June 1685.

67 Monmouth raised his rebellion in June and was executed on 25 July.
In mid-May 1697 Leibniz informed Duke Ernst August of Hanover,
'It is certain that it was the death of the King of England which
encouraged France to take this strange resolution [i.e. the revocation]:
Allgemeiner politischer und historischer Briefwechsel, IV (Berlin, 1954)
p. 434.

68 For the English minister in Paris congratulating Harlay on the vote
on the 'four articles' see Martimort, *Le gallicanisme de Bossuet*, p. 505 n.,
522; my *Origines du Jansénisme*, III, p. 145, n. 1 and my *Louis XIV
contre Innocent XI*, p. 49, n. 223.

69 Cf. my *Louis XIV et les Protestants*, p. 105, n. 65.

70 'The Clergy does not insist on this at present': B.N., MS. Fr. 7044,
ff. 120, 122.

71 Gaultier de Saint-Blancard points out that, until the very end of the
summer, delays of six months, three years, even twelve years were
suggested: *Histoire apologétique*, I (Mainz, 1688) pp. 365–70, 390–9.

72 Benoist, *Histoire de l'Edit de Nantes*, v, p. 863ff asserts that these
measures are strongly anti-Huguenot, but in my opinion Rulhière is
right in interpreting them as typical of the anti-revocation sentiment
which for so long persisted at Versailles; cf. Foucault's *Mémoires*, ed.
F. Baudry (no place of publication, 1862) 125; *Mémoires de Noailles*,
ed. J. F. Michaud and J. J. F. Poujoulat (Paris, 1854) p. 10.

73 For these reports see e.g. the Venetian envoy's letter of 17 October
1685: B.N., MS. Italien 1897, ff. 357ff.

74 See Louis' letter to Cardinal d'Estrées of 10 August 1685: A.A.E.,
C.P., Rome, vol. 294, f. 185r. Note ibid., vol. 296, f. 142v, Louis'
letter to the duc d'Estrées of 27 September 1685, in which he speaks
of 'the glory of having succeeded in an enterprise which seemed
impossible to the king's predecessors'.

75 *Journal de Dangeau*, ed. A. Soulié *et al.*, 19 vols (Paris, 1854–60) I,
p. 218; *Mémoires de Sourches*, ed. De Cosnac *et al.*, 13 vols (Paris,
1882–93) I, pp. 303–7.

76 *Copie de L'Edit de Révocation de l'Edit de Nantes, tel qu'il avait été dressé par
le Conseil de Conscience et envoyé à feu Monsieur le Chancellier pour le sceller,
lequel obligea le Roi de le faire examiner de nouveau dans le Conseil, et de le
réformer dans la manière qu'il parait aujourd'hui*, 8 pp., a copy of which was
discovered by I. Noye in the Bibliothèque de l'Histoire du Protestantisme, R.1240.

77 See Louis' letter of 21 Sep 1685 in E. Esmonin, *Etudes sur la France du
XVIIe et XVIIIe siècles* (Paris, 1964) p. 360. Cf. the letters of pastor

Claude of 7, 21 Sep and 12 Oct printed in E. O. Douen, *La Révocation de l'Edit de Nantes à Paris*, I (Paris, 1894) p. 568ff.

78 See Louis' letter of 24 Sep in Esmonin, *Etudes sur la France*, p. 360; Dangeau, *Journal*, I, pp. 223, 236; the nuncio's letters of 17 Sep, 9 and 16 Oct printed in Gérin (ed.) p. 404; and those of the Venetian ambassador of 5, 19 and 26 Sep, B.N., MS. Italien 1897, ff. 305, 323, 332. See also Louis' letter to Cardinal d'Estrées of 8 Nov 1685, A.A.E., C.P., Rome, vol. 294, f. 336r.

79 Spanheim, *Relation de la Cour de France*, p. 182.

80 B.N., MS. Fr. 17,420, f. 140r.

81 See his letters of 2 and 3 Oct in Esmonin, *Etudes sur la France*, p. 360ff.

82 *Mémoires de Saint-Simon*, ed. A. M. de Boislisle, 43 vols (Paris, 1879–1930) VII, p. 410; cf. my *Louis XIV et les Protestants*, p. 107.

83 Louis' letters prove that the archbishop of Paris was present; see also Ph. Legendre, *La vie de P. du Bosc* (Rotterdam, 1694) p. 146. Legendre is alone in asserting that Père de la Chaise was present, but this is probable in view of his membership of the *Conseil de Conscience*. The chancellor was too ill to attend, but – since the edict carries the signature of Le Tellier and Colbert – the three other ministers (Louvois, Colbert de Croissy and Le Peletier) must have been present. Chateauneuf, secretary of state for the *R.P.R.*, must also have attended. As for Seignelay, the other secretary of state, it was he who on 19 October sent the edict to the chancellor, and to the *procureur-général* the *lettres de cachet* necessary for the registration of the edict. Cf. the letter from Le Tellier to Achille III de Harlay of 20 Oct 1685: B.N., MS. Fr. 17,420, f. 144r.

84 He became a member of the *Conseil des dépêches* (though without voting right) only in 1688 and of the *Conseil d'état* not till 25 July 1691: see Boislisle (ed.), *Mémoires de Saint-Simon*, IV, pp. 443, 469.

85 L. B. Proyart, *Œuvres complètes* (Paris, 1819) II, pp. 105–7. *Mémoires de F. T. de Choisy* (ed. M. F. A. de Lescure) II (no place of publication, 1888) pp. 175–7 differs, but it would seem that his account has been influenced by later happenings. For the danger of armed revolt see *Mercure galant*, Jan 1706, and my *Louis XIV et les Protestants*, p. 112, n. 7.

86 Written long after the event, his account tries to put responsibility for the revocation on Colbert towards whom the Le Tellier clan (to which he himself belonged) was hostile. Cf. L. André, *Deux mémoires historiques de Cl. Le Peletier* (Paris, 1906).

87 See Louvois' letters of 5 Mar and 8 Sep 1685: Rousset, *Histoire de Louvois*, III, pp. 474, 459.

88 Legendre confirms that the *Conseil* of 8 October 'was held for the purpose of deciding if the pastors should be confined between four walls': *Vie de P. du Bosc*, p. 146.

89 See *Mémoires de François Hébert*, ed. G. Girard (Paris, 1927) p. 55ff for the archbishop's views.

90 Legendre, *Vie de P. du Bosc*, p. 146; cf. Rulhière, *Eclaircissements historiques*, I, p. 151.

91 Esmonin, *Etudes sur la France,* p. 364; Rulhière, *Eclaircissements historiques,* II, p. 65. Public opinion in 1685 (for which see the newsletter of 24 Oct 1685 printed in Griselle, 'Avant et après la Révocation', p. 28) erroneously believed that there would be no change in respect of Huguenot marriages and burials.

92 Rousset, *Histoire de Louvois,* III, p. 477 n., and L. André, *M. Le Tellier et Louvois* (Paris, 1942) p. 308; cf. B.N., MS. Fr. 7044, ff. 170ff.

93 Benoist, *Histoire de l'Edit de Nantes,* v, p. 862; André, *M. Le Tellier,* p. 508 shows that Croissy and Chateauneuf had been forewarned by Louvois on 16 October.

94 B.N., MS. Fr. 17,420, f. 145r. According to a contemporary newsletter the premier président was summoned on the same date and the declaration was officially sealed and issued on the eighteenth: Griselle, 'Avant et après la Révocation', p. 27. For the declaration having been sent to the intendants in the evening of that day see *Mémoires de Foucault,* ed. F. Baudry, p. 136; Louis communicated it to his ambassador in Rome on the nineteenth: A.A.E., C.P., Rome, vol. 296, f. 181.

95 For Louis' answer of 20 October to the archbishop see Esmonin, *Etudes sur la France,* p. 362.

96 See Benoist, *Histoire de l'Edit de Nantes,* v, p. 904 and Douen, *La Révocation de l'Edit de Nantes,* I, p. 569.

97. For Louis' efforts to keep the dialogue with the Huguenots going see Esmonin, *Etudes sur la France,* p. 363: Louis' letter to the archbishop of Paris, 22 October; and Seignelay's letter to *procureur général* de Harlay of 23 October: B.N., MS. Fr. 17,420, f. 48r. For the change of course, since success was despaired of, see ibid., f. 149, Seignelay's letter of 28 October.

98 Neither Louis XIV nor Innocent XI were intransigent on the issue of Huguenots partaking of the wine at communion; but Louis – because of the position he had taken in respect of Rojas de Spinola – did not wish to demand this from the pope. For his part Innocent XI, while prepared to make this concession to Protestants in other countries, did not wish to do so for France where he feared a religious schism: see my *Louis XIV et les Protestants,* pp. 88 (and n. 28), 120.

99 This was particularly evident in the case of Oloron, Montauban and Lyon: see my *Louis XIV et les Protestants,* pp. 86, 119–22 and my *Correspondance de Fénelon,* III, (Paris, 1972) p. 53ff, letter of 28 Jan 1686. For the efforts of the bishop of Grenoble (Monseigneur Le Camus) at conciliation see *Mémoires de l'abbé Legendre,* ed. M. Roux (Paris, 1863) p. 67 n.; Esmonin, *Etudes sur la France,* pp. 362, 364.

100 For these alterations see Benoist, *Histoire de L'Edit de Nantes,* v, p. 847, corroborated by the contemporary printed document in B.N., Ld 176/539: the essence of the changes was to replace the word 'believe' with weaker terms such as 'confess' and 'testify'.

101 For a printed formula see B.N., MS. Joly de Fleury, 1679, f. 255.

102 Louis' letter of 20 November, Archives National, O^1 29, f. 509v; cf. Douen, *La Révocation de l'Edit de Nantes,* II, p. 756 and III, p. 402ff.

Seignelay seems to have been the driving force since he wished to avoid using the *dragonnades* on Parisian Protestants: see my *Louis XIV et les Protestants*, p. 121. That La Reynie was taken by surprise can be seen from his letter to *procureur général* de Harlay of 20 November, B.N., MS. Fr. 1,420, f. 159r.

103 See my *Louis XIV et les Protestants*, table and p. 135ff.

104 Ibid., p. 70, n. 137.

105 See Martimort, *Le gallicanisme de Bossuet*, table, and my *Louis XIV contre Innocent XI*, table; cf. above, note 54.

106 Spanheim, *Relation de la cour de France*, p. 248.

107 See my *Louis XIV et les Protestants*, p. 27, n. 66.

108 Ibid., p. 116, n. 33; see also above, note 89 ff.

109 This is the thesis of the Huguenot propagandists: as e.g. in Claude Brousson, *Etat des réformés de France*, 2nd ed. (The Hague, 1685) p. 81. Gaultier de Saint-Blancard in the sixth *Dialogue de Photin et d'Irénée* (Mainz, 1685) p. 349, uses the phrase 'the treaty between Henri IV and his subjects in respect of religion'. For Ancillon's view see above, n. 3.

110 Dreyss (ed.), *Mémoires*, ı, p. 228.

111 See his letter of 27 July 1680 in Michaud and Poujoulat, ıv, p. 471.

112 The grievances complained of in the *Dialogue de Photin et d'Irénée*, p. 346, are upheld by Abbé Legendre, pp. 62–3 who speaks of a 'destruction by degrees' which has left only 'a shadow of the Edict', and by Rulhière, *Eclaircissements historiques*, ı, p. 14; see also my *Louis XIV et les Protestants*, pp. 97–8.

113 Rulhière, *Eclaircissements historiques*, ı, p. 13 (cf. above, note 6).

114 For his attitude see Benoist, *Histoire de l'Edit de Nantes*, v, pp. 733, 787; *Mémoires de Legendre*, ed. M. Roux, p. 82; E. G. Léonard's article in *Revue Historique* (see above, note 1) p. 173 ff; cf. above, note 12.

115 See above, text, for 1643, 1652, 1669, for June 1680 (the edict) and 10 July 1682 (letter to the bishops).

116 Rousset, *Histoire de Louvois*, ııı, p. 433.

117 Such a change has been demonstrated by A. Dupront in the attitude of Cardinal Chigi (Pope Alexander VII): see his 'De la chrétienté à l'Europe', *Forschungen und Studien zur Geschichte des westfälischen Friedens* (Münster, 1965) ı, pp. 48–84.

118 See my *Louis XIV et les Protestants*, pp. 15–19, 93, n. 17.

119 There was a rumour on 10 November 1685 that this phrase would be explained in a new declaration: ibid., p. 128, n. 7.

120 Ibid., pp. 24ff and 67ff.

121 Blet, *Le clergé de France*, ıı, pp. 367ff, 378, 383, 388. It should be noted that at least from 1679 the requests of the clergy were in effect dictated by the ministry: see *Mémoires de l'abbé Legendre*, p. 62.

122 Rousset, *Histoire de Louvois*, ııı, p. 437ff.

123 Cf. Ranuzzi's despatch of 15 March 1689 in Latreille, *Société de l'histoire de Protestantisme français, Bulletin historique et littéraire* (1957) 236.

124 C. G. Picavet, cited ibid., p. 99, n. 38.

125 Ibid., pp. 49ff and 96; see also above, notes 33, 37, 40.

126 Ibid., p. 75, n. 163.
127 Ibid., p. 110 and Rulhière, *Eclaircissements historiques*, I, p. 182ff.
128 Ibid., p. 184.
129 Fr Puaux, 'De la responsabilité de la Révocation', *Revue Historique* (1885) 242.
130 See my *Louis XIV et les Protestants*, pp. 112–16.
131 The harsh judgements of Innocent XI, Vauban and Daguesseau (ibid., p. 45ff., 156 and 166 n.; cf. also above, note 46) are possibly less significant than later efforts of those responsible for the revocation to make contemporaries and posterity believe that they had disapproved of the Edict of Fontainebleau; e.g. the controller-general Le Peletier (see above, note 86) and the intendant Lamoignon de Bâville (see J. R. Armogathe and Ph. Joutard, 'Bâville et la guerre des Camisards', *Revue d'histoire et de philosophie religieuses* (1972) 62, 67).

9 Royal Administration in a Frontier Province: the Intendancy of Alsace under Louis XIV*

G. LIVET

Besides the *pays d'élection* and *pays d'état* usually recognised by historians of French institutions, the Ancien Régime in France might be understood better if one also recognised a third category, the frontier provinces. At that time the frontier was not so much a dividing line – demarcated by fortresses and fortified lines – as a zone of contact; and because of conquest, and royal policy, these provinces show a strange mixture of old institutions and new administrative realities. Alsace is a good example of this kind of province, and a study of it will also be of interest for our knowledge of the comparative institutions of France and the Holy Roman Empire. The essential agent of royal power, the intendant of justice, police and finance, was introduced there in 1643, and it was around this new institution that the complex play of the forces of change and those of conservatism took place. This interplay determined the administrative and social evolution of the province between 1634 – the time of 'the appeal of the towns to France' – and 1714, when the wars which had gone on almost continuously along the Rhine throughout Louis XIV's reign came to an end with the peace treaties of Rastadt and Baden.

I   FORCES MAKING FOR CHANGE

The intendancy of Alsace in these years was forged through a development of the status of the institution itself and by the continuing systematisation of its functions. These two closely

* Specially commissioned for this volume.

related aspects will serve as criteria for an explanatory analysis
of the different evolutionary periods, which will be examined
one by one: the creation of the intendancy during the Thirty
Years War, its extension after the treaties of Westphalia (1648),
the incorporation of Strasbourg (1681), the recognition of the
Rhine by the Treaty of Ryswick of 1697 as the 'frontier between
France and the Empire', and – finally – its consolidation within
the administrative system as well as in the new social, religious,
political, economic and provincial entities which were strongly
influenced by the absolute monarchy of Louis XIV.

1. *The army intendants and the indeterminate scope of administration*

Between 1634 and 1648 five intendants, or men with intendant
duties, followed each other in Alsace. The scope of administration
was not yet clear. The word intendancy has several meanings. It
can denote first of all those agents of the central government
called intendants of the army, who only concerned themselves
episodically with the province. No such appointment was made
until 1637, when Alsace was joined to Lorraine and the three
bishoprics (Metz, Toul and Verdun). In 1639 Alsace appeared
for the first time as an independent district; but after the capture
of Breisach and the death of Bernard of Saxe-Weimar there was
a reversion to an administrative and territorial dualism, which
lasted till the end of the Frondes. It can also denote commissary-
deputies charged with executing the court's orders and acting as
representatives of the king. These originated from various levels
of the government machine. Some, with the office of *maître des
requêtes*, were responsible to the council; others, military men or
clerics, combined authority in judicial and financial matters with
their ordinary duties. The latter ranked as secretaries and did not
have the powers of real intendants. Finally, persons of very different origins and standing exercised some of the functions of intendants: royal commissaries acted, in their capacity as extraordinary commissioners in a province under military occupation,
both as intendants of the army and provincial intendants, their
commissions putting them on a par with magistrates and
governors.

How successful were they? As they lacked any preliminary
training for their work some of them only came to terms slowly

with the complex traditions of Alsace : the end of the archducal (i.e. Austrian Habsburg) administrative system, the absence of accessible records, ignorance of the language – all these hampered their activities. Although there was no opposition from native judicial and financial officers, they came up against the regional supremacy of the governors of local fortresses who proved jealous of their prerogatives : their 'protection' of Alsace was a juridical fiction but a military reality. The followers of Bernard of Saxe-Weimar, led by the governor of Breisach, asserted their loyalty to the king but claimed that they were free to ignore his intendant. Also, despite the wide powers given them by their commissions, the commissioners found their duties limited to certain precise tasks : to look after the welfare of the garrisons and inhabitants, to take care of provisioning and to supervise the regular collection of contributions. It is hardly possible to talk of a genuine intendant administration when the intendant had no fixed place of residence, when there was no established procedure laid down, and no real impact on the province by the central power. The institution was therefore slow to break away from the intendant-of-the-army image. Its position and duties were still at an empirical stage.

2. *The annexation of Upper Alsace and the work of the Colberts*
After the signature of the Peace of Westphalia and the suppression of the Frondes the institution took on distinct characteristics and its scope increased. Alsace became the preserve first of the Colberts, under the protection of Mazarin, and then of the Le Telliers. Both families put their own creatures into this distant province, using it as a training school. After the death of de Baussan, which marked the end of the Weimarian and quasi-feudal transitional stage, the intendancy served as a useful apprenticeship for the two Colbert brothers, Jean-Baptiste and Colbert de Croissy. With Louis XIV's accession to personal power a distinct policy developed and fruitful exchanges were established between the province – reduced to Upper Alsace and a protectorate over the ten towns (*Décapole*) – and its administrators.

What did the Colberts learn in Alsace ? A keen sense of what mattered in the provinces, an essential for good government. Jean-Baptiste Colbert might have been able to develop his talents to the full without this, but it was in Alsace that he experienced

G

the daily cares of the people. His brother, Colbert de Croissy, did not hide from him his difficulties with the governors – Comte d'Harcourt, a *grand seigneur* with inordinate pretensions, and the duc de Mazarin, who thought of nothing but religion – nor his clashes with the king's lieutenant, Marquis de Saint-Geniès, who was intent on making himself master of Breisach. He also provided information of an administrative kind about the exercise of power and the obstacles that it met, the role of the clerks, the weakness of the revenues, and the appointment of *subdélégués*. Political issues evoked reports on relations with the powerful Catholic clergy, with the proud nobility who had been pandered to in the past by the House of Austria, and with the towns which were intent on maintaining their privileges. It was also through the Alsace intendant that the misery of the countryside, still prostrate from the sufferings of war, was brought directly to the attention of the king. Colbert de Croissy, though he would have denied it himself, together with the future *contrôleur général*, were the best spokesmen for the people of the province; and one can assume that those measures which Colbert inspired in Louis XIV after 1661 might not have seen the light of day but for the reports from Ensisheim.

Jean-Baptiste Colbert for his part influenced the province through the instructions he gave his brother : in these we can discern the spirit of Richelieu's *Testament politique*. Croissy had a quick and hot temper but he was loyal in carrying out his instructions, and in Alsace he laid the base for a new tradition which combined the best of archducal and Weimarian experience with the maxims of the French monarchy. The sovereign council was solemnly established in 1657 and assumed control of the province in the king's name. The general outlines of the institution of the intendancy, which had been sketched by d'Oysonville and de Baussan, were now filled in. The financial administration was strictly regulated. Customs duties were defined and tax farming of crown land introduced. Thanks to ceaseless police activity, backed up by frequent tours of inspection, the roads became safer and order was re-established in the countryside. The cession of the archducal lands to Cardinal Mazarin gave the royal administrator – manager of his excellency's domains – much experience in economic matters. The publication followed of the great edicts for reconstruction of the province in the administrative, religious, judicial and economic fields. The arrival of numerous immigrants, especially Swiss, caused problems; while the general decline in agricultural prices and the great food crises, for example of 1637 and 1661, did not make the royal administrator's task any easier.

At this time, however, and through the work of Jean-Baptiste Colbert, the broad lines of future policy were laid down: the treaties of Westphalia with their differing German and French interpretations[1] had to be resolved sooner or later. The Austrian representative at Münster, Volmar, had said that 'the stronger will win'. In the event France proved the stronger, though there was some delay in putting the French interpretation into effect; partly due to the Frondes but also partly due to the good relations established between France and the elector of Mainz through the League of the Rhine. A first step along the road to success was the enthronement in Strasbourg in 1663 of a bishop well-intentioned towards France, Franz Egon von Fürstenberg.

With his military base and bridge over the Rhine at Breisach and his administrative centre at Ensisheim, the old archducal capital, the intendant enjoyed in this period a nice balance between his personal power and his statutory duties. Although appearing to be dependent on the ministers at the centre, the intendant, who had diplomatic and political as well as administrative duties, was able to influence the way provincial unity developed. Colbert de Croissy's departure temporarily destroyed this balance. His successors were lesser men: Charles Colbert was maintained entirely through being in favour at court and Poncet de La Rivière's appointment was due to his father's services The Alsace intendancy therefore suffered an eclipse which was made worse because of differences between the intendancy and the *Grand Bailli* of Hagenau. The rivalry between the two institutions harmed the smooth running of the king's government. It was at this time that the great Condé, during a tour of inspection of the Alsace fortresses, referred to the province as 'a plough with a badly harnessed horse'. The outbreak of the Dutch War in 1672, however, necessitated a concentration of powers and ended this period of equivocation and caution towards the German princes and the towns of the *Décapole*, where Colmar was the centre of resistance.

3. *The forming of the province of Alsace and the seizure of Strasbourg (1681)*

The appointment of Jacques de La Grange in 1673 inaugurated a period of expansion for the intendancy. La Grange was neither a *maître des requêtes* nor a councillor of state. A commissioner for war, who had been noticed by Louvois, he became the devoted and skilful agent of the secretary of state for war when the latter's department took over Alsace. As with Colbert de Croissy he was given power by stages, different commissions extending his original brief. The frequent journeys of the king and his minister to the province testify to the direct impact of the central government.

By 1698 the Alsace intendancy had changed in two ways. First, it had been enlarged by successive incorporations of the territories of Lower Alsace as far as the river Queich and had, by its establishment in Strasbourg, been brought into easier communication with Versailles. Secondly, its administrative organisation had been modified as the experienced Louvois introduced into Alsace his own ways of acting, quick, brutal and intent on immediate and tangible results. The intendant acted as Louvois' agent: he collected information on disputed matters and helped prepare for the *Réunions* which covered not only Alsace but the whole area of the French frontier in the north east, the Saar and Franche-Comté. At the same time, however, the intendant also carried out orders: the minister's letters were short and to the point, his memorials brief, and the opportunity for independent initiative was restricted to the manner in which the orders were obeyed. Louvois knew how to mix absolute inflexibility in defending the monarchy's military and religious interests with intelligent concern for the economic and financial needs of the province, and especially for the town of Strasbourg. He helped its recovery and fulfilled as easily the role of a supreme master, submissive only to the king, as that of an attentive tutor. During the Nine Years War the needs of the military also stamped the pattern of the province's economic life. Ties with the Empire were broken, though smuggling persisted on both sides of the Rhine and allowed the Swiss towns – especially Basle – to profit appreciably.

The Treaty of Ryswick which set the seal on Strasbourg's incorporation into France was soon followed by the departure of the intendant La Grange. His recall by the secretary of state for war, Barbezieux (Louvois' son and successor), seems to have been due to his lack of support at court : unlike the *maîtres des requêtes*, La Grange did not have the backing of this powerful body of men and he remained isolated. An effective and creative administrator, though somewhat negligent in financial matters, he had been irreplaceable during the *Réunions* and the Nine Years War; but fell when he was no longer indispensable, despite his personal reputation and experience.

4. *The testing time and the War of the Spanish Succession*
With the intendants La Fond and above all Le Peletier de La Houssaye the functions of the institution created empirically by La Grange were brought into shape and defined. The links with the ministers were relaxed. La Houssaye, a near relation of the *grand commis* d'Arguesseau, was a *maître des requêtes* and became a councillor of state. La Grange's long period in office had strengthened the intendancy. The commissioner who had never been off horseback was succeeded by a static administrator who had secretaries and clerks working for him as well as several *subdélégués* to carry out his orders. Benefiting from this inheritance, La Houssaye exercised to the full powers which, while remaining wide, were gradually systematised. Vauban remarked that 'the perfect engineer had at one and the same time to be carpenter, mason, architect, artist, political orator, soldier and good officer and, moreover, to be kind-hearted, well-disposed and very experienced'. These requirements can be applied to the provincial intendants with even greater justification. His powers demanded knowledge of basic questions. He had not only to be capable of mastering general ideas, as did de Baussan, but also of acting as a technician who could supervise and delegate the details of assessments and supplies to his departments while being enough of a statesman to propose bold solutions for the problems of the hour to his minister. He could use his initiative, but the loneliness of responsibility was also his.

The administration created, or maintained, distinct but not rival powers around the intendant. In the absence of the governor – the duc de Mazarin was kept away from the province – the commander-in-chief of Alsace had a prestige denied to him in other areas of France : Montclar had actively promoted the

Réunions; Huxelles possessed the confidence of Louis XIV and Mme de Maintenon. During La Fond's intendancy it was Huxelles who undertook the task of general co-ordination and, after some clashes on La Houssaye's arrival, he stayed in the forefront of government. In the fields of justice the intendant had to reckon with the powers of the sovereign council. The change in the *présidial* of this tribunal set up at Ensisheim, and its reversion in 1679 to a superior court of justice, reveals the special character of this court; less costly to set up than a *parlement* and more tractable through the choice of the magistrates commissioned, the sovereign council was from its very inception a political rather than a judicial institution. But after 1698, when it was moved to Colmar, the sovereign council was transformed by the introduction of the sale of offices; it now enjoyed real independence and played an important part in the development of French law, providing the necessary judicial framework for the province. Yet, though it paved the way for future influence, it was at this time in no position to prevent the intendancy's immediate policies. In the financial sphere the intendant's powers also remained all but absolute. The old provincial estates no longer met and the supervision of the nearest financial department (at Metz) remained remote and theoretical, Alsace being one of the provinces directly subject to tax. The province benefited from progressive policies in the economic sphere even in the seventeenth century but did not escape hardships. As a frontier province it had to provision the troops which defended Alsace and were deployed in Germany. The fortresses of Strasbourg, Neuf-Brisach, Fort Louis, Landau and the Lauter lines played an important part in the many exhausting wars of Louis XIV's reign. The crisis of the terrible winter of 1709 brought suffering for the civilian population as well as for the soldiers. The treaties of Rastadt and Baden in 1714 ensured that Alsace and Strasbourg stayed within the French community : the French interpretation of 1648 was not to be reversed.

Administrative life evolved along the triple path of the development of the intendant's personal position, the regulation of rights which had grown up empirically, and respect for local customs. The concentration of powers granted by successive commissions would have proved a hollow formula if it had not corresponded to established facts. The individuality of the region created certain practices and French bureaucracy imposed others. A kind of customary legislation developed which accommodated both the forces making for centralisation and those making for decentralisation. The intendant saw to the suppression of abuses and used his regulating power to clarify the new decrees and edicts which the central government added to existing laws. The towns and the countryside were subject to administrative control through the ubiquitous police who saw to the maintenance of public order. By systematising his powers and developing administrative machinery, the technical efficiency of which had been tested in other provinces, the intendant acted as a veritable force for change, modifying the old order and absorbing the traditional strengths of Alsace. Like the eyes and ears of Darius and the *scrinia* of Augustus and Tiberius which symbolised the supremacy of the civil power, the intendants can be compared to the lifelike scribe on exhibition in the Louvre : the hub or armature at the centre of the modern as of the ancient state.

II THE FORCES OF CONSERVATISM OR OF RESISTANCE: THE REPUBLICAN SPIRIT

I will not enlarge on the town of Strasbourg, Monseigneur, which you have visited several times. Its inhabitants are still gripped by the spirit of republicanism and their hope of returning to their original state has not, as yet, been completely extinguished; they still need more time to appreciate monarchical government . . . they are a little more used to it in the other towns of Alsace.

These lines, written by a member of the duke of Burgundy's retinue in 1703, confirm Jacques de La Grange's statement in an earlier period that 'the government of Strasbourg is too republican'. A little later La Houssaye had noted that 'the magistracy of Strasbourg has great difficulty in believing that it has done more than change protectors. . . . Their attitude is very awkward and, if we allowed it to persist, all business would become a matter of bartering.' He added the shrewd comment : 'Expressions of respect, zeal and affection for His Majesty are common enough, but those of obedience are rare.'

These quotations illustrate the special problems of French administrators in Alsace. Its frontier position encouraged the survival of old traditions from the time of the Austrian archdukes (as Charles Colbert once said : They wish 'to follow in everything the example of the Archdukes') and also of Imperial ones, such as appeals to the Chamber at Speyer or to the Aulic Council. Moreover, it also limited royal action, religious as well as political, and subjected economic matters not only to the many and pressing demands of war but also to the more discrete and complex demands of diplomacy.

1. *The importance of diplomacy*
Diplomacy was necessary above all in respect of the town of Strasbourg; but throughout the province there was a need to counteract by diplomatic means a mentality which brought the risk (far greater than that of the distance involved and the remoteness of the capital) of checking the development, if not the introduction, of the essentials of absolute monarchy. In 1648 the cession of Alsace to France was neither complete nor immediate : the terms of the Peace of Westphalia authorised the transfer of sovereignty but at the same time limited it. The capitulation of Strasbourg, the edicts of the *Réunions*, the special letters-patent which followed, and the various treaties concluded with various potentates, including the bishop of Strasbourg, had similar effects. Diplomacy therefore laid down the law for the administration.

It was not till the treaties of Ryswick (1697) and Baden (1714) that international law recognised the complete cession of the province of Alsace; by then the French interpretation of the Treaty of Münster had triumphed completely.

2. *The law of 'territorial superiority': the territories of previous and new domination*
The law of political development in the mosaic of Alsace was territorial superiority. If the lords and the towns thought little of the ties which united them so tenuously to the Empire, they proved very attached to their own traditions. In distinguishing between sovereign and useful rights the monarchy refrained from generalising. Each case was treated separately on the basis of certain guiding principles : (a) to keep what was in use, to destroy nothing *a priori* and to maintain as much as possible the façade the people knew; (b) to use the existing system, adapt it in the way desired, correcting it sometimes, often changing parts of it,

and always controlling it : in this way the administrative revolution was effected secretly and in depth; (c) to change men rather than institutions; to employ those natives won over by a show of confidence in them and to avoid bringing in non-essential personnel from the interior of the kingdom; (d) never to condone scandal or abuses and to maintain free access to the intendant, to the king and his council.

These measures and the prevalent spirit of compromise explain the heterogeneous appearance of the edifice. Indeed the historian must be well acquainted with the original architecture to understand the lines of its exterior. Some privileges were continued, such as the tax due to the *Grand Bailli*, the *Steuergeld* or *Schirmgeld*. The privileges of towns remained, as is evidenced by the fact that in 1789 they petitioned their then protector, the duc de Choiseul, to have their own privileges maintained. The *baillis* might be thought to have kept excessive powers : they dispensed justice, presided over the drawing up of tax rolls, saw to it that taxes were collected and sent these to the king's collectors. As councillor Goezman said, 'The customs of the Empire were maintained in Alsace'. These remarks could also be applied to the regents and magistrates who were allowed to keep their privileges, even though the provincial estates had disappeared at the same time as the petty courts in the villages : here professional jurists replaced the assessors who had customarily had civil and criminal cases referred to them for trial. While keeping the notables – municipal technicians and active *seigneurs* – involved in public duties, the monarchy intended to suppress all elements of opposition or even of simple dissent. But it thus also destroyed a means of control at various levels of the bureaucratic hierarchy and deprived itself of knowledge of public opinion. The maintenance of the traditional façade brought with it the danger of hiding the new administrative reality from the people, while the institutions – seigneurial or municipal – which had been created formed a screen separating the king from his subjects. The Imperial tunic could still be seen beneath the cloak, made up of bits and pieces of monarchy.

3. *Catholic crusade and Protestant resistance*

The Peace of Westphalia had established mutual toleration between the Catholic and Lutheran states by law. The Lutheran

G*

magistracy of Strasbourg did agree to return the town's cathedral to the Catholics, but with this exception Alsace seems to have escaped religious persecution. In fact, the Revocation of the Edict of Nantes was never imposed openly in the province and any anti-Lutheran legislation in Alsace presupposed, for various reasons, voluntary conversion.

Although conversion was voluntary, political inducements and administrative pressures can be found : the alternating of Catholics and Lutherans within the magistracy, the equal position of the two religions which was decreed for Protestant churches as soon as there were seven Catholic families in a parish. Jesuit and Capucin activity was intense and often decisive. But after 1698 there was some relaxation in respect of Calvinists also, although toleration was not extended to Anabaptists or to Jews. On the Protestant side an autonomous organisation persisted. It did not operate in a diaspora of cells as inside France, but in organised groups under seigneurial or municipal authority. The secularisation of lands, carried out at the time of the Reformation, was respected. The consistories, where divines and laymen met, stayed supreme for temporal and spiritual matters. Appeals against sentences were not transferred to a superior authority but from one consistory to another. Recruitment of clergy was provided by the University of Strasbourg which was allowed to keep its privileges under the supervision of a royal *préteur*. The maintenance of a powerful Lutheran university on the banks of the Rhine, loyal both to the doctrine of St Paul and, at least in theory, also to its sovereign, the Most Christian King, is symptomatic of the religious position in Alsace.

Two prelates shared Catholic spiritual authority in Upper and Lower Alsace. One, the bishop of Strasbourg, remained an Imperial prince with a diocese which stretched also along the right bank of the Rhine; the other, the bishop of Basle, had his seat at Porrentruy, a town which had not submitted to the French king's authority : in 1662 he had refused to appoint a vicar-general to Ensisheim. The sovereign was unable to control either the elections to the episcopal sees of Strasbourg and Basle or the appointments to benefices in the monasteries of Alsace; nor could the 1516 *concordat* be introduced into the province which remained subject to the German *concordat*. Despite his attempts in 1661 and 1700 Louis XIV was unable to prevail on the pope to grant him an *indult* for Alsace; diplomatic activity and administrative pressure were necessary at every election. Forewarned by constant disputes between the bishop of Basle and the House of Austria, the French monarchy introduced the procedure of appeal by writ of error into the province, tried to prevent the appointment of priests of foreign extraction, and did its utmost to create an indigenous clergy. It did not, however, act forcefully enough to achieve decisive results. Control of the clergy was a matter of great importance for the monarchy at a time when the parish priests were the leaders of the rural society. Religion primed politics, but it appears that Louis XIV and his ministers expected too much from the election of a well-intentioned bishop and did not take into account that the majestic façade of the Catholic hierarchy did not, by and large, coincide with the feelings and needs of the parish priests who were in closest contact with the faithful.

4. *A province 'to all intents and purposes outside France'*

Alsace was one of the provinces which were 'to all intents and purposes outside France', offering a wide breach in the mercantilist fortress. This resulted from the actual geographical and economic position of the province. Astride the great road stretching from Italy to the Low Countries through the Rhine valley, Alsace owed its prosperity to the carriers who, after loading up at Strasbourg, made their way to Switzerland. If this trade were disrupted and customs posts placed on the bridge at Kehl, the carriers and merchants would be provoked into deserting the route through Alsace and moving to the other side of the Rhine to unload their goods in Baden. But how could the province be allowed to stay outside the defensive commercial system that the monarchy had set up on the frontiers of the kingdom? Colbert's creation of the 'five great farms' in 1664 (the first step towards a much more comprehensive protective project) aimed at establishing a single import and export tariff and was a rational concept which satisfied the requirements of a minister intent on uniformity. Artois, Flanders, Dauphiné and Brittany were not at first included in the tariff of 1664: they were provinces 'considered foreign'. One ought perhaps to add 'foreign to the tariff of 1664'; though it would be more correct to call them 'provinces with local rights' instead of 'provinces to all intents and purposes outside France'. The latter is an ambiguous expression especially if used in a non-fiscal sense. The application of the 'outside' concept to Alsace was complex. In wartime foreign trade was subject to a toll at the bridge at Kehl, and at all times some duties were levied on various categories of goods at the frontier posts. Everything passing through Upper Alsace still paid the old tolls levied by the arch-dukes at a tariff rate fixed by Colbert de Croissy in 1663. A novel idea, first applied to Strasbourg, was that of a free river port on the model of free maritime ports; but the change made the town seem like a fortress besieged by the activities of crown financiers, while the provincial administration intervened whenever it saw fit. The intendant now appeared under a double guise : he was the agent for the monarchy's political and financial policy, yet he remained 'patron of Strasbourg's commerce' – the splendid title which the guild of city merchants had bestowed on La Houssaye.

5. *Bourgeois resistance and the new social hierarchies*

The Peace of Westphalia laid down that personal privileges and legal status should be maintained in Alsace as they existed at the time of cession. Undoubtedly the social problems of the province could not be solved by means of diplomacy, but diplomacy was extensively used in attempts to solve them. Alsace had its own rules deriving from feudal law, notably those relating to the *seigneurie* : the reversion of fiefs to their overlords in the absence of direct male heirs; provision for investitures which restricted the rights of creditors and only allowed the transfer of freehold land; marriages free from the loss of noble rights and privileges; and, for certain families, the indivisibility of property for which the eldest son alone did homage to the overlord. Despite some isolated attempts Alsace refused to accept that law of 'no land without a master' which was generally admitted in the interior of the kingdom. The bourgeois class similarly stuck to old customs : citizenship brought with it important privileges. The bourgeoisie of Colmar, Strasbourg and Hagenau considered themselves the equals of the nobles whom they had long since stripped of political power in their towns. The peasants owned their land but it was divided into a multiplicity of plots and was heavily burdened by various charges. Estates owned by absentees were numerous; many vineyards, fields, meadows, woods and manor houses were owned by the bourgeoisie and testify to the accuracy of the picture drawn by the elder Brentel in his *Officium beatae Mariae Virginis* of 1647.

The balance which had existed initially between the bourgeoisie and the nobility tended to shift through the agency of the French intendancy. An essential trait of monarchical society was the importance given to the *noblesse*. While in Alsace there were numerous shades of distinction within the bourgeoisie itself, in France the only one which counted was the difference between gentlemen and commoners. To Versailles the local customs of Alsace seemed strange and spurious. The reactions of the ladies of the court during Louis XIV's progresses reveal a determination to have the supremacy of the nobility recognised, and the king's entourage set the tone for the province. Nobility brought profit as well as honour. Through exemption from taxation, except for personal contributions, the Alsatian nobleman was now assured of a permanent benefit denied to the bourgeois.

The attitude of the monarchy affected all social classes. In Colbert de Croissy's time the monarchy had tended to follow its traditional line of reducing the power of the nobles and of limiting their jurisdiction over the peasants as regards justice, finance and police. Then comes a second period – very noticeable under La Houssaye – when the monarchy seemed inclined to favour the nobility (especially its leading members, the princes and other great landlords), whom it needed to control the flat country of Alsace. It tended therefore to ignore the rural masses who had to wait till the French Revolution to reach political maturity and have their importance in society recognised. The bourgeoisie was also affected by the monarchy. At first the great majority of the Protestant bourgeoisie turned in on its own traditions and customs, entering into only the most necessary official relations with the new power, avoiding private contact and fearing the billeting of troops. But later on they began to succumb to the temptation of office and participation in royal business. Office brought tax exemptions and made entry into the nobility easier. Office was, however, reserved for the Catholic sector of bourgeois society. On the other hand business became the preserve of the Lutherans thanks to the perpetually insolvent monarchy's need for financial help; among the Alsatian financiers of Louis XIV's reign one need only mention Dietrich. Louvois' brutal policy of conversion was resisted, but a Protestant alliance with the new power – especially with the intendancy – came about in the world of banking and industry : Protestant capital was invested in mines and ironworks and this led to concessions and privileges of various kinds.

In this way a new social class was born in Alsace, one expert in the art of administering cities and people to its own advantage. It provided a permanent following for the monarchy outside the administrative machine. It had its experienced leaders, the royal *préteurs* and *syndics* of Strasbourg and the big towns, the Obrechts, Klinglins, Hatzels and Dietremanns; its subalterns, the *subdélégués* like Noblat de Belfort and the *baillis* like Oberlin de Benfeld; its non-commissioned officers, the registrars, attorneys, secretaries, copyists and interpreters who ensured future recruits; and its irregulars, the bankers and university professors of the Lutheran faith who at the very least flirted with authority. In this way both townsmen and countrymen were linked with the monarchy. This class, of very varied origins, was distinguished by two qualities : a Protestant core, and bilingualism in German and French. As there was no general public education, a knowledge of French strengthened positions acquired through birth and money and helped to confirm the ascendancy of the bourgeois over the peasant.

The monarchy responded to the various paradoxes it found in Alsace by a series of compromises. Despite its absolutist principles it allowed intermediate bodies to persist in the province; intent on religious uniformity, it became in Alsace Lutheran and Calvinist but not Anabaptist; while wanting a mercantilist system, it permitted the great stream of north–south trade to pass through a 'province to all intents and purposes outside France'. This policy of compromise and of tolerating the traditions of the country (which, as in other French frontier provinces, can be traced back to military requirements and diplomatic contingencies) led to a productive alliance with the local notables but to some extent also helped to keep the 'republican spirit' alive. It might be debated how far the administration developed by the monarchy in Alsace was at the mercy of the following it had created.

III THE FRONTIER PROVINCE : A DEFINITION AND A POLICY OF 'LEAVING THE CUSTOMS OF ALSACE ALONE'

In 1715, at the death of Louis XIV, the Alsatian balance-sheet shows how the forms of absolute monarchy and the medieval tradition of the Holy Roman Empire had merged. The tendency toward integrating the province into the kingdom – developed via the powers of justice, police and finance given to the intendancy – had an effect on the 'republican spirit' intent on preserving traditional privileges. The conquered province had become a frontier province: the absolutist demand for assimilation had given way to a policy of compromise. This success in the creation of new values, tending towards the transformation of institutions, is explicable by the ability of the protagonists on both sides and by the dynamism of two main ideas: that of unity based on considerations of security and that of the prestige of the monarchy, asserted by intellectual rather than by military means.

Security first of all. The transformation of Europe and the appearance of powerful military monarchies confirmed the new role of frontier regions, which changed from places where peoples were privileged to come into contact with each other into battle-fields for hostile forces. Control of routes became a precondition of power. The devastation of the Thirty Years War period had been a traumatic experience for Alsace: periodic invasion had been the price paid for political fragmentation. The monarchy of Louis XIV had to ensure the safety of the province and to defend the eastern frontier. This task was undertaken by the great generals, but also by the intendant and his helpers.

Chamillart wrote to La Houssaye when Landau was captured: 'The King owes the success of this campaign to you. You well deserve that he should show how satisfied he is with you.' Jacques de La Grange was praised with similar words when Freiburg was captured by Crequi. From 1642 d'Oysonville was actively employed in supplying Turenne's army. The two functions of army intendant and provincial intendant had become inseparable. In peacetime the royal administrator worked with future battles in mind. The intendant knew full well the cost of the extra-ordinary effort needed to ensure victory. La Houssaye painted a striking picture of the zeal of the people of Alsace: 'An infinite number of sappers immediately repaired to the siege of Kehl and to the works at Huningue and Fort Louis . . . the ploughman, as though on manœuvres, made his horses double their step . . . the inhabitants were tireless in relieving each other in defending the Rhine.'

How far did the cereal crises, which caused so much suffering towards the end of the reign, contribute to the birth of a new consciousness through an intimate alliance between the people and an administration bent on minimising distress? The evidence available seems to cut both ways. Because of the proximity of the frontier any loss in the monarchy's power would affect it nationally and have dangerous local repercussions. But, without the rural or urban masses always being fully aware of this, common distress and suffering tended to produce a deep unity tempered by the spirit of common resistance to France's external enemies.

The wars thus appear to have been a melting-pot for particularism. Various institutions bear witness to a desire for unity long before the French period : the *Décapole* in which the ten towns came together,[2] and the estates of Upper and Lower Alsace which met intermittently. Strasbourg and Mülhausen had remained outside the *Décapole* and the estates had proved to be impotent and impermanent. The idea of defending the frontier – of the province as well as of the realm – proves the efficacy of monarchical effort.

This concept was presented as rooted in a distant past. 'It would not be out of place to remark that Alsace was formerly part of France', Obrecht had commented. La Grange recalled 'that the town of Strasbourg was built by the Romans 2000 years ago'. Scholars emphasised old traditions and politicians magnified them to give French ascendancy the necessary perspective and patina of time to increase its prestige. The ties between the kingdom and the province were from the first non-material ones. The magistracy of Colmar wrote to the minister à *propos* one of its first governors : 'You know, Monsieur, the strength of the people's love and what it is to have won their affection.' The complex sentiments and interests making up public feeling can only with difficulty be reduced to cartesian formulae; nonetheless it appears that Louis XIV's monarchy brought to the Rhine the new ways of thinking implied in *Le Discours de la Méthode*. At the end of the reign the results were not yet striking. Language differences did not make for easy understanding of abstract matters : the theatre, fashion and education only affected a limited public in this French province with its German dialect. To reach Strasbourg the influence of Versailles still went through Frankfurt and the Rhineland towns. But the administrative spirit which developed in Alsace was also inspired by classic rules of clarity and precision. Moreover, as the desire for lucidity and truth had animated such Alsace humanists as Sebastian Brant and Beatus Rhenanus in their fight against medieval scholasticism centuries ago, there was a native tradition with which the French example could interact. In time, the population could see the advent of the new spirit in the sober lines of the civil and military edifices, in the language of the decrees of the sovereign council and in the orders of the intendancy.

In the seventeenth century the political concept cannot be separated from the sciences and literature, for it found a common merit in both : moderation in everything. Huxelles wrote to Puysieulx, 'We must avoid using the King's power too much, for people who love their liberty easily resist what they believe interferes with it.' After the first offensives – and the dual confusion of spiritual and temporal matters and of the impossible and the possible which characterised the anti-Protestant struggle – royal policy developed in a way more suited to the realities of Alsace : the absolute monarchy itself set limits to its power in the province. Monarchical centralisation did not mean uniformity throughout the kingdom. Its guideline was to leave the province all privileges compatible with the king's sovereignty. Louis XIV, who symbolised the continuity of this activity, said so when he sent La Houssaye to Strasbourg. This concept of national unity, which largely accorded with the immediate and distant demands of a centralised monarchy, relied on the king's leading representatives in the provinces; it found support in loyalty to the monarchy and was justified by the special position of the frontier provinces within the national community.[3]

Amid the din of battle, convoys and manufacturing activities the intendancy of Alsace represented values, was a symbol of order and the creator of a new environment. By its very moderation it is an achievement of that classical spirit which reached the height of perfection in the eighteenth century when peace reigned along the Rhine.[4]

NOTES

1 For a brief explanation of these interpretations see R. Hatton, *Europe in the Age of Louis XIV* (London, 1969) p. 92ff. and authorities there cited.

2 The *Décapole*, the *Zehnstädtebund* of 1354, consisted of the towns of Münster (Munster), Weissenburg (Wissembourg), Hagenau (Haguenau), Rosheim, Oberehnheim (Obernai), Schlettstadt (Sélestat), Kaysersberg, Turkheim, Colmar and Mülhausen (Mulhouse). In 1510 Landau was included, to replace Mülhausen which had become part of the Swiss cantons.

3 See my 'Louis XIV et les provinces conquises. Etat des questions et remarques de méthode', *XVIIe Siècle* (1952) 481–507, which defines the role of Flanders, Franche-Comté, Roussillon and the Lorraine bishoprics of Metz, Toul and Verdun in the French monarchy. See also: R. Dion, *Les frontières de la France* (Paris, 1947); Owen Lattimore, 'The Frontier in History', *Relazioni* of the International Congress of the Historical Sciences at Rome (1955) vol. I, pp. 103–38; G. Zeller, *Les Temps Modernes*, I and II, in 'Histoire des relations internationales', ed. P. Renouvin (Paris, 1953, 1955).

4 These ideas are discussed more fully in my *L'intendance d'Alsace sous Louis XIV, 1648–1715* (Paris, 1956). For a more recent treatment, with bibliographical references to works which have appeared since 1956, see my chapters VII and IX of *Histoire de l'Alsace*, in 'Univers de la France', ed. P. Wolff (Toulouse, 1970) and my chapters IX, X and XI in *Documents de l'histoire de l'Alsace*, same series (Toulouse, 1972).

Part III

ECONOMIC AND
FINANCIAL MATTERS

10 Fiscalism and Public Opinion under Louis XIV*

J. MEUVRET

In the seventeenth century certain conceptions inherited from the medieval past were still a living force. By tracing their development we can estimate their scope and importance. One such conception was that in normal times the king should be able to live off the revenues of his 'domain'. But what had become of the 'royal domain' by the seventeenth century? Originally it had been easy enough to define; it comprised the lands owned by the king and the income he drew from those of which he was immediate lord. But as time went on the royal power had extended its area of operation and gathered in strength. The domainial revenues had come to include an extremely wide variety of taxes.[1] Nevertheless, from the old idea that any revenue from a source other than the domain was in itself abnormal, there survived the view that any new tax could only be temporary.

Another question connected to this was that of the consent of the taxpayers. From the fourteenth century onwards certain taxes had been approved by assemblies, the 'Estates' made up of representatives of the three orders of society – Clergy, Nobility and Third Estate – either in the Estates-General for the kingdom as a whole, or more usually in the provincial estates composed of deputies from a single province. In actual fact for a long time already the monarchy had been creating new taxes, or extending the area in which old ones were levied, without the least consent from an assembly and even without opposition. Yet on almost every occasion when this occurred the preambles of royal edicts were full of excuses. The needs of the moment were invoked, but at the same time, more or less explicitly, there was an undertak-

* Specially commissioned for this volume.

ing to abolish the new tax as soon as circumstances should have changed. Even in the later seventeenth century this was still the accepted principle, and the way that it was disregarded in practice by the government did not overcome a reluctance to abandon it even among those who were the most devoted to the king's service. Vauban's *Plan for a Capitation*, which anticipated the tax established under that name in 1695, allowed no doubt on this point:

> What appears to me most essential in setting up this poll tax is to find a means of getting the public to understand that His Majesty only intends to make use of it until peace is made, and then he will restore matters to their former state, together with every possible measure of relief that he can add. This so much concerns his honour and his conscience that I can find no words strong enough to express it.[2]

In fact, during the long process of extending the royal domain to all the provinces and reducing the whole realm to obedience, the king had sometimes got his way by force but just as often by negotiation. The result had been a mass of compromises. Sometimes, to gain acceptance for certain innovations he had had to limit their extent; dividing in order to rule, he had granted to some what he had refused to others. On other occasions, he would grant a reduction of one tax to compensate for an increase in another. These partial or total exemptions formed so many distinctive types of government. Hence nothing varied more widely than fiscal institutions from place to place and according to social category. It can be said that their ruling principle was the exemption provided by privilege.

For ourselves, the notion of privilege contravenes that of equality before the law and is tainted with injustice. But in old France, as more generally in old Europe, it was conceived as being based on contracts which bound the monarchy. Respect for privilege raised the question of faith in royal promises, often solemnly and explicitly proclaimed. The attempts made to uphold privileges were for a long time part and parcel of a larger obsession: that of placing rights already acquired outside the scope of arbitrary power. Although it preserved anomalies that could be harmful, particularism was nonetheless the concrete shape assumed time and again by the struggle for liberty. Here we reach the borderline between monarchy and despotism, a borderline that was often unclear, but one which has been of the liveliest concern to the French people in every age.

Where they survived the provincial estates were the guardians of regional privileges; so their role in the resistance to fiscalism ought not to be overlooked. In Brittany and in Languedoc the necessity of their approval in taxation matters remained theoretically in force.[3] In practice, a sort of comedy was played out at each meeting. The king's commissioners asked for more than they wanted and the estates offered less than they knew they would have to give, until in the end offers and demands met somewhere in between.[4] No doubt we are dealing with formalities whose actual effect was limited. But the care taken by the estates' desire to preserve these formalities was no more than a pale reflection of the real passion which inspired provincial opinion in business such as this.

Even in the regions that were most firmly under royal control, moreover, local privileges had to be taken into account. Through diverse deals towns as well as provinces had often enough succeeded in replacing a fluctuating tax on revenue with a fixed sum which was always considerably lower. This was known as 'compounding' (*abonnement*). Better still, some towns were completely tax-exempt.

Besides the citizens of these privileged towns, there were whole social categories that escaped the direct taxes grouped under the name of *taille*.[5] The most obvious case was the total exemption enjoyed by the first two orders of society, the clergy and nobility. In areas where the system of *taille personnelle* held good, the *taille* formed a general tax on incomes, and clerics and noblemen paid nothing under this head. In areas subject to the *taille réelle*, the tax was levied on non-noble lands, whoever the current owner might be.

But exemptions went far beyond this. We know how the monarchy, in the search for additional resources, placed public functions on sale. Now a great many of these 'offices' carried a fiscal privilege, thus people with tax-exemptions were to be found in remote rural areas and little country towns.[6]

The system by which the *taille* was raised rendered these myriad exemptions very harmful. The king's council set the total amount to be collected and apportioned it among the various fiscal dis-

tricts, the *généralités*. Then within each *généralité* the sum required was divided up between the secondary fiscal areas, the
élections. Finally, in each *élection* the amount to be paid was
shared out among the parishes. This sum had to be obtained,
whatever the cost. Within a parish all taxpayers were held collectively liable : what was not paid by some people had to be paid
by the rest. The existence of exemptions caused the weight of
taxation to bear still more heavily on the body of the inhabitants,
often in less easy circumstances than the exempt.

But if the inequity stemming from privilege, that is from legal
tax-exemptions, entailed serious abuses, it was complicated by
evils that were still harder to eradicate. Most of the well-to-do
(*notables*) leased their lands to farmers, themselves subject to the
taille. The consequences of exemption would have been considerably reduced had the farmers who rented land from the
clergy, nobility or other privileged persons paid their share. But
this in turn would have drastically affected the level of rents. The
privileged knew how to get round the problem : they claimed
that they were working their rural estates themselves and pretended that their leaseholders were no more than personal servants. Of course ways had to be found to limit the number and
extent of lands they could claim to be farming for themselves,[7]
but it was difficult to prevent them from using their influence to
obtain favourable conditions for their farmers. In the countryside, those who were in a lord's service in any capacity took large
advantage of their position, first and foremost in fiscal matters.
The 'assessor-collectors' elected in each parish to draw up the
taille registers were humble people, scarcely able to stand up to a
nobleman determined to secure a relief for his dependants; and
most of them preferred not to provoke his anger, which could be
dangerous for them.[8] For all that it was less blatant, the protection afforded to their clients by the officials of the *élections* who
apportioned the levy between parishes could be just as effective.

It was the peasant masses that suffered from these abuses, although they were readier to protest against the weight of taxation than to dispute its distribution. Being accustomed to inequality they accepted its excesses in a spirit more of resignation
than of indignation. Further, the poor people of the countryside
could not express their discontent, still less revolt, unless they
were supported by other groups; nor could such rebellion take

a dangerous turn unless the local notables connived or took a hand in it.

In any case, the most violent anti-fiscal outbreaks were above all addressed to the indirect taxes, duties on the movement of goods and fiscal monopolies. One reason for this was that the collection of customs and excises was leased out to tax-farming companies. Judging by the mass of pamphlet literature and the intensity of popular outbreaks, this was the aspect of the fiscal system that was almost always under attack. The most prominent and therefore obvious motives for these outbursts of fever in the body politic, but also the most specious, were the scandalous profits reaped by the tax-farmers, the proliferation of their parasitic agents, and the endless vexations to which they subjected the populace.

Throughout history ordinary people have been easily convinced of the dishonesty of intermediate agents. It is a convenient and usually successful procedure to blame them for all the ills whose real cause it would often be more difficult or less expedient to disclose. On many occasions it is hardly to be questioned that the negotiation of the crown's leases gave rise to some dubious transactions. Long before the age of the 'general farm' the same criticisms were being levelled at the crown's office-jobbers and financial contractors, the *traitants* and *partisans*.[9]

There is another aspect to consider. Solidarity between notables and the generality was most easily achieved in opposition to taxes of this sort. As a consumer, neither nobleman nor bourgeois drew any benefit from privilege when he bought articles whose price embodied the king's taxes. Against the duties on the transport and sale of wine (the main taxes included in the category of the *aides*) wine-grower and tavern-keeper stood together, ceaselessly cursing the collectors. But the owner of a high-quality vineyard was similarly affected in so far as he sold his produce. In a city like Dijon such proprietors formed a sizeable interest-group; in 1630 the wine-growers occupying some of its district formed an assembly at the mere rumour that the *aides* were to be introduced into Burgundy.[10] Such stirrings were helped by the more or less tacit connivance of large sections of the bourgeoisie and, on occasions, of the nobility. The agitation that began in the towns against the 'tax-men' and their agents was a movement of the lower classes,[11] but it was often encouraged by the protests of local or provincial authorities against the royal edicts. Thus one might argue that the crown had good cause to fix the blame for the rebellion in Normandy in 1639 on the Parlement of Rouen, the highest magistracy of the province.[12] We shall observe a similar pattern in the events of 1675 at Rennes and Bordeaux.

Resistance of this kind, deriving from a rudimentary but deep-rooted collective psychology, explains why the king's government could never contemplate far-reaching changes in the fiscal system. At most it could try to increase the yield of a particular tax; for the rest, it had to live by expedients and anticipate future revenues. Moreover, the state's financial needs had grown considerably since the beginning of the seventeenth century; and with no real reform in the basis of taxation, its weight was felt more and more by the whole country.

In comparison with their predecessors and successors, Henri IV and Louis XIII spent little on their own account, but they were faced by massive internal debts and the cost of an active foreign policy. From 1635 France became actively involved in a European war. The last years of Louis XIII and Richelieu were marked by a desperate effort to overcome the external enemy, and at the same time to suppress domestic conspiracies in which the king's own brother was implicated. Meanwhile, at the crisis of the war, there were three great rebellions, fiscal in origin and exceptional in scope : the *Croquants* (Crunchers) of the south west in 1636, the *Croquants* of Périgord in 1637, and the *Nu pieds* (Barefeet) of Normandy in 1639.[13] Each bears witness both to the accumulating load of royal taxation and the traditional opposition to any increase.

The methods worked out to meet the state's needs left enduring marks on Louis XIV's reign. Many fiscal expedients amounted to an almost irredeemable mortgaging of the future. Caught between the pressing necessity for ready cash and the difficulty of improving taxation, the crown could only attempt to borrow directly or indirectly. The sale of offices was one of the innumerable combinations which released fresh resources; it formed an impressive structure whose importance cannot be exaggerated. It flourished in the period of Henri IV and Louis XIII, at least down to 1638, after which date indeed this kind of income fell off.[14] In subsequent years the government managed to live from hand to mouth thanks to the monies loaned by the *partisans* – that is to say, those who signed a contract or *parti* for the farming of this or that tax.

The victories won between 1640 and 1643 may be regarded as having produced a dividend for Richelieu's daring enterprise. But it is impossible to deny that the financial situation resulting from it was disastrous.

On one point however, the importance of which seems largely to have been missed by contemporaries, these crucial years brought a real improvement. The clergy did not pay taxes in the normal sense of the word, but instead contributed to the crown's support by means of a 'free gift', voted by their own assemblies and collected by their own autonomous administration. The very term 'free gift' indicated the necessary consent of the representatives sent to the assemblies and, to begin with, the exceptional character of these subsidies. And yet the pretext or occasion for them were royal demands, which would usually be justified by the interests of the Catholic faith. In the sixteenth century crusading projects had given way to requests for aid in the struggle against heresy. When Richelieu was attacking La Rochelle this argument had seemed valid; but after 1635, when France was the ally of Sweden and the United Provinces against Catholic powers, it became clear that national solidarity was the real motive for the king's demands.[15] Besides being a statesman, Richelieu was also a prince of the church, which allowed him to make use of the assemblies of the clergy. He proceeded empirically, moreover, negotiating with the ecclesiastical leaders and as far as possible avoiding direct conflicts over issues of principle. Nevertheless in 1641 he made a display of authority when he ordered his opponents back to their dioceses.[16] Thus were the ways cleared for that real subjection of the clergy which was to come later.

When Louis XIII died in 1643, his son was still a child and the regent relied completely on Mazarin. Temperamentally more accommodating than his predecessor had been, he faced powerful interests with which Richelieu had clashed and which sought to take advantage of the regency to free themselves from the constraints they had undergone. Across Mazarin's correspondence we can follow the incidence of state penury in political life – of special gravity was the anxiety to pay the regiments fighting outside France, above all the foreign regiments.[17] Necessity imposed an endless invention of new financial expedients. It also led to attempts to tax the privileged classes – less out of a zeal for social justice than a need to obtain results.

The countryside which paid the *taille* almost unaided could no longer bear the burden while it was customary to try to make the towns contribute as well. In 1644 the authorities noted that buildings had been erected just outside the walls of Paris in a zone where an ancient law forbade construction. This was how the suburbs of Saint-Antoine and Saint-Germain had developed. A royal edict laid fines on the areas so built up. At this juncture the Parlement of Paris stepped in. To us its role, like that of the provincial parlements and the other so-called 'sovereign courts' (the *cour des aides*, the *chambre des comptes* and the *grand conseil*), may seem surprising, but is to be explained by the constitutional formality of 'registering' royal edicts, and the practice of 'remonstrances'. Although the members of the Parlement owed their positions to the king, and their function was to dispense justice in his name, they arrogated to themselves the right to censor royal legislation before entering it in their registers. During the recent reigns, indeed, fiscal edicts had almost always required the presence of the king at a special session known as a *lit de justice* before they could be registered. But now the government gave way. The *taille* was increased and attempts made to float a loan secured on the proceeds of a tax levied on those 'in easy circumstances'[18] – the rich and the notables. The self-interests of the parliamentary magistrates came out into the open, while the Paris Parlement manœuvred to deflect popular anger towards the financiers. The new tax was only approved on condition that the judicial office-holders should be exempt from it, and that it should be shared 'between those who had been employed for twenty years in the financial administration or who had advanced money to the king or who had engaged in commerce'.[19]

In September 1646 the so-called 'edict of the tariff' laid tolls on the various articles of general consumption entering Paris, without distinction of persons. The preamble emphasised that this was 'the most equitable assistance' that the king could expect from his subjects, since it was being asked of privileged city-dwellers, whereas 'those who paid the *taille* have suffered so many impositions that it is not reasonable to ask them to give any further aid'. Here again, government ran into opposition from the Parlement. The queen mother was ready to resort to her authority, but Mazarin preferred to negotiate. 'The proposed tariff was modified by agreement to exclude coal, wood fuel, every kind of grain, wine, and whatever the citizens grew for themselves . . .' The exemption of the citizens' own produce could only have been dictated by a selfish and very culpable motive; it meant the exemption of the rich and deprived this tax henceforward of its main advantage. This is the opinion of Forbonnais,[20] a man of the eighteenth century. But such thoughts were already present in the minds of the more intelligent government servants, as official documents prove.

Meanwhile, the majority of the people of Paris saw the Parlement only as their chief defender against the fisc. It is in any case surprising that the government's financial management should have been held to ransom by the businessmen who advanced incessant loans at outrageous rates of interest. But the government's weakness in face of the Parlement's demagoguery was also revealed when, at the critical moment, it sacrificed the man who had juggled the whole system of lending. On 9 July 1648 Particelli d'Emery received notice of dismissal – he who since Richelieu's last years had directed the state finances with a bold resourcefulness not unmixed with devices both of dubious honesty and in the long run dangerous. Coming at that moment, such a sop to public opinion aggravated the crisis. A series of bankruptcies followed one another. Observing on 22 August 1648 that the Parlement had issued a decree against the *traitants*, Goulas remarked that 'everyone was amazed at this imprudence . . . for the king has no other source of revenue if he does not cultivate the business world'.[21] It can be said that the government had alienated the only support which remained to it. This date marks the opening of a revolutionary period. In Paris there was general discontent, but it would not have assumed an extreme form had it not been for the attitude of the Parlement. The government had given way to most of the 'remonstrances' and yet succeeded in arousing the resentment of the body of office-holders. In multiplying the offices which it sold for ready cash, it had reduced their intrinsic value and prestige. By indirect means it had tried to attract money from privileged groups who felt their privileges to be threatened. Some of them had gone as far as to combine for the defence of their interests.[22]

We shall not describe the events of August 1648 and all that

followed. Known by the general and deceptive name of the
'Fronde', they were a mixture of many-sided intrigues and disorders whose disastrous effects were hardly palliated by the presence of any constructive programme.

Paralysed by their contradictory roles as officers of the king
and leaders of the opposition, the members of the Paris Parlement
were unable to go very far with their plans for reform as long
as they remained among the principal beneficiaries of the established order. They were content to extend the authority they had
won in fiscal matters through the practice of 'registration', transforming it into a real power of veto. They demanded control of
the whole crown administration, but without offering any evidence that they would run it better. Their most constructive point
was a denunciation of abuses which was only too well-founded.
They insisted on the need for clarity and honesty in the presenta-
tion of the public accounts. They showed how a variety of tricks
were used by the tax-receivers, and especially the tax-farmers, to
line their own pockets. In this way they joined forces with popular resentments.[23]

Particelli d'Emery was an Italian by birth, as were a number
of financiers. Worse still, the all-powerful minister, Cardinal
Mazarin, was also of Italian origin. Veneration for the monarchy,
still a powerful force, meant that attacks were rarely directed at
the regent herself, unless it were obliquely, through the influence
that the cardinal had over her. Mazarin conveniently personified
the adventurer who had achieved power, the more so since he
made good use of his position to increase his private fortune. From
1648 to 1652 the Parisian press enjoyed exceptional liberty, and
printed or handwritten pamphlets and libels circulated freely. A
large number of these *Mazarinades* have survived.[24] As usual with
writings of this type, much is pure burlesque or sensational tale-
bearing, but there are some pamphlets that rise above this level,
as Naudé, Mazarin's own librarian, observed.[25] But even the most
elaborated and thoughtful criticisms are always set in a traditional mould : royal absolutism, of divine origin, is limited by the
subjects' property rights and by the crown's own obligation to
keep its promises.[26]

In these circumstances we may well wonder whether the
Estates-General, the only legal representatives of the nation as a
whole, could have served any useful purpose. On several occa-

sions there were demands that they should be summoned, and the regent even agreed to this. But she then postponed their meeting and in the end it never took place.

In 1653 Mazarin returned to Paris after two periods of exile, more powerful than ever. He remained master of the state for another eight years, until 1661. The general weariness and the sorrowful experiences of the preceding years made thinking men crave for a strong government. All that the cardinal's extreme caution could accomplish was to conciliate the most important interests and win their support. The financial chaos persisted, none the less since the cardinal and his colleagues profited from it. The Treaty of the Pyrenees in 1659 aroused hopes of a long period of peace, and it seemed as if the hour of reform had struck at last. Public opinion was virtually unanimous in placing all its hopes on the young king. He would have to rule in person, without a first minister, and use his power to scrutinise the inner workings of the administration. If he could avoid being fleeced himself, he should have revenues enough to be able to relieve his subjects.

In 1661 Louis XIV appears to have been aware of the role that on all sides it was hoped to see him play. Savinien d'Alquié's propaganda tract, *Les délicies de la France*, summarising in 1670 the results that had apparently been achieved, announces in the course of its unstinted praise of the monarch: 'He has redeemed the royal domain so that he need no longer call upon his subjects' aid, save in pressing emergencies . . . Now that his chests are full, he wants to reduce the *taille* to what it was in the time of Henri the Great.'[27]

This programme for return to a past which was in part mythical is naturally presented here in a highly simplified form, but it nonetheless represents what public opinion expected from the new government inaugurated by Louis XIV's personal assumption of power in 1661.

On Mazarin's death the king in effect reserved to himself the authorisation of all expenditure. Although there was no public budget, accounts were kept to be shown to the king and examined by him. In principle he directed the finances in person, assisted by a special council. But in practice Jean-Baptiste Colbert managed most of the financial business, first as a mere *intendant* and then as comptroller-general. He alone had the capacity for work

which was essential for understanding it. The king lacked time
and inclination to go into all these questions, and relied on the
clear arguments presented by the man who was tending to become his chief minister.

There is consequently, in these matters in particular, an element of fiction in the satisfying, officially propagated image of the
king ruling on his own. Equally fictitious is the idea – to which
many historians have succumbed – that the methods employed
in running the finances changed profoundly and immediately in
1661. And there is even less reason to think that the attitudes of
the taxpayers were transformed in the space of a few years.

To escape from the legacy of the past, it was necessary not
only to redeem the royal domain but also to reduce the multiple
debts that had accumulated. In actuality, many of the state's
creditors had profited from a period of confusion when money had
had to be borrowed at usurious rates of interest, and during which
the most deserving creditors had often been forced to sell their
claims at a loss to those with ready cash and sufficient influence
to obtain repayment, at least in part. In this complex financial
jungle, the notion of respecting one's pledges could seem far-
fetched. The desired result was therefore obtained through a series
of partial bankruptcies, of which the writing down by one quarter
of the value of state bonds (*rentes*) is only the best-known episode.
These manœuvres injured a variety of interests indiscriminately;
in the main they were urban and made up of businessmen.

The latter were the victims, besides, of a spectacular measure
which had numerous precedents and responded to public resentments. This was the special Chamber of Justice set up to investigate the corrupt use of public funds by the financiers and to make
them disgorge their most outrageous profits. It was a highly selec-
tive and inadequate instrument for the correction of past abuses,
involving persons who could claim to have been acting under
Mazarin's authority, and as such it carried no great moral weight
with the well-informed people. It provided Colbert with the
opportunity to get rid of Fouquet, the former superintendent of
finances, whose loyal friends nevertheless continued to voice their
opposition. And it also served no doubt as a weapon of intimida-
tion to influence future negotiations with the financial community.

Some of the tax-farming contracts were consolidated and re-
negotiated on better terms for the king. There was an attempt to

draw up a complete list of the resources available to the government and of the inroads made upon them by private citizens. These measures would probably have been enough to fill the coffers of a king of economical habits who would have restricted his expenses as the need arose. But this did not last long and from the early years of Louis XIV's personal reign there were intermittent but increasing attempts by the government to overstep the limits imposed on it by ancient privileges. The little province of the Boulonnais, bordering on Flanders and Artois, enjoyed exemption from many taxes because of its strategic position; in return it was supposed to provide a sort of military service. Its fiscal exemptions – solemnly affirmed by Louis XI in 1478, confirmed by Henri II in 1552, by Henri III in 1575, and again in 1656 – had their defenders in the provincial estates. But when the local militias had proved inadequate, professional troops had been brought into the Boulonnais; and their billeting was annoying and at times intolerable to the local population. In 1657 the estates voted a 'free gift' to pay and maintain the troops, while a solemn promise was made that this abnormal imposition would not be levied after the war was over. But in 1661 the government decided to keep it in force, and it was enforced indeed against the protests of the estates. Louis XIV's *Mémoires* contain a curious passage dealing with this. 'I desired', he wrote, 'to tax them a very small sum, merely to show them that it was within my power and my right to do so.'[28] Perhaps the king, and more particularly his ministers, acting upon some private conception of absolutism which they would not express openly, already believed that local and provincial privileges were destined to disappear. Louis XIV's great caution, however, in conflict with his authoritarian temper, prevented him from turning this venture into a general maxim of policy. In any case opposition remained lively and sometimes alarming.

The revolt that these measures provoked in the Boulonnais is typical of the contradictory nature of such movements and the successive stages by which they developed. It began as a legal dispute between the local estates and the central government; provincial opinion was unanimous as represented by its leaders. But in June 1662 a peasant rising opened a new phase in the drama. The anti-fiscal propaganda which preceded it probably helped to spark it off, but very soon the notables felt themselves

H

to be threatened, partly because of their dislike of mob violence, but also because popular resentment now began to turn increasingly against them. The use of military force quickly crushed the rebels and was followed by severe repression. The tax remained in force and was made permanent, even though it had to be approved anew each year by a special act registered in the *chambre des comptes*. The Estates of the Boulonnais, which Colbert wanted to abolish, were preserved, but the government took care not to convoke them too frequently.[29] In such manner was respect for the form of traditional liberties reconciled with their violation in practice. It is worth noting, besides, that the subsidy for the troops' winter quarters levied in the Boulonnais affected neither the gentry nor their farmers, nor those who held exemptions, nor the citizens of Boulogne. The monarchy indulged the upper classes, while allowing itself to reprove them for not taking better care of public order themselves whenever it was menaced by the lower classes.

The various popular risings noticed here and there every year could stem from widely different causes. The peasants complained of the *taille* and sometimes soldiers had to be brought in to make them pay it. In market-towns the high price of grain would provoke short-lived '*emotions*'. In the Pyrenean regions where the salt-tax (*gabelle*) was introduced for the first time in 1664, the ensuing rebellion lasted a long time, thanks to the geography of the area and to a skilful partisan leader.[30]

'This year is undoubtedly a brilliant one for the financial administration . . . for in no other were there fewer permanent charges on the state's revenues and lighter taxes on the people.'[31] The year that Forbonnais calls 'brilliant' was 1670. Yet it was in this very year, in time of peace, that one of the most serious antifiscal revolts broke out, the revolt of the Vivarais. The rumour of a tax on clothes, hats and the number of babies born was obviously absurd. But the taxes on hired horses and taverns, and on receipts for payments, were only too real; they bore especially on carters and tavern-keepers, who were in a good position to spread news, true or false. At Aubenas the first victim of popular vindictiveness was an agent of the tax-farmers; then an open revolt of the country parishes made it far more serious. The song sung by the rebels was a variant of one from the time of the Fronde, attacking 'the avarice of the lesser tax-farmers, financiers, businessmen'. The revolt was brutally repressed and the town of Aubenas lost its right to send a deputy to the estates.[32]

The relative stability of the royal finances could not last. After describing the 'brilliant' year of 1670 Forbonnais goes on : 'The heavy expenditure on furniture, diamonds, paintings and buildings, at Versailles, at the Louvre, at the Observatory and elsewhere, began after that year to exceed what had been planned. Then came the war, and the state lived by continually anticipating its revenues, apart from sales of offices (*affaires extraordinaires*).'[33] Not only was this a return to the former hand-to-mouth existence; it also meant a spreading fiscalism. The original programme was far from fulfilment.

The war against the Dutch Republic in 1672 opened as a lightning campaign, but dragged on and developed into a struggle against a large coalition. Greater ingenuity than ever was required to discover new sources of revenue. In 1674 three novel measures were introduced. A duty was levied on pewterware, which was to be stamped with a punch, as was already done with gold and silverware. Then there was the stamped paper. A special type of paper, marked with an official stamp, was henceforward made obligatory for all legal transactions, the proceeds from its sale going to the crown. Finally a monopoly was set up for the sale of tobacco. The marking of pewterware struck at the prosperous artisans who produced it, and affected a large part of the population which, for lack of an alternative, collected articles made of this semi-precious metal as a true means of saving. The obligatory use of stamped paper for all documents drawn up by proctors, notaries, ushers and registrars threatened to reduce the profits of the entire legal profession. And the consumption of tobacco had been spreading far and wide, particularly among seamen.

The essentially anti-fiscal and above all urban nature of the popular risings of 1675 appeared clearly in the events at Bordeaux[34] – the invasion of part of the city by country people from the surrounding districts was only a brief episode. The other movements reported from the south west took place in towns : Périgueux, Bergerac, Pau, Montségur, La Réole. There was nothing like the old peasant insurrections of the *Croquants*. At Bordeaux it was the artisans who led the violent opposition. The king's representative, the intendant of Guyenne, tried to negotiate with the bailiffs and syndics of the guilds, but he accused the

juridical corporations of working all the time 'to keep the fire
going'.[35] The parlement of Guyenne went so far as to issue a decree
suspending collection of the new taxes. In the end fresh disorders
led to military intervention. The harshest punishments were reserved for rioters from the lower classes. But the notables, although
most of them had themselves been terrified, did not get off scot-
free. Bordeaux lost its fiscal privileges and had to suffer the billeting of a large number of soldiers, while the parlement of Guyenne
was exiled to Condom.

The Breton troubles of the same year[36] are often described as a
rural movement, and this is certainly a striking feature of them.
The feelings that stirred the country people have been preserved
more or less accurately in the articles of the famous 'Peasants'
Charter', where they appear as a curious mixture : the stamped
paper is to be burned, tobacco to be distributed free; the salt-tax
figures as a symbol of oppression, but also as a mysterious living
monster, creature of a coarse imagination. But beside all this, as
has been frequently observed, there were articles which formulated fairly definite social claims, attacking clerical and noble
impositions which were onerous to the peasants.[31] None of this
should however detract from the importance of the urban agitation, in little towns like Guingamp or Chateaulin, but above all
in Rennes, the provincial capital and seat of the parlement. It was
there in April 1675 that the riots broke out with the pillaging of
the offices where tobacco and stamped paper was sold. Psychological echoes of the events at Rennes can be traced even in the
placards distributed by the rebels at Bordeaux. Seen from Rennes,
the revolt was anti-fiscal and secretly fostered by the provincial
authorities. The fact is that the estates had been given a solemn
promise the year before, in return for an increase in their 'free
gift', that no new taxes would be imposed. The parlement of
Brittany sympathised with the opponents of stamped paper. For
this reason the city was punished, and the provincial court was
moved to Vannes.

There can be no doubt that the government feared that this
tentative alignment of the magistracy with bourgeois and popular
forces might lead to a recurrence of the Fronde. In reality the
times were very different. Clergy and nobility had been tamed;
opposition in the parlements was no more than a shadow of what
it had been; the new taxes had come to stay. Authority was trium-

phant, but it had not changed its methods. Discontent could only find expression in a negative and anarchic manner, in ways that recalled age-old slogans of rebellion such as 'long live the king, down with the *gabelle*'.[38]

The years following the Peace of Nijmegen could perhaps have been a period of reform, but instead there was only a partial restoration of financial stability and this was undone by the resumption of a major war ten years later. For matters to have been otherwise, strict measures of retrenchment would have been necessary. But Louis XIV maintained surprisingly large military forces for that age, and was far from reducing his other expenditures. It is therefore all the more remarkable that down to the end of the reign there were no anti-fiscal revolts comparable to those of the earlier period. Even the great famines of 1693 and 1709 provoked no more than sporadic and ephemeral reactions to the high price of grain.

The reason is that the royal administration, step by step, had acquired an ever-increasing practical effectiveness. The government's real authority was no longer exercised by *officiers*, with a property in their posts and roots in their own locality, naturally prone to defend its interests, but by commissaries, agents nominated for their reliability, transferable or revocable at will. The king was now represented by these *commissaires départis* – that is by commissaries sent out to each *généralité*, known increasingly by the name of *intendants*. This institution went back in origin to Richelieu. It was naturally unpopular with the *officiers* whose powers it curtailed, and was suppressed for a time during the Fronde. Now it was to be even more firmly established and respected. It culminated in the person of the comptroller-general of finances, who was gradually assuming control over all the internal affairs of the kingdom, and to whom the intendants addressed their correspondence. The latter had their own colleagues, occasionally at first but then permanently, distributed throughout their *généralité* : these were the subdelegates (*subdélégués*). They and their superiors delved into every sort of question. Their original function was the supervision of financial matters, but since everything has its financial aspect they came to have a finger in every pie.

This administrative machine made for greater precision, regularity and promptness in the levy and collection of taxes, but to contemporaries it seemed only to aggravate the burden. In fact it achieved a real pursuit of abuses. Hence, in default of equity, the evils of tax-distribution were cut down in practice. Without being able to abolish fiscal privilege, the intendants lessened the harm done by it. As the taxpayers became accustomed to dealing with them, the intendants received an increasing flow of complaints and arbitrated in the disputes of taxpayers with the agents of the tax-farmers and with the assessors and receivers of the direct taxes. They developed the habit of revising the *taille* registers and by means of *cotes d'office*, or sums fixed by themselves, they secured payment from the better-off farmers who sheltered behind the legal exemption of privileged landlords, even though the latter still escaped. To this extent there was a net gain in revenue, if no benefit to other taxpayers.

Faced by the silence of the traditional corporations – the estates that were never summoned, the muzzled parlements – the historian has great difficulty in discerning the outward signs of public reactions. Strict control of printing had early taken effect. In consequence we should have only the vaguest idea of what even a minority of the French people were thinking were it not for the indirect evidence afforded by pamphlets printed abroad, or by those of similar inspiration printed secretly at home. This literature it is true, is highly miscellaneous and sheds only a partial light on our problem. Almost always the main themes of the rising polemics are the king's aggression in matters of religion and foreign policy : the persecution of the Protestants, Louis XIV's quarrels with the pope, the arrogance of the 'reunion' of frontier lands – all these offered rich material for the expression of discontent.

One of the best known of these pamphlets, and one of the few that deals with every subject of grievance including fiscal problems, was the anonymous work published in 1689 under the title of *Soupirs de la France esclave*.[39] It is worth pausing to consider it. The author displays admirably all sides of the development of absolutism. But it is evident that his outlook on taxation is altogether conservative and, according to modern ways of thinking, reactionary.

Monsieur Colbert drew up a plan to reform the finances and caused it to be carried out with the utmost rigour. But of what

does this reformation consist? Not in reducing taxes for the
relief of the people, but in a great increase, and in spreading
taxes over all those who formerly sheltered from it through
their own influence or that of their friends. A gentleman no
longer has the influence to obtain a reduction of the *taille* for
his parish. His farmers pay as much as the others, and more.
Magistrates, lords and other persons of repute today no longer
have influence where the king's revenues are concerned. Every-
body pays.[40]

As we read this today, it may well strike us as one of the most
convincing testimonials in favour of administrative absolutism. In
fact, to speak bluntly, it was nostalgia for the past.

Another order of problems was bound more and more to attract
the attention of the best thinkers of the time. The proceeds of a
fiscal system depend not only on the merits and failings of its
system of apportionment, but also on the level of national income.
In this connection there is no escape from the effects of the general
economic situation on a state's revenues. Historians have latterly
realised that many of the difficulties experienced by the governments of the seventeenth century can be ascribed to the phases of
economic stagnation, indeed recession, generally on an international scale. Of the various indicators of economic activity,
grain prices (the easiest group in continuous series) are among
the most conclusive. Now grain prices in France, prone to fluctuations of sometimes surprising magnitude, displayed frequent falls,
especially after 1664, with an underlying downward tendency.
This hurt the interests of nobles and landowners, and not least
those of the clergy, whose essential income depended on the sale
of grain; not only they, but the rich peasants and leaseholders
were also injured. At the same time the deflation slowed down the
tempo of commerce and industrial production.

The different social groups blamed all this on different causes.
At all events, the economic situation restricted the state's ability
to increase revenue at a time when its needs were far from declining. Long before a great new war came to exacerbate the financial
chaos, the situation was already grave.

It took the genius of Boisguilbert to perceive the links that connected the different sectors of production and consumption. A
slump in the agricultural market causes farmers and landowners

to reduce their expenditure, bringing about a contraction in all forms of employment and, by a sort of chain reaction, a decrease in all incomes, including ultimately those of the king. Boisguilbert's *Détail de la France*, published in 1695 but apparently written in the first years of the Nine Years War, is a polemical work, as its obvious exaggerations and passionate tone suggest. Besides a comprehensive view of economic circulation, however, it contains a concrete and lively description of abuses in the system of the *taille* and the *aides* which must have struck its readers with particular force. But if Boisguilbert was attacking the existing taxes, what innovation had he to propose? Not very much, let it be said, in 1695 : merely a hearth-tax which he did not work out in detail. The rest would be achieved by the reform of abuses, by making the *taille* everywhere fall on land and not on persons (*taille réelle*), by alleviating and simplifying transit duties, and by a commercial policy which would facilitate the export of grain.[41] Later on, during the War of the Spanish Succession, Boisguilbert was to put forward a more radical fiscal reform, but here he was anticipated by Vauban and by the royal administration itself.

The idea of a poll-tax (*capitation*) was not new. Foreign states could provide examples. For seventeenth-century France, however, to tax every subject in the kingdom without respect for rank amounted to an innovation indeed. The tactics adopted by Pontchartrain, the comptroller-general, prior to its introduction, are indicative of the misgivings it aroused.[42] A circular letter was sent to the intendants, instructing them to sound out the sort of reception that could be expected for the proposal. But the minister's political dexterity was particularly evident in the manœuvres carried out by the intendant of Languedoc, who managed to get the estates of the most independent of all provinces themselves to suggest a tax that they could have been expected to oppose. The Capitation Edict of 1695 divided the whole population into twenty-two classes,[43] with the dauphin, the heir to the throne, heading the first class. The classification was determined by titles and official position, and by professional qualifications, so that within the same class men of widely differing incomes would find themselves taxed at the same rate. The obvious advantage of this elementary classification, however, was its use of ready-made criteria in a country where a great many professions, to say nothing of the office-holders, were incorporated like the guilds. The king, moreover, promised solemnly that this extraordinary tax would be levied only for the duration of the war. The promise was kept and the tax abolished in September 1697. The prospect of a resumption of hostilities led to its revival in 1701. The manner of its application had demonstrated none the less that the agents of government still favoured the privileged. Arthur de Boislisle, the historian, noted that the proportion paid by the nobility during the first period of the *capitation* decreased every year in comparison with that of the payers of the *taille*. The poll-tax of 1695 proved no more than a passing expedient.

The financial situation was bound up with the war. Peace was urgently desired; even at court, in the king's innermost circle, a number of influential people were pressing very hard in that direction. Mme de Maintenon, the dukes of Beauvilliers and Chevreuse, and the abbé Fénelon were all close allies for a few years. Fénelon, whose spirituality charmed them, was nothing less than guide to their conscience.[44] He was tutor to the king's grandchildren, whose governor was the duke of Beauvilliers. His teaching of Christian morality inevitably involved a certain view of politics, mediated through his conception of the duties of a king. The Quietist controversy led to Fénelon's departure from court, but in his episcopal see of Cambrai he was less inhibited from voicing with some authority his criticisms of Louis XIV's conduct. His papers, discovered in the nineteenth century, are remarkable for their boldness and eloquence, particularly the famous 'Letter to the King' of 1694.[45] But he always spoke in his capacity as a leading figure of the church, and what he said was not for publication. The letter was sent to his friends at court, the duke of Beauvilliers and Mme de Maintenon, and was probably never seen by Louis XIV. It is a guide to the remonstrances that the king's closest associates were expected to make to him. Fénelon advises the conclusion of peace at any price, if necessary by abandoning earlier conquests, which were in any case unjust; the domestic situation, far worse because of the famine of 1693–4, making this imperative. There remains the question of the reforms that were needed. But here it appears that the great and brilliantly intelligent nobleman contemplated no more than the restoration of a past which was itself in part a myth.

When the *capitation* was renewed, in March 1701, the king justified it by pointing to the imminent threat of war. If we

H*

remember that peace was not signed at Utrecht until 1713 and at Rastadt until 1714, we can visualise the burden that the country was called upon to bear; it was as if the clock had been put back fifty years. More than ever the state lived on loans, anticipating future revenue as security for advances from whoever would provide them. More than ever it was at the mercy of the financiers. Samuel Bernard is an extreme example, flattered by the king who personally conducted him on a tour of the royal gardens. Not all the financiers could measure up to him. Several of these *parvanus* were of lowly origin. Once again the speculator battening on the state becomes a stock figure; Lesage's comedy *Turcaret* features a former footman turned financial jobber. The concomitant evils were real enough, but the satire amused the public. These practices and the reactions they provoked were of old standing. Yet the state needed something more solid to rely on. The renewal of the poll-tax itself announced a new policy. The tax was not intended to disappear again. Could it be improved? Might it even be possible to discover a universal system of taxation based on this model? Boisguilbert had become an officious adviser of the government – not without difficulty – and wrote a great deal. The tracts published during his lifetime, it is true, only repeat the main themes of the *Détail de la France;* but among his unpublished works written for the comptroller-general Chamillart, there is a 'Memorandum on the distribution of the *taille* and the *capitation*' which contains some original suggestions about the new tax.[46] Boisguilbert criticises the system of classes on which it was based, but far from rejecting this system he seeks to transform it into a tax on the different kinds of income. He thinks it will be an easy matter to ascertain these incomes : each individual will be assessed 'in the eye of his neighbours' (*à vue du pays*), in other words by guesswork. If he feels he is being over-taxed, he will only need to prove it by 'authentic documents' – that is by contracts sworn before a notary. Merchants will be able to cite the evidence of 'import registers and customs paid, and their own books, which they are under an obligation to keep in good order'. Likewise the productivity of artisans can be measured according to the number of machines they employ, and so on. The memorandum is dated 1705, and the rate suggested for this improved version of the *capitation* was a twentieth. Boisguilbert's *Factum de la France* was published in 1707,[47] at which time he must already have been aware of Vauban's fiscal schemes, although he made it a point of honour to distinguish them from his own. Instead of a 'royal tenth' in kind he proposes a tenth in money. While not describing in detail how the tax is to be collected he maintains that 'it is nonsense to allege that it is difficult to discover the taxable portion of an individual's possessions, or cruel to oblige him to give an account of them'.

Vauban had for long been working on the final draft of the system presented in his most important work, *La Dixme Royale*.[48] A much more balanced mind than Boisguilbert, he based his proposals on research and statistical conclusions. The marshal proposed a tax on every type of income, a single tax (*impôt unique*) capable of superseding all others. He echoed the bitter criticisms of the *tailles* and the *aides* that had appeared in the *Détail de la France,* of which he reproduced certain passages almost word for word.

Boisguilbert's advice was passed over. Copies of the *Dixme Royale* were seized; it had in any case been printed in secret. Even so, the counsels of these exceptional personalities cannot be said to have been lost to sight by those who at first had not wished to follow them.

It is true that the Tenth (*dixième*) of 1710 was a gamble ventured at the moment of a most sombre crisis,[49] but it must all the same be placed beside the projects of the reformers. The king had hesitated a long time. Advancing age and misfortunes brought out scruples that at one time he would have been able to stifle more easily. His confessor had to assure him that he was within his rights before he made up his mind. On 14 October 1710 he decreed an annual levy of a tenth of the income from all the property 'owned or possessed by our subjects and others, of whatever rank or condition they may be. . . . And in order to establish fairly what must be paid as a tenth on the property so liable, we require the owners of the said property, to furnish, within a fortnight of the publication of this present Edict, declarations of their property to the persons appointed to receive them'. Fraud was to be punished by a fourfold increase in the tax.[50] But there was no indication of how the declarations were to be verified. Given the social mores of the time, the methods recommended by Boisguilbert could hardly have been implemented there and then. As the consulate of Lyons asked, what would become of business secrets? Thirty years later an indignant Saint-Simon exaggerated the zeal with which the commissioners set themselves 'to require incontrovertible proof' and the despair of taxpayers forced to divulge the secrets of their own 'families'.[51] It is, however, clear that the results of this bold departure were far from what it should have produced. It is clearer still that public opinion was not ready to accept it. In his *Politique tirée de l'Ecriture Sainte*, published posthumously in 1709, Bossuet wrote: 'Reason tells us that the whole state should contribute to those public needs that are in the prince's care.'[52] It was his love of logic as much as his devotion to the monarchy that led the bishop of Meaux to a conclusion always evaded by others. The idea of taxation as a contribution by the whole nation to ensure the orderly running of public services, and therefore payable by everyone, is an idea that is not only modern but relatively recent. In the age of Louis XIV, only a few chosen spirits could glimpse it.

NOTES

1 Marcel Marion, *Dictionnaire des institutions de la France, aux XVIIe et XVIIIe siècles* (Paris, 1923) entry on *'domaine'*.
2 Vauban, 'Projet de capitation', printed A. M. Augoyat, *Oisivetés de M. Vauban*, reprinted by A. M. de Boislisle in *Correspondance des Contrôleurs Généraux des finances*, 3 vols (Paris, 1874–97) I, Appendix, and by E. Coornaert in his edition of *Projet d'un Dixme Royale* (Paris, 1933) pp. 254–73.
3 See *Histoire générale de Languedoc*, new ed. (Toulouse, 1889) vol. XI, book XLIII, chs 73, 74, pp. 1003–4, for taxes levied in 1635 without the consent of the estates; for Brittany see the letters of the duc de Chaulnes and the bishop of Saint-Malo in 1675, printed in G.B. Depping, *Correspondance administrative sous le règne de Louis XIV*, 4 vols (Paris, 1850–5) III, p. 225ff. See also Richelieu's letter to the prince de Condé of 24 April 1632, in which he expresses his fears that there will be disputes when the estates meet in Brittany: Georges d'Avenel, *Lettres, instructions diplomatiques et papiers d'état* (Paris, 1853–77) IV, p. 287 and Avenel's note on the subject.
4 Depping, *Correspondance administrative*, I, pp. 60, 63–5.
5 Marion, *Dictionnaire*, entry under *'taille'*.
6 For exemptions see E. Esmonin, *La taille en Normandie au temps de Colbert* (Paris, 1913) ch. 5, para. II, 'Les exempts par la fonction' (pp. 231–64) and para. III 'Les exempts par le domicile' (pp. 264-73).
7 Limited to one farm in a single parish situated in the *élection* where the owner resided; the extent of the farm to correspond to a scale of

privileges ranging from one to four ploughlands included in the land which those exempt from the *taille* could claim to exploit 'by their own hands'. Anthologies of jurisprudence give some information on lawsuits about this, the archives of the *Cours des Aides* furnish more. We can note as an example the 'gentils-hommes de Beauce' who in 1650 asked that a number of their home farms be so counted when cultivated by their servants.

8   Striking examples of the brutality of seigneurs and their agents in cases where their protégés had been taxed can be gathered from a variety of sources and places. Here are two taken from a single session of the king's council on 10 March 1663 (Arch. Nat. E 352A, ff. 142, 202). In the Noyon region a parish collector-assessor had been imprisoned by the seigneur's widow in an unheated room at the height of winter for having taxed individuals she had forbidden him to touch. On the same day the council dealt with a more serious case from Berry: here masked men had cut off the ears and the nose of a tax collector and among them the collector had recognised the personal valet of the marquis to whom the parish belonged. The summary of the council's decree, declaring that such violence could not be tolerated, goes on to say: 'no more than various other cases of violence extorted by gentlemen and parish seigneurs on the collectors and others employed in the recovering of the *tailles* and taxes'. This addendum has been crossed out of the record in case it came to be published.

9   Cf. *Dictionnaire de Trévoux*, entry under '*traitant*' (contractor): 'This is a name now given to men of business who manage the King's taxes . . . it replaces that of *partisan* (favourite) which has become odious . . . the Chamber of Justice has been established to investigate the malpractices of the contractors. The King's coffers grow heavy from the contractors' ruin.'

10   C. Fevret, *De la sédition arrivée en la ville de Dijon le 28 février 1630* (Paris, 1630).

11   The term *maltôte* (extortion) to characterise a bad tax is found from the middle of the fourteenth century. The *maltôtiers* (extortioners) were the collectors of the bad taxes.

12   For the responsibility of the Rouen authorities in the events of 1639 see F. de Vertha Mont, *Diaire ou journal du chancelier Séguier en Normandie*, ed. A. Floquet (Rouen, 1842).

13   The researches of Roland Mousnier and his pupils have defined and clarified the complex character of these revolts, see R. Mousnier, *Fureurs paysannes* (Paris, 1967) pp. 87–121.

14   See the same author's *La vénalité des offices sous Henri IV et Louis XIII* (Rouen, 1945) p. 175.

15   P. Blet, *Le clergé de France et la monarchie* (Rome, 1959) I, ch. 6.

16   Ibid., ch. 7.

17   *Lettres de cardinal Mazarin pendant son ministère*, ed. A. Cheruel and G. d'Avenel (Paris, 1902–6).

18   This is the term regularly used at the time. In reality it was a forced loan, secured on the farm of the *aides*. The preamble to the declaration

of September 1644 which introduced it is worth quoting: 'After having maturely considered that the nobility has so generously contributed with its blood, and that those liable to our *tailles* have suffered so many impositions since the beginning of this war that it would not be reasonable to demand further assistance from them, we have concluded that we cannot devise a fairer subsidy than one drawn from the inhabitants of our good town of Paris and the other good towns the citizens of which possess the greater part of the wealth of this Kingdom': Isambert *et al.*, *Recueil général des anciennes lois françaises*, xvii, p. 45; cf. O. Talon, *Mémoires*, ed. Michaud and Poujoulat (Paris, 1839) p. 124 ff.

19   Talon, *Mémoires*, p. 128.

20   [—] Forbonnais, *Recherches et considérations sur les finances de la France* (Paris, 1758) ii, p. 88.

21   *Mémoires de Nicolas Goulas*, ed. C. Constant, 3 vols (Paris, 1879–82) ii, p. 349.

22   R. Mousnier, 'Quelques raisons de la Fronde', *XVIIᵉ Siècle*, no. 3 (1949) 33–78.

23   Cf. the text adopted by the assembly of deputies from the sovereign courts (*chambres des comptes, cours des aides, grand conseil, parlements*) which met, on the initiative of the Parlement of Paris in the chamber of Saint-Louis in June 1648: Isambert *et al.*, *Recueil général*, xvii, pp. 71–84.

24   C. Moreau, *Bibliographie des Mazarinades* (Paris, 1850).

25   Gabriel Naudé, *Jugement de tout ce qui a été imprimé contre le cardinal Mazarin* (no place, no date).

26   C. Moreau, *Choix des Mazarinades* (Paris, 1863).

27   S. d'Alquié, *Les délices de la France* (Paris, 1670) p. 122.

28   *Mémoires de Louis XIV*, ed. C. Dreyss (Paris, 1860) ii, p. 482.

29   P. Heliot, 'La guerre dite de Lustucru et les privilèges du Boulonnais', *Revue du Nord*, xxi (1935).

30   A. Communay, *Audijos. La gabelle en Gascogne* (Paris, Auch, 1893-4).

31   Forbonnais, *Recherches et considérations*, iii, p. 54.

32   De Vissac, *Chronique vivaroise, Antoine du Roure et la révolte de 1670* (Paris, 1895). For a penetrating analysis see E. Le Roy Ladurie, *Les paysans de Languedoc*, 2 vols (Paris, 1966) pp. 607–11.

33   Forbonnais, *Recherches et considérations*, iii, p. 56.

34   'Documents sur l'émeute de Bordeaux en 1674–1675', *Archives historiques de la Gironde* (1906) i, pp. 145–90.

35   Letter of the intendant of Sève to Colbert (24 Apr 1675), published by Clément in *Histoire de la vie et de l'administration de Colbert* (Paris, 1846) p. 365.

36   J. Lemoine, *La révolte du papier timbré ou des bonnets rouges en Bretagne* (Paris, 1898); cf. Mousnier, *Fureurs paysannes*, pp. 123–56.

37   Texte of the *Code paysan* (Peasants Code) in Arthur de La Borderie, *La révolte du papier timbré* (Saint-Brieuc, 1884) pp. 93–8.

38   This cry was traditional in the south west. There are echoes of it in the letter which the assistant to the receiver-general of Bordeaux wrote to

Colbert on 30 March 1675: Clément, *Histoire de la vie . . . de Colbert,* p. 359.
39 *Les soupirs de la France esclave qui aspire après la liberté* (Amsterdam, 1689).
40 Ibid., Mémoire II, p. 28.
41 For a complete edition by the Institute Nationale d'Etude Démographique of Boisguilbert's manuscripts and earlier printed works, see *Pierre de Boisguilbert ou la naissance de l'économie politique* (Paris, 1966).
42 For a detailed study of the capitation of 1695 see A. M. de Boislisle's edition of the *Mémoires de Saint-Simon*, 43 vols (Paris, 1879–1930) II, appendix IV.
43 Text published by Boislisle in appendix to his *Correspondance des controleurs généraux*, I.
44 Boislisle (ed.), *Mémoires de Saint-Simon*, II, p. 342.
45 The most recent edition of the *Lettre à Louis XIV* with a facsimile is that of Henri Guillemin (Neuchâtel, 1961).
46 Manuscript published in the edition of Bousguilbert cited in note 41 above, II, p. 663.
47 Ibid., p. 879.
48 Vauban, *Dixme Royale*, ed. Emile Coornaert (Paris, 1933).
49 Boislisle (ed.), *Mémoires de Saint-Simon*, XX, appendix V.
50 Ibid., pp. 455, 458.
51 Ibid., p. 166.
52 J. B. Bossuet, *Politique tirée des propres paroles do l'Ecriture Sainte*, ed. Jacques Le Brun (Geneva, 1967) bk. VI, proposition II, para. 3.

11 Manufacturing Industries in Seventeenth-Century France*

P. DEYON

A great deal has been written on the industries of seventeenth-century France, but ignorance and uncertainty still envelop many aspects of the subject. Although we are well informed about state intervention in the industrial sector, we still lack essential information on prices, profits and the volume of production. There are few studies of great industrial families and their achievements, or of the merchants and financiers who periodically helped Colbert in his work. I propose to sketch in the information that we do possess, and will then pose some questions and suggest some hypotheses, not just on the probable trends of industrial development but also on the leading groups and organs of production.

When we look at the general conditions of manufacturing, one point immediately strikes us: although France was the foremost European power and possessed considerable natural resources, it did not make the most of its advantages and was even rather backward in comparison with some of its neighbours.

The advantages were: forests and mineral deposits sufficient to meet the requirements of the technology of the time, except perhaps in the case of non-ferrous metals; an abundant population; and a system of government better organised than in the neighbouring countries. Yet in spite of these favourable preconditions, the men in charge of the French government seem to have been obsessed by foreign competition and distressed by the backwardness of French methods.

* First published in *XVIIe Siècle*, nos 70–1 (1966) under the title 'La production manufacturière en France au XVIIe siècle et ses problèmes'.

As a result of the Wars of Religion of the sixteenth century, of the Thirty Years War and of the seventeenth-century domestic Frondes, the French economy had suffered some serious setbacks. The coinage was adversely affected by continual debasements and by the failure of the government to fix a rate of exchange which would balance internal and external purchasing power. There was no banking system and thus no real centre for international exchange. French manufactures had lost that excellence of quality which certain luxury industries in Italy still retained, while failing to adopt those methods of large-scale production which were transforming certain sectors of the English economy. Foreign trade still clung to its out-of-date organisation; the merchants were unable on their own to form those great companies which had brought commercial success to England and the Dutch Republic. Finally, the crown had abandoned the few colonial trading posts set up by Admiral Coligny, and the French navy at the beginning of the seventeenth century still lacked large, ocean-going ships.

Eager to achieve real power for France, the central government under Louis XIV soon realised the contradiction which existed between the grandeur of its political ambitions and the economic and industrial organisation of the country. Keen to become the first power in Europe in the seventeenth century, the monarchy followed a policy of state support, regulation and economic control; and we must therefore take into account its intervention and efforts in any study of the organisation of manufacturing in France.

1. THE FORMS OF ORGANISATION OF PRODUCTION
In our classification we shall use purely geographical and technological criteria : urban as opposed to rurally based industry, concentrated as opposed to dispersed organisation. Other distinctions, arising out of juridical status or social organisation, will also be noted.

(a) Dispersed urban industry
This generally implies family workshops with one or two journeymen and an apprentice, using artisan or manual methods, with the processes of production split up by the rivalries of guilds and crafts. In a system like this the apprentice or the journeyman

could hope one day to take over the master's position and achieve independence.

But certain distinctions must be made within the urban artisan class. The most important difference was that between guild or sworn crafts and the regulated crafts. In towns all artisan work was controlled by the state or by the urban administration though the relevant authorities in many respects left the craftsman relatively free; as long as he complied with public regulations, he could do as he pleased within his own craft. This is the system of regulated crafts. In the guild or sworn craft there was also control of artisans from within by groups which had organised themselves in craft guilds, comprising in theory both masters and journeymen. These guilds enjoyed a monopoly of production and controlled their recruitment by means of the institution of the master's piece.[1] The craft guild thus assumed the form of a corporate defence and mutual assistance organisation; and it also took part in certain religious festivals as a brotherhood. In some French towns all crafts were regulated with no sworn guilds; in others some were organised into guilds, while others remained regulated and therefore open. This indicates that the edicts of 1599 and 1673, which proclaimed sworn guilds obligatory, were not enforced.

There is another distinction to be noted within the organisation of urban artisans : whether the artisans were economically independent or not. If they were, they would work with materials which they had bought for themselves, and they would sell the finished product on the open market. This was true for a large number of the smaller crafts catering direct to customers such as coopers, soap-boilers or tailors. But if they were not economically independent, they were in reality reduced to the level of piece-workers, paid according to contract by merchants for the amount of work they completed. This was the case, for example, in the silk industry of Lyons. Merchants also frequently succeeded in establishing control over rural workers, whose activity they often initiated.

(b) Dispersed rural industry
This industry enjoyed comparative freedom from restrictions; rules were infrequently enforced and guilds were extremely rare outside the towns. Where they did exist, their structure was very

loose. The guild set up in 1666 by the rural workers of Aumale did not require a master's piece and gave the masters complete freedom in the selection of their journeymen. This weakness in organisation and the lack of regulations help to explain the central role which the putting-out merchants were able to play. Despite the existence of the known barter relations between farmers and weavers (about which we have little detailed information), it seems that few rural craftsmen were in a position to profit directly from their work. One certain exception were the pin-makers of the region of Laigle, Conche and Breteuil in Lower Normandy, examined by J. Vidalenc.[2]

Piece-work and putting-out systems were the basis of the rural textile industries. That almost all the spinning industry in the seventeenth century was rurally based has long been realised, but wool and linen weaving were also widespread in the countryside. These industries provided a supplementary source of income to the people of western France (Picardy, Dauphiné and many other regions) where the sound of looms was heard in most villages.

The country weaver often worked at a loom which did not belong to him and his wages were half those of the town craftsman. Bignon, intendant of Picardy, in a memorandum of 1698 estimated daily wages at 10 or 15 *sous* for town craftsmen and 5 for those of the countryside.[3] In Dauphiné the condition of rural weavers was just as precarious; and the inspector of manufactures observed in 1728 that the workers to whom the merchants sold their wool on credit were absolutely dependent upon the latter, who forced them to sell their products at whatever price the merchants fixed.[4]

It would be necessary to draw a map of the locations of the rural textile industries in order to determine the relationship between the overpopulation of certain districts, the inadequate resources of others, and the presence of alternative sources of income. The craft activity of the rural workman remained secondary and seasonal. He was more often than not still a peasant; and the reports of the inspectors of manufactures never fail to differentiate between the work of the first and second half of the year : the productivity of the second was always less because of the labour necessarily withdrawn for the sake of harvesting, ploughing and sowing.

Town guilds disliked the competition of rural workshops and took measures against it, but in vain : they forebade urban workers and masters to settle in the countryside, and dyers in the towns were prohibited from dyeing cloth produced in the villages. But despite this hostility and these prohibitions rural industry increased during the seventeenth century. This allowed merchants to cut costs and maintain the level of profits in a period of economic difficulties and falling industrial prices. Gradually a division of labour appeared between the towns and the surrounding country areas : the countryside specialised in spinning, wool-washing, linen-weaving and low-quality cloth-making; while the town retained the quality manufactures. This kind of system allowed great flexibility in the organisation of production. It would be wrong to imagine, however, that there was a clear distinction between the dispersed rural industry and the more concentrated industry which we shall speak of in a moment. Between the operations of the country hat-maker on the one hand, and the factories producing Point de France [lace] at Auxerre or Alençon, there were workshops which the wives of prosperous farmers organised during the winter months; between the little shop of a weaver at Amiens or Abbeville, and the Van Robais factory, there would be more substantial workshops where a dozen or so masters and workmen were employed by a small-scale cloth merchant.

(c) Concentrated industry
In both town and country concentrated types of industry appeared as the result of certain conditions. Sometimes it was the nature of the techniques themselves which required a concentrated labour-force. This was so for the new type of furnaces adopted in many provinces during the sixteenth century : these required far more men than the older type of iron works. Metallurgical establishments which used the power of running water (such as tilt-hammers, steel works, wire-drawing mills, cannon-foundries or factories for making anchors), were also by their very nature larger and more important. Glassmaking and printing in the cities followed a similar pattern.

A second factor causing a more concentrated form of organisation was the application of the poor laws which created the workshops of poor-houses and hospitals. Charity this may have been, but it was also work under close supervision in grim hostels where the paupers were subjected to a near-military discipline. Colbert was in favour of this system and tried to use it, for example, in the manufacture of lace and serge. Concentration made it easy to introduce new techniques and provided a few privileged contractors with a particularly cheap and docile labour-force: so cheap, that in some workshops (at Rheims for example) the young inmates received nothing but their board and lodging.[5]

The preoccupation with training and discipline also gave rise to a third type of concentrated industry. I am referring here to those establishments of which the Van Robais factory is a prototype: large-scale operations producing high-quality goods to compete with foreign manufactures – fine cloth comparable to the best English or Dutch products, Venetian mirrors, Flemish tapestries. They demanded a large capital outlay, experienced workmen, raw materials of high quality and a director eager to succeed in the particular type of work involved, ready to reach perfection by stages. These were long-term projects, and also risky ones, so that state support was required from the start.

(d) State intervention

Historians have devoted most attention to state support in creation of large-scale, concentrated industries. But it would be a serious mistake to assume that all privileges for the establishment of manufactures were for the benefit of concentrated operations. This was undoubtedly true in the case of establishments belonging to the crown, like the Gobelins, the arsenals or some of the state cannon-foundries, or certain famous foundations like the royal mirror factory or the Van Robais factory. But manufacturing privileges could be granted to a merchant or a group of merchants making use of a scattered labour-force, in which case the 'manufacture' was no more than the office from which the putting-out or shipment was handled.[6] In certain cases a whole locality might be given a privilege for a type of manufacture, as with some of the centres of the cloth industry in Languedoc or in Sedan. We should note that in that town the masters who benefited from the privilege already figured as small entrepreneurs in the cloth trade, providing work for a considerable number of poor masters and journeymen.

A manufacturing privilege had two essential characteristics. The state demanded concern for quality, the observance of detailed regulations,[7] and a certain volume of production. In return the state gave loans at advantageous rates, tax-exemptions, favourable conditions for foreign workers, and almost always a temporary monopoly. State intervention was meant to be temporary, and was to cease as soon as the new industries began to make a profit. The state was not wedded to concentration. Sometimes, when the technical conditions permitted, a centralised industry was broken up. In 1666, for example, the workmen of the silk stocking manufacture at the Château de Madrid were set up as independent masters and formed into a craft guild.

2. FRENCH INDUSTRY IN THE SEVENTEENTH CENTURY : THE VOLUME OF PRODUCTION

We still have much to learn on this subject. The sets of statistics which we possess are incomplete and as yet do not allow of a general interpretation. We know some of the factors which affected the rhythm of industrial activity : there were periodic short-term crises caused by inadequate harvests, then the high price of foodstuffs reduced the level of consumption of a wide range of manufactured products and touched off a crisis in the availability of ready cash and credit, which in turn temporarily paralysed the whole economy. We can also follow the effects of certain fluctuations in international and overseas trade and note disturbances due to outbreaks of plague, rebellions and wars.

The study of the long-term economic situation poses far more complex problems. In our present state of knowledge we are forced to conclude that there were great variations and inequalities between one province or sector of the economy and another. The information we have from the second part of the century in particular seems often so contradictory that it is hard to speak of an overall trend of industrial production. Let us summarise the information we possess :

(a) The large number of studies on prices, and some sets of figures on the volume of production, permit us to conclude that a long period of expansion in the manufacturing sector continued down to the 1630s. The silk industry of Lyons progressed; at the time of the royal visit of 1575 it comprised just over 200 master artisans, and by 1621 the number had risen to 716. Similar progress can be seen in the muslin industry at Rheims, where the tax of 4 *deniers* levied on each piece reached its highest level between

1625 and 1635. In the same period the cloth industry of Picardy was at its most active, as is revealed by the returns from the taxes levied upon it and the number of apprentices taken on.[8]

(*b*) We find general agreement also in the figures for the movement of production during the second third of the century. After 1630–5 production slowed down or declined everywhere. Industry at Lyons went into a temporary phase of stagnation. In some industries there is not merely decline, but collapse : between 1636 and 1653 the number of masters in the cloth trade at Beauvais fell by more than one half; the returns from the tax on muslin at Rheims declined by five-sixths; the textile industry at Amiens and the cloth industry of Languedoc show comparable drops in activity.

All sectors of the economy must have been similarly affected, for protectionist measures were used to succour all types of production. Long before Colbert the new tariffs of 1644–54 heralded a new policy. The situation must have been particularly serious in the French textile industry, for in a period of ten years the import duties on Dutch and Flemish camlets rose fivefold, those on fine English cloth went from 6 to 35 livres per piece of 24–6 ells, whilst serges which had only paid one livre per piece in 1643 had to pay almost seven after 1654. The seriousness of the depression certainly justified Colbert's wide-ranging plans and the energy with which he pursued them throughout his ministry.

(*c*) Unfortunately, from the beginning of Colbert's period in office we know far less about the volume of French industrial production. This is not as surprising as it might appear. During a 'B' phase, with a continual fall in the price of gold, once the first moment of collapse has passed there follows a period of efforts to adapt to the changed conditions and to restore profits. The various branches of production manifest different degrees of flexibility and ability to adapt to the new economic situation. To quote just one example, the ability of the journeymen and homeworkers to resist a lowering in their real or nominal wages varies according to the degree of cohesion within their trade organisations and the state of the labour market.

Let us briefly summarise what knowledge we have at present. Colbert did not achieve results to match his hopes anywhere, or hardly anywhere. In some fields he met with complete failure, in others there was a slow but progressive improvement; new methods were introduced, beacons and bases for future advances set up. The second half of Louis' reign does not in fact seem as dark, economically speaking, as some historians have suggested : the figures for the exceptional crisis years of 1693 and 1709 have been given too much prominence and too little attention has been paid to statistical theory. The movement of prices in the second half of Louis' reign indicates a shift in the general situation, and there are signs of a rise in prices each decade. Seaborne trade was increasing. Devaluations, the growing use of bills of exchange, and increased monetary circulation all combined to raise the nominal level of profits and lower the cost of real wages. State expenditure, resulting from involvement in two major wars, also stimulated various kinds of production. Some industries grew : cloth-making in Languedoc, several manufactures in Picardy, the linen industry in the west, muslin-production at Le Mans. But others were in a state of continual crisis : glass-making in Langue-doc, the metal industries in general and those of Dauphiné in particular. Once again we must stress that we do not have reliable statistics for the metal industries, though we know that their problems resulted not so much from the contraction of the market as from inherent organisational weaknesses in the industries themselves.

3. FRENCH INDUSTRIES AT THE END OF LOUIS XIV'S REIGN (a survey limited to the textile and metallurgical industries).

(a) *Mining and metallurgy*
In the seventeenth century these industries were still very scattered. Wherever there were forests or easily worked deposits of ore we find iron foundries or new furnaces, especially in the Pyrenees, Angoumois, Périgord, Dauphiné, Berry, Lower Alsace, Champagne and Normandy. But despite this widespread geographical dispersion, production was beginning to be concentrated in more substantial units. The replacement of the old type of iron-smelting plant by the new high furnace in some regions during the sixteenth century made such a development inevitable. In the old type of furnace, still used in Roussillon and the Pyrenees, the 'pig' of crude iron was removed from the ashes of the fire and then had to be refined and purified. The process of liquefaction and casting did not come until the introduction of the high furnace, which

increased production tenfold but required a large investment of capital and a continual and regular supply of wood fuel. This was a source of worry for the iron-masters. They had to pay more and more for wood, and at the same time were forced to respect royal laws which gave greater protection to the forests than in the past. Many had to request letters-patent from the king to ensure a regular supply of fuel for their operations. Similar problems faced the iron-founders, who needed wood to re-heat ingots and 'pigs' because in France – unlike England – coal was not yet used in the secondary metallurgical industries.

Here and there the first signs of concentrated organisation began to appear in response to the pressure of technological developments. In 1634 the company formed by the iron-masters Damvillier, Gendre and Laisné was granted the exclusive right to build forges and iron-furnaces in Burgundy, with permission to take all the materials, wood and ores it needed, on condition that it compensated the property-owners. For its part the company agreed to supply a given quantity of cannon balls per year for the army.

The needs of the armed forces largely explain the government's preoccupation with this type of industry under Colbert. Royal iron-foundries were established at Douai, Metz, Strasbourg, Besançon, Narbonne, Pinerolo, Perpignan and other places. Some cannon-foundries remained private concerns but received state subsidies: Dallicz de la Tour, receiver-general (*receveur-général*) of the *taille* in Dauphiné and one of Colbert's most important collaborators in industrial development, formed a big company with the Swede Besche to produce cannons and anchors for the navy. The manufacture of armaments was not the only industry which benefited from state support. In 1666 a royal company was formed combining all mines and foundries in Languedoc; at the same time another company was formed for the Nivernais to build a tin-plant at Beaumont-la-Ferrière with the help of German specialists.[9]

The premature disappearance of many of these enterprises poses a problem. Why did they not succeed in effecting a radical change in the methods of production, and raising the French metallurgical industries to the level of their competitors in England or Liège?

One reason lies in the fact that the shareholders of such companies were often recruited under duress: Colbert obliged tax-farmers and other officials connected with finance to buy shares, which they then hastened to dispose of. Furthermore, the companies and co-operative enterprises which we have mentioned were often only superficially commercial. The participants were more interested in profiting from a monopoly than in building up a new and technologically superior enterprise. The best example of this mentality is a company founded in Dauphiné in 1657 by the iron-masters of Moirans, Vienne, Rives and other places, along with certain merchants from Lyons.[10] The stated purpose of the consortium with a capital of 100,000 livres was to regularise the production and marketing of steel. But it proceeded to halt production at eleven out of its sixty-eight plants and limit operations at the others to nine months in the year.

More long-lived but not fundamentally different were the enterprises of J. de Barral, who from 1675 took control of all foundries, high furnaces and tilt-hammers in the Allevard region, and Jean Maslin, bourgeois and merchant of Nevers, who assumed direction of all iron-works in the valleys of the Nièvre and Ixeure – buying a forge in one place, providing the money for a high furnace in another, and making a long-term supply contract with an apparently independent iron-master.

(b) The textile industries
At this period textile manufacturing was by far the most important sector of French industry, comprising the woollen, linen and silk manufactures.

The woollen-cloth industry had two main sectors: the older, essentially urban high-quality cloth manufacture and the newer, coarse-cloth industry, which was started towards the end of the fifteenth century and located mainly in Picardy and Champagne.

The older type went through a serious crisis in the mid-seventeenth century. Colbert was much concerned about it, both because of the decline in sales and the drop in quality. He called in Dutch or Flemish entrepreneurs and craftsmen, trained in the methods of Leiden, Brussels and elsewhere, to bring the production of the cloth towns up to the standard achieved by the best foreign producers. Massieu and Jemblin were installed at Caen, Van Robais at Abbeville, Abraham Cossart, Denis Maréchal and Isaac de la Tour at Fécamp and Dieppe. Their privileges included loans and subsidies, often proportional to the number of looms set up, and a temporary monopoly of sales. The guilds opposed the new foundations and proved hostile to the foreigners who ran them, but could not adopt the new methods as their master-craftsmen were unwilling to face the risks involved in technical innovation. Colbert's efforts were crowned with success, at least as far as the standards of quality were concerned : in 1681 he could write that 'the King will no longer give the same privileges and exemptions as in the past, because there are now enough manufactures for the whole kingdom'.[11] The new types of cloth gradually gained ground with the older craftsmen as well, and many of the privileged manufactures were allowed to disappear once they had fulfilled their educative function.

The products of the luxury cloth industry were destined for the domestic market and were protected by almost prohibitive customs duties. This was not the case in respect of the cloth industry of Languedoc and the light cloth manufactures in general. The Languedoc output was intended mainly for export to the Levant, where it faced powerful competition from English and Dutch products. Colbert's persistence succeeded in laying the foundations for the future prosperity of this industry, which gained on its competitors in Mediterranean markets during the first half of the eighteenth century.

The light-cloth industry of northern France was able to survive without direct intervention by the state. It benefited from a shift in demand towards cheaper types of cloth. It was able to produce a great many varieties and gained new customers when the 1686 ban on importation of printed foreign cloth came into force : the domestic cloth was found to be an excellent light and attractive substitute. The weavers of Amiens used endless combinations of wool, silk and even goat- and camel-hair in their cloth; and Jean Véron introduced the manufacture of muslin to Le Mans, where it was to have a brilliant future.[12] As the towns concentrated on new processes, the countryside was able to take over the coarser cloth manufactures; cheap, rural cloth-production spread in Champagne, Normandy and Picardy. Thanks to their flexibility and willingness to adapt to new fashions and methods, the light cloth manufacturers of northern France recovered markets in Spain and the Americas which they had lost at the time of the great depression. From the beginning of the eighteenth century

cloth from Rheims, Le Mans, Amiens and Châlons came second
only to linen on the list of French exports to Cadiz.

Linen was the most important French export. The main centres
of the industry were in Upper Picardy, Normandy, the *bocage*
country round Le Mans, Brittany and Dauphiné. Linen-weaving
was overwhelmingly rural and had grown up in comparative
freedom from guild restrictions. At Le Mans in 1667 several
merchants, a glass-blower, an iron-master, two notaries and two
lawyers formed a company to start linen-weaving in the town,
having first arranged for the dissolution of the guild of master-
weavers. Everywhere it was the merchants who developed this
industry, and they also introduced new methods of bleaching at
Beauvais, La Ferté-Macé and Laval.

Mercantile initiative was also important in the Lyons silk industry which experienced a remarkable stage of growth in the
seventeenth century. Reports from the periodic inspection of the
workshops indicate that there were 1648 looms in 1621, double
that number in 1660 and 5067 by 1720. In this instance too,
prosperity was the reward of diversification. The introduction of
special frames permitted the production of figured materials –
brocades, damasks, brocatellos and so on. The increase in
productivity was achieved under the direction of merchants who
at the beginning of the eighteenth century numbered from two
to three hundred. They controlled about two-thirds of the looms
and provided silk, gold thread and patterns to the weavers, who
were called master workmen. Not unnaturally these merchants
provoked the enmity of those craftsmen who remained independent.[18]

In the most dynamic areas of the textile industry, therefore –
in those sectors which managed to adapt and prosper without
state support – the old guild system was severely shaken. A large
number of proletarianised artisans had appeared, indigent masters
or master-workmen, and this facilitated the takeover of the industry by the merchants. Struggles developed between the merchants and the masters who remained independent, since the latter
were also trying to concentrate looms and workers under their
control, to expand their workshops and put out work for the poor
to do at home. At Lille, at Amiens and at Le Mans the merchants
managed to prohibit the masters from selling cloth which they
themselves had not made. The conflict was most acute at Lyons,

and dominated the industrial life of the city until the mid-nineteenth century with tragic results.

Many other sections of French industry in the seventeenth century deserve discussion: the glass industry, wood-working, leather manufacture, pottery, paper-making and printing, furniture-making and tapestry, the last two particularly cherished by the government.

But as space will not permit, we must draw some general conclusions from our analysis of the metallurgic and the textile industries. We noted that one of the most striking characteristics of French industry in the seventeenth century was its extreme dispersion. There were factories and workshops everywhere, and every province showed a wide range of different industries.[14] Colbert's administration encouraged this diversity in order to give all regions a measure of economic and monetary autonomy.

It is difficult as yet to assess the effectiveness of Colbert's policies since for this we need statistical information not yet available; but we can give him credit for having diagnosed the sickness which threatened to destroy French greatness: that of idleness. Everything conspired to divert the sons of the bourgeois and merchants from economic activity – the general acceptance of aristocratic prejudices, the suspicion of the Catholic reform movement of 'trafficking in bills of exchange and usury', the backwardness of commercial and financial methods, the setbacks to trade in a time of recession, and the place which the nobility of the robe enjoyed within the state. To live nobly, in other words in the manner of the nobility, idly and without following a trade or craft, was in itself a claim to honour and social esteem. All Colbert's energy was needed in the struggle against this combination of interests, predilections and snobberies, and for his fight to get France back to work after the exhaustion of the Fronde.

We still have to explain why such an effort, unique in the history of seventeenth-century Europe, did not achieve a more far-reaching transformation of the methods of production. French industry in fact remained blocked in its development by three significant obstacles.

(a) It was still seriously affected by periodic agrarian crises which produced a drop of from one quarter to one third in demand. These recurring crises hindered the accumulation of working capital; industry in seventeenth-century France lacked a great internal market. The cyclical or permanent poverty of a section of the peasantry could not sustain a regular and adequate demand.

(*b*) The consequences of these periodic crises were all the more serious since the credit system in France was still rudimentary. There was a shortage of long-term investment in industry as capital was attracted by more profitable opportunities, and there was also a lack of short-term commercial credit. Discounting remained, if not exceptional, at least semi-secret, condemned by theology and ignored by law until the end of the seventeenth century. In general, official attitudes in economic matters remained tradition-bound for a long time. Colbert and his contemporaries did not realise the advantages which would derive from a general system of freedom of labour. Their outlook was still marked by a corporate and regulatory spirit inherited from the Middle Ages. Nor did they understand the advantages which England and the Dutch Republic were obtaining from a more flexible and liberal monetary system, and from a more sophisticated system of exchange.

(*c*) Finally, the crucial problem would seem to have been that seventeenth-century France was short of entrepreneurs. Neither the well-to-do craftsman nor the merchant-trader was a real entrepreneur. The artisans naturally clung to their time-honoured procedures; in the woollen-cloth industry, for instance, the material was worked on by eight or nine men in succession, each belonging to different crafts or guilds. This fragmentation of the manufacturing process prevented an artisan from devising or implementing a new technique or a more economical method of production. Guild regulations, royal ordinances and protectionism all helped to make technological progress and invention more difficult and less attractive. The exceptional master craftsman who was intelligent and ambitious was hampered in his efforts, not only by regulations but also by the united opposition of his co-workers and the merchants.

Even the merchants could not provide industry with a stable and progressive group of entrepreneurs. Progress requires ingenious, tenacious personalities, willing to take risks. The merchant-trader putting out work for craftsmen and peasants at home was not of this type. He often did not have a precise knowledge of the techniques, let alone the desire to improve them. For him, the only way to lower costs was by reducing wages and piece-rates. The comparative over-population of the countryside, and improvements in the government machinery, favoured his policy. Furthermore, he only invested a small amount of capital in his operations. Although he provided part of the mobile capital in the form of the product being worked up, he would not invest any fixed capital without invoking state aid, in the form of privileges, monopolies or subsidies.

The merchant manufacturer, where he did in fact exist, was too often fickle and unfaithful to his profession. After fifteen or twenty years of manufacturing he would shift his capital to an investment in property or a *seigneurie* or into the purchase of an office or a tax-farming contract. Here we touch the fundamental problem of mental outlook, for manufacturing was not considered a means of social advancement in seventeenth-century France, and even suffered under hostile prejudice. A typical instance of this is the attitude of many mine-owners and proprietors of iron-works who, behaving more as stockholders than as entrepreneurs, preferred to lease out their operations rather than direct them in person.[15] The state apparatus offered, through the sale of offices or grants of privilege, greater rewards for vanity than could be found in a career in manufacturing. Its fiscal administration also offered more profitable opportunities for investment than the difficult operations of industry or trade. The financial officials and tax-farmers whom Colbert obliged to invest in his manu-facturing companies sought to withdraw their capital as soon as they could, in order to re-invest in transactions offering a higher return, like tax-farming contracts, state loans and other financial ventures. In this way part of the country's wealth was rendered unproductive and the spirit of enterprise was discouraged. This indicates, if any further proof were required, that the history of industrial activity cannot be separated from the history of mental attitudes and social structures.

NOTES

1   The *chef d'oeuvre* to establish that a given standard of craftsmanship had been reached.

2 J. Vidalenc, *La petite métallurgie rurale en Haute-Normandie sous l'Ancien Régime* (Paris, 1946).

3 Bibl. Mun. Amiens, MSS. 505, *Mémoire* by the intendant Bignon.

4 Report of the inspector of manufactures in 1728, quoted by P. Léon, *Naissance de la grande industrie en Dauphiné* (Paris, 1952).

5 When a manufacturer enjoys a monopoly, this almost always involves the lowering of wages in comparison with previous levels.

6 This happened frequently with manufactures of lace and bonnets, and particularly in the case of the Point de France lace and the London serge manufactures.

7 The old municipal regulations provided the model for this by specifying, for the cloth industry, the size of pieces of cloth, the number of threads, the sequence of dyeing operations, and so on.

8 See my article, 'Variations de la production textile aux XVIe et XVIIe siècles', *Annales: Economies, Sociétés, Civilisations* (Sep–Oct 1963).

9 B. Gille, *Les origines de la grande industrie en France* (Paris, 1947) and C. W. Cole, *Colbert and a Century of French Mercantilism* (New York, 1939) p. 320ff.

10 Gille, *Les origines*, p. 31.

11 Quoted in Cole, *Colbert*, p. 155.

12 F. Dornic, *L'industrie textile dans le Maine et ses débouchés internationaux* (Le Mans, 1955).

13 J. Godart, *L'ouvrier en soie, monographie du tisseur lyonnais* (Lyon, Paris, 1899) and E. Pariset, *Histoire de la fabrique lyonnaise* (Lyon, 1901).

14 The different manufacturing regions can be classified according to the foreign or domestic market for their products, their location in town or country, their legal status and regulations, and the relations between merchants and manufacturers prevailing within them.

15 The duc d'Aumont, the marquis de la Vrillière, the duchesse d'Uzès and the duc de Montausier, who all received important concessions, did so.

12 The French Navy under Louis XIV*

ARMEL DE WISMES

By reason of its geographical position at the far end of the European continent, France has frequently been threatened by invasion. The French have therefore from early days sought security in the possession of a powerful army. The desire for a strong navy came much later. It was Philip the Fair who created the first French navy, but his sons allowed it to decay, and the naval defeat of Sluys (24 June 1340) led directly to the Hundred Years War.

There have always been great French seamen, but a properly organised naval force did not really exist until the time of Richelieu and Colbert. For centuries France had few maritime frontiers: Normandy and Gascony were English possessions, Provençe was a separate appanage, and Brittany maintained its independence as a Grand Duchy with meticulous stubbornness.

French kings therefore usually leased ships, as the need arose, from peoples with a maritime tradition. Since it was easy to convert a peaceful merchant ship into a man-of-war, they could spare themselves the burden of maintaining a fleet, always a heavy drain on royal finances.

● Until the seventeenth century no real corps of naval officers existed. Ships were run by pilots or sailing-masters, and the man who held the title of captain would often be an infantry or cavalry officer. He delegated his powers to the sailing-master, and only took over himself in periods of danger (in battles or boardings) to direct the fighting as a soldier. He was in effect only the leader of an expedition. All this helps to explain why the king's ships were at first largely commanded by officers drawn from the

* Specially commissioned for this volume.

Knights of Malta, who were experienced sailors. In addition to the usual qualifications of bravery, they possessed nautical skills which were rare and precious at that time : schooled in pitiless warfare against Turkish or Algerian corsairs, the Knights of Saint John (successively of Jerusalem, Rhodes and Malta), displayed an incomparable skill. France's resources were severely strained to maintain fleets in both the Mediterranean and the Atlantic, and when Richelieu began to create a navy he often called upon these knights of the sea.

The fleets of the 'Ponant' and the 'Levant'
One must never forget that the French fleet was always divided into two sections: that of the 'Ponant' for the Atlantic, the Channel and the North Sea, and that of the 'Levant' for the coasts of the Mediterranean. When there was no Admiral of France, a mainly honorific office and title granted to a prince of the blood, the two sections of the fleets were under the orders of the two vice-admirals of Ponant and Levant.

The Mediterranean had always been considered the centre of the seafaring world. Had not the greatest civilisations flourished on its shores? But by the seventeenth century the Mediterranean galley was outclassed by the ocean-going sailing ship. In 1684 the warship *Le Bon* provided striking proof of this by defeating a fleet of thirty-seven Spanish galleys off the island of Elba. Clearly it was no longer enough to know how to pursue the enemy into a creek and then capture him by boarding. The great sailing ships were already fighting in formation, and this new technique of naval warfare required specific training.

The Atlantic coasts of France became increasingly important as the state encouraged maritime trade. In 1626 Louis XIII gave his approval to plans for a company with a strange name : 'The Company of the Vessel of Saint Peter of the *fleur-de-lys*'. In 1654, 'The Company of the Continent of America or Equinoctial France' began to send ships to the West Indies. Richelieu built arsenals at Le Havre, Brest and Brouage, although this last port (in Poitou) soon silted up and had to be replaced fifty years later by Rochefort. These Atlantic ports became the bases for a large number of shipowners and merchants. As Spain declined, France began to play the role of a major colonial power. For too long the careful French bourgeois had allowed foreigners to monopolise the profits – and risks – of trade with distant lands. Now they began to acquaint themselves with the ocean trade-routes, and a book by Jean Eon, entitled *Honourable Commerce*, urging the French to take part in this trade made a strong impact.

'Sail away, seek adventure ...'

From the seventeenth century onwards the French became a maritime people. They hunted whales in the northern seas, sailed to New France (Canada), to the West Indies and to Guinea, and sometimes even followed the Cape of Good Hope route, touching at Brazil and Madagascar on the way to the East Indies, the Dutch Eldorado.

Because sailing ships had to follow certain routes, particular waters were especially frequented, and it was here that corsairs and pirates gathered. Once the great river of gold, silver and precious stones had begun to flow from the Americas to the Old World, English, Dutch and French freebooters attacked the Spanish *flotas del oro y de la plata* and the Portuguese vessels coming from Brazil, Asia or the East Indies.

In their little ships men set sail from Bordeaux, Saint-Malo and the Basque country, hoping to intercept the galleons on their way home from Havana. The Spaniards had to sail as far north as the Bermudas to find the regular westerly winds which would take them to Cape Saint-Vincent. The corsairs would lie in wait near the Azores, ready to fall swiftly on their prey. They boarded : grappling-irons were thrown, hulls ground together and sailors leapt to the attack with pikes, axes, sabres and cutlasses. Those who fell were immediately replaced, as if by magic. A fight without quarter began, and all too frequently the victors proved cruel even in victory. It was a struggle with no holds barred, for 'a share in the riches of the Indies'.

Richelieu plans for a regular navy

Even though the French coast favoured the creation of corsair bases to threaten enemy merchantmen bearing the wealth of Asia and America to Europe, Richelieu did not think it advisable to encourage this type of warfare. His foremost aim was to create a regular navy, and this meant that he had to bring as many seamen as possible under royal authority. He therefore forebade 'all captains, masters and owners of ships from taking sailors away from the ports of this kingdom, and all seamen and gunners from signing aboard a ship, unless the king's ships had their complement of men; and this on pain of death'. He wanted France to take part in the struggle between the great powers of western Europe – England, France, Spain and the Dutch Republic – for control of the seas, a struggle which necessitated huge fleets. Richelieu undoubtedly staked out the road that Colbert was to follow, but at first his efforts were mainly directed towards increasing 'the dignity and prestige of the King' by the conquest of colonies.

It was an economist, du Noyer de Saint-Martin, who convinced Richelieu of the commercial value of colonies. The gains of distant territory would enrich French merchants, develop the re-export trade and lead to industrialisation in the French port regions. Such acquisitions required a strong navy and Richelieu was not given the time to create it. After his death the royal fleet was still so weak that Duquesne, to stop the Spaniards from entering the mouth of the Gironde, had to reinforce the squadron of the duc de Vendôme with several ships 'equipped at his own expense'. But the existence of French overseas colonies and trading-posts certainly gave an added importance to operations at sea, and during Louis XIV's personal reign all the seas became theatres of war : in the Dutch War, in the Nine Years War and in the War of the Spanish Succession.

At the outset of his personal reign (from 1661) the young Louis had visualised military operations as a well-ordered promenade, with parades of carriages through the streets of conquered cities. The uncertainty of war at sea did not tempt him; in his eyes the money required to maintain a fleet was wasted. Only once was he persuaded to go aboard one of his ships, the *Entreprenant*, at Dunkirk. All the ceremonies organised for that occasion had one purpose : to interest the king in his ports and warships. It was at this stage that Colbert intervened.

Thanks to the genius of Colbert

Colbert intended 'to restore the glory of the kingdom by maintaining a considerable number of vessels at sea'. In this great task his most important helper was his son, the marquis de Seignelay, and the admiral who best suited his purposes was Tourville. Colbert's temperament led him to attempt regulations for all areas of statecraft, and his great ordinance of 1681 became the basis of naval organisation. From 1661 to his death he worked unceasingly to build up the navy, and after 1683 Seignelay carried on the task with the same passion as his father had shown.

Colbert knew that it was not enough just to build ships, and laid down a three-part programme of naval development :

1. The creation of vast stocks of all types of naval supplies, and the organisation of large numbers of workmen to supply the needs of the fleet.
2. The building of several arsenals for the protection and up-keep of the fleets.
3. The construction of the necessary ships, the formation of an officer corps, the recruitment of crews and their regular training by means of frequent manœuvres and operations.

Colbert was always careful to direct the use of the French navy to the advantage of French trade. To him, naval strength and economic prosperity were synonymous, for he argued that colonies, overseas trade and a merchant marine all required a powerful and well-trained navy. At first he repaired the few warships he found in French ports fit to be mended while he bought ships in Sweden, Denmark and the Dutch Republic. By 1667 France had sixty warships; by 1672 this figure had risen to a hundred, and by 1681 it had reached two hundred and thirty.

It was the Basque Bernard Renau d'Eliçagaray who demonstrated to Colbert how dangerous it was to allow the shipwrights to follow their own personal methods in the construction of ships, since this made it almost impossible to repair a ship except in its home port. Colbert took this advice. He also tried to standardise the calibre of the guns used aboard ship, as the supply of ammunition for many different sizes raised enormous difficulties. He wanted to know everything and control everything, down to the calibre of the guns on ships of the line as well as those on light craft.

The arsenals of Dunkirk, Brest, Le Havre, Rochefort and Toulon were renovated; the harbour at Marseilles was enlarged, that of Sète was dredged. The navy of this time employed a total of one hundred and sixty thousand men, made up of sailing crews and supporting naval personnel.

Professional naval officers

In 1672 Colbert obtained Louis XIV's approval for the establishment of the *Gardes de la Marine*, young men specifically recruited
to be trained as naval officers. At Brest, Rochefort and Toulon
the companies of these guards developed into naval academies.

Thanks to Colbert, naval officers began to form an élite. Captains had to show 'application, diligence and dash', for 'the king
only awards commissions in the navy on merit, and not by recommendation'. There was thus only one way to obtain promotion :
'service and actions of note'. Colbert demanded that naval officers
be men of the highest probity. Captains were not permitted to
contract debts, but they were expected to live in a style commensurate with their rank : a commodore, M. de Mericourt, was
reprimanded for having set up his dining table in a tavern. Colbert
did not approve of the use of force except against the enemy : M.
de Forbin was sent to prison for thrashing a burgher, and edicts
against duelling among officers were scrupulously enforced.

Colbert reduced the gulf between career officers ('reds') and
officers who had come from the merchant service or privateering
(the 'blues').[1] The former were proud of their caste and schooling,
but the latter – trained as privateers from Dunkirk, Saint-Malo,
Nantes or Saint-Jean de Luz – provided energetic individuals for
the regular navy : Jean Bart became a commodore, and Dugauy-
Trouin rose to the rank of lieutenant-general in the navy.

Recruitment for the fleet

Colbert and Seignelay, and their successor Pontchartrain, all experienced difficulty in finding recruits for the king's ships. Colbert
had devised a crucial reform : he had replaced the press-gang with
a system of maritime inscription by the ordinances of 1669 and
1673. Before his reforms, press-gangs would close off a port and
seize the sailors found within it and one may easily imagine the
lack of enthusiasm for the king's service among such unwilling
recruits.

The establishment of the maritime inscription marked a great
step forward. The definition of a sailor ran, 'Any man who has
sufficient experience to be able to work a ship'. All such sailors
were to be listed and divided into three classes, each class to serve
for a given term in the navy every year. Aboard ship, good treatment was recommended in order that men from different

provinces 'would become accustomed to serving'. Careful attention was given to their pay – part of which they received on board
ship, part at home – to protect them from usurers who offered to
advance loans on their wages, greedy tavern-keepers and prosti-
tutes.

Discipline, however, remained harsh. Under the 1693 regulations the least infractions were punished by flogging or the pillory.
The men were often poorly lodged and fed. On the biggest ships
crews had to be large because of the need for rapid and precise
movement of the sails to change course during combat, for man-
handling the heavy guns, and for a reserve in case of boarding.
One hammock was provided for every two men – one man asleep
below, the other on deck to help manœuvre the ship, or on
watch.

Frequently warships had to transport as many troops as there
were sailors in the crew; this also made for overcrowding.

Life on board was governed by the availability of space, by
standards of hygiene and the quality of the food. The crews
suffered all the diseases common to seamen : typhus, dysentery,
syphilis and scurvy. Chronic dysentery was often accompanied by
persecution mania. Scurvy claimed huge numbers of victims.
'Syphilis', it was said, 'comes from the north, scurvy from the
south, and where they meet they mingle and blend their viruses.'
Gangrene killed large numbers of wounded.

On long voyages the filthy conditions on board and the poor
food – biscuits, salt pork, dried fish and water – decimated the
crews. Jean Bart, preparing for winter campaigns in the rigorous
conditions of the North Sea, understood that success would depend
on the health of his men. He therefore gave them extra rations of
bread, butter, cheese and beer, for most of his sailors were from
Flanders. Thanks to his example, the Dunkirk shipmasters followed Dutch practices in victualling. But it was not till the next
century – the age of the great circumnavigations – that we find
captains like Cook and Bougainville who were expressly concerned with hygiene and careful of their men's comfort.

After his expedition to Cartagena in 1697, Pointis brought
home an enormous booty, but also many cases of yellow fever.
He may be deemed fortunate, however, in having his hospital
ship captured by the Anglo-Dutch fleet, which soon became in-
fected by the disease.

But even though the sailors suffered much at sea, it is clear that Colbert was the first naval minister to be seriously concerned with the physical and moral health of the crews. And from his time onwards French sailors preferred to sail on one of the king's ships, where they could be certain of receiving their pay, rather than aboard a merchantman, where they were often abused and exploited by dishonest captains and owners.

Seaborne trade

At the same time as he was laying the foundations of maritime legislation in his great ordinances, Colbert was encouraging the colonisation of Guyana, Madagascar, New France and the West Indies. Although the famous India Company may not have brought its investors much profit at the outset, its ships helped provide trained seamen. The port which it had been allocated was eventually handed back to the crown and developed into the great naval base of Lorient.

The commerce of the Levant seemed far away, and the northern seas were already controlled by the English, but 'the Isles' – St Kitts, Martinique, Guadeloupe and Santo Domingo, bought from their owners by Colbert – attracted French merchants and even the noblemen of the coastal provinces. A royal edict, registered by the Parlement on 13 August 1669, stipulated that 'nobles may engage in trade without derogation of their rank . . . commerce, and particularly seaborne commerce, being the fertile source of abundance in a state . . . there is no way of acquiring wealth which is more innocent and more legitimate'. It was in these years that French ports became the impressive spectacle they were to remain for so long, their merchantmen 'trafficking all over the world'. A fleet setting sail, the great ships, grey-blue and gilt, putting out to sea before a favourable wind, was a magnificent sight. The king's great men-of-war could be recognised by their rich ornamentation. They were majestic vessels, short, broad in the beam and round-hulled. The biggest, carrying one hundred and twenty guns, were called ships of the line, since they alone were able to take their place in the line of battle; their cannon represented a tenth of their total tonnage. Tourville developed a system of signals for them: a square blue flag at the mizzen yard meant 'Board the enemy'; a red pennant on the mainmast, 'Begin combat'.

The strength of the Atlantic fleet lay in the two lines of warships anchored in the harbour of Brest; from Toulon the 'spiders of the Levant' protected the Côte d'Azur. To command these new fleets, France, in Louis' reign, found two great seamen : Duquesne and Tourville. Although both had learned much from the Dutchman de Ruyter, the founder of naval tactics, the two admirals had little in common. Duquesne was supreme at Toulon, whereas Tourville sailed the Atlantic.

Abraham Duquesne (1610–88)

Duquesne was a plain sea-dog from Dieppe. Contrary to what is generally believed, nobility was not an essential qualification for becoming a naval officer and the 'Regulation for the order of senority of naval officers' of 1675 indicates that thirty per cent of the officers at that time were non-nobles. Duquesne had helped build the *Couronne*, the first French sailing ship of war, launched at La Roche-Bernard in 1638. In the Mediterranean he had fought the Spaniards and the Barbary corsairs with equal success. He became a vice-admiral in the Swedish navy and inflicted defeat on the Danes. Recalled to France, his victories of Stromboli (1675), Agosta (1676) and Palermo (1671) contributed to the advantageous Peace of Nijmegen. Tough, proud and sharp-tongued, this great man was never popular with those in authority. Colbert considered him inferior to de Ruyter and found him difficult to deal with; Louis XIV disliked him for remaining a Protestant. As a reward for his services the sailor from Dieppe was made a marquis, but he never received the marshal's baton which he so richly deserved.

Anne Hilarion de Cotentin, Comte de Tourville (1642–1701)

Tourville also came from Normandy. He was born of an old-established noble family at Agon-Coutainville in the Cotentin. As a young man he served under the white cross of the Knights of Malta; this experience gave him a love of striking hard, and he was conscious of having from the time of his adolescence been a brave seaman always willing to risk his life.

He was polite, elegant, perhaps even a little dandified. He created the ideal naval-officer type, who combined a knowledge of his craft and administrative ability with the gift of command. He codified into axioms what de Ruyter and Duquesne had dis-

I*

covered about the art of war at sea. He drew up the first regular fighting instructions and demanded that his codes be committed to memory so that officers and sailors could replace each other in an emergency. His signal-code was officially adopted in 1687. Tourville's innovations produced excellent results, and his victory at Beachy Head (1690) was a glorious date in the history of the French navy. But it was as a reward for his having followed the royal orders which led to the disaster of La Hougue (1692) that Louis XIV made him a marshal of France.

Naval tactics

Under Tourville the system of fighting in line of battle became normal tactics. The large ships moved in line at intervals of about sixty yards, while behind this moving wall – which became the firing-line – the smaller craft moved in relative security, carrying messages and acting as auxiliaries. The opposing fleet would take up the same formation, sailing parallel while exchanging fire. Then both fleets would go about and renew the battle. Fleet actions were thus fought in moving parallel lines, very different from the individual tactics of the privateer who sought to immobilise his enemy in a surprise attack and then capture him by boarding and the use of 'naked steel'. Such tactics made it necessary for the admirals to manœuvre for the advantage of the wind. This called for skills which Tourville worked very hard to develop. The admiral who held the weather-gauge could dictate the course of the battle.[2]

Main fleet actions

Let us now describe briefly the role played by the navy during the half century which comprised Louis XIV's personal reign.

In the second Anglo-Dutch war France was allied with the Dutch Republic, but Colbert was quite happy to let the two most powerful navies of the time destroy one another fighting for control of the North Sea : the French navy took no part in the Four Days Battle (11–14 June 1666).

In the war that broke out in 1672 the French had England as their ally against the Dutch. The combined fleets operated in the Channel and the North Sea, meeting the Dutch at Solebay (1672) and The Texel (1673). The French fleet was commanded by the admiral Comte d'Estrées, a great nobleman employed in the army and without any aptitude for naval combat. He gave his ally little support, and at The Texel the Dutch won a clear victory. Soon afterwards England dropped out of the alliance, leaving France to continue the struggle against the Republic and Spain. The French fleet was sent to the Mediterranean to support the revolt of Messina against Spanish rule. The aged de Ruyter commanded the allied fleet in those seas, and several glorious actions were fought off the coast of Sicily. Dutch sea-power was not destroyed, but de Ruyter was killed (29 April 1676) and for a time the French appeared to be in control of the western Mediterranean.

A decade later, in the Nine Years War, France had to fight alone against the two most powerful navies of the age. The victory at Beachy Head (10 July 1690) was the first great action won by the French navy: south-west of the Pas-de-Calais Tourville inflicted a serious defeat on the Anglo-Dutch fleet. 'The enemy have taken flight', he wrote after the battle, 'abandoning ten disabled ships so close to us that we should be able to take them if we get the least breath of wind'. This victory should have served to prevent the transport of troops from England to Ireland, but the English recovered quickly and James II was not restored. Nevertheless, Tourville's memorable success was a source of grave concern to the English.

Another invasion of England was projected in 1692. Basing its plan on false assumptions, the government ordered Tourville to give battle: on 29 May 1692 forty-four French ships faced ninety-seven Anglo-Dutch vessels off Barfleur. For twelve hours Tourville held his own, inflicting losses on the enemy and holding them off. But he was not within reach of a port where he could repair his damaged and dismantled ships and rest his exhausted crews. Should he try to reach Brest? But if he did, how could he work his way back against the wind and weather off Cape Ushant? With the enemy in pursuit, twenty-two ships managed to reach Saint-Malo. Three which put into Cherbourg were burned, among them the magnificent flagship, the *Soleil Royal*. Tourville had to beach twelve others at La Hougue, where they were destroyed by enemy fireships and small craft. The defeat of La Hougue led to the loss of no more than fifteen ships – a loss which could quickly have been made good. Was it in fact a defeat, when during the actual battle the French fleet did not lose a single ship? Of Tourville's conduct one of his lieutenants, Villette, was to write : 'All that the Comte de Tourville did on that day was so fine, so great, that there was nothing to excuse or defend. In an action lasting twelve or thirteen hours he gave proof of the highest heroism.'

After La Hougue, however, the king and his ministers lost faith in main fleet actions. Despite Tourville's success off Cape Saint Vincent in 1693, the French government believed that a decisive victory at sea was impossible. Privateering and commando raids on the enemy coast seemed to promise more rapid results.

During the War of the Spanish Succession, the French fleet under Châteaurenault was given the task of conveying the Spanish galleons from the New World. On their way from Havana to Cadiz they were forced to seek shelter in the bay of Vigo (1702), where – despite a staunch defence – they were defeated by Sir George Rooke. By the end of Louis XIV's reign the fleet had been reduced to half its strength. Velez-Malága in 1704 was to be its last notable action, though it is not likely that the French recognised this at the time since privateers and corsairs scored successes and maintained a redoubtable reputation.

The king's buccaneers

The buccaneers, for the most part bold scoundrels, were recruited in the West Indies and rendered useful service in time of war. They attacked enemy shipping, but also the viceroyalties of Spain. Baron de Pointis used them in his attack on Cartagena in 1697; and Porto Bello, Vera Cruz, Maracaybo and Panama likewise suffered from their exploits and outrages. Like their English comrade-in-arms Morgan – later Sir Henry Morgan, governor of Jamaica – some of the French buccaneers were colourful figures. There was the terrible François le Nau, called 'l'Olonais', who was captured and eaten by Indian braves. There was the chevalier de Grammont, beloved by 'the brotherhood of the coast' for his invincible courage. Other extraordinary adventurers were Roc van Dorn, Montbart, Laurent de Graf – the latter married to a beautiful woman, Anne Dieulevant, who could handle a pistol as well as her husband. Exquemelin, a surgeon who served in the West Indies, has described for us the seething world of black, white and Indian buccaneers whose centre was the island of Tortuga. What reckonings must have been settled off those beaches, by day under a blazing sun, and at night when the stars shone unconcerned over the ocean.

Colbert, Seignelay, Vauban and regular privateering warfare
We should define our terms clearly: the buccaneers stood half-way between privateers and pirates. Though their exploits were impressive, they were difficult to control, and even when peace returned to the Antilles they continued to pillage, rape, burn and kidnap for ransom. As long as they fought a national war they were technically privateers, but their activities in defiance of peace agreements sent many of them to the gallows. By the end of the seventeenth century the French government deemed it unwise to encourage them.

In respect of privateers Emile Boisseul's judgement is a valid one: 'all the infractions of which neutrals complained during the seventeenth century were the work of privateers legitimised by unsound laws and abetted by the connivance of the courts'.[3] Because he sailed under a letter of marque, was subjected to inspections by the naval authorities and had to render account of his actions when he returned to his home base, the seventeenth-century privateer could consider his ship as a man-of-war with a volunteer crew. Weakening the enemy and seizing his merchantmen for profit was a recognised part of the right of privateering.

Colbert included the use of privateers in his great programme of naval development. But he and his son succeeded where their predecessors had failed: they were able to organise privateering on a regular basis. Their edicts, ordinances and encouragements gave birth to the legitimate, regular privateer. Many officers of this auxiliary fleet served only for the honour, and the most famous of them were entrusted with important missions and operations of great scope. In this way the Fleming, Jean Bart, the two Bretons, Dugay-Trouin and Cassard, and a Provençal, the chevalier de Forbin, took their places in the ranks of France's naval officers – a group of brave, skilful men of courteous temperament.

The great age of privateering
After the defeat of La Hougue, the moral effect of which was more significant than the actual material losses suffered, Vauban was able to have his programme of intense privateering warfare

against enemy trade adopted, though the value of it is a matter
for debate. Pontchartrain, who had succeeded Seignelay as
minister for the navy in 1690, now loaned the king's ships to
private citizens, or allowed the use of them fully equipped and
crewed in return for a quarter of the prizes taken.

This was the golden age of privateering in every port; at Dunkirk, Saint-Malo, Nantes and Bayonne dynasties of shipowners
formed a powerful plutocracy whose services were rewarded by
the state. Their captains, who were often young men (at Nantes
their average age was thirty), were very skilled seamen. Some,
however, out of vanity, sailed in company and wasted their
powder on salutes, flying the banners and pennants of warships.

'Commercial announcements', published in the ports, gave
private individuals the opportunity to invest in privateering
ventures. A share of one thousand livres seems to have been the
normal unit of participation, but it could be divided into halves,
quarters or eighths, giving even people of modest means a chance
to 'try their fortune'.

The privateers' best ships were light frigates, rarely above two
hundred tons, armed with from eight to thirty small-calibre guns.
But 'it is not guns which take [an enemy]; it is the determination
to board him'. Jean Bart loved these swift ships, easy to manœuvre,
which could negotiate shoal water and outstrip the great blue and
gold warships with their massive poop-works designed by Pierre
Puget. Long before he became a chevalier, Bart, like so many
other privateers, risked his fortune in small craft of fifty tons. The
size of their vessels meant that for many privateers boarding was
the only possible offensive tactics.

Jean Bart

Descended from a long line of corsairs, Jean Bart was born at
Dunkirk in 1650. Dunkirk was a port frequented by *capres*, that
is sailors who lived by a combination of fishing and privateering.
Paradoxically, Bart as a young man learned his trade aboard the
great brown and black warships of de Ruyter; later his ambition
was to fight his way into the Thames estuary as the great Dutch
admiral had done. When war broke out between France and the
Republic he returned to his native town. In 1675 the *Gazette de
France* first mentions 'Captain Bart'. In recognition of ten successful actions and on Vauban's recommendation he was promoted

lieutenant. In 1689 he was involved, with Forbin, in a hard-fought action off the Isle of Wight, protecting a convoy of twenty merchantmen sailing from Le Havre to Brest. Defeated by weight of numbers and taken prisoner, the two corsairs escaped from Plymouth in a skiff, with Bart manning the oars. In 1691 he attacked Newcastle. As examples of his innumerable exploits we may mention that he commanded the *Alcyon* at Beachy Head, and the *Glorieux* at Lagos.

One of his most spectacular victories, which came at a crucial moment when France was ravaged by famine, was the battle of The Texel in 1694. Bart was in command of seven warships detailed to meet and escort thirty merchantmen bringing wheat from Poland and Russia. While he was still on his way, the convoy was intercepted. An enemy squadron of eight ships, one of which was flying the flag of Rear-Admiral Hiddes de Vries, turned west and bore down on Bart. The two squadrons came alongside one another within gunshot. The sea was rough. Bart decided to 'retake the convoy or perish'. The French ships captured three of the Dutchmen and scattered the rest. Bart attacked the *Prince of Friesland*, the enemy flagship, and his son François boarded her. After half an hour the battle was over. From Dunkirk the dying Hiddes de Vries wrote home to the Republic 'that he had never been in so fine a fight'. His only consolation was that 'he had been defeated by heroes'.

In France the price of wheat fell from thirty livres to three. Louis XIV granted the corsair skipper letters of ennoblement, and the naval minister Pontchartrain prophesied 'that he would rise higher still'.

Forbin pictured Bart as 'an illiterate sailor, a bear'. During the revolutionary wars Bart's panegyrists turned him into a sturdy peasant smoking his pipe in the salons of Versailles. Eugène Sue spun the legend of a hero sprung from the bosom of the people, struggling against royal absolutism.[4] Faulconnier, a Dunkirker, has left us a factual but possibly truer portrait of his fellow-towns-man :

He was above the average height, well-built, strong, able to resist all the fatigue of life at sea . . . His features were strongly formed, his eyes blue, his complexion fine, his hair fair, his expression cheerful and open. He was sober, watchful and bold; he was as quick and sure in deciding his course of action as he was cool in issuing his orders in the heat of battle; and he always retained that presence of mind so necessary on such occasions. He was a master of his craft, and he practised it with such detachment, such general approbation and glory, that he owed his fortune and advancement solely to his own ability and his valour.[5]

In 1701 Bart was commissioning his new ship, the *Fendant*, at Dunkirk. 'This brave officer, pleased with his ship, worked with such ardour that he fell victim to a pleurisy which carried him off at the age of fifty-two, much regretted by all men and by the King in particular.'

De Jonghe, the Dutch naval historian, has summed up the achievement of the great corsair with fine impartiality : 'He died lamented by every Frenchman, but not by the English and Dutch who, while paying due respect to his outstanding services to France, could not hide their joy at being safe from one of their most dangerous enemies.'[6]

Duguay-Trouin

Along with Jean Bart, and following in his footsteps, René Duguay-Trouin made his reputation via privateering and thus got his chance to win fame. His career was rapid and hazardous. For centuries the men of Saint-Malo had been considered by the English as 'the greatest thieves who ever lived'. Duguay-Trouin went to sea at the age of sixteen and at eighteen he was already in command of a ship. He became a commodore at thirty-nine and ended his career as lieutenant-general of the fleet and commander of the Order of Saint Louis.

In 1711 he captured Rio de Janeiro, in reprisal for the governor's killing of some French citizens : a victory which consoled the aged Louis XIV amid the many defeats of the last decade of his reign. Duguay-Trouin brought an enormous booty home, but 'this was of so little concern to him that although he had captured innumerable ships and taken a Brazilian city, he left only a very middling fortune'. Pierre Jazier de la Garde, Duguay-Trouin's nephew, informs us in a foreword to his uncle's *Mémoires* that 'he was never devoted to wine or the pleasures of the table', though he continues : 'one might have wished that he had observed the same restraint with regard to the other pleasures of life; but since he could not overcome his passion for the fair sex, he sought instead to avoid serious and long-drawn affairs which would have preoccupied his affection too heavily'.[7]

Duguay-Trouin's success with women was sometimes useful to him. His escape from Plymouth, after being captured by Sir David Mitchell, admiral of the blue, for instance, was effected with the help of a beautiful young girl. That he was charming and amiable, is revealed by his memoirs. As modest as he was bold, in war he exhibited a chivalry that testifies to his high moral standards. After his bloody victory over the heroic Dutch admiral Baron Wassenaer, Duguay-Trouin showed himself deeply concerned for the health and well-being of his vanquished enemy.

Proud, sensitive, noble, attractive to women, somewhat given to melancholy, Duguay-Trouin seems in much a typical Breton. 'His character tended to a kind of sadness which prevented him from engaging in much conversation, and his habitual preoccupation with great plans encouraged a certain detachment.'

Jacques Cassard

Though not as well known as Jean Bart or Duguay-Trouin, Jacques Cassard of Nantes was, like them, received at Versailles and given a commission in the regular navy.

In 1709 the town of Marseilles appealed to Cassard to escort a convoy of grain to relieve the city from the English blockade. South of Toulon he met a fleet of fifteen enemy sail. He ordered his merchantmen to scatter while his ship, the *Eclatant*, poured broadside after broadside into the enemy ships which engaged him in rapid succession. 'After the action had lasted eleven hours, the English squadron gave up the pursuit and disappeared from view.' But when he presented his bill for services rendered to Marseilles, he was told that the convoy had reached port without him, so that it would seem that the merchantships had not after all required an escort. This sort of ill-luck continually dogged him and was to cause his ruin, for his creditors made him pay for the cost of equipping his ships out of his own pocket. After the Peace of Utrecht, desperate and in debt, Cassard made many appeals to be reimbursed for his services. He became an embarrassment and was imprisoned by Fleury in the fort of Ham (1737), where he died three years later, forgotten.

The astonishing Monsieur de Forbin

The younger son of an old Provençal family the chevalier de
Forbin was a shrewd adventurer, courtier and hero. His life seems
like a historical melodrama, complete with love-affairs which from
time to time caused him trouble.

He went to sea at twelve in the galley fleet, fought in the West
Indies with d'Estrées and at Algiers with Duquesne. Next he went
on a long voyage to the Far East, returning as grand-admiral of
Siam with the title 'Opra-sac-dison-cain'. Since this carried little
weight in France, he took to privateering as a way to glory and
fortune. In his memoirs he makes fun of Jean Bart and criticises
Duguay-Trouin and even Tourville, under whom he served with
great distinction at La Hougue. On Bart's death he took over command of the Dunkirk frigates; in 1702 he attacked the Dutch
Baltic convoy at the Dogger Bank and won a fine victory. But
he was less successful when ordered to land James Stuart in England in 1708. In his long retirement he wrote his memoirs, which
make fascinating reading. They prove him arrogant, vain and
slanderous but are full of wit. His accounts of maritime affairs
are most precise : at times the unadorned pages of the sailor give
the lie to the assertions of the romancier.

Quite apart from the actions of the well-known heroes we have
many examples of great feats accomplished by privateers and corsairs whom history has passed by, but who played a vital part in
the later wars of Louis XIV.[8] In this connection it should be
stressed that privateers and corsairs from Saint-Malo found a
most fruitful field of operations in the South Seas, along the western shores of South America and as far away as China. During
the War of the Spanish Succession Louis XIV had not been able
to place a Catholic king on the throne of Great Britain, but Louis'
grandson, Philip V – called to the Spanish inheritance by the will
of Carlos II in 1700 – maintained his position with French help.
The Spanish navy and merchant fleet had been neglected in the
second half of the seventeenth century and the presence of Philip's
French ships in the South Seas was, though not welcomed, tolerated. From this relaxation in practice if not in principle of the
Spanish monopoly, the inhabitants of Saint-Malo benefited
enormously : Breton textiles found ready markets and were paid
for in ready cash. Their interloping trade, supported by the French
navy, in areas hitherto closed and thus little known to French

navigators, also helped France. It is no exaggeration to say that Louis XIV was saved from bankruptcy by the large influx of coins which this trade brought to France.

Yet, the sum of the achievements of the great names and the unsung heroes during the war of 1702–13 could not prevail against the growing power of England with its rich arsenals and inexhaustible supply of sailors. By the time of the peace treaties of Utrecht and Rastadt, England had won control of the seas. The English flag flew over Gibraltar, Minorca, Newfoundland, Acadia and St Kitts. English merchants had obtained a monopoly of the slave trade to the Spanish empire for a period of thirty years. To protect their merchant fleet the English government demanded the destruction of the port of Dunkirk, thereby recognising that the war conducted by the privateers, although less effective than the actions of a battle-fleet, had been for them a serious threat.

The Peace of Utrecht was a compromise one. Even if it marks the beginning of English ascendancy, a Bourbon occupied the Spanish throne and France had been able to strengthen its northeast frontier. During Louis XIV's reign France had begun to figure as a sea-power on the international scene. At Colbert's death the French fleet was as big as that of England or the Republic. Why had it failed to win victories commensurate with its strength? Principally because it lacked an admiralty, a body of trained personnel such as England had. The French navy was controlled from Versailles. By the time orders reached their destination they were often out of date or hopelessly arbitrary, as at La Hougue. When orders did not arrive in time, the commanders on the spot were forced to make decisions in complete ignorance of the overall strategy determined by the king and his ministers. The ministers had been able to build up and organise a fleet of the highest order; but they did not know how best to use it. The moment came when, under Vauban's influence, Louis XIV accepted that 'privateering was the only form of naval warfare which can be [of] any service to us'. From then on the French fleet never risked combat with an enemy who was superior in numbers. To see the French navy once more holding its own against England one must wait for the reign of Louis XVI and the resurrection of French naval power. In the War of American Independence, and in the battles fought by the bailli de Suffren in the Indian Ocean, the French navy recovered its lost glory.

The reputation of the French navy dates, however, from the seventeenth century. It was based upon the achievements of a few noblemen, some commoner captains and thousands of seamen who manned the light privateering frigates and the lumbering three-decker men-of-war with their towering spars. Whether they live on in men's memory by some great action or whether their sacrifices have remained unknown, they are now part of French naval history.

NOTES

1   Both naval career officers and officers who had come from the merchant marine wore blue uniforms, but the former were easily distinguished by their red facings, waistcoats and stockings.

2   During the eighteenth century this type of naval battle became stereotyped and declined into 'ornamental parades' till Suffren revitalised tactics and Nelson in his turn further developed Suffren's revolutionary changes.

3   E. Boisseul, *La course maritime, son influence dans les guerres* (no place of publication, 1904).

4   M. J. E. Sue, a popular novelist and former naval surgeon, wrote a history of the French navy in five volumes, *Histoire de la marine française* (Paris, 1825–7).

5   Pierre Faulconnier, grand bailli of Dunkirk and president of the Dunkirk chamber of commerce during Louis XIV's reign, wrote a history of Dunkirk from which this characterisation is taken.

6   G. B. T. de Jonghe, *Histoire de la marine néérlandaise* (Paris, 1886).

7   *Mémoires de Monsieur du Guay-Trouin Lieutenant-général des Armes Navales* was published, anonymously, in Amsterdam in 1741. It is worth pointing out that in an age which saw many fictitious or adulterated memoirs the authenticity of the above edition is vouched for by contemporaries, a claim supported by the high opinion of their value expressed by Sir John Knox. See V. Laughton, *Studies in Naval History* (London, 1887) p. 289. The quotation in the text is from p. 20 of the *Mémoires*.

8   One of these is Jean Doublet, of Honfleur, who left a lively journal. Among his exploits was the boarding, capturing and sailing away at night of a Dutch pinnace off Saltash in Cornwall; also the victorious outcome of his battle with three Dutch ships whose captains had ordered him, off Elsinore, to lower his flag in salute.

13 The Protestant Bankers in France, from the Revocation of the Edict of Nantes to the Revolution*

JEAN BOUVIER

H. Lüthy: *La banque protestante en France, de la Révocation de l'Edit de Nantes à la Révolution*. Vol. 1 : *Dispersion et regroupement (1685–1730)*; Vol. 2 : *De la banque aux finances (1730–1794)*. Published by S.E.V.P.E.N., in the series 'Affaires et gens d'affaires', nos 19 and 19 *bis*; 454 and 861 pages respectively, with alphabetical tables of names and companies. (Paris, 1959 and 1961).

One thousand three hundred and fifteen pages of close type : that makes a vast undertaking in two volumes, but it is without doubt a great one. The volumes are not always clearly constructed or easy to follow, digressions, parentheses, appendices, flashbacks, changes of key succeed one another. But in the end, the reader is swept along by the flow; he follows the story with pleasure, and that is what counts. The author knows how to paint on a wide canvas; he makes broad judgements and etches fine, detailed studies under the microscope. His style is lively and his pen somewhat sharp, so that the reader not only follows, but enjoys himself as well – very necessary over so long a stretch.

Bibliography and sources take up only eight pages. This is be-

* This review article was first published in *Annales: Economies, Sociétés, Civilisations*, vol. 18, no. 4 (1963).

cause Herbert Lüthy's aim is not to write scientific, economic or
religious history, but rather to describe the fate of 'a social group
which by reason of the constantly false or ambiguous position in
which it was placed – ambiguous in its legal status, its nationality,
its religious affiliation, even its civil position – played a separate
part in the society of the Ancien Régime'.

The author sets out to examine, by means of social analysis,
the 'myth' of the 'international' or 'cosmopolitan' Protestant
bankers, who are not to be 'confused with the 'financiers', those
'financial administrators, tax-farmers and contractors who were
the managers and sometimes the masters of the economy of the
Ancien Régime'; to these latter the author refers only briefly in
the course of his work. His real subjects are not the Paris family,
but Samuel Bernard and the Necker clan. Hence his meticulous
research on individuals, into names, genealogies and families, and
into those myriad links which hold together individuals and
groups, becoming stronger or weaker according to the climate of
business or the needs of the moment, political or economic. The
book therefore assumes the form of a continuous, and apparently
exhaustive, enquiry into this 'marginal' group whose history during the eighteenth century moved through several long phases of
development. There are few earlier studies on this topic, apart
from the pioneer work of A.-E. Sayous, which has inspired important economic and social historical investigation, and the
studies of J. Bouchary, which however deal only with the Revolutionary and the immediate pre-Revolutionary periods. H.
Lüthy has worked – and had to work – from hitherto untouched
archival material : the State Archives of Geneva and Zürich, the
city archives of Saint Gall, certain private collections in Switzerland which possess papers of bankers of the period and, above all,
the National Archives in Paris, particularly the notarial papers
and sequestrated documents, and the records of the bankruptcy
division of the former consular jurisdiction of Paris (now in the
archives of the Department of the Seine). Altogether, an enormous amount of research undertaken and a vast panorama un-
folded.

The volumes cover two chronological periods (1685–1730 and
1730–94) but deal with three major developments. In Volume 1,
the formation and growth of the 'Huguenot international' as a
result of the Revocation of the Edict of Nantes in 1685 and the

entry on to the French financial scene of the Huguenot bankers at the end of Louis XIV's reign, the ascendancy of Samuel Bernard and the emergence of Isaac Thellusson are covered. The second volume, by far the larger, chronicles two subsequent developments : the activity of the Huguenot firms of Paris, and of their international connections, in the middle of the reign of Louis XV, and their renewed growth at the time of Necker. How did a 'self-made man', a heretic into the bargain, climb to the top of the tree of state finances? And what was the exact role of the Protestant bankers in the financial orgy at the end of the Ancien Régime?

Although a review should not be a detailed summary of the work considered, I have decided to stick close to the author in the hope of saving his future readers from the feeling of having been cast adrift in mid-ocean.

In the hefty introduction to the first volume Lüthy embarks upon a series of polemics, including one on the question of the relationship between 'Protestantism and capitalism'. We shall have to come back to this, as Lüthy returns to this theme in his conclusion. But it is worth stressing at once that the author maintains that Calvinism did not of itself predispose its adherents to banking or finance 'either by its doctrine or its practices'. International banking was not a Huguenot 'invention', but grew naturally from the traffic in bills and drafts between financial centres of international trade : the Medicis (among others) engaged in transactions on a European scale long before Calvin's time. The origins of the so-called Protestant bankers are not so much religious as historical; they were spawned by the diaspora, the scattering of Huguenots caused by the revival of French persecution at the end of the seventeenth century, and took part under duress – or near duress – in the great international financial manœuvres and exchanges of the European wars of 1689–97 and 1702–13/14 : in subsidies and in contracts for the supply and provisioning of armies. War and the financial strain it brought to belligerents, and particularly to France, and exile on religious grounds – these were the conditions which produced the 'Huguenot international' since the Huguenot, because of his ambiguous social position in seventeenth-century France, could only make a career in trade, banking or industry. Noble rank, whether of robe or sword, was not really open to him, and definitely closed after 1685.

Events thus created the Protestant bankers; the coincidence of
the Huguenot exodus with the distress of French state finances
providing in Lüthy's words 'a badly guarded door' through which
appeared a Scot, a Genevan and many others. Thus the late seventeenth century brought the first French Protestant banking 'networks', utilising family and business connections established in
western and central Europe and along the northern shores of the
Mediterranean. The system had its foundations, its reserves and
its centres of activity – and new points of growth – in the Protestant commercial centres of Germany, the Dutch Republic,
England and the Swiss cantons.

French Calvinism after 1685 assumed three forms : the 'desert'
and the southern provinces, orientated towards Geneva; bourgeois Protestantism, turned in upon itself, located in the area
around Paris and orientated towards London and Amsterdam;
and the 'refuge'. This last is the diaspora which forms the object
of Lüthy's researches. It was an 'international' of private bankers
usually known by the convenient if vague title of 'the Geneva
bankers', a group composed of business connections, alliances and
links outside France, while within the country it comprised 'a
penalised national minority, a tiny sovereign republic and a cosmopolitan society with far-flung contacts'. The author concludes
his introduction with an assessment of the position of Protestants
in France after the Revocation of the Edict of Nantes. He describes Huguenot families divided 'by abduration, persistence in
the faith, or exile', and his examination of these separate groups
leads him to question whether this decision amounted to 'a religious split or a division of labour'. He finds the sons of French
Protestants sent to the Dutch Republic, England, Germany or
Switzerland to learn the business, and stresses that abjurations of
the ancestral faith – like that of Samuel Bernard – in no way
destroyed the contacts with those who had fled abroad from persecution in France. This in turn explains the power of certain
bankers in France, chief among them Bernard, as trustees and
guardians of the assets and property of the exiles and émigrés;
they enjoyed the advantage of contacts, friends, clients, debtors
and creditors all over Europe, placed there by the very fact of
the diaspora. Louis XIV had to make use of these men for payments and transfers of funds : Samuel Bernard is in fact the har-

binger of Necker, or rather of 'the growing hold of Huguenot bankers over French finances'.

Volume 1 is made up of three imposing chapters : the 'take-off', the financial operations during the War of the Spanish Succession, and the Regency and the episode of John Law.

The 'take-off' begins with the establishment of groups of Protestant bankers at Geneva, Lyons and Paris; Lyons was the 'half-way house in the movement of the Genevans to Paris'. The author traces the careers of various individuals, families and firms, relating their activity as bankers and traffickers in bills of exchange to the economic life of these commercial centres and more particularly also to the political developments and the financial needs of the French government. Geneva became 'a clearing-house for contraband and an extraterritorial bank for France', its upper bourgeoisie increasingly choosing the rich profits of international trade and banking, at the expense of most of the local industries. At Lyons the famous system of 'payments', dating from the fairs of exchange of the fifteenth and sixteenth centuries, declined; and borrowing by the French government was eventually disguised as fake drafts on the fair – fakes since they lacked the normal basis of real goods. This led to the use of 'cavalry', an inflationary issue of paper notes secured by nothing more than 'the promises of a notoriously insolvent Treasury'. The repayment of the four issues during the years 1700–9 became increasingly difficult because of the 'snowballing mass of obligations of financiers and court bankers, their agents and sub-agents', which caused the postponement, indefinitely renewed, of each 'payment' as it became due. Such postponements culminated in the great crash of 1709, which destroyed the international position of Lyon, a disaster that explains why banking activity from then on became concentrated in Paris. In the capital sixty-five Huguenot bankers and merchants had in 1685 abjured before Seignelay and renounced their faith, and in 1705 the first 'Genevans' – Mallet, Tourton and Guiguer – made their appearance in Paris. Lüthy's fascinating sketch of the Tourtons and the Guiguers, one of the first international networks based on the 'refuge', is typical of the vignettes with which his volumes are adorned. In this group we first meet Isaac Thellusson.

The basic organisation of the Huguenot banking system having

been laid down, the author goes on to show it at work in two
excellent chapters entitled 'Financial operations during the War of
the Spanish Succession' and 'The Regency and John Law's experi-
ment'. Here the main phases of the history of France in the first
half of the eighteenth century unfold, seen through its financial
and banking operations and focused on the important position
enjoyed by Protestant bankers and merchants. In a sub-section,
modestly labelled 'A glance at the monetary and financial situation', Lüthy offers suggestive insights into the shortage of currency, the manipulation of the coinage, the various means used
to maintain the state's credit, and the administration of its
finances. France had no public banks such as existed in Italy,
in Hamburg, Amsterdam or London. Therefore 'the system of
repayments was the only means of alleviating the shortage of
currency', which in the main resulted from economic contraction
and hoarding, and not only from the very real decline in French
monetary reserves between 1680 and 1710. 'The temptation to
print paper money thus inevitably presented itself', and the 'notes'
of 1701 anticipates the solution adopted by Law after 1715. The
monetary situation also dictated the close relationship engineered
by the merchants of Saint-Malo between 'the two wings of the
world's commerce', Spain and the Far East, the problem being
to secure enough currency to pay for the trade with the Indies.

The government tampered with the currency fourteen times
between 1686 and 1709, thus effecting 'a partial cancellation of
debts by a fiscal expedient, a trick of the Treasury'. To such time-
honoured and inadequate procedures were added others, as
ancient and disastrous in the long run, like the issue of *rentes* –
'that most ordinary of extraordinary expedients to get money'.

What the French monarchy had always lacked was a 'Treasury
fund' from which to meet emergencies, especially in wartime:
hence its dependence on financiers – whom Lüthy deliberately
excludes from the latter part of his study – and on bankers.
Although there were two distinct types of financier – the administrative officials on the one hand, the tax-farmers and contractors
on the other – these 'publicans' formed in fact one great family,
with some members managing the state funds and others collecting them – save (as is well known) in the case of direct taxes.
Everywhere, in posts connected with government finance, in tax-
farming, in state contracts, the same family names occur and

nepotism, speculation and monopolies shamelessly flaunt themselves.

But such faults are in the eyes of the present-day beholder. At the time such a system reflected certain pressing and practical needs; it conformed to the structure of contemporary society and politics and ultimately to a fiscal edifice which depended upon the state of the annual harvest. The most difficult question in respect of the financiers is that of their own credit : where did they obtain their capital? Lüthy stresses the importance of the 'note payable to bearer', their favourite instrument of credit which permitted them to draw money from 'the business conducted for the king' – the sale of offices, and in many special tax-farms which supplemented the general farms. But at the end of the reign of Louis XIV these notes partook of the unsavoury reputation of all paper money.

It was then that the bankers came into their own, as 'merchants more or less specialising in the traffic in currencies'. Their role was in no way new : the need for long-distance payments brought forth businessmen in the service of princes, popes, kings or emperors long before our period. What is new about them, their specific function at the end of Louis XIV's reign, is in Lüthy's words their 'discounting of public and semi-public revenues'. Purchase may be a more fitting word than discounting, since the use of the latter word might lead the reader to assume that commercial discounting in the modern manner was then practised in France, when in fact it was used only in England. The French bankers took as payment or in deposit the promises of the Treasury and its agents, making them advances for which the bankers used, thanks to the system of letters of change (the basic instrument of credit), 'more or less illegally the funds of their clients and correspondents'. They drew on the 'floating mass of available commercial funds', swamping the various financial centres – starting with Lyons – with their 'cavalry drafts', paper notes which were not secured on any merchandise, but only on the promises of the state. Samuel Bernard, the Hogguers and many other Huguenots operated in this way. The normal classical traffic in bills of exchange was thus overwhelmed by a deluge of inflationary paper, and the public debt was transformed and extended into a floating debt which, in form at least, was private. In other words, the result was disguised inflation. The whole structure ultimately rested on shaky foundations, on the 'limitless credit' of some banker or army contractor like Bernard or the Paris brothers, whose reputation of being well placed in court circles was thought to ensure that their claims for payment would be honoured. Just how shaky these foundations were was demonstrated by the Lyons catastrophe of 1709.

Lüthy illustrates how this mechanism worked by a study of the role of Samuel Bernard. According to 'a probable hypothesis' he was the banker of the Protestants in exile, which would explain his contacts and the international scope of his credit. From 1701 to 1708 he presided, almost unchallenged, over the external payments of the French government with its insatiable need for foreign funds to support the armies beyond its frontiers and to provide the subsidies required by its allies. In these transactions Samuel Bernard was nearly always associated – the exception proving the rule – with Huguenots or Genevans. He never borrowed in France itself, but always abroad, from Protestant bankers who included a number of recent refugees : 'What might at first have been a means for removing capital from France now became a powerful network of banking and exchange.' The foundation of his wealth, and the whole of his business operations, did not fit 'the usual uncomplicated model of the tax-farmer or contractor who had grown rich'. 'His power was the first sign of the victory of the bankers – cosmopolitans and heretics as they were – over the old-style financiers, now relegated to the modest role of tax-collectors.' This goes far to explain the suspicion and jealousy directed against this 'banker of the Protestants' which produced the reaction against Samuel Bernard after 1709, and the return to the 'old financiers' during the administration of Desmarets.

Having discussed this question (pages 126–275), Lüthy executes a series of those micro-analyses of which he is so fond, detailing the various Protestant banking groups and their dealings with the Treasury, from the Nine Years War to the close of Louis XIV's reign. The most important ones are those describing the role of Geneva as the link between the French Treasury and the outside world; the penetration of the 'Protestant bankers' into the Royal Mirror Manufactures (the ancestor of the present company of Saint-Gobain); the clash between Samuel Bernard and Huguetan, a Protestant from Lyons who had emigrated to the Dutch

Republic after 1685, next moved to Switzerland and England, and who ended an adventurous life in 1749 as a baron of the Empire; the story of the collaboration between Samuel Bernard and the Genevan banker Nicolas, which covers interesting projects for a 'bank of issue'.

In the last chapter of Volume 1 Lüthy rewrites the history of the John Law period, agreeing with Harsin that 'this is still a long way from completion'. 'Historians', Lüthy stresses, 'have studied Law only and not examined the men who moved around him.' Although Law had the support of merchants from the Atlantic ports, most of the French financiers and bankers were arrayed against him. Lüthy gives diverse convincing reasons for this. If Law's projects had reached fruition, it would have meant the end of most of the profits of the royal bankers and financiers. But Law came too early; the economic and political situation in France which gave him his chance paradoxically ensured that he would not succeed.

Lüthy draws a parallel between the failure of the Mississippi Company and the crisis of the English South Sea Company. If total collapse was the outcome on one side of the Channel, while the other experienced only a severe shaking, this was because the French financial system could not withstand certain kinds of shock whereas England, more advanced financially, could live through a crash without investors losing confidence in the Bank of England.

In France things were very different, and could not be otherwise in the absence of sound public credit, parliamentary control of the budget and a strong monetary system. The Huguenot bankers (there were forty-seven Genevan and Swiss bankers in Paris during the period 1714–16) escaped the clutches of the Chamber of Justice of 1716–17 which struck at the financiers, and for the most part they became deeply involved in the manœuvres and speculations which accompanied Law's 'System'. Their operations with royal paper notes led many of these bankers, particularly the Genevans, to exchange the notes for Law's shares (in the General Bank or in the Mississippi Company), to speculate in the shares and finally make a profit. Lüthy has been able to reconstruct, in particular by using the notebooks of the Genevan Calandrini, some of the ways in which groups of Huguenots used the 'System'. Many were prudent enough to end their speculations in time. One who stood apart was Thellusson. His attitude was that of a 'conservative banker with cautious and inflexible principles'; he refused to speculate and lent his effective support to Law's opponents.

To sum up : by its involvement in government finances during the last twenty years or so of Louis XIV's reign, the group of Protestant bankers was gradually drawn to Paris. The collapse of Law's 'System' brought a certain lethargy and financial affairs resumed their traditional forms. But by this time the 'Huguenot international' was an established fact.

Volume 2 sets out to 'build a bridge' between the work of A.-E. Sayous and that of J. Bouchary across 'our great gulf of ignorance of eighteenth-century French economic history'. As in the first volume, Lüthy organises his research around the careers of the Huguenot banking groups. He starts with a long chapter, 'An outline of the age of Louis XV', full of acute observations on the years of prosperity which form the middle of the reign of Louis the Well-Beloved. Lüthy's commentary on Quesnay's *Economic Survey* may be reread with pleasure and profit, and he makes good use of this work to describe the social order of the Ancien Régime, in which the 'receivers' consist of the whole 'class of proprietors', the holders of land, offices and titles.

Driving closer to his central theme, the domain of the bankers, the author treats of new developments in the area of prices, money and exchange. The decisive development was the achievement of monetary stability, in England after 1719, in France from 1726. As the economy recovered and the currency became stable, the traffic in 'letters of change' lost the risky character which it had possessed during the years of shortage and instability, and speculation became less profitable as the sudden shifts in value of bills of exchange diminished. The practice of discounting which had arisen from the conditions of the English internal money-market in the seventeenth century could now take root on the Continent. Such profits were regular, predictable and modest. A similar change can be observed in the trade in gold and specie which had been one of the favourite activities of the international bankers in the earlier period. The trade continued, but was now conducted within fixed norms. The ready circulation of money, and the lack of strain on the budget during Fleury's administration, made this a time of 'lean pickings for speculation and stock-

manipulation'. The fiscal system could now meet its own needs
and men like Samuel Bernard were no longer needed. The Paris
brothers, who symbolise the classic type of financiers closely
involved with the monarchy, ran all the financial operations of
the War of the Austrian Succession, and 'Protestant bankers were
almost totally eclipsed in the mid-eighteenth century in the
management of the king's business'. They did better in colonial
and overseas trade. But not till the very end of the Seven Years
War do we find a recurrence of 'the incredible ascent to positions
of power by formerly peripheral groups, led by the Genevans, as
control starts to slip from the hands of the established elements of
monarchical society'.

In three hundred rich, dense pages (Chapters II and III) Lüthy
continues his investigation of the activities of the Protestant
bankers between 1726 and 1763, producing a series of short
studies or *Firmengeschichte*. He starts with a description of the
financial and economic life of Geneva, the centre for floating
foreign loans at mid-century. During the 1760s Genevan investments were carefully balanced between French and English
securities – Bank of England shares, state bonds, shares in the big
trading companies. After 1770 comes 'the strange and rather
unhealthy shift' to investment in French securities alone. The
second feature of Genevan finance was 'the development of a
Genevan network in international trade' based on various
Huguenot colonies all over Europe. The author is particularly
concerned with the great crossroads of Marseilles (where his
work is complemented by that of Dermigny), with the Huguenots
at Genoa (he has some excellent pages on the André family),
and with the 'Genevan companies' at Cadiz and in the Americas.
This section teems with families, individuals and business deals;
they demonstrate in a realistic and lively manner how professional
banking practice combined mercantile trade, maritime investment, exchange and normal banking on an international scale.

Next come the great names of 'banks and business partnerships'
from the time of Thellusson to that of Necker, centred mainly in
Paris. By 1770 the major banking firms of the capital were the
Catholic Lecouteulx, and the Protestant companies of Thellusson,
Necker and Co., and Tourton and Baur. We follow Thellusson's
career in detail (pages 177–205), and after his death in 1755 the
continuance of the firm is ensured by the partnership of his son,

George Tobias, with Jacques Necker, who had learned his trade with Isaac Vernet at Paris. (There is an excellent summary of Necker's early career on pages 228–32). The firm of Thellusson and Necker offered credit to overseas traders and managed the deposits and accounts of about three hundred and fifty foreign clients in the year 1759, most of whom dealt in French government loans; this was the first stage in what was later to become a very big operation. It was in those years that Necker built up the clientele of international capitalists and stockholders on whom he later relied.

Having covered Necker's career to the point where he was about to 'become a public figure and aim higher than the counter of his bank', the author deals with some of the smaller banks, a few of which were to achieve fame subsequently. He discusses in some detail (pages 246–73) the Mallet family, attracted to Paris by 1711 by government business; for their activities Lüthy has some interesting evidence, in particular part of the accounts for 1770–1.

Chapter iv ('The Apogee', 380 pages) brings us to the heart of Volume 2 : the resurgence of the Protestant bankers from their earlier 'anaemia', the rise of Necker, and the financial crisis (or rather the general crisis of the Ancien Régime) and the loans and speculations of the 1780s. In Necker we have 'a man without antecedents, without a title, without connections, without an office, never in the king's service . . . a heretic and a foreigner into the bargain . . . a man completely outside the established structure of society under the monarchy' who came to power at the end of 1776 – first as director-general of the Royal Treasury and then, in July 1777, as director-general in charge of all public finance. How are we to explain the astonishing rise of this banker-minister, the key man who could transmit to 'an international clientele of capitalists the demands of a heavily indebted Treasury which could no longer be sustained by tax-revenues and the traditional resources of the financiers'?

Necker's career was the result of his ability; his rise to power was due to his mastery of his trade, and to his clientele. Lüthy holds that the explanation of 'the obscure progress which led to his amazing entry into the royal entourage' lies in the part Necker played in the Company of the Indies (pages 376–97), which the abbé Raynal called 'a company of tax-farmers rather than merchants'. Important facts about Necker's role as a private

banker have been uncovered. In January 1772 we find the abbé
Terray, the then controller-general, writing to Necker, 'We beg
you to help us before the day is over. Please come to our assistance
with a sum which is absolutely necessary to us. Time presses and
you are our only hope' – a significant passage.

Following Necker (for whom Lüthy, by the way, has little
sympathy and for whom he at times shows an intense dislike),
comes the figure of Isaac Panchaud who deluged Necker with his
pamphlets and was one of the founders, with a group of Huguenot
bankers from Switzerland, of the Discounting Fund (March 1776).
This fund was set up at the very end of Turgot's ministry, and
Lüthy sees it as 'the first attempt after Law's, to turn the technique
of discounting into general practice'. It was diverted from its
initial purpose in part by Necker himself who, as minister, found
it a useful instrument for his policy of borrowing. It also fulfilled
the purpose of being a bank for private bankers, who borrowed
from it at four per cent in order to make loans at six per cent and
thus obtained finance for 'the great waves of speculation of the
1780s'. Panchaud himself characterised it as 'a fund for borrowing
rather than a discounting fund'.

Lüthy next (pages 464–591) tackles the part of his work which
evidently gave him most pleasure to write : an analysis of Necker's
methods of borrowing through his Huguenot connections, 'the
thirty immortal ladies of Geneva and their annuities' : 'He managed the apparent feat of plugging the deficit and financing the
American War without recourse to new taxes, leaving his successors the problem of paying the bill.' Necker was here playing the
– limited – part for which he had been chosen : as a negotiator of
loans. He was naive enough to believe himself indispensable and
was surprised to be sent packing after the war. He had planned
that the interests on his loans should be paid from taxation alone,
but the French fiscal system was neither as regular nor as efficient
as the English, and he left to his successors a public debt which
had risen from 500 to 600 million livres. His famous statement of
account was, Lüthy argues, strongly doctored.

Most of Necker's borrowings – 386 out of 530 million livres –
took the form of life annuities. This was not Necker's own invention : it conformed to the practice of his friends and clients and
provided him with 'eager subscribers within easy reach' in Geneva

K

or among the Genevan bankers at Paris. Such annuities enjoyed an enormous popularity at Lyon, in Switzerland and in Holland; there were infinite variations on the theme of speculating on human longevity : 'one bets on the length of lives as one bets on racehorses'. His Genevan system rested on bankers acting as inter-mediaries between bondholders and the state which wished to borrow money. Once Necker's system of borrowing had gained momentum, Calonne's policy after the former's fall is easy to understand; he just followed the system in which annuities re-mained the dominant element and Huguenot bankers did the work – among them Girardot, Haller and Co. (Necker's old firm), Delessert, Mallet, Bontemps, Lullin, de Candolle, Calandrini.

Borrowing was the most important factor in the financial crisis which led to the events of 1789. In the spring of that year the interest on the public debt accounted for more than half the revenue of the state, and most of this was paid on annuities con-tracted on the Genevan system. But 'the insidious bankruptcy through inflation', and the conversion decreed by Cambon in 1793, upset the far-sighted calculations on the longevity of the young ladies of Geneva – those 'thirty immortals' on whose heads rested the whole system of annuities. Bondholders suffered in France, but there was disaster in Geneva, where millionaires and petit-bourgeois alike had snapped up French state bonds : 'The Genevan bondholders lived like parasites on the French Treasury.' Since a whole edifice of credit had been built up on the foundation of these bonds, many banking firms went bankrupt after 1792.

In the last two sections of his vast Chapter iv Lüthy attempts to describe the activities of the Huguenot bankers outside the realm of state finance in the years before 1789. We watch the operations of trade and finance during the War of American Independence through the correspondence of Louis Greffulhe, a banker from Amsterdam, but Genevan by birth; through the activities of bankers like Grand, one of Franklin's supporters at Paris; through Haller who joined Girardot in succession to Necker in the summer of 1777. From here the author goes on to chronicle the affairs of Girardot, Haller and Co., from the spring of 1789 replaced by the firm of Greffulhe, Montz and Co. The story of this company during the Revolution (pages 631–42) is especially illuminating. Its directors were able to adapt to the new order of things, for a time at least : they supported the political schemes of the duke of

Orléans, speculated in commodities and state lands, but finally gave way to the great fear that had gripped the business community. In March 1793 Greffulhe emigrated to London; he resumed operations at Paris in 1810, now much richer, at the moment when the young James de Rothschild made his appearance.

After disposing of the later vicissitudes of Greffulhe, Montz and Co. the author returns to the period following the War of American Independence and studies overseas trade, and the new Company of the Indies of the 1780s. He gives us a series of separate studies, each one interesting, on the spread of 'Indian fever' in France, and on the fate of the Company of the Indies, which was 'the object of greed and clan rivalries on an increasingly international scale'.

The last part of Chapter IV deals with 'the great speculations and the twilight of the Ancien Régime'. In the author's view 'the final orgy of the Ancien Régime was . . . [that] of the upper reaches of established society, their agents and financial experts'. All the polemics of the last years of the monarchy – on the Company of the Indies, the Paris Water Company, the Discounting Fund and the Bank of Saint Charles, in which Mirabeau, Brissot and their Genevan 'brains trust' distinguished themselves (Clavière in particular) – should not make us forget that 'the real managers of the kingdom's money' were not the Huguenot bankers, but the 'financial directors of the king and the court . . . the high financial officials . . . the Farmers-General . . . the Treasurers for War and the Navy . . . the financiers of the high nobility'.

We know very little about these circles which formed an integral part of high society. But the author feels sure that 'neither the Genevan bankers, nor the Huguenot international, nor international high finance in any form whatever, played a decisive part in the last fling of the dying monarchy'. Without going over ground already covered by Bouchary, Lüthy wishes to strike a balance to 'restore a certain sense of proportion and hierarchy'. The petty speculators, or the bigger men who played the market under Calonne (and the Huguenots did not hold aloof from speculation), can not be regarded as the gravediggers of the Ancien Régime. The final budgetary collapse was the result of a cumulative process of indebtedness unsecured by expanding resources. The economic situation in the 1780s was full of contrasts : false

prosperity in the luxury trades, in the great ports and on the
Bourse, accompanied by agrarian crises and general stagnation
in industry and commerce.[1] Lüthy's analysis is impressive. He
concludes that too much attention has been paid to the freebooter
of the stock-market, when in fact the big speculations of the time,
either in property or in bonds, were essentially controlled and
dominated by the ruling elements of the Ancien Régime. Panchaud, whom earlier writers have portrayed as the tutor of
Calonne, was not important according to Lüthy; the Discounting
Fund, which was initially a 'syndicate of bankers put together by
Necker', was subsequently taken over by the financiers, including
the farmer-general Lavoisier. The Huguenot bankers, unlike the
financiers, weathered the storm of the Revolution without suffering too many losses.

The Committee of Public Safety had its own banker, Perrégaux.
The revolutionary government could not do without currency and
notes for its foreign purchases since the French *assignats* were not
accepted abroad. Circumstances restricted normal banking transactions a great deal. Lüthy quotes in full a most interesting 'Note
on an establishment for banking and trade', drawn up by Montz
in March 1795, which recommends the limitation of all activities
(the classic reaction of a banker in a time of crisis) : 'Land, real-
estate and stable objects which are not affected by the ups and
downs of events', he writes, 'are almost the only investments which
one would choose'. But after the tumult, in the year V, the pre-
Revolution firms reappear – Cottin, Delessert, Girardot, Ful-
chiron, Hottinguer, Lecouteulx, Mallett, Perrégaux, Tourton. The
bankers of the ninetenth century were not new men – not even
the Rothschilds.

At the end of Volume 2 Herbert Lüthy offers his readers a
section of about sixty pages which should not be overlooked. First
comes an Appendix which supports the author's disbelief in the
existence of a 'Genevan party' in Paris in 1789. Space has been
given to this theme above (pp. 275–6) and the present writer
prefers to concentrate on Lüthy's conclusion, his 'Final Remarks',
in which he questions his own approach : is it not perhaps
arbitrary to separate a Protestant bank from the whole system of
banking activities? 'Were the Protestant bankers an independent
phenomenon in their own right?' And more generally, 'Are we
justified in linking commercial and religious terms?' – particularly

as the Protestant bankers were not united but split among themselves (Thellusson against Law, Clavière against Necker), and there is no sign of a 'Protestant party' advancing to conquer France.

Here Lüthy returns to the problem of 'Protestantism and Capitalism' which he posed at the beginning of Volume 1. He skilfully and powerfully rejects the findings of Marx and Max Weber. It should be pointed out that before Lüthy, Lucien Febvre made a significant contribution to this debate.[2] Febvre did not claim to be a Marxist, but he rendered to Caesar – or rather to Marx – what was due to him. To the present writer he seems to have been more clear-sighted than Lüthy and to have arrived at more decisive conclusions. Lüthy ends on a note of indecision (page 773 : 'In this confused whirlpool where are we to divide the waters?'). He also resorts to formulations too dogmatic to be acceptable, as for example, 'To describe the Reformation as a bourgeois movement is historical mystification which makes nonsense of the most obvious facts.' Here Lucien Febvre is more helpful, and clarifies the basic problem. The new ideas contained in the message of Luther and Calvin were, he stressed, put forth by men reflecting on questions of faith; but 'as soon as they were formulated, the men of the time seized upon them, absorbed them, digested them and turned them to their own uses'. The bourgeoisie, the leaders of the time, transformed the Reformation, but at the same time the Reformation had its effect on the bourgeois mentality. As Febvre pointed out, 'it strengthened, refined and accentuated in them a certain capitalist attitude to business'.

It is a truism that, at certain times, a new idea will triumph. The Protestant theologians did not intend this, or plan it at the outset; but their originally religious message encountered echoes which were amplified, distorted or in harmony, because society and the economy were in the process of changing. There was cross-fertilisation between the ideas of the reformers and capitalism, reciprocal relations between the sphere of society and economics and that of ideology.

Lüthy is on firmer ground in the excellent pages (773–7) where he draws the distinction between bankers and financiers, and where he analyses the 'social fact' which the Huguenot international undoubtedly represented. If the 'Protestant conspiracy' which for some explains 1789 is no more than a 'legend', none-

theless 'French Protestantism taken as a whole formed part of
the Third Estate, and even the liberal élite of that Estate'. This
is understandable when one analyses the Huguenots as a group.
The circumstances of the diaspora at the end of the seventeenth
century; the strengthening of the international banking network
which went with it; the forced uprooting from the land, and the
shift to more mobile sources of wealth; all this meant that in
general – though there were of course individuals who did not
conform to type – the Huguenot bankers were not part of the
'establishment' like the traditional type of financiers (the king's
men), but remained outsiders. Viewed in this light, the arrival
of Necker to political power is indeed a totally new phenomenon :
here was a banker in control of the finances. To the historian,
Necker represents the future, or a form of it. The financial edifice
of the Ancien Régime disappeared completely after 1789. But the
bankers are still with us in this world of 1963, and very much
alive, which gives Herbert Lüthy's work a contemporary interest.
Let us make a wish by way of conclusion : when will there be an
equivalent work on the finances and financiers of eighteenth-
century France?

NOTES

1   On page 690 Lüthy flogs a dead horse with his ironic remarks on the
    'enigma' of agrarian underconsumption and – more generally – on
    the problems connected with statistical studies for the eighteenth
    century.
2   Lucien Febvre, 'La première Renaissance française', *Revue des Cours et
    Conferences*, nos 11, 12, 13 and 15 (1925) and the same author's
    'Capitalisme et Réforme', *Foi et Vie*, LVII (1934), both reprinted in the
    collected version of his articles and essays, *Pour une histoire à part entière*
    (Paris, 1962) pp. 562–604 and 350–66 respectively.

Glossary

Absolutus legibus: (literally released from the laws) above the law.

Agrières: a due to be paid in kind to a direct lord.

Aides: indirect taxes on consumer goods, especially on the transport and sale of wine.

Avocat-général: there were two of these, who, with the *procureur-général*, represented the king in the Parlement of Paris; collectively the three were called the *gens du roi* (the king's men).

Bailliage: a legal unit (entity) centred on a major town in which the *bailli* would be situated.

Bailli: petty court in northern France.

Bishoprics, the Three : (*Trois Evêchés*) Metz, Toul and Verdun, occupied by France in 1552 as a reward for helping German Protestant princes against Charles V; sovereignty over them was granted to France in 1648.

Bourse: exchange.

Cahier: resolution, memorandum, claim; usually a memorandum embodying a grievance or request.

Capitation: poll tax.

Cens: quit-rent.

Chambre des comptes: sovereign court for accounting of taxes, etc.

Chambre des requêtes: there were two of these courts among the ten chambers of the Parlement of Paris; their function was to hear subjects' requests for justice

Chambre des vacations: a skeleton body of judges to conduct business when the Parlement of Paris was in recess.

Champarts: dues levied by a seigneur in kind on the produce of land.

Château: palace.

Château de Madrid: a former palace, transformed into a factory where silk stockings were produced.

Code Michau: this code, framed by Michel de Marillac, keeper of the seals in the late 1620s, was never enforced.

Collège: (as e.g. Collège de France) a state institution – as opposed to a church institution – for education.

Commissaire: one who has a temporary commission and serves at the king's pleasure, as opposed to an *officier*, a permanent official.

Concordat: agreement or treaty arrived at with the papacy.

Conseil: council.

Conseil d'en haut: the high council, small council (inner cabinet), advising the king on policy; before Louis XIV's personal reign similar councils had been known as council of the chamber, council of affairs, secret council.

Conseil d'état privé: also called *conseil des parties*, during Louis XIV's reign this council drafted letters, edicts, etc.

Conseil de conscience: a council dealing with religious matters and especially with Huguenot affairs.

Conseil des dépêches: 'council of despatches' in which letters from intendants were discussed.

Conseil des finances: council dealing with allocation of revenues.

Conseiller d'état: councillor of state, a member of any one of the *conseils.*

Constable: title held, till 1626, by supreme army commander under the king.

Controleur-général: controller- (or comptroller-) general of finances.

Corvée: service without pay, obligatory labour imposed either by the central government or by a seigneur.

Coucher: (literally to sleep) the ceremony of the king's retiring for the night.

Cour des aides: a sovereign court to settle tax suits.

Cour des comptes: a sovereign court of accounts.

Croquants: (literally crunchers) nickname for poor country folk in revolt in south-west France in the 1630s.

Curia regis: king's council.

Dauphin: (literally dolphin) title usually given from the early fourteenth century to heir apparent of king of France.

Décapole: (literally the Ten Cities) ten cities of Alsace which at the peace in 1648 had been ceded to France only in respect of 'provincial overlordship', but which were occupied and later ceded to France with full sovereignty : Colmar, Haguenau, Kaysersberg, Landau, Munster, Obernai, Rosheim, Sélestat, Turkheim, Wissembourg. The German names of the *Zehnstädtebund* of 1354 are : Kolmar, Hagenau, Kaysersberg, Münster, Oberehnheim, Rosheim, Schlettstadt, Türkheim, Weissenburg, and Landau replacing Mülhausen which in 1510 joined the Swiss cantons.

Denier: fraction of a livre.

Deniers parisis: the deniers of Paris.

Deniers tournois: the deniers of Tours.

Dixième: (literally the tenth) annual tax instituted on 14 October 1710, meant to constitute one tenth of income from all property.

Don gratuit: (literally free gift) voted to the crown by a body, as e.g. by the assembly of clergy.

Donneurs d'avis: (literally providers of information) paid informers.

Dragonnades: use of dragoons to exert pressure on households where they were quartered.

Droit d'avis: fee paid for information useful to the state.

Droit divin: divine right (of kings)

Ducs et pairs: dukes and peers, highest ranking nobles of France.

Election: secondary fiscal area within a *généralité.*

Elus: officials entrusted with the assessment of taxes.

Emotions: popular uprisings.

Esprit: literally spirit, used for a quickwitted, intelligent person, a man of parts.

Fermier général: tax-farmer.

Firmengeschichte: (literally history of firms) business history.

Flotas del oro y de la plata: the Spanish fleets carrying silver and gold from Spain's overseas empire to the mother country.

Gabelle: salt tax.

Gallicanism: insistence on the local and national rights of the French Catholic church *vis-à-vis* the papacy, as expressed in the four Gallican articles of 1682.

Généralité: a fiscal district for tax purposes.

Gens de robe: lawyers, judges, officials, usually ennobled.

Gloire: literally glory, indicating also reputation, the verdict of history on a person.

Grand bailli: (great bailiff) an official in Alsace.

Grand conseil: a sovereign court which adjudicated ecclesiastical disputes.

Grand dauphin: the court title of Louis XIV's son, Louis, after he himself had a son.

La grande mademoiselle: court usage for Gaston d'Orléans' daughter Anne, Louis XIV's cousin (*see* list of persons under Montpensier).

Hôtel de Ville: Paris town hall, housing the municipal administration.

Hôtels: town houses of noblemen and others.

Impôt unique: single tax.

Intendant: intendant, king's commissary sent to provinces.

Justaucorps à brevet: a special coat denoting king's favour to a courtier.

Laboureur: farmer.

Lettres de cachet: warrants of arrest or imprisonment by the king's authority.

K*

Lever: (literally to rise, get up) the ceremony of the king's getting dressed in the morning.

Lit de justice: session of Parlement where the king is present (a symbol of majesty since royal beds were canopied; here a seat of cushions under a canopy).

Livre: the money of account.

Livres tournois: the *livre* of Tours which in the sixteenth century superseded the *livre parisis* (of Paris).

Maître des reqûetes: 'master of requests', holders of a legal office (which could be purchased) used to provide the councils of the state with pertinent information and opinions.

Maltôte: extortion.

Monsieur: court title for brother of the king of France, e.g. for Louis XIII's brother Gaston, and for Louis XIV's brother Philippe.

Monsieur le Grand: court usage for the king's grand equerry.

Noblesse de robe: nobility of the robe, men who had been ennobled because of their office and especially for legal office.

Nu pieds: (literally barefoot) poor country-folk in revolt, Normandy 1639.

Parlements: sovereign courts based in Aix (for Provence); Bordeaux (Guienne); Dijon (Burgundy); Grenoble (Dauphiné); Metz (for the Three Bishoprics); Paris (for the central provinces); Pau (Navarre); Rennes (Brittany); Rouen (Normandy); Toulouse (Languedoc).

Partisan: financial contractor under the crown, one who has signed a contract (*parti*).

Paulette: annual levy or tax on office which gave the holder the right to transmit the office by sale or leave it to a designated successor.

Pays d'états: French provinces with local estates.

Pays d'élection: French provinces without local estates.

Placets: petitions to the king.

Point de France: a type of lace.

Preliminary question : the preparatory stages of a judicial process.

Presidial courts (*presidiaux*) : regionally based intermediate courts midway between bailiwick courts and *parlements*.

Procureur de l'intendance: procurator, attorney, working in the intendant's office.

Procureur général: procurator-general, attorney general; the king's representative in the Parlement of Paris, who — with the two advocates general — was known as the *gens du roi*.

Procureur du roi: the king's attorney or representative.

Receveur général: receiver-general.

Régale: the king's right, especially used in respect of his right (ceded by the papacy) to income from certain bishoprics between the death of one incumbent and the appointment of the next.

Religion Prétendue Réformée: (literally the religion which calls itself reformed) often abbreviated to *R.P.R.*, the Huguenots.

Rentes: annuities or interest-bearing bonds in return for capital investment or loan, paid by an institution or an individual; best known are those of the Hôtel de Ville of Paris which date from 1522.

Réunions: 'reunions' of land to France resulting from claims to dependencies and rights of newly acquired conquests pursued via the *Chambres des Réunions.*

Roturier: a commoner, a non-noble.

Schirmgeld: (literally protection money) a tax.

Seigneurie: land bought or inherited with title to fiscal and judicial powers (e.g. quit-rent, oath of fidelity, homage), a sign of social superiority because of its implication of allegiance and service.

Sénéchal: old French title for one who helps the king lead the army.

Soulèvements populaires: risings involving the poorer sections of society.

Steuergeld: literally tax-money, tax.

Subdélégués: 'subdelegates' who helped the intendants, especially in the financial administration in the major towns of a *généralité.*

Survivance: reversion (of office).

Taille: direct taxation, payable by those not exempt, in proportion to their income. In the Midi ownership of the land was the base for the tax and the nobility were not exempt.

Taille personnelle: a general tax on income.

Taille réelle: tax on non-noble land, even if the owner happened to be a nobleman.

Terrages: dues to be paid in kind to a direct lord.

Traitants: financial contractors under the crown, tax-farmers.

Trésoriers de France: 'treasurers' organised into bureaux who, under the *chambre des comptes,* supervised the royal domains, roads and the work of the *élus.*

Trésoriers de l'Epargne: 'treasurers' for savings.

Chronology

1576, 1577 and 1598	Edicts of Beaulieu, Poitiers and Nantes (defining Huguenot rights).
1610	Confirmation of Edict of Nantes after death of Henri IV.
1620s	French indirect involvement in the Thirty Years War (1618–48).
1629	Grace of Alais (limiting Edict of Nantes) to lessen danger of Huguenots being a state within the state.
1635	French declaration of war against Spain (war lasted till 1659).
1636	French declaration of war against Austrian Habsburgs (war lasted till 1648).
1638	*5 September*. Birth of Louis, later Louis XIV, son of Louis XIII and his wife Anne (Ana) of Austria.
1643	*14 May*. Death of Louis XIII, accession of Louis XIV, regency of his mother—having set aside the will of Louis XIII—with Mazarin as 'first minister'.
1648	Peace of Westphalia (or of Münster where France had presided, while Sweden had presided at Osnabrück) between France and the Austrian Habsburgs: France obtains sovereignty over bishoprics of Metz, Toul and Verdun and gains the city of Breisach and the Landgravates of Upper and Lower Alsace.
1648 53	Civil war in France, the Fronde (or Frondes, distinguishing between the parliamentary Fronde, or Fronde of the judges, and the Fronde of the high nobility) directed against the power of the crown and the influence of Mazarin and his nominees.
1651	Louis XIV declared of age.
1654	Louis XIV crowned and consecrated at Rheims.
1654 onwards	Louis XIV takes part in war against Spain on northern, north-eastern and eastern frontiers of France.
1658, 1659 and 1660	Louis XIV's journeys to southern and south-western France.
1659	Peace of the Pyrenees between France and Spain: France has Roussillon and Cerdagne (ceded in 1493)

returned and gains land in the Spanish Netherlands.
From Spain's ally Lorraine France obtains the duchy
of Bar and military routes across the duchy to keep
communications open with bishoprics ceded in 1648
and with Alsace.

1660   *9 June*. Marriage of Louis XIV with Maria Teresa,
infanta of Spain; she renounces her right to the Spanish
throne against a promised dowry (which was never
paid).

1661   France returns the duchy of Bar to the duke of Lorraine, the duke in his turn accepts the military routes
and French fortifications along them.
The Assembly of the Clergy condemns Jansenism.
9 March. Death of Mazarin; henceforth Louis governs
(on Mazarin's advice) without a first minister; cabinet
and *conseil* government develops and the civil service
is increasingly bureaucratised.
July. Louise de La Vallière becomes Louis' mistress.
September. Arrest of Fouquet; his trial 1662–3, imprisoned for life at Louis' insistence in 1664.
1 November. Birth of Louis, dauphin of France. Between 1662 and 1672 five more children (two sons,
three daughters) are born of Louis' marriage to Maria
Teresa, none of whom survived infancy or early childhood.
Birth of Louis' first illegitimate child; between 1662
and 1678 ten acknowledged illegitimate children are
born to him; those who survive early childhood are
legitimised.
Beginning of military reforms; these continue throughout reign with improvement in discipline and organisation, abolition of venality, introduction of new
weapons, and fortresses built on new principles.
Tax gathering by tax-farmers introduced experiment-
ally; contracts bought back the next year but system
re-established in 1680.
Work begins to expand the gardens and the palace at
Versailles; intensified 1668, completed 1695.

1662   Charles II sells Dunkirk (which Cromwell had won
from Spain with French help) to Louis XIV for five
million francs.
Institution of hospital services throughout France.
Boulonnais peasant revolt.

1663	Sorbonne's declaration against papal infallibility confirmed by Louis and the Paris Parlement. Intendants take over administration of indirect taxation. French colonists in New France (Canada) reach 25,000 in number.
1663–71	French academies founded or recognised : 1663, Inscriptions and Medals, and Paintings and Sculpture; 1666, Science, and Academy of Rome; 1669, Music, Dancing; 1671, French Royal Academy; Architecture, and Botanical Garden.
1663 onwards	French trading companies founded and commercial treaties to promote trade signed. Companies : 1664, French West India Company and East India Company; 1665, French North Africa Company; 1669, French Company of the North; 1670, French Levant Company; 1673, French Senegal Company; 1682, French Hudson Bay Company; 1698, French China Company; 1701, French Guinea Company. Treaties : 1662, with the Dutch Republic; 1663, with Denmark-Norway and Sweden; 1671, with German Baltic free cities; 1683, with Morocco; 1684, with Algiers and Tunis; 1713, with all ex-enemies of the War of the Spanish Succession.
1664	*Grande enquête* into the resources of France. Port Royal closed to stop the spread of Jansenism. French soldiers take part in the war against Turks in Hungary (victory of St Gotthard). Silk manufactures begun at Lyons. Regulations for the 'free crafts' (i.e. the non-guild ones) in respect of hours of work, prices, holidays, etc. Containment of Huguenots begins. French protective tariff to promote own manufacturers.
1664 and 1665	*Grandes fêtes* at Versailles.
1665	Colbert restores council of commerce. Bull (*Regiminis Apostilici*) against Jansenists registered by Parlement. French bombardment against pirates of Algiers and Tunis preying on French commerce.
1665 onwards	Council of justice founded to edit and formulate French codes, *ordinances*; work completed by 1685 : 1669, for water and forests; 1679, for criminal cases;

1671, for civil cases; 1673, for commercial matters; 1681, for maritime matters; 1685, for colonial matters (*code noir*).

Special tribunals sent to Clermont–Ferrand to deal with the nobility's harsh treatment of commoners (Grand Jours d'Auvergne); another to Forez next year.

French occupy western half of Santo Domingo.

Construction of the arsenal at Brest and the port of Rochefort.

1665–67   French participation in Anglo-Dutch war on Dutch side. At Peace of Breda France obtains Acadia, but cedes to England Antigua, Montserrat and St Kitts.

1666   The Paris Parlement forbidden to discuss or vote on royal edicts before their registration.

Silk manufactures begun in Paris at the Château de Madrid.

Wool manufactures begun at Carcassonne.

1667   Construction of the Languedoc canal (Canal des Deux Mers) connecting the Atlantic and the Mediterranean, completed in 1684.

The Gobelins factory established.

Work begun on Louis' *Mémoires*.

Creation of post of lieutenant-general of Paris (minister for Paris) with a great variety of responsibilities.

Françoise (Athenaïs) de Montespan replaces La Vallière as Louis' mistress.

French protective tariffs directed against England and the Dutch Republic.

Workers' associations banned after revolts in Rheims and Lyons.

Reduction in number of printers, to facilitate censorship.

1667–8   War of Devolution (of Queen's Rights) after negotiations with Spain over the unpaid dowry had failed; Flanders offensive (Louis present) successful and French gains made at Peace of Aix-la-Chapelle in respect of the northern frontier (twelve fortified places); Franche-Comté (conquered 1668) restored to Spain.

1668   French establishment in Surat (India).

Louis orders 'Church peace', forbidding public controversy between Jansenists, Gallicans and Ultramontanes.

Secret partition-treaty with Leopold I for the Spanish inheritance.

Creation of militia by Louis (by drawing of lots in parishes).

The maritime inscription of sailors between the ages of 20 and 60 to serve one year in three or four in navy.

1669   Chamber of Commerce for Marseilles.

First general *règlement* for the textile industry. Colbert takes over the administration of the navy.

1669–77   Southward exploration and expansion from the Great Lakes into the Missouri valley by Marquette, Jollet and La Salle; westward expansion from New France by Jesuit missionaries from 1671.

1670   Antifiscal revolt in the Vivarais.

French factory established at Magilipatam (India).

French preferential duties aimed at Dutch sugar refineries.

Dutch virtual boycott of French goods.

1671   Town of Versailles started. Chapel begun, not completed till 1710.

1672–   Dutch war, beginning with French invasion of the ter-
1678/9   ritory of the Republic and developing into a general war. French gains : from Spain, Franche-Comté and western Española (renamed Haiti); from emperor and Empire, sovereignty over Metz, Toul and Verdun, and French interpretation of sovereignty in respect of Alsace, including the *Décapole*, all confirmed. French concession : restoration of less harsh tariff (that of 1664) for the Republic.

1673   Controversy with papacy over *régale* begins.

1674   French re-coinage.

French factory established at Pondichery (India).

1675   Antifiscal revolts in Bordeaux and in many towns in the south and west.

Urban and rural antifiscal revolts in Brittany.

1676   The 'poisoning scandal' (the diabolist affair) breaks in Paris; investigation from 1679.

1677   Vauban put in charge of fortifications; *barrière de fer* begun in 1679.

1679   Chair of French law established at the Sorbonne.

Palace at Marly started.

French persecution of the Jansenists.

1679–85   Increasing persecution of the Huguenots.

1679–99   The Mississippi valley to mouth of river explored by La Salle, Folliette, Marquette, Hennequin and the Iberville brothers; French colony of Louisiana (named after Louis XIV) established in 1682.

1680   Taxes farmed again (*gabelle, aides, traites* and royal domains).
           City of Paris bestows title 'Le Grand' on Louis XIV.

1680–3   Reunion policy to annex to France or to claim sovereign rights over dependencies which formerly belonged to the gains of 1648, 1659, 1668 and 1678/9.

1681   Strassburg (which opened its bridge to Imperial troops in 1674 and 1677, permitting invasion of France) joins France under pressure (henceforth Strasbourg); local autonomy and religious freedom survive.
           The duke of Mantua sells Casale to France.
           French bombardment of Tripoli pirates.

1682   Birth of Louis' first grandchild, a boy from the marriage of the dauphin in 1680 with the Bavarian princess Marie-Christine; in all three legitimate grandchildren were born alive or survived infancy; by his legitimised children Louis had nine grandchildren.
           Louis moves his court and central administration to Versailles.
           The four Gallican articles attack papal authority in France.

1683   Death of Louis' wife Maria Teresa.
           Reduction in *taille* benefits peasants.
           Spain declares war on Louis to stem the French reunion policy in the Spanish Netherlands, and in the duchy of Luxembourg, where the fortress of the city of Luxembourg seems threatened; after the war has started the fortress is taken by the French.

1683–7   Louis sends expeditions against Algiers, eventually an undertaking is given that French shipping will not be molested.

1684   French bombardment of Genoa, Spain's ally, to deny Spain use of Genoese fleet.
           Probable date (1682 and 1689 also possible ones) of Louis XIV's second (morganatic) marriage to Mme de Maintenon.
           Truce of Ratisbon (Regensburg) for twenty years with Spain and the emperor; Louis is to keep his reunions

	and conquests (such as Luxembourg) for that period and hopes to make the settlement permanent at a later date.
1685	French influence established in Siam. *16 October.* Revocation of the Edict of Nantes. *22 October.* Edict of Fontainebleau permitting 'liberty of conscience'. Water pumped from the Seine to Versailles.
1686	Persecution of the Protestant Vaudois in Savoy encouraged by Louis XIV; Louis forbids Geneva to protect French refugees. School of St Cyr (Hôtel de St Cyr) founded by Louis XIV and Mme de Maintenon for the education of 250 girls, noble and commoners; by 1692 converted into a religious institution. Madagascar annexed by France.
1687	Revolts in Maine, Orléans and Touraine. Conflict with the papacy over the franchise (*quartiers*), that is, right of asylum in embassies in Rome.
1688	Dutch encourage revolt against French influence in Siam. Journey of French explorer Grefillon through Mongolia. French militia arrangements improved. William III lands in England; his invasion leads to the flight of James II to France and the establishment of a Jacobite court at Saint-Germain.
1688/9– 1697	Nine Years War (also called War of Orléans because of Liselotte's claim to the Palatinate; or the War of the League of Augsburg, somewhat misleadingly, after the 1686 league since not all the signatories took part in the war. The aim of the league was to confine Louis to his 1659 boundaries by moral solidarity and diplomatic pressures.)
1689– 1717	English embargoes and/or prohibitive duties on French goods (wine hit in particular).
1693	Famine year in France. Louis XIV ends the *régale* dispute with the papacy, setting aside the Gallican articles. Saint-Simon arrives at court; begins notes for his memoirs, 1694. Establishment of French factory in Senegal.
1694	Vauban suggests capitation tax; it is enforced in 1695

	according to class (twenty-two classes), not income; abolished in 1697, reinstated in 1701.
1695	Fénelon's letter to Louis XIV.
1696	Duke of Savoy signs separate peace with France (obtains Casale and Pignerol) and opens the way to a general peace; marriage arranged for the duc de Bourgogne, Louis' eldest grandson, to Marie-Adélaïde of Savoy.
1697	Peace of Ryswick : Louis XIV restores the reunions, but keeps Strasbourg, Longwy and Saar-Louis.
	Fénelon exiled from court.
	Quietism is condemned by Pope Innocent XI.
1697–	
1715	Senegal conquest is completed.
1698–9	Relaxation in persecution of Huguenots by Louis XIV.
1698 and	Partition treaties between Louis XIV, William III and
1700	the Dutch Republic to solve the Spanish succession problem : France stands to gain important areas both by first (Naples and Sicily) and second (Milan to be exchanged for Lorraine, Naples and Sicily) treaties.
1699	*Conseil de Commerce* revived; inquiry into methods to encourage trade, great efforts in respect of overseas trade and exploration.
	Louis' emissary Poncet travels overland from Cairo to Ethiopia.
	Attempts to establish lieutenant-generals of police also in provincial towns.
1700	*2 October.* Carlos II of Spain, on the advice of the pope, nominates Louis XIV's second grandson, Philip, duke of Anjou, his heir on the condition that no partition shall take place.
	1 November. Death of Carlos II.
	16 November. Louis XIV accepts the will of Carlos II.
	Greater freedom of trade permitted to Dunkirk, Marseilles and Bordeaux.
	France buys the unexpired portion of the asiento held by a Portuguese company.
1701	*March. Capitation* reintroduced.
	April-July. Unsuccessful negotiations at The Hague in which the Maritime Powers fail to obtain cessions of Spanish land and commercial advantages from Louis XIV acting on behalf of Philip V of Spain.
	Paper money introduced in France.

	July. The emperor invades Italy.

July. The emperor invades Italy.
September. France prohibits entry of English textiles.

1702   Jansenists struggle to the fore once more.
Revolt of the Protestant Camisards in the Cévennes, put down 1704 but flares up again in 1710.

1702–   War of the Spanish Succession in Europe; in America
1713/14   Queen Anne's War. The English conquered Acadia in 1711 and kept this at the peace, as also Newfoundland and Hudson Bay. In Europe Philip V had to cede the Spanish Netherlands, Naples, the Tuscan ports and Sardinia to Austria; Sicily to Savoy, and Gibraltar and Minorca to England; but only minor losses were suffered in Spanish America (to Portugal). The asiento trade in slaves was awarded to England for thirty years.

1703   Unrest ('terror') in Casrais, Albigeois and Toulouse and Languedoc.
Introduction of the *centime denier*.

1704   Birth of Louis XIV's first great-grandchild, a boy who died in 1705; another great-grandson who survived till 1712 was born in 1705; a third great-grandson (later Louis XV who became king in 1715) was born in 1710; there were also three great-grandsons from the marriage of Philip V to Marie-Louïse of Savoy.

1705   Papal bull (*Vineam Domini*) condemns Jansenism once more.

1706   Riot at Cahors, another in 1709.

1707   Circulation of paper money enforced.

1708   Hard winter (bad harvests 1708 and 1709).

1709   Freer French trade with both Indies.

1710   The razing of the church and the convent at Port Royal; 1711 destruction of the cemetery which had been worshipped as a shrine.
14 October. The *dixième* tax on all Frenchmen irrespective of privileges (the idea owed much to Vauban and Boisguilbert).

1711   Capture by a French naval force of Rio de Janeiro (restored at peace).
14 April. Death of the grand dauphin.
Louis XIV extends the advantages held by the Dutch in respect of French tariffs since 1678 to Britain, Denmark-Norway and the free Baltic cities of the Empire.
Louis XIV withdraws his promise of freedom of worship in the principality of Orange.

1712   Foundation of the *Académie Politique* to train foreign
            office officials and diplomats.
            Death of Louis' eldest grandson (18 February), the
            grandson's wife (12 February) and their elder son (8
            March).
            Opening of official peace congress at Utrecht after sep-
            arate negotiations with the English Tory government
            after 1710 had led to the peace preliminaries of Octo-
            ber 1711 and to the Anglo-French separate armistice
            of 17 July 1712.
            Free exchange re-established in France.

1713   *March-July.* Peace treaties signed between France and
            her enemies, except the emperor and Empire.
            September. Papal bull (*Unigenitus*) condemns Jansen-
            ism; Louis XIV orders Parlement to enforce the bull in
            February 1715.
            November, to March 1714. Peace negotiations between
            Louis XIV and the emperor. Treaty of Rastadt (6
            March) whereby emperor gives up claim to Metz, Toul,
            Verdun and Alsace and lets France keep Landau.

1714   *4 May.* Death of Louis' youngest grandson, the duke
            of Berry.
            July. Louis makes it possible for his legitimised sons,
            the duke of Maine and the count of Toulouse, to suc-
            ceed if the Orléans and Condé families should die out
            in the male line; both are declared princes of the blood.
            2 August. Louis XIV's will, establishing a regency
            council of fourteen members, the president of which is
            to be his nephew, the duke of Orléans, on which his
            two legitimised sons shall have seat.
            7 September. Peace treaty between France and the
            Empire (at Baden in Argau) confirms the Rastadt
            peace.

1715   *August.* Louis XIV's illness and final arrangements for
            the governorship and education of his heir, his great-
            grandson Louis.
            1 September. Death of Louis XIV.

List of Persons

Alquié, François Savinien d' (1669–1691), French writer and translator.

Althusius (Althaus), Johannes (1557–1638), Netherlands-born German academic jurist and political theorist.

Anjou, duc d', see Philip V.

Anne of Austria (1600–66), Spanish infanta, queen of France on her marriage to Louis XIII, regent for Louis XIV from 1610.

Antin, Louis-Antoine de Pardaillan de Gondrin, marquis d', later duc d' (1665–1736), superintendent of royal works from 1708.

Anton Ulrich, duke of Brunswick Wolfenbüttel 1685–1714.

Argenson, René-Louis, marquis d' (1696–1757), minister to Louis XV 1744–7.

Arnauld, Antoine (1612–94), Jansenist writer.

Arnauld, Robert d'Andilly (1588–1674), intendant general for Gaston d'Orléans.

Arnauld de Pomponne, see Pomponne.

Avaux, Jean-Antoine Mesme, comte d' (1640–1709), French diplomat.

Barbezieux, Louis-François-Marie Le Tellier, marquis de (1688–1701), French war minister, son of Louvois.

Bart, Jean (1650–1702), French privateering captain and naval officer.

Bayezid II., Sultan 1481–1512.

Bayle, Pierre (1647–1706), French philosopher who in 1681 settled in the Dutch Republic.

Beauvillier (Beauvilliers), Paul, comte de Saint-Aignan and duc de (1684–1776), minister of Louis XIV from 1691–1712.

Bernard, duke (*Herzog*) of Saxe-Weimar (1604–39), Protestant commander in Thirty Years War.

Bernard, Samuel (1651–1739), French financier.

Berri (Berry), Charles de France, duc de (1686–4 March 1714) Louis XIV's grandson.

Bertin, Henri-Léonard-Jean-Baptiste (1719–92), French controller-general of finances 1759–63.

Berulle, Pierre (1575–1629), French theologian and educator, cardinal from 1627.
Bodin, Jean (1530–96), French political theorist.
Boileau (more correctly **Boileau-Despréaux**), **Nicolas** (1636–1711), French writer, historiographer-royal to Louis XIV.
Boisguilbert, Pierre le Pesant, Sieur de (1646–1714), French economist.
Bolingbroke, Henry St John (1678–1751), 1st viscount from 1713, English statesman.
Boniface VIII, pope 1294–1303.
Bossuet, Jacques-Bénigne (1627–1704), French theologian and political theorist, bishop of Meaux.
Boucherat, Louis (1616–69), chancellor of France 1685.
Bougainville, Louis Antoine, comte de (1729–1811), French navigator.
Bouillon, Robert de la March, duc de (1492–1556), marshal of France.
Bourgogne, duc de, *see* **Burgundy.**
Bourjon, François (d. 1751), French jurist.
Brienne, Louis Henri de Loménie de, comte de (1635–98), French secretary of state for foreign affairs.
Brissot (de Warville), Jacques Pierre (1754–93), French jurist.
Broglie, Victor-Maurice, comte de (1646–1727), marshal of France 1724.
Brunswick (Braunschweig), dukes of, more correctly **Brunswick-Lüneburg.**
Burgundy, Louis de France, duke of (1682–1712), grandson of Louis XIV, dauphin 14 April 1711 to 18 February 1712.
Burgundy, duchess of, Marie Adélaïde of Savoy (1685–1712) wife from 1697 of the above.
Bussy, François de (1699–1786), French diplomat.
Byng, George, from 1721 Viscount Torrington, (1663–1733), British admiral.

Calonne, Charles-Alexandre de (1734–1862), French statesman in reign of Louis XVI.
Cambon, Jean-Louis-Auguste-Emmanuel de (1737–1807), procureur-général in 1786.
Carlos, Don (1545–68), eldest son of Philip II of Spain, who was unstable, plotted against his father and died (possibly executed) in prison.
Carlos II, king of Spain 1665–1700 (b. 1661).
Cassard, Jacques (1679–1740), French naval officer.

Catherine the Great, tsaritsa of Russia 1762–96.

Catherine de Medici, queen of France by her marriage to Henri II, king 1547–59, influential during the reigns of their sons.

Chamillart, Michel (1652–1721), member of the *conseil d'en haut* 1700–9; his son Michel II (1689–1716).

Charles I, king of England, Scotland and Ireland 1603–25.

Charles II, king of England, Scotland and Ireland 1660–85.

Charles V, Holy Roman emperor 1519–56 (b. 1500); ruler of the Burgundian state 1506–56; of Spain (as Carlos I) 1516–56; of the Austrian Habsburg dominions 1519–56; abdicated 1556; died 1558.

Charles, Austrian archduke (b. 1685), Charles III of Spain to the anti-French side in the War of the Spanish Succession, later Charles VI, emperor and ruler of Habsburg dominions 1711–40.

Châteauneuf, Pierre Antoine de Castagnéry, marquis de (1647–1728), French diplomat.

Chateaurenault, François-Louis de Rousselet de (1637–1716), French naval officer.

Chevreuse, Charles Honoré d'Albert de Luynes, duc de (1646–1712), adviser to Louis XIV.

Choiseul, Etienne–François, duc de (1719–85), French statesman.

Chorier, Nicolas (1612–92), French advocate.

Christina, queen of Sweden 1634–54 (b. 1626, d. 1689).

Cinq-Mars, Henri Coeffier Ruzé, marquis de (1620–42), favourite of Louis XIII.

Clement XI, pope 1700–21.

Colbert, Charles, *see* Croissy.

Colbert, Jean-Baptiste (1614–83), member of *conseil royale des finances* 1661, of *conseil d'en haut* 1669–83, important minister of Louis XIV.

Coligny, Gaspard de (b. 1515), French admiral, assassinated 1572.

Concini, Concino (d. 1617), favourite of Marie de Medici between 1610 and 1617.

Condé, 'le Grand', Louis II de Bourbon (1621–86), prince de Condé from 1646, before his father's death known as duc d'Enghien, French commander.

Corneille, Pierre (1606–84), French dramatist.

Créqui, Charles II de Blanchefort de (1623–87), son of Marshal Crequi.

Croissy, Charles Colbert, marquis de (*c.* 1626–96), French secretary of state.

300 *List of Persons*

Daillé, Jean (1594–1670) Protestant pastor.
Dangeau, Philippe de Courcillon, marquis de (1638–1720), Louis' aide-de-camp in 1672, author of a journal for 1684–1720 which was published in 19 volumes in 1854.
D'Aquin, Antoine (*c.* 1620–96), chief physician to Louis XIV 1672–93.
Delessert (Gabriel), Etienne (1735–1816), banker at Lyons and Paris.
Descartes, René (Renatus) (1596–1650), French philosopher and mathematician.
Desmarets (also Desmaretz), Nicolas, marquis de Maillebois, member of the *conseil d'en haut* 1709–15.
Dubois, Guillaume (1656–1723), French statesman, former tutor to Philippe II of Orléans, cardinal 1721.
Dubourdieu, Jean-Armand (*c.* 1680–1726), Lutheran pastor.
Duquesne, Abraham II, le grand Duquesne (1610–88), French admiral.
Duguay–Trouin, René (1673–1736), French naval commander.

Eliçagerey, Bernard Renau d' (1652–1719), French engineer.
Elizabeth, queen of England 1558–1603 (b. 1533).
Enghien, duc d', *see* Condé.
Estrées, César d', cardinal 1674 (1628–1714), French cleric, used on diplomatic missions.
Estrées, Jean, comte d' (1624–1707), French admiral.
Eugéne, prince of Savoy (1663–1736), army commander in Austrian service.

Fagon, Guy Crescent (1638–1718), Louis XIV's premier physician 1693–1715.
Fénelon, François de Salignac de la Mothe (1651–1715), French cleric, archbishop of Cambrai from 1695, writer.
Ferdinand II, king of Aragon 1479–1516 (b. 1452), m. 1469 Isabella, queen of Castile 1474–1504.
Ferdinand of Styria (1578–1637), younger Habsburg prince, elected king of Bohemia 1617, king of Hungary 1618; inherited Austrian Habsburg dominions and was elected Emperor Ferdinand II in 1619.
Ferdinand II, Holy Roman emperor and ruler of Austrian Habsburg dominions 1619–37 (b. 1578).
Ferdinand III, Holy Roman emperor and ruler of Austrian Habsburg dominions 1637–57 (b. 1608).
Ferdinand, archduke, infant son of Emperor Leopold who died in 1668.

Ferdinand-Maria, elector of Bavaria 1651–79.
Fléchier, Esprit (1632–1710), bishop of Nîmes (1632–1710), celebrated preacher and theological writer.
Fleury, André Hercule de (1653–1743), cardinal, first minister from 1726.
Fontenelle, Bernard Le Bouyer (1657–1757), French writer.
Forbin, Claude, chevalier de (1656–1733), French naval officer.
Fouquet, Nicolas, marquis de Belle-Ile, comte de Melun et de Vaux (1615–80), French superintendent of finances 1653–61.
Francis (François) I, king of France 1515–47 (b. 1494).
Frederick William (Friedrich Wilhelm), elector of Brandenburg 1640–88 (the Great Elector).
Frederick William I, king in Prussia 1713–40.
Fürstenberg, Franz-Egon (François-Egon) von, prince of the Empire (1626–83), bishop of Strasbourg 1663–82.

Gaston d'Orléans, *see* **Orléans.**
Gregory XIV, pope 1590–1.
Grotius, Hugo (1583–1645), Dutch political philosopher.

Harcourt, Henri, marquis de Beuvron, duc de (1654–1718), marshal of France, used also on diplomatic missions.
Harlay de Champvallon, François de (1625–95), archbishop of Paris 1671–95.
Henri II, king of France 1547–59 (b. 1519).
Henri III, king of France 1574–89 (b. 1551).
Henri IV, king of France 1589–1610 (b. 1553).
Henry VII, king of England and Ireland 1485–1509.
Hobbes, Thomas (1588–1679), English philosopher.
Huber, Ulrich (1636–94), Friesland jurist and academic teacher.
Huguetan, Jean-Antoine (1647–1750, French librarian and financial speculator.
Huxelles, Nicolas de Laye du Blé (Bled), marquis d' (1652–1730), marshal of France 1703, also used on diplomatic missions.

Innocent III, pope 1160–1216.
Innocent XI, pope 1676–89.
Innocent XII, pope 1691–1700.
Isabella, queen of Castile 1474–1504 (b. 1451), married to Ferdinand of Aragon 1469 (q.v.).
Ivan III, ruler of Muscovy 1462–1505.

James I, king of England and Ireland 1603–25; king of Scotland 1567–1625 (b. 1566).

James II, king of England, Scotland and Ireland 1685–8 (b. 1633, d. 1701).

'James III', son of James II and Mary of Modena (1688–1766); in England known as James (Francis Edward) Stuart and later as the 'Old Pretender', in Catholic countries (including France after 1713) as the Chevalier de St George.

John Albert (House of Jagiello), king of the Polish-Lithuanian Commonwealth 1492–1501.

John III Sobieski, king of the Polish-Lithuanian Commonwealth 1674–96.

Joly, Claude (1607–1700), French theologian, writer of memoirs.

Joseph, king of the Romans, Austrian archduke (b. 1678), elected king of the Romans and in 1705 succeeded his father Leopold I as Holy Roman emperor and ruler of the Austrian Habsburg dominions. Died 1711.

Joseph Clement of Bavaria, archbishop elector of Cologne 1688–1723.

Joyeuse, Anne, duc de (1561–1587), French admiral.

Jurieu, Pierre (1637–1713), French Protestant theologian living in the Dutch Republic.

La Bruyère, Jean de (1639–96), French writer and moralist.

La Chaise, François d'Aix de, père (1624–1709), Louis XIV's confessor.

La Milletière, Théophile Brachet de (*c.* 1596–1665), French Protestant controversialist.

Lamoignon, Guillaume de (1617–77), premier president of Parlement of Paris.

Law, John (1671–1729), Scottish financier active in France at the time of the Mississippi bubble.

Le Bret, Cardin (1558–1655), French political theorist.

Lebrun (Le Brun), Charles (1619–90), French painter and architect.

Lecouteulx, Jean-Barthélemy de Cantelou (1749–1818), French politician.

Legendre, Louis (1655–1733), French historian.

Leibniz, Gottfried Wilhelm (1646–1716), German philosopher, mathematician and historian.

Leopold I, Holy Roman emperor and ruler of the Austrian Habsburg dominions 1658–1705 (b. 1640).

Le Peletier, Claude (1630–1707), controller-general of finances.

Lesdiguières, François de Bonne, duc de, (1543–1626), [last] French constable from 1622.

Le Tellier, Michel (1603–85), member of the *conseil d'en haut* from 1661; also secretary of state.

Lionne, Hugues de, marquis de Berry (1611–71), member of *conseil d'en haut* from 1663.

Locke, John (1632–1704), English philosopher.

Loisel, Antoine (1536–1617), sixteenth-century French advocate.

Loménie de Brienne, *see* Brienne.

Louis VII, king of France 1137–80 (b. 1119).

Louis XI, king of France 1461–83 (b. 1423).

Louis XII, king of France 1498–1515 (b. 1462).

Louis XIII, king of France 1610–43 (b. 1601).

Louis XV, king of France 1715–74 (b. 1710).

Louis XVI, king of France 1774–92 (b. 1754).

Louis, dauphin of France (1662–1711), son of Louis XIV, 'the grand dauphin'.

Louvois, François le Tellier, marquis de (1641–91), member of *conseil d'en haut* from 1672, designated successor to his father (*see* Le Tellier, Michel) at the War Office in 1655.

Lude, duchesse de, wife of Henri de Daillon, duc de Lude, who died in 1685.

Luynes, Charles, marquis d'Albret, duc de (1578–1621), *connétable* of France on 2 April 1621.

Maine, Louis-Auguste de Bourbon, duc de (1670–1736), natural (later legitimised) son of Louis XIV.

Maintenon, Françoise d'Aubigné, marquise de (1635–1719), second (morganatic) wife of Louis XIV.

Maria Teresa (Marie-Thérèse) (1638–83), queen of France after her marriage to Louis XIV in 1661, daughter of Philip IV of Spain.

Marie de Medici (1574–1642), wife of Henri IV, regent for Louis XIII after 1610.

Marillac, Michel de (1563–1632), French minister for planning reform (code Michau).

Marlborough, John Churchill, 1st duke of (1650–1722), English soldier and diplomat.

Maupeou, Charles-Augustin de (1714–92), French chancellor.

Maximilian I, Holy Roman emperor and ruler of the Austrian Habsburg dominions 1493–1519 (b. 1455).

Maximilian (Max) Emmanuel, elector of Bavaria 1679–1726 (b. 1662), governor of the Spanish Netherlands 1691–1706.

Mayenne, Charles de Louraine, duc de (1554–1611), French nobleman, active during civil wars.

Mazarin, Armand Charles, duc de (1632–1713), courtier, married niece of Jules Mazarin (q.v.) and became duke by an entail in his favour.

Mazarin, Jules (Guilio Mazarini) (1602–61), Italian-born French statesman, cardinal from 1641.

Mercoeur, Philippe-Emmanuel de Lorraine, duc de (1558–1622), French nobleman active in civil wars.

Mesmes, Henri de (1531–96), French magistrate.

Mirabeau, Victor Riguette, marquis de (1715–89), French statesman.

Monmouth, James Scot, duke of (1649–85), natural son of Charles II.

Montaigne, Michel de (1533–92), French essayist.

Montausier, Charles de Saint-Maure, marquis, later duc de (1610–90), governor of the grand dauphin.

Montespan, Françoise (Athénais) de Rochechouart Montemart, marquise de (1641–1707), Louis XIV's mistress.

Montesquieu, Charles de (1689–1755), French philosopher.

Montmorency, Henri II, duc de (1595–1632), governor of Languedoc, plotted to secure Richelieu's dismissal.

Morgan, Sir Henry (1635–88), Welsh buccaneer, governor of Jamaica.

Motteville, Françoise Bertaut, dame de (*c.* 1621–89), lady-inwaiting to queen Anne of France, memoir writer.

Naudé, Gabriel (dates unknown), librarian to Cardinal Mazarin.

Necker, Jacques (1732–1804), French financier and statesman.

Noailles, Anne–Jules, duc de (1650–1708), marshal of France.

Noailles, Louis-Antoine (1651–1729), archbishop of Paris from 1695, cardinal from 1700.

Orange, William, prince of (1650–1702), stadholder of the Dutch Republic 1672–1702, king of England, Scotland and Ireland 1689–1702.

Orléans, Gaston, duc de (1608–60), uncle of Louis XIV.

Orléans, Philippe I, duc de (1640–1701), brother of Louis XIV.

Parker, Henry (1607–52), English writer.

Pellisson, Paul (1624–93), royal *lecteur* from 1663 and historiographer from 1671 to 1678.

Péréfixe, Hardouin de Beaumont de (1605–70), tutor to Louis XIV in 1644, archbishop of Paris 1648–62.

Phélypeaux, *see* **Pontchartrain.**

Philip IV (the Fair), king of France 1285–1314.

Philip II, king of Spain 1556–98.
Philip V, king of Spain 1700–46 (b. 1681), grandson of Louis XIV, title of duc d'Anjou 1683–1700.
Philip II Augustus, king of France 1180–1223 (b. 1165).
Philippe I, duc d' Orléans, brother of Louis XIV, *see* **Orléans.**
Pithou, Pierre (1559–96), French jurist.
Pius IV, pope 1559–65.
Pointis, Jean-Bernard-Louis Desjean, baron de (1645–1707), French naval officer.
Pomponne, Simon Arnauld, marquis de (1618–99), secretary of state for foreign affairs, disgraced 1679, restored to *conseil d'en haut* 1691.
Pontchartrain, Jerôme, comte de (1674–1747), French secretary of state for the navy 1699–1715.
Pontchartrain, Louis Phélypeaux, comte de (1643–1727), French controller-general of finances 1689, later chancellor.
Puget, Pierre (1620–94), French sculptor.

Quesnay, François (1694–1774), French economist and physician.

Racine, Jean (1639–99), French dramatist, historiographer royal to Louis XIV.
Rákóczi, Franz (Feranc, Francis, François) prince (1676–1735), leader of Hungarian and Transylvanian independence movement 1703–11.
Retz, (Jean François), Paul de Gondi (1613–79), coadjutor archbishop of Paris, cardinal 1649.
Richelieu, Armand Jean du Plessis duc de (1585–1642), French statesman, cardinal from 1622.
Richelieu, Armand-Jean-Wigncrod du Plessis (1629–1715), French courtier.
Rivet, A. (1573–1651), Protestant theologian.
Rooke, Sir George (1650–1709), English admiral.
Rose Toussaint, seigneur de Coye (1615–1701), Louis XIV's private secretary.
Ruyter, Mich. Adrianszoon de (1607–76), Dutch admiral.

Saint-Réal, César Vichard, abbé de (1639–92), French historian.
Saint-Simon, Louis de Rouvroy, duc de (1675–1755), French courtier and memoir writer.
Salvinien d'Alquié, *see* **Alquié.**
Savary, Jacques (1622–90), French merchant, writer on economic matters.

Séguier, Pierre III (1588–1672), chancellor of France 1635, keeper of seals from 1633.

Seignelay, Jean-Baptiste Colbert, marquis de (1651–90), member of *conseil d'en haut* from 1685.

Sévigné, Marie de Rabutin-Chantal, marquise de (1626–96), celebrated letter writer.

Sixtus V, pope 1585–90.

Sobieski, *see* John III Sobieski.

Soissons, Charles de Bourbon, comte de (1566–1612), French nobleman active in the civil wars.

Spinoza, Baruch (1632–77), Dutch philosopher of Portuguese Jewish descent.

Suffren, Pierre André, duc de (1726–88), French naval officer.

Sully, Maximilian de Béthune, duc de (1559–1641), French statesman.